Plays by
Tom Robe

SOCIETY
OURS
CASTE
SCHOOL

Edited with an Introduction and Notes by
William Tydeman

CAMBRIDGE UNIVERSITY PRESS
Cambridge
London New York New Rochelle
Melbourne Sydney

Published by the Press Syndicate of the University of Cambridge
The Pitt Building, Trumpington Street, Cambridge CB2 1RP
32 East 57th Street, New York, NY 10022, USA
296 Beaconsfield Parade, Middle Park, Melbourne 3206, Australia

First published 1982

Printed in Great Britain at the
University Press, Cambridge

Library of Congress catalogue card number: 81-10249

British Library cataloguing in publication data

Robertson, Tom
Plays by Tom Robertson. – (British and American
playwrights, 1750–1920)
I. Title II. Tydeman, William III. Series
822′.8 PR5232.R5

ISBN 0 521 23386 0 hard covers
ISBN 0 521 29939 X paperback

GENERAL EDITORS' PREFACE

It is the primary aim of this series to make available to the British and American theatre plays which were effective in their own time, and which are good enough to be effective still.

Each volume assembles a number of plays, normally by a single author, scrupulously edited but sparingly annotated. Textual variations are recorded where individual editors have found them either essential or interesting. Introductions give an account of the theatrical context, and locate playwrights and plays within it. Biographical and chronological tables, brief bibliographies, and the complete listing of known plays provide information useful in itself, and which also offers guidance and incentive to further exploration.

Many of the plays published in this series have appeared in modern anthologies. Such representation is scarcely distinguishable from anonymity. We have relished the tendency of individual editors to make claims for the dramatists of whom they write. These are not plays best forgotten. They are plays best remembered. If the series is a contribution to theatre history, that is well and good. If it is a contribution to the continuing life of the theatre, that is well and better.

We have been lucky. The Cambridge University Press has supported the venture beyond our legitimate expectations. Acknowledgement is not, in this case, perfunctory. Sarah Stanton's contribution to the series has been substantial, and it has enhanced our work.

Martin Banham
Peter Thomson

TO MY MOTHER
ELIZABETH TYDEMAN
Gentlest of prompters
Kindest of critics

CONTENTS

List of illustrations page viii
Acknowledgements ix

Introduction 1
Biographical record 31
The texts 35
SOCIETY (1865) 39
OURS (1866) 85
CASTE (1867) 135
SCHOOL (1869) 185

Appendices: I The source of CASTE 227
II Mr Eccles's musical and literary allusions 232
The principal plays of Tom Robertson 234
Select bibliography 236

LIST OF ILLUSTRATIONS

I		Tom Robertson (from a drawing by W.H. Kendal formerly in Peterborough Museum)	*page* x
II	a	Squire Bancroft and Marie Wilton in act I, scene 2 of *Society* (1865) (Guy Little Collection, British Theatre Museum)	17
	b	Marie Wilton and John Clarke in act III of *Ours* (1866) (Guy Little Collection)	17
III		Artist's impression of the Owl's Roose scene from *Society* (1865) (Billy Rose Theatre Collection, New York Public Library at Lincoln Center, Astor, Lenox and Tilden Foundations)	40
IV		Artist's impression of act III of *Ours* (1866) (*Illustrated London News*, 20 October 1866)	86
V	a	John Hare as Sam Gerridge in *Caste* (1867) (Guy Little Collection)	136
	b	George Honey as Eccles in *Caste* (1867) (Guy Little Collection)	136
VI		The Prince of Wales's Theatre, Tottenham Street (*Windsor Magazine*, December 1911)	186

ACKNOWLEDGEMENTS

I should like to thank the general editors of the British and American Playwrights series for their friendly support and encouragement; the staff of the Cambridge University Press, and Sarah Stanton in particular, for their advice and expertise; the staff of the British Theatre Museum; Ronald Pearsall, D.H.A. Redway of Imperial Tobacco Ltd, George Rowell, Don Roy, Martin Smith and Vivien Thomas, who all assisted my researches; the college authorities and my colleagues in the Department of English, University College of North Wales, for enabling me to enjoy two terms' study leave during which this edition was completed.

WMT

From a drawing by Mr. W. H. Kendal.

T. W. ROBERTSON.

I Tom Robertson

INTRODUCTION

It has never been a simple matter to deal justly with even the best plays of Tom Robertson. Excessively admired and lavishly praised in their own generation, often for features whose lasting merit has proved dubious, they have since that time been sadly undervalued and harshly denigrated for lacking qualities to which they never made pretence. If Robertson's popularisation of certain fruitful innovations in the character and presentation of English stage plays once led effusive disciples to link his name with Ibsen's, his role in establishing a vogue for genteel, amiable, optimistic comedies of respectable middle-class life has frequently doomed him to unjustified dismissal. Yet, if both attitudes seem misguided, it is equally mistaken to ignore Robertson's place as both pioneer and influence.

To appreciate the work of Tom Robertson truly, we have to reconstruct not only the prevalent tendencies of the stage he helped to reform, and the constitution of the principal dramatic company for which he wrote his best plays, but also the changing preferences of the age in which he lived. His brief life coincided with a transition in British theatrical taste from a penchant for the heroic and exotic to a preoccupation with the native and domestic, from a love of the overtly histrionic to an obsession with the ostensibly lifelike, and his personal share in bringing about this significant shift in public demand must not be forgotten. Like Bernard Shaw, who was later to commend Robertson's novelty of approach, he too endeavoured to replace the extravagant and outworn conventions of the drama of his day with portrayals of human behaviour and conditions more closely related to actuality. Admittedly, unlike Shaw's, Robertson's intellect was unoriginal, his moral and social thinking orthodox, but at his best he established the dramatic validity of placing unextraordinary people in recognisably mundane settings, of involving them in everyday situations to which they responded in credible ways while conducting their affairs through convincingly authentic conversation. His is still far from being a literal imitation of life, but if with hindsight Robertson's 'revolution' seems only a timid step in the evolution of the naturalistic movement in the theatre, it should not be written off as unsound in principle.

To cater for the new predilections of Victorian theatregoers, the playwright was in one sense amply equipped, his impeccable theatrical pedigree supplementing possession of an intimate personal knowledge of current stage practice and popular requirements. But this familiarity did not bestow on Robertson those automatic advantages which some commentators have claimed for him. His experience of the early nineteenth-century equivalent of 'provincial rep' exposed him to the tried and tested formulae of dramatic literature at a young age, so that he might have been forgiven for remaining inhibited for ever by the conventions accepted by many of his contemporaries. As it is, given the number of Victorian authors from outside the playhouse who professed an interest in 'reviving the drama', it is curious that perhaps the most successful individual 'reformer' of nineteenth-century English plays not only emerged from within the ranks of the profession, but achieved his results by promulgating the ideal of a theatre which would take its subject-matter and artistic criteria from contemporary life rather than from hallowed stage tradition.

In this he was neither unique nor alone: we should never forget that there were precedents for Robertson's practices, or that he was supported in his aims by a 'production team' whose concern for accuracy, refinement, and detail was fully equal to his own. It was his good fortune to have his first play with any genuine claim to originality accepted by an enterprising and youthful management prepared to take risks in pursuit of high standards of theatrical artistry, and all his subsequent triumphs were gained through adherence to the same principles and allegiance to the same personnel which had unexpectedly made *Society* the talk of London in 1865. The complaisance and gentility of proceedings at the Prince of Wales's Theatre should not be allowed to detract from the courage and integrity with which the Bancrofts carried through their reforms in stage management and playhouse procedure, just as the obviousness and popularity of Robertson's comedies should not obscure their innate stageworthiness or their author's instinctive understanding of what makes for satisfying theatre.

For it is not enough merely to urge the historical importance of what Robertson accomplished; any true assessment of his quality as a playwright must depend eventually on the intrinsic pleasure and satisfaction obtained from his plays when viewed from the auditorium or recreated in the imagination. Apart from periodic revivals of *Caste*, the modern stage has largely elected to pass Robertson's work by, yet many of his pieces possess immense latent theatrical appeal, and would repay respectful (which is not the same as pedantically reverential) revival. Most of them feature 'well-made' if slender plots with watertight *dénouements*, a broad range of personages memorable for their distinctive characteristics and vitality, and a wealth of effective and pleasing scenes encapsulating fundamental aspects of Victorian society, its values, conduct, and beliefs. If it be objected that they also abound in dramatic contrivances and coincidences, in trivial fooling or sentimental banter, in tritely sententious maxims, in arbitrarily achieved conclusions, and in facile solutions to complex problems, it must be remembered that these are also the weaknesses of much Victorian writing, even outside the playhouse. Affronted zealots have never been slow in sneering at Robertson's 'teacup-and-saucer' or 'bread-and-butter' school of playwriting; what they tend to ignore is that Robertson's wholesome bread-and-butter enraptured a public surfeited with cheap cake, and his homely brew, if oversweetened, can still prove distinctive enough to placate even today's sophisticated taste-buds.

I

Nothing could be more erroneous than to assume that Robertson launched himself as a dramatist with a clearly-defined programme of theatrical reforms mentally mapped out in advance. Arthur Wing Pinero's semi-portrait of the aspiring playwright in *Trelawny of the 'Wells'*, staged in 1898, celebrates a man with an already distinct vision of the kind of plays he wishes to compose and, indeed, with many of them already written. The sentiments of Tom Wrench, with his ambitions of making his characters 'talk and behave like live people', of fashioning heroes out of 'actual, dull, everyday men', and of having 'locks on the doors, *real locks*, to work', are undoubtedly faithful to the spirit of Tom Robertson, but it is doubtful if his prototype had ever formulated such a positive plan of campaign even by the time he reached Wrench's age of 'about thirty'. The early career was devoted to attempts at hitting on a compelling recipe rather than to confidently awaiting recognition.

Certainly Robertson's apprenticeship to the stage was long and arduous, and it did not leave his sensitive personality unmarked. Born in January 1829, he was thirty-five before achieving even a modest theatrical success with *David Garrick*, and nearly thirty-seven before *Society* received its London première: most of his short life was spent in circumstances of constant labour, frequent penury, and abject disappointment. The strain of bitterness and sarcasm which many noted in his character is not difficult to explain; indeed, some commentators felt that even his sunniest comedies were marred by a taint of worldly cynicism, incredible as this view may now appear to those more apt to be offended by Robertson's idealised fairy-tale conclusions with their affecting reconciliations and genial pairings-off. Daryl's indictment of poverty as an impediment to marriage, or the musician's complaint in *Dreams* that youth is an inevitable disqualification for success, may certainly be construed as expressions of authorial disillusionment, yet both Harfthal and Daryl are dismissed to happiness at the end by a writer who bestows his rewards with transparent sincerity untinged by irony.

Money or the lack of it is of course a common preoccupation in Victorian literature, and it is found playing a prominent role in almost all Robertson's plays, affecting personal relationships as well as more mundane areas of existence. Like his older contemporary Dickens, who predeceased him by less than nine months, Robertson was acutely aware of his own financial responsibilities, working desperately hard at first from necessity, and, on achieving fame, from the need to capitalise on it in order to secure his family's future. He fully understood the economic hazards of both performing and writing for the stage, depending as they did on the whims of public favour, and the years of subsistence living and low salaries, which partly accounted for the death of his first wife, made him prudent and shrewd, and he never became even modestly well-to-do. Robertson's young men without prospects and young women without fortunes are plentiful enough in nineteenth-century fiction, but in his case they reflect their creator's personal misfortunes only too well.

The branch of the theatre into which Robertson was born was the provincial 'circuit' system which enjoyed its greatest vogue in England during the late eighteenth and early nineteenth centuries. Under this set-up a 'stock' company of players would base itself on a large provincial town or city such as York, Bath, Worcester, or Norwich, but undertake to tour at frequent intervals in the outlying district, providing three or four weeks' performances at as many centres as could boast even a modest playhouse. Occasionally a leading London professional might slot with little or no rehearsal into the resident cast and give a number of guest appearances, but normally presentation was in the hands of a peripatetic company composed of actors experienced at filling the various type-cast roles in their repertoire. The arrangement involved the circuit companies in much travel and no little hardship, especially if spectators were sparse or spasmodic in their attendance, but it was a scheme which enabled apprentice actors to learn their craft in an imitative but intensive school; it permitted audiences in remote districts to enjoy live performances; it ensured that celebrities such as the great Macready occasionally made contact with audiences drawn from outside the metropolis.

It is tempting to associate the methods of every company playing on the circuits with those of that colourful, obstreperous troupe led by Mr Vincent Crummles, and doubtless many productions were hit-or-miss affairs, but often a surprisingly high standard of presentation appears to have resulted from this makeshift manner of proceeding; John Ryder, a London-based actor summoned to appear in the provinces, confessed himself humbled by the experience:

> I was engaged for walking gentlemen and 'utility' at a guinea a week, commencing at Hull in January, 1838. Having seen all the great people in town, I thought I knew all about it, and I flattered myself that I was going to astonish the wretched country actors; but, by Jove! they astonished me! . . . On the night of my arrival, the play was 'Macbeth' . . . The piece was capitally mounted, and the music admirable. When I saw this specimen of country acting, I felt that there was not much chance of my setting the Humber on fire . . .[1]

John Coleman, in whose *Fifty Years of an Actor's Life* there appears a lively description of his brief sojourn with the Lincoln circuit company then managed by Tom Robertson's father, also testifies to the striking quality of performances in the provinces; of the playwright's mother he says:

> Mrs Robertson was a remarkably fine woman and an accomplished actress. Her Portia, Constance, and Helen Macgregor were about as good as anything that was done in those days . . . Mr Butler [the company tragedian] 's performance of King John, The Stranger, William Tell, Shylock, Robert Tyke, and Richelieu, to my immature mind appear to be of the highest order of excellence, and I have since heard the same opinion expressed by persons far better qualified to form an opinion than I was at that period.[2]

However, by the 1840s, when Robertson began to participate seriously in the affairs of the Lincoln company, the heyday of the provincial circuits was over. Their repertoire of plays was necessarily dictated by what could be mounted effectively on a variety of unelaborate stages with restricted facilities, and the general populace, motivated by what Wordsworth had censured as a 'degrading thirst after outrageous stimulation',[3] were now demanding less traditional and more spectacular entertainment. This thirst could only be slaked at theatres with more sophisticated equipment than most on the circuits, and the opening-up of the country districts by the rapidly-expanding railway system meant that spectators could now travel further in search of pleasure. Moreover, the patronage of the influential local squirearchy, on which the system had for long depended, could no longer be relied upon, and as their clientele fell away, so many of the old companies declined and were disbanded.

This was certainly the fate of the Lincoln troupe with which the fortunes of the Robertson family were so closely bound up. Its sphere of influence included the towns of Boston, Grantham, Newark, Oundle, Peterborough, Spalding, and Wisbech, as well as the city of Lincoln itself, and in its latter-days efforts were made to extend its range to include Leicester, Sheffield, Malton in Yorkshire, and even Stockton and Darlington. Here the young Tom Robertson learnt the business of theatrical factotum, combining the skills of actor, adaptor of plays, stage manager, writer of comic songs, prompter, scene painter and designer, business manager, and the rest. It is therefore strange that theatrical life features so rarely in his writings: Amanda in *Play* is an actress, Polly and Esther Eccles ballet-girls, Jack Randall in *Birth* is a struggling playwright, and Chudleigh Dunscombe from *MP* longs to star in burlesque, but of the major plays not even *David Garrick* has a stage or a dressing-room as its setting. It is almost as if Robertson kept the playhouse and its peculiar customs and aura out of his pieces deliberately, though few could have known the atmosphere of sleazy digs and leaky greenrooms as intimately as he.

Yet it might well have proved impossible for Robertson to bathe his memories of theatre life in a sufficiently rosy glow to delight his audiences. From the time the Lincoln company broke up in about 1848–9, until he scored a hit with *David Garrick* in 1864, his professional life was one of unrecognised obscurity and unmitigated drudgery. A short spell as an English-speaking usher at a school in Utrecht, where he fell foul of the original of Krux in *School*, had preceded the demise of the Lincoln troupe, and from then on Robertson pursued a variety of journalistic and theatrical activities without notable success. Whenever engagements offered themselves at the 'minor' London theatres he served as prompter or acted for a guinea a week, and although he does not seem to have been an outstanding performer, he was evidently competent enough to act with Macready, and to become a member of Samuel Phelps's Sadler's Wells company then pioneering popular performances of Shakespeare at a playhouse formerly devoted to water spectaculars.

In the literary field Robertson obtained casual work as a journalist on a number of London newspapers and magazines, but his most regular source of income seems to have been derived from the common practice of adapting and translating a wide variety of plays from the French, a chore which fell to many aspirants for theatrical success at a period when it was cheap and profitable to crib from the latest Parisian sensation. Much of Robertson's work was done for the leading theatrical publisher of his day, Thomas Hailes Lacy, and most of his products are indistinguishable from the average low-quality commercial pieces then in fashion. From such hackwork

Robertson may have assimilated the principles of sound construction on which the contemporary 'well-made play' of Scribe and Sardou was built, and it has been argued that when he came to write his own original plays Robertson did little more than anglicise and humanise the *pièce bien faite* of his Gallic forerunners, transposing it for middle-class tastes. At all events his early excursions into the world of original creation are not memorable for any remarkable qualities of construction or invention: none of his early plays, whether original or adapted from French, strikes one as being the work of an author with anything unusual to say or with any unusual talent for saying it, even if one includes the more prestigious *David Garrick*. The Victorian stage may have been slow to recognise exceptional ability, but it may be said with equal justice that Robertson was slow in demonstrating it: the success of *David Garrick* and *Society* did not release a flood of rejected masterpieces from the bottom drawer of the dramatist's desk.

It is tempting to argue that Robertson only began to evolve a distinctive approach towards dramatic composition and a matching performance style during his brief period as prompter at the Lyceum Theatre in 1854, but the influence of his experiences there remains conjectural. By then the Lyceum was effectively managed by Charles James Mathews, the most celebrated light comedian of his day; but it was his wife and partner, Madame Lucy Eliza Vestris, who, inspired by Parisian models, had transformed popular entertainment of the burlesque and farcical type into an elegant and stylish display of histrionic and decorative skills during her tenancy of the Royal Olympic Theatre between 1831 and 1839. Vestris's major innovation had been to ensure that Olympic presentations achieved a coherence and a harmony of effect whereby the exaggeration and vulgarity which had formerly dominated comic entertainment were firmly excluded and the accent placed instead on artistic delicacy and restraint. These were most obviously manifested in the relaxed, unaffected acting style employed, and in the Olympic's carefully planned and executed designs for costumes and settings, often the work of J.R. Planché, a qualified antiquarian and a skilled deviser of tastefully-mounted extravaganzas and burlettas. In the view of Vestris and Mathews (who joined her at the Olympic in December 1835), elegance and fidelity to life, far from being incompatible, were inseparable; as a leading theatre historian has written:

> Vestris certainly gave verisimilitude to everyday rooms by abolishing the unconvincing wings and by furnishing them with real, not painted, furniture of taste and quality. She took pains to supply good carpets, fine draperies, real blinds over practicable glass windows and props such as clocks, fireplaces, mirrors and even actual door knobs . . . The public did in fact flock to the Olympic to see scenes of contemporary life in close imitation of the drawing rooms and gardens they knew. Vestris created an illusion of reality and imposed a unified conception by the attention she lavished on every detail of the staging.[4]

Vestris and Mathews also agreed on the deficiencies of prevalent styles of acting, the result of the practice of categorising dramatic roles into a number of recognisable standard types, which encouraged actors to execute parts according to traditionally sanctioned principles. Henry Barton Baker, deploring in 1878 the disappearance of the old provincial circuits, unwittingly exposes the dangers arising from the 'stock type' system as it was imposed on a 'stage-struck youth' taught by circuit methods:

> In all his engagements he had played the same round of characters, and when he stepped upon the London stage it was not in some new part in some new play, written for the occasion, in which he was to *experiment*, but in some old part of which years before he had carefully studied every point, gesture, tone, look, in which great actors before him had delighted generations of audiences, and by their excellences he was now to be sternly judged.[5]

Of the histrionic style encouraged by Vestris, none is so well qualified to speak as Charles Mathews, whose memoirs record the attractions of the Olympic for an aspiring novice anxious to begin his career by avoiding the standardised and artificial methods of acting long familiar to the public:

> The theatre for my *début* as an actor was chosen without a moment's hesitation. I had no passion for what was called the 'regular drama'. I had no respect for traditional acting, and had no notion of . . . undertaking for so much per week all the characters in comedy and tragedy, whether fitting or not, played by Mr. Charles Kemble, or Mr. Jones, or Mr. Elliston, whose every movement was registered in the prompt-book, and from whose 'business', as it is technically termed, no deviation was allowed. The lighter phase of comedy, representing the more natural and less laboured school of modern life, and holding the mirror up to nature without regard to the conventionalities of the theatre, was the aim I had in view. The Olympic was then the only house where this could be achieved, and to the Olympic I at once attached myself. There was introduced for the first time in England that reform in all theatrical matters which has since been adopted in every theatre in the kingdom. Drawing rooms were fitted up like drawing rooms, and furnished with care and taste. Two chairs no longer indicated that two persons were to be seated, the two chairs being removed indicating that the two persons were not to be seated. A claret-coloured coat, salmon-coloured trowsers with a broad black stripe, a sky-blue neckcloth with a large paste brooch, and a cut-steel eye-glass with a pink ribbon no longer marked the 'light comedy gentleman', and the public at once recognized and appreciated the change.[6]

The criteria of charm, grace, polish, stylistic unity, and 'truth to life' accompanied Vestris and Mathews to Covent Garden, where in 1841 they staged Dion Boucicault's first success *London Assurance*, and after an interval to the Lyceum which they occupied from 1847 to 1855. Ill-health was by then dogging Vestris who died in 1856, and Robertson would probably have seen little of Madame herself, but the standards she had evolved were everywhere apparent, and it may have been at the Lyceum that the future master of domestic realism discovered those principles at work which he was later to apply in the field of 'straight' comedy.

But by the 1850s the Lyceum was far from being the only London theatre in which 'more natural and less laboured' techniques might be studied. Certain sectors of the Victorian stage at least were weaning themselves by degrees from their more raffish and rumbustious antecedents, acquiring in the process, it must be owned, not a little social pretentiousness and pseudo-gentility. But on the credit side there was an appreciable gain in artistic finish and subtlety, a rejection of any excess or imbalance which might mar the imaginative integrity of a production, and an increasing willingness to consider a dramatic presentation as a totality.

That Robertson was acutely conscious of the direction in which the main cultural and social impulses of the age were carrying the Victorian theatre is evident from a series of articles he contributed to the *Illustrated Times*, entitled 'Theatrical Types'. Here he waxes satirical at the expense of managers, stage carpenters, scene painters, and so forth, but reserves his deepest scorn for performers who undertake the hackneyed stock roles of tradition. Robertson's contempt for set formulae and conditioned responses which impede the emergence of a drama based on carefully observed behaviour is manifest; he says of the 'Light Comedian':

> The Light Comedian is the actor who represents the character of young patricians, volatile lovers, voluble swindlers, well-dressed captains, swells in and out of luck, and the upper classes generally on this side of forty years of age. He is purely and entirely the creation of the dramatist; for neither in nature nor in society was the like of this bustling, talkative creature ever seen, for which let nature and society be thankful; for, not excepting neuralgia, snakes, or earnest men with missions, the presence of a high-spirited, high-voiced, highly-dressed hero of comedy is the most intolerable nuisance . . .[7]

Jack Randall in *Birth* also ridicules stock characters in a similar manner, and it was in this spirit of disillusionment with the outdated conventions of contemporary stage practice that Robertson created his best work. Yet it is clear from the historical evidence now available that others had already begun the campaign for a dramatic art which would relate more closely to the habits and appearance of the workaday world. Obviously the reforms of Vestris and Mathews, Charles Kean and others, upon which Robertson and the Bancrofts capitalised, represented only the first hesitant steps along the path to thoroughgoing naturalism as understood and practised in Europe by the end of the century, and Robertson was not the first to initiate such steps, but as the first important English playwright to exploit them, he deserves his due measure of esteem.

II

It was in 1855 that Robertson met his first wife, Elizabeth Burton, an actress whom he encountered at the playhouse which was to prove the scene of all his own major successes. The Queen's Theatre off the Tottenham Court Road suffered a variety of vicissitudes and changes of name for many years until its occupation in 1865 by Marie Wilton (later Bancroft) and her company under its new designation as the Prince of Wales's. The Robertsons married in 1856, and together the couple fulfilled a number of engagements. After these experiences, however, Robertson in about 1859 seems to have abandoned the boards for full-time journalism and play-doctoring as offering a slightly less unstable means of earning a livelihood, and although he continued to produce translations and adaptations for Lacy along with some original works, the largest portion of his modest income was now probably derived from articles for various periodicals including the aforementioned *Illustrated Times*, of which he eventually became the drama critic under the pseudonym 'Theatrical Lounger'. When Thomas Hood the Younger launched the comic magazine *Fun* in 1863, Robertson like W.S. Gilbert became one of its first contributors, and all three men contributed to two Christmas miscellanies edited by Hood, *A Bunch of Keys* (1865) and *Rates and Taxes* (1866), in the latter of which appeared Robertson's short story 'The Poor-Rate Unfolds a Tale' which he was to convert into his dramatic masterpiece *Caste*.

He was soon a familiar figure of London's literary and artistic 'fringe', and a popular member of a set of authors, actors, artists, and journalists who frequented slightly Bohemian, convivial clubs such as the Savage and the Arundel which provided the inspiration for the celebrated Owl's Roost scene in *Society*.[8] Of his friends, H.J. Byron was probably the closest; a Mancunian some five years younger than Robertson, Byron had originally intended like W.S. Gilbert to pursue a legal career, but the lure of writing for the stage and acting had proved too strong, and after some years of struggle he made his reputation as a writer of burlesques and extravaganzas distinguished (some might say disfigured) by their outrageously inventive punning. It was as the author of such works that Byron came to know Marie Wilton, then London's leading exponent of the sprightly art of burlesque performance, and it was partly through Byron's good offices that Robertson's *Society* was brought to Miss Wilton's attention soon after she ventured into management at the Prince of Wales's in the spring of 1865.

By the time Robertson's play was accepted by Marie Wilton, his adaptation of the French play *Sullivan* had been staged at the Theatre Royal, Haymarket, under the title *David Garrick*. The composition of this piece pre-dated its London première of April 1864 by some six or seven years, and its staging came about almost by chance. Edward Askew Sothern was a gifted character actor who, in the part of Lord Dundreary in Tom Taylor's comedy *Our American Cousin*, 'stole the show' with his portrayal of an affected English peer which so captured the popular imagination that for a time 'Dundreary whiskers' and other accoutrements became the rage. The part was virtually Sothern's own creation, expanded from the barest of authorial hints, and it established the player's prestige to such an extent that vehicles to display his talent as an actor were anxiously sought. Robertson, who had adapted his source to make the great actor Garrick its hero, saw Sothern as ideal for the role, and found both player and J.B. Buckstone, manager of the Theatre Royal, Haymarket, responsive. The romantic tale of the creditable manner in which Garrick endeavours to disillusion the infatuated play-going daughter of a London dignitary through a display of assumed drunkenness was a stale one, but it appealed to a profession eagerly seeking to improve its public image, and captured attention in a way that no previous piece of Robertson's had contrived to do, so that a modest triumph ensued. It is again significant that the *Athenaeum* for 7 May 1864 should choose to praise the *restraint* of Sothern's performance:

> His action was everywhere elegant and unobtrusive . . . We were glad to find there was no exaggeration in his style, but that all was genuine acting. Even in the drunken scenes he was moderate; while the delineation was complete, a certain boundary was not overstepped. His acting was a perfect bit of art . . .

Indeed, it may be fairly said that the applause for *David Garrick* was rather more due to actor than author. However, while there is little novelty or verisimilitude apparent in a work whose techniques are still distinctly old-fashioned, here and there (as in the tender love scene between Garrick and Ada Ingot in the final act), the Prince of Wales's 'house dramatist' is faintly foreshadowed.

Whether the success of *David Garrick* encouraged Robertson to write or merely to complete *Society* is uncertain: however, the manuscript of his most original play hitherto is dated 12 August 1864, and the leading parts in *Society* were intended for the Haymarket company, including Sothern as Sidney Daryl, a further opportunity for the actor to appear inebriated being provided in act II, scene 2. However, although Sothern liked his role, Buckstone, to whom the part of John Chodd Senior had been allotted, reputedly dismissed the whole offering as 'rubbish', and refused to stage it at any price. The piece was then successively considered and rejected by a number of London managers, doubtless dissuaded by the generally unpretentious nature of the play's theme and execution, the relative restraint of its characterisations, the low-key informality of much of its idiomatic, even slangy, dialogue, and the emphasis given to realistic scenes such as the London square and the Owl's Roost. There was also some apprehensiveness lest the latter might offend the real-life prototypes of O'Sullivan, MacUsquebaugh, and the other denizens of Robertson's Bohemia.

Not that the dramatist had entirely shaken off as yet the dead hand of stage tradition: Chodd Senior, and Lord and Lady Ptarmigant[9] are scarcely products of independent observation, while Maud Hetherington is closely related to hundreds of ardent but insipidly virtuous Victorian heroines. The absurd misunderstanding which breeds between Maud and Sidney concerning Little Maud's paternity is laboured, and Sidney's sudden acquisition of cash and a title seems a final surrender to values and attitudes which the play has been at pains to deride, though it does create the ultimate irony that the social hypocrisy practised by Lady Ptarmigant eventually works to the lovers' advantage. The style is unequal, even the usually offhand and laconic Sidney lapsing into passionate rhetoric more typical of the abortive tragedies of the past half-century, most flagrantly in his 'denunciation' speeches at the end of act II. However, managers were evidently not reassured by these remnants of the 'old style', and it seemed for a time as if the author of *David Garrick* was likely to be plunged back into obscurity. But a provincial fool was prepared to rush in where metropolitan angels feared to tread, and to his credit Alexander Henderson of the Prince of Wales's Theatre, Liverpool, accepted *Society* for production by his company in May 1865. Its undeniable success on Merseyside brought it to the notice of Marie Wilton, and despite Byron's misgivings, *Society*'s London opening, arranged for November 1865, proved a turning-point in the careers of both Robertson and his actress-manager.

Marie Effie Wilton was, after Ellen Terry, the most popular and respected woman on the late Victorian stage. Born in Doncaster of theatrical parents in 1839, she achieved prominence as a child actress in Bristol before coming to London in September 1856, where her boyish figure and manner, her tuneful voice and nimble dancing, made her the natural choice for the burlesques and extravaganzas popularised by Vestris and Planché which were still in vogue. She graduated to the Strand Theatre, where she rapidly became the principal attraction with its predominantly male clientele. Her first role at the Strand as Pippo in Byron's *The Maid and the Magpie* won the praise of Charles Dickens who confessed to John Forster in a letter that he regarded her as 'the cleverest girl I have ever seen on the stage in my time, and the most singularly original'.

Despite her appeal as a burlesque performer, Marie Wilton's ambition was to attempt the subtler art of comedy, and she sought in vain to break down managerial prejudice against her capabilities as a straight actress; thus in 1865, financed by a loan of £1000 from her brother-in-law, she broke away from the Strand to become the tenant of the Queen's Theatre in Tottenham Street, with Byron as her resident playwright, moral support, and partner, although he was legally indemnified against sharing any pecuniary loss incurred from such a risky venture. Just how risky may be imagined from the fact that the playhouse selected, familiarly known as the 'Dust Hole', stood surrounded by fried-fish shops in an unsavoury part of London, and had specialised for many years in lurid melodramas attracting a far from select type of spectator. Marie Wilton was to leave a graphic account of a visit paid just prior to assuming control:

> . . . oh, the audience! My heart sank! Some of the occupants of the stalls (the price of admission was, I think, a shilling) were engaged between the acts in devouring oranges (their faces being buried in them), and drinking ginger-beer. Babies were being rocked to sleep, or smacked to be quiet, which proceeding, in many cases, had an opposite effect! A woman looked up at our box, and seeing us staring aghast, with, I suppose, an expression of horror upon my face, first of all 'took a sight' at us, and then shouted, 'Now, then, you three stuck-up ones, come out o' that, or I'll send this 'ere orange at your 'eds.' Mr. Byron went to the back of the box and laughed until we thought he would be ill. He said my face was a study. 'Oh, Byron!'

> I exclaimed, 'do you think that people from the West End will ever come into those seats?' 'No,' he replied, 'not *those* seats.'[10]

And Byron was right. Not only was the little playhouse renamed the Prince of Wales's, to exorcise something of its former reputation, but the month before its reopening was devoted to extensive reconditioning and redecorating which ran through nearly all the enterprise's capital, but whose favourable impact upon the theatre's new up-market patrons found mention in the *Illustrated London News*'s report of the opening night, 15 April 1865:

> The doors were literally besieged, and admission was scarcely possible. The prices are, however, on an aristocratic scale, and many carriages were among the crowd assembled at the door. The interior of the house has been entirely reconstructed and richly decorated . . . The front of the boxes presents an ogee, with white and gold trellis picked out with blue; and the ceiling is divided into six panels, with gold stars and a blue centre. The arch of the proscenium is framed with white enamelled scroll, the panels in blue, and the Prince of Wales's feathers in white relief forming the centre. A niche with an ornamental stand of flowers graces each side of the proscenium – an arrangement, we understand, due to the taste of Miss Wilton. There are four commodious rows of stalls, consisting of fifty-four in number, all spring-stuffed and cushioned, and covered with blue leather and white-enamelled studs. The box seats, entirely new, are similarly stuffed and covered; and the whole circle, brilliantly illuminated, is lined with rose-bud chintz. The saloon has been entirely reconstructed and decorated with panel ornament embellished with appropriate statues . . .[11]

Despite the elegance and novelty of these appointments, the dramatic fare offered was disappointingly traditional: the triple bill staged on the first night consisted of nothing more daring than a new 'comedietta' with the prophetic title *A Winning Hazard*, an original operatic burlesque by Byron, and a farce. It had been the advice of J.M. Levy, owner of *The Daily Telegraph*, that, notwithstanding her reluctance, Marie Wilton should continue to appear in the burlesque roles for which she was adored, until support for the new venture was assured; but comedies became a prominent feature of the repertoire, including Byron's *War to the Knife*, first staged on 10 June, the cast including many who were to star in *Society* in November.

Of these the most important (in his manager's eyes at least) was a tall, nonchalant, well-bred young man, his aristocratic air enhanced by a monocle, who rejoiced in the name of Squire Bancroft Bancroft, although at this stage in his career he used the less flamboyant Christian name of 'Sydney', the legacy of a Cork printer's error. He was just twenty-four and had begun his acting life by playing a wide range of parts at the Theatre Royal, Birmingham; he had performed with Charles Mathews and E.A. Sothern as well as with Charles Kean and Samuel Phelps, and after gaining further experience, established himself at Alexander Henderson's theatre in Liverpool in 1864, where he first encountered Marie Wilton on tour with the Strand company, acting with her in Planché's *Court Favour.* An invitation to join the Wilton team for the Prince of Wales's venture swiftly followed, and Bancroft made his London début in *A Winning Hazard* at the start of the season. He went on to create many central Robertsonian roles, beginning with Daryl in *Society*, but, more significantly, came to assume a vital place in the affairs of the Prince of Wales's company as Marie Wilton's *confidant* and adviser, encouraging her to abandon burlesque entirely for comedy, a course of action H.J. Byron had always been reluctant to countenance. Moreover, Byron's Liverpool commitments took him out of London a good deal, and in April 1867 his business partnership with Marie Wilton was dissolved. On 28 December 1867 the Bancrofts were married; their theatrical association continued until their retirement in 1885, while their domestic relationship endured until Lady Bancroft's death in 1921.[12]

The original Prince of Wales's company included several other reputable actors, but the season (resumed on 25 September 1865) not only brought the troupe two valuable players in J.W. Ray from Sadler's Wells and Sophie Larkin who created Lady Ptarmigant, Lady Shendryn, and the Marquise de St Maur, but the actor who was to make a greater single contribution to the success of Robertson's comedies than any performer other than Marie Wilton or Squire Bancroft. The twenty-one-year-old John Hare was, like Bancroft and Sophie Larkin, an ex-member of the Liverpool company, and his talents as a character player were to be utilised to the full in such varied parts as Lord Ptarmigant, Prince Perovsky, Sam Gerridge, and Beau Farintosh. In providing for the winsome high spirits of Marie Wilton, the innate breeding and easy confidence of Bancroft, and the chameleon versatility of Hare, Robertson encouraged the less forced, more self-generated type of characterisation he wished to see replace the broader, overemphasised, more stereotyped modes he felt to be anachronistic in the mid-century theatre, and the relaxed 'natural' underplaying of Hare and Bancroft was to influence such actors as Charles Wyndham, George Alexander, and Gerald Du Maurier.

The season recommenced with a further triple bill, but *Society*, first staged on Saturday 11 November 1865, was accompanied only by Byron's already popular burlesque version of *Lucia di Lammermoor*, or, *The Laird, the Lady, and the Little Lover*. The skit was always well received, but it was rapidly clear that *Society* represented a major triumph for both author and company. John Oxenford in *The Times* of 14 November praised the play's 'Englishness' of tone and construction as a welcome remission from French adaptations; he admired its 'perfect freedom from conventional trammels', and its healthy tendency to strike a blow for plays of character, wit, and humour, in an age seemingly dominated by a penchant for the sensational and the spectacular. *The Daily Telegraph* commended Robertson's shrewdness and observation, describing the piece as 'a clever, sketchy picture of modern men and manners, dashed off in a spirited style, and giving perhaps a new view of some of the gradations in the social scale'.

With the passage of time it is impossible to say whether what struck *Society*'s early audiences as novel was truly so: certainly many inaccurate claims have since been made for Robertson on the grounds that his was the first English piece in which box-sets and real ceilings, actual door-knobs or coat-hooks or genuine food for stage meals, were employed. In productions at the Prince of Wales's no doubt part of the attraction lay in the good taste of the management in supplying 'everything of the best', but that *Society* was innovatory or even satisfactory in this particular is belied by the *Pall Mall Gazette*'s tart observations of 17 November 1865:

> In a comedy which aims at realism, and the essential character of which demands *vraisemblance*, the furniture and accessories are of great importance. For these the author is not altogether accountable. Few dramatists are allowed to be stage managers, and one does not expect to find in Tottenham Court-road the elegance which Madame Vestris exhibited at the Lyceum; but we may reasonably expect to see a fashionable drawing room in the 'noble mansion' of Lord Ptarmigant furnished with more than one chair and with a carpet of visible proportions, especially as there are some allusions to the wealth of the British nobleman . . .

Yet, setting aside financial limitations on *Society*'s budget, perhaps the reviewer, in drawing adverse comparisons with Vestris, was missing the point: Vestris had been required to make her art one of diversion; Robertson aimed to do a little more than amuse and give pleasure. Despite its romantic interest, *Society* seems intended to offer some serious observations on modern civilisation: that hard cash is no substitute for generous impulse and considerate behaviour; that snobbery and hypocrisy are to be despised at whatever class-level they occur; that the press wields immense power for good or evil; that good fellowship and loyalty count for more than social prestige. Sidney with his hatred of pretensions, folly, and cant, Tom Stylus with his deflationary horse-sense, are descendants of the men of honesty and honour from Restoration comedy, while the collision between the vulgar *nouveaux riches* and a scion of the old aristocracy prefigures dramas yet unborn, including Galsworthy's *The Skin Game* of 1920. Robertson's plays are not High Art, but they are not mere *jeux d'esprit* either. Moreover, although Vestris had introduced a measure of realism to her presentations, practically all her dramatic material was highly unrealistic: in *Society* and its successors not only were set, costumes, and properties 'lifelike', but dialogue, situations, stage business, theme, and character usually combined harmoniously with the mounting of the production to achieve a total effect, namely that of conveying the illusion that spectators were witnessing a faithfully recorded, unexaggerated series of events taken from ordinary life in all its flat normality. The size of Lord Ptarmigant's carpet was a detail.

But verisimilitude was not the only key to *Society*'s success: partisans such as Clement Scott were inclined to regard the freshness and youth of the company as significant:

> the young, good-looking, well-dressed actors and actresses on the stage were a change indeed after the . . . old fossils who persisted in playing young lovers and dashing sparks when they were rapidly qualifying for the

> role of grandfather . . . '*Society*' was never intended for the fossils of the old school, but for the bright young fellows of the new . . .[13]

Scott was notoriously prone to overstate the novelty of Robertson's methods and achievements, yet playwright, management, and public certainly came to believe that *Society*'s success heralded a new movement in the English theatre; whatever the secret of its appeal, it held the stage for over 150 performances and paved the way for Robertson's other Prince of Wales's ventures. Bancroft himself accounted for the dramatist's impact in the following terms:

> In those now far-off days there had been little attempt to follow Nature, either in the plays or in the manner of presenting them. With every justice was it argued that it had become a subject of reasonable complaint with reflective playgoers, that the pieces they were invited to see rarely afforded a glimpse of the world in which they lived . . .
>
> The Robertson comedies appeared upon the scene just when they were needed to revive and renew intelligent interest in the drama. Nature was Robertson's goddess, and he looked upon the bright young management as the high-priest of the natural school of acting. The return to Nature was the great need of the stage, and happily he came to help supply it at the right moment.[14]

It is easy now to smile at Bancroft's earnest assertions: the belief that Robertson's plays, with their fortunate coincidences and lucky contrivances, their just deserts and happy endings, constitute 'a return to Nature' seems ludicrous. He may have persuaded the denizens of Mayfair that it was safe to re-enter a playhouse, but it would be several decades before even society's more intelligent and perceptive elements would accept an unvarnished portrait of *true* social and economic conditions on the stage. Yet Robertson unwittingly paved the way to that goal: his plays do convey something of the quality of everyday existence where meals are eaten, watches consulted, pipes smoked, peas shelled, half-crowns borrowed, and galoshes fetched; behind the fiction some of the domestic and ethical pressures of the age can be dimly discerned, and in his far from facile characterisations intimations of psychological complexity filter through. In introducing even a hint of these factors into his pieces Robertson cautiously unbolted a door which bolder spirits were to fling wide. *Society* and its sequels are no more 'like life' than the plays Robertson strove to displace, but they are a little less 'unlifelike' and that is part of their claim on posterity's attention.

III

When *Society* was produced in London Robertson had just over five years left to live, and into this period he crammed a fierce amount of work. In addition to his labours as a playwright, he also directed a number of those pieces he composed, becoming the virtual founder of a new school of organised, authoritative, meticulous 'stage management', and an important forerunner of today's director of plays. The fact that he was thus able to dictate, not only what was said on stage, but how it was spoken, not only what was done but the manner of doing it, obviously ensured for him a greater degree of control over his work than most dramatists could command. It also enhanced the reputation of the Prince of Wales's as the home of tastefully homogeneous productions and polished ensemble playing where egocentricity was not tolerated. Because they found such carefully-presented fare to their liking, the well-to-do and better-educated continued to be the Bancrofts' chief patrons, notwithstanding the presence in the gallery of the former clients of the 'Dust Hole', and it was their preferences and prejudices that Robertson seems increasingly to have catered for. Gradually prices were raised, the pit eroded by successive extensions of the stalls, and the 'smart little bandbox' refurbished on more than one occasion. The 'carriage trade' also expected the dramatic accent to be placed on restfulness and respectability: the harrowing or vulgar was to be avoided at all costs, and Robertson's later work tends to be, like his dress circle, 'lined with rose-bud chintz'.

He wrote five more comedies for the Prince of Wales's company after *Society*: *Ours* (1866), *Caste* (1867), *Play* (1868), *School* (1869), and *MP* (1870). All enjoyed enormous acclaim, although *Play* and *MP* were generally felt to be less satisfactory than the others, even if their popularity with the public was only slightly less marked. Robertson's plays for other theatres are, however, a different matter: he achieved little success with old-fashioned melodramas such as *Shadow-Tree Shaft*, *For Love*, and *The Nightingale*, and while there are effective and typical episodes in *Home*, *Dreams*, *Progress*, and *Birth*, none of them possesses the sustained power of the Prince of Wales's comedies by which Robertson must stand or fall. It is certainly difficult to deny the suggestion that he never obtained his best results away from the Bancrofts' intimate, miniature playhouse,[15] however sternly Bancroft might point to *Caste*'s popularity at the vast Standard Theatre, Shoreditch, in 1873, or John Hollingshead claim that *Dreams* did excellent business at the Gaiety. As Dutton Cook remarked in his review of *School*:

> It may be noted that the limited size of the Prince of Wales Theatre is of real advantage to the class of plays Mr. Robertson is fond of producing; a story gains in strength and significance by being brought so closely to the view of the spectators; and the players are not constrained to unnatural shouting and grimacing in order that their speeches may be heard and the expression of their faces seen from distant portions of the house. Both author and actors are thus enabled to avoid the exaggeration of language and manner which has long been a prominent failing in dramatic writing and representation.[16]

The preparations for *Ours*, the sequel to *Society* completed during the summer of 1866, did not augur well: the piece, said to have been inspired by Millais's Academy picture 'The Black Brunswicker', was certainly infused with Robertson's perennial fascination with things military, a brother having actually served in the

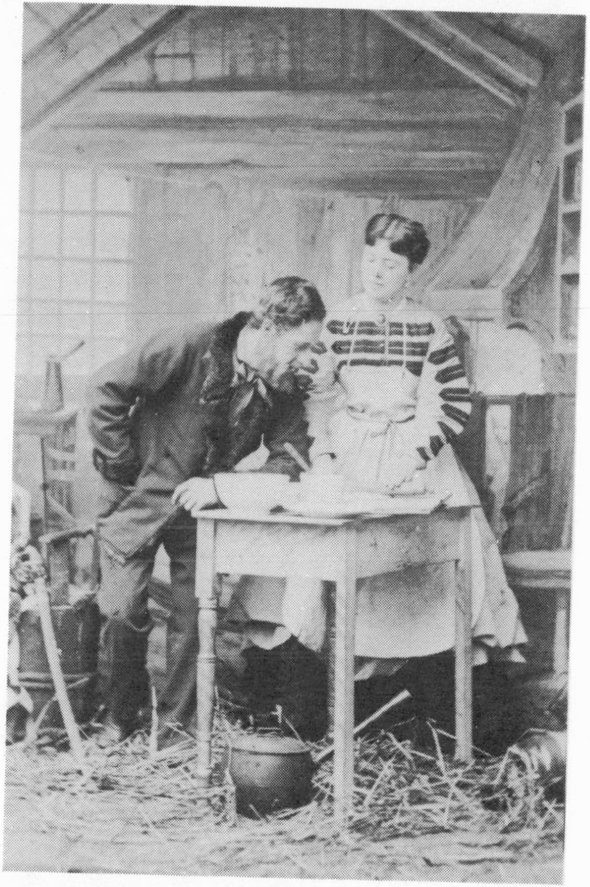

II a Squire Bancroft and Marie Wilton in act I, scene 2 of *Society* (1865)
b Marie Wilton and John Clarke in act III of *Ours* (1866)

Crimea, but dissension followed the initial reading of *Ours* to the Prince of Wales's company who were to give the play its pre-London try-out in Liverpool themselves. The part of Hugh Chalcot (assigned to John Clarke) was felt to be too dominant; Hare only agreed to play the 'insignificant' role of Prince Perovsky as a personal favour to the author; Marie Wilton was disappointed with the character of Mary Netley, and much of the 'business' developed during act III was devised by her with Robertson's consent in order to 'flesh out' a figure which, as a result, tends to eclipse that of the more mature Blanche. Furthermore, in her efforts to sparkle, Marie Wilton resorted to the somewhat pointless techniques of burlesque, a fault critics were quick to reprove. On the other hand, the device of matching a quiet, introverted girl with a more mercurial, 'sparky' companion is effective, and Robertson was often to repeat it, so much so that these female pairs became something of a trademark, whose influence lingers in James Albery's *Two Roses* (1870), Gilbert's *Engaged* (1877), Pinero's *Dandy Dick* (1887), and even *The Importance of Being Earnest.*

It is not surprising, in view of the preliminary unrest, that Robertson supervised rehearsals for *Ours* in a state of some anxiety, or that by the opening night in Liverpool he was in a condition of high nervous tension as to the play's fate, which was only dispelled when it became clear that *Ours* was a hit. Before the production opened in London on Saturday 15 September 1866, alterations were made to the troublesome third act, and Frederick Younge, a long-standing friend of the playwright, replaced Fred Dewar as Sergeant Jones. The capital's response to the new piece was overwhelming: *The Times* for 19 September, in describing it as 'an exact specimen of the ultra-real school of comedy', singled out for particular praise examples of 'the minute regard for detail which is so indispensable to this species of comedy', which included the pattering of the rain on the leaves of the trees in act I, the sounds of bands and marching columns off stage in act II, and the military and domestic paraphernalia in the hut for the final act. Most remarked upon, however, were the now-legendary 'realistic' flurries of driven snow which accompanied the opening of the hut-door, which startled with their novelty. In summing up, *The Times* gave its opinion that 'the success of *Ours* is complete beyond the shadow of a doubt'.

For all but the most captious, *Ours* retains its charm and appeal, though it is a more markedly 'period piece' than *Society*, where the bluff humour of the Bohemians and the satirical exposure of the vulgar *parvenus* can still be relished. In *Ours* genteelly flirtatious romance is made more of, and the *ambience* is high Victorian, without those Regency touches which enliven *Society* with its duns and drunks, its prize-fighters and its Pickwickian election. The pictorial element in *Ours* often appears posed: the lovers under the great trees of an English park, the 'Black Brunswicker' tableau and 'The Girl I Left Behind Me' off stage, the song at the piano, the captured colour, all are reminiscent of Victorian book-illustrations or song-covers, stimulating an unthinking response by their picturesque blandness. Even the very real hardship of the Crimean winter is rendered merely piquant, its miseries almost flippantly transformed into petty irritations, while war is glamourised, yet trivialised too. To be just, *Ours* is romantic comedy whatever its pretensions to realism; for the military heroes Hugh and Angus love finds a way, just as the resource of British womanhood rises superior to the rigours of the Crimean campaign and the urgent necessity for roly-poly pudding.

In terms of construction, however, *Ours* represents a considerable advance on *Society* with its episodic development, laboriously interwoven narrative threads, and diffuse cast: the three couples introduced in act I of *Ours* retain the centre of the stage throughout, with Sergeant Jones and the enigmatic Perovsky acting as foils rather than distractions; the dialogue often has real pace, and Robertson's ingenious method of juxtaposing the exchanges of his paired protagonists for the purpose of ironic comment arouses an interest not unlike that found in *Much Ado About Nothing* or *A Midsummer Night's Dream*. Admittedly, Scribean tactics are once again clumsily employed to set Lady Shendryn and her husband at loggerheads in acts I and II, in order to effect their tearful reconciliation in act III, and some of the extraneous foolery jars, but these are minor flaws, even the apparent improbability that a trio of women could be brought to within a short distance of so much as a skirmish with the Russians being rendered less damaging by the knowledge that some serving officers *were* joined in the Crimea by their wives.[17] Not that *Ours* is in any sense literal documentary: it is rather a set of interrelated contrasting love stories, coloured by some fairly realistic tints, and it must be judged as a piece of light fiction in a non-fictional setting. Discrepancies were perhaps inevitable.

Several relatively unsuccessful works intervened before *Caste* was presented at the Prince of Wales's on Saturday 6 April 1867: all the players had previously appeared in *Ours* with the exception of Lydia Foote who played Esther and George Honey who made a superb Eccles. Robertson was now able to provide every member of the small cast with a role geared to his or her known talents and personality, the parts of Hawtree, Polly, and Sam Gerridge being allocated with particular felicity, so that it is doubtful if the Bancrofts or Hare were ever better fitted. The slight surprise, perhaps, is that the part of George D'Alroy, the juvenile hero, should have gone to Frederick Younge, who had previously tackled Sergeant Jones in *Ours* and was scarcely the youthful-looking actor which the part seems to require. Bancroft has an amusing anecdote on the subject, which simultaneously throws light on the era's *idées fixes* which Robertson did so much to destroy:

> All that had been said . . . by the author when he read his comedy by way of describing George D'Alroy and his friend Captain Hawtree, was that he wished one of them to be fair, and the other dark.
>
> Fred Younge was amazed when I went to him and asked if he would mind being the fair man. He said how on earth could he do such a thing! He was the sentimental hero, and of course was intended to be dark; while, as what he described as the comic dandy or fop, I was equally compelled to be fair, and wear long flaxen whiskers. I eventually succeeded in touch-

> ing a very pardonable vanity – his only drawback to his ever-to-be-remembered performance being that he had already partly lost his *première jeunesse* – by suggesting that a chestnut-coloured wig would give him youth. At any rate I got my way; but I believe, at the time, I was by more than one person thought to be mad for venturing to clothe what was supposed to be, more or less, a comic part in the quietest of fashionable clothes, and to appear as a pale-faced man with short, straight black hair.[18]

By such minute changes the Robertsonian revolution took place, and *Caste* illustrates the perfect fusion of a literary style and its theatrical expression. Lisping George is far removed from the customary dashing soldier-lover, and Hawtree, the 'heavy swell' of tradition, while retaining some of his conventional traits, turns out to have a generous heart as well as a 'Pall Mall manner' and a supercilious stare; honest Sam Gerridge is idealised to the extent that his political quiescence has embarrassed radicals ever since, but his presence is at least a reminder of just how few credible working men appear on the stage at all at this period. Esther is tolerable even if, as Max Beerbohm once said, it is a mystery where she acquired her air of refinement; if the Marquise is the least convincing figure in the play, the gloriously disgusting Eccles is a genuine comic creation and a constant pleasure, the author's perfect revenge on all the benevolent aged parents cluttering the stock dramas of the past century. Throughout the action Robertson is concerned to undercut any tendency to sentimentalise the love story of George and Esther, counterpointing their amorous ardour with the sharp physical and verbal combats of Sam and Polly, just as in *Ours* he allows the Shendryns' marital strife to make a wry commentary on the courtship of Blanche and Angus. Similarly the pathos of Esther's widowhood is prevented from becoming mawkish by the grotesque comic jealousy of Eccles, and anything potentially cloying in George's story-book return is skilfully rendered semi-farcical by his impersonation of the milkman and the disruption of the meal which his 'ghostly' arrival provokes. Passionate intensity cannot be long maintained with a mouth full of bread and butter.

Although based on Robertson's short story 'The Poor-Rate Unfolds a Tale', *Caste* also appears to owe a debt to a true story of the courtship of one of Robertson's innumerable sisters in similar circumstances to Esther's, although the final details remind us once again that his purposes never involved the direct transcription of actuality.[19] Whatever the spark which kindled *Caste*'s cheerful flame, there can be little doubt that this honest-to-goodness, plain comedy remains the high point of Robertson's achievement, and that he never wrote as good a play again: it is the only one of his pieces even remotely familiar to theatregoers today, and the reasons are not difficult to comprehend. Firstly, it is an extremely economical play in terms of plot and characters, even the utter simplicity of its basic narrative making for a coherent and craftsmanlike structure where the resolution of one problem creates the next. Each memorably-etched character may only be a modification of a stock type, as Shaw was later to stress, but nonetheless each is clearly defined, nicely discriminated from its associates, and forms part of an attractive pattern of contrasts and conflicts, of which the combinations are endless: George and Hawtree; Esther and Polly; Polly and Hawtree; George and Esther; Sam and Hawtree; Eccles and the Marquise; the Marquise and Esther. Moreover, in true ensemble spirit the acting honours are equally divided, and the rich quality and variety of the characters unequalled in the entire Robertson canon: Polly, Sam, Eccles, and the Marquise (with a little help from Froissart) are interesting as much for what they say as what they do, and their distinctive speech styles divert attention from the occasional plunge into the older grandiloquent manner, of which the injured Esther is the most frequently guilty. But such lapses are rarer in *Caste* than elsewhere in Robertson's works: here he perfected the apparently natural, semi-colloquial, telegraphic conversational manner which in *Society* and *Ours* was sometimes at the mercy of the declamatory highfalutin' strain considered *de rigueur* at moments of great emotional tension, and the idiom of Eccles, however Dickensian at base, is unforgettable.[20] Finally, there is in *Caste* genuine comedy, chiefly but not exclusively emanating from Eccles whose comic rascality can be richly savoured still; the sparring of Polly and Sam may be only mildly amusing, but there is Hawtree who is caricatured just sufficiently for the purposes of laughter, but never to the point of ridicule, so that his deeper qualities are revealed as a surprise but not as a flagrant impossibility. The Marquise, too, while a figure of fun for much of the action, retains a measure of justification for her conduct and attitude, so that the final reconciliation can be endorsed and not sneered at.

Naturally, it is not hard to sneer at *Caste* if one chooses: Robertson does not really close with the question of class distinctions and their validity: he prefers to drown any exploration of the issues in a sea of sentimental tears over a bassinet. His faith in emotional outpouring and the impulses of the tender heart to overcome awkward social and moral problems is typical of countless writers of his day, not always excluding Dickens, and his admiration for Sam is symptomatic of an age prepared to tolerate working-class aspirations so long as the artisan 'knew his place'. *Caste* and plays like it helped to hypnotise the Prince of Wales's clientele into the comforting illusion that a class system which permitted society's Georges and Esthers to marry and live happily ever after was in little need of restructuring or abolishing, and that the maintenance of the *status quo* was the best guarantee of a healthy and contented populace.

But we do not have to endorse a play's premises in order to admire it, and as a technical accomplishment for the theatre of any age one must admire *Caste.* Granted the permissible objection that George is reported killed rather than merely missing, there is little that cannot be accepted as credible; there are few artificial contrivances of a Scribean nature, and if the finale with its mock-ballet[21] seems unnecessarily protracted, it may perhaps be attributed chiefly to Polly's sense of theatre. In its geniality, its economy, its domesticity, *Caste* is the happy apotheosis of the new comedy.

Robertson's next work for the Bancrofts was *Play*, staged on 15 February 1868; in the interim he had married for a second time, his new wife being of German origin (his first wife died in 1865), and *Play* is set in a German watering-place amid gamblers and tourists. It was the least well-liked of the Prince of Wales's pieces, never being revived, and a reading soon makes it clear why. For one thing Robertson had reverted to the looser type of construction eschewed in *Ours* and *Caste*, and peopled the stage with a heterogeneous cross-section of society engaged in miscellaneous adventures not all of which coalesce. The sole function of several farcical figures of a kind Robertson had been at pains to humanise elsewhere seems to be not so much to supplement the main action as to distract attention from it. Even the principals are not built on the natural lines of their predecessors, but are mostly unconvincing clichés: rich brave young man; sweet apparently penniless girl; heartless philandering aristocrat; devoted, deserted actress-wife. One can understand Robertson's desire to produce a more panoramic canvas than had been possible in *Ours* or *Caste*, but in so doing he betrayed the principles that had brought him success. Hawes Craven's sets were highly commended as capturing the essence of the German landscape, but the only episode in the play to match them for delicacy and 'truth to life' was the love scene between Frank Price and Rosie in the castle ruins.

The relative failure of *Play* was however redeemed by the runaway commercial success of *School*, the most popular of the Prince of Wales's group of comedies, which opened on Saturday 16 January 1869 and ran to crowded houses for an amazing 381 performances. This fact is an interesting comment on Robertson's work, for, though less sprawling than *Play*, *School* is only a little more distinguished as a dramatic creation; the difference is basically that *School* is more typically 'Robertsonian'. It embodies the most characteristic aspects of his art: an idealised English setting; sharp characterisations and flowing dialogue; gentle humour; pretty stage pictures; the sentimental charm of schoolgirl heroines; a whiff of aristocracy to satisfy the sycophantic instincts of middle-class spectators. *The Times* for 18 January 1869 once more led the chorus of critical approbation, observing that the presentation of a new play by Robertson at a theatre which had now become one of the most fashionable in London was to be regarded as one of the most important events of the dramatic year. It was acknowledged that *School*'s plot was of the slightest, yet this was felt to be no defect: 'four pictures, all striking and full of significance, though of unequal merit, are connected with an artistic hand, and when all is over an unwearied audience is aware that a perfectly organized whole has been contemplated with uninterrupted pleasure'. Particular praise was bestowed on the lovers' moonlit duologue in act III:

> by the mere force of treatment it is worked into an episode which for simple gracefulness is altogether unique. The dialogue between the young lord and Bella, while they converse in the moonlight, contemplating their own strongly-cast shadows, and fancifully commenting upon them, is replete with the prettiest conceits, in which it is hard to say whether wit or sentiment has the mastery, and the effect of the situation is heightened by the perfect arrangement of the decoration and the contrivance of dioramic

> effect . . . the peculiarity of *School* is a certain idyllic character, to which it would be difficult to find a parallel in any other work. The first scene in the wood, the interview between the two pairs of lovers in the grounds of the school, seem pervaded with a spirit which suggests a reminiscence of Watteau, though employed not on the conventions of an imaginary Arcadia, but on the manners of the period to which we belong . . .

The *Athenaeum* of 23 January was equally generous, believing *School* to be in point of dialogue and situation 'its author's masterpiece', though it both criticised the slowness of the concluding act and censured the classroom riot which ends act II as 'unnatural and farcical', involving a sacrifice of 'both art and probability to obtain a situation which is out of keeping with the rest of the play'. However, the overall impression was approved of, and Robertson's works summed up as

> simple almost to baldness in plot, and altogether free from improbable incident or melodramatic situation. Their hold upon an audience is due to three gifts which Mr. Robertson possesses in a remarkable degree, – power of characterization, smartness of dialogue, and a cleverness in investing with romantic associations commonplace details of life. Mr. Robertson's plays are brilliant, epigrammatic, and amusing. They fall short of greatness, but their cleverness is remarkable.

The general enthusiasm of *School*'s critics was scarcely cooled by the allegation that the author had annexed without acknowledgement a play entitled *Aschenbrödel* (Cinderella) by the prolific German playwright Roderick Benedix, and merely supplied it with an English colouring. A long article in *The Times* for 1 February 1869 endeavoured to arbitrate in the matter, pointing out that while there were certainly resemblances between the German play and Robertson's – the Cinderella motif, the school setting, the orphan-pupil heroine, the examination, the jealous wife, frustrated usher, and noble suitor – *School* had enough original elements and omitted sufficient of Benedix's ingredients to be deemed, if not an independent invention, at least as much Robertson's creation as his mentor's. *The Times* pointed to the different spirit of the English work whose comicality and wit contrasted with *Aschenbrödel*'s more Germanic sentiments and mystery, to the prominence given Naomi and Jack whose counterparts are mere sketches in the German play, to Robertson's invention of Beau Farintosh, and to his failure to make the parallel with *Cinderella* more than an incidental feature of *School*. The writer concluded that Benedix's piece was 'very pretty and romantic' while Robertson's comedy was 'extremely smart'.

Whatever its origins, *School* contains the quintessence of Robertson, however inferior to *Society*, *Ours*, and *Caste* it may be adjudged to be. Here we meet in their most undisguised form his blend of fairy tale and everyday life, his mixture of sweetness and mild satire, the latter chiefly conveyed in Beaufoy's somewhat contradictory strictures on women, and in the ridicule of the antiquated Beau. Unfortunately, in *School* the two contrasting elements do not coexist happily, so that the revelation of Bella's ultimately impeccable antecedents seems more contrived than it should, while Beaufoy's worldly cynicism renders the awe and deference his presence inspires even more uncongenial. Indeed, one's sense of justice as well as credibility is strained when at the end of act III the chivalrous lord calmly permits Bella to be dismissed at the vindictive Krux's instigation, without attempting to defend her moonlight activities to which he was (to say the least) a party: clearly his non-intervention is tolerated simply to engineer the laboriously-contrived *peripateia* of act IV with its orange-blossom tableau and comforting reassurance that Lord Beaufoy has not only not seduced Bella, but has not allied himself to a penurious waif either. Even by Victorian standards Beaufoy and Jack Poyntz are clearly the least satisfactory heroes in Robertson; Krux may be despicable, and deserve his final thrashing, but it is difficult to resist the conclusion that Jack is a Philistine hearty whose sole talents appear to be throwing his weight about, eating other people's food, and fortune-hunting, while Beaufoy seems little more than an opinionated and useless British peer with little consideration for the feelings of others, even those of his bride. Add to these a pair of heroines embarrassing in their archness, and the implausibly jealous Mrs Sutcliffe, and one senses that *School*'s weaknesses of motivation and characterisation were only masked from its early audiences by the somewhat facile charm of its schoolgirlish romping, and the 'idyllic character' of its staging which owed much to the artistry of Hawes Craven. As in *Ours*, atmosphere and youthful innocence, quiet humour and naturally-moving dialogue, compensated for inconsistencies of character and contrivances of plotting, but *School* remains not for all time but of an age, a flaw several reviewers emphasised when the piece was revived at the end of the century.

School was the first of five new plays by Robertson staged in 1869, but none of the others enjoyed the tremendous acclamation which greeted *School*: potentially the most interesting of the group was *Progress*, presented at the Globe Theatre on 18 September; though based on Sardou's *Les Ganaches* (The Stick-in-the-Muds), Robertson anglicises quite naturally the rivalry between the long-established but anachronistic Mompessons and the rising young railway engineer Ferne, whose development plans threaten their ancestral abbey home. While Arthur Mompesson discourses on the drawbacks of material progress, Ferne descants on its inestimable benefits, and Robertson makes some attempt to arbitrate and seek refuge in a compromise, but the social and economic issues are soon subsumed in the inevitable love interest which develops, and the extravagance of the comic diversions in the shape of Bob Bunnythorpe, an incompetent poet, and his father, a dyed-in-the-wool reactionary, ultimately disqualifies the play for the compliment of serious attention.

Two Robertson plays stand out among those performed in 1870: *MP* was his last piece for the Bancroft management, but it was written with some difficulty, under the pressures of what was to prove his fatal illness: the Bancroft team worked ceaselessly to prevent the production from becoming a total disaster, Robertson himself being unable to supervise rehearsals and the final presentation. Curiously, elements in *MP* remind one forcibly of *Society*: once more the action turns on the rivalry for political honours between the self-made man, one Isaac Skoome, a Chodd-like character of no breeding, and the representative of the *ancien régime*, Talbot Piers (a role which again fitted Bancroft to perfection). Once more there is misunderstanding between lover and beloved, though in this instance Cecilia Dunscombe is an incomparably more enterprising creature than Maud Hetherington, capable of acting independently (even unwisely) in order to help her lover win the election. Once again any discussion of serious questions is baulked in favour of presenting the rival attentions paid by Skoome and Chudleigh Dunscombe to Ruth Deybrooke, a rich Quaker heiress, in order that Skoome may ultimately be deprived of the girl he courts as well as of the parliamentary seat he aspires to. Hero and heroine quarrel so that they can be reconciled, and their impassioned utterances disturb the more casual tone in which the other parts are written; there is also some irrelevant comedy in the antics of Chudleigh whose ambition to tread the boards as a drag artist in burlesque enables him to quote favourite lines from a recent hit at intervals throughout. Present now is a good deal of repetition of effects from past successes, notably in the tender duologue between Ruth and Chudleigh in act II, which reads like an attempt to recapture the magic of the 'milk-jug episode' in act III of *School*. It is indeed hard to avoid the impression that with *MP* Robertson (with some excuse) was simply constructing a play on approved lines, conscious that 'the mixture as before' was all that was required of him.

His last important play was *Birth*, staged at Bristol in October 1870, in which a highly promising topic is again tantalisingly toyed with, and then whisked from view. The action turns once more on a common theme of the period, the confrontation between ancient birth and modern brains, in that Paul Hewitt's factory is about to encroach on the feudal estates of the Earl of Eaglecliffe and his sister Lady Adeliza, and deprive them of their family heritage, and for a time the stage seems set for an intriguing conflict of the *Skin Game* kind as to the relative merits of hereditary and acquired abilities when put to the test. But the interest is never sustained: Robertson soon resorts to melodramatic tactics, with an incongruous murder attempt on Paul and the eruption of an angry gang of factory hands seeking revenge on the Earl who lies under suspicion of guilt for the crime. But the real obstacle to a meaningful climax is romance: a symmetrical arrangement of reconciliatory love affairs between Hewitt and Adeliza, and Hewitt's sister Sarah and the Earl, ensures that the serious interest withers away, and even the irreverent facetiousness of Jack Randall, the would-be playwright, becomes irritating by the close of an action which winds up with a general flurry of condescension and deference. A promising subject founders between the rocks of romantic and of melodramatic inconsequence, and the constant reminders of the Earl's status – 'Let those people who despise rank despise it – I like it' announces Sarah smugly – make it clear that Robertson was not concerned to expose to vulgar gaze the human foibles of the occupants of the House of Lords. Indeed, *Birth* betrays that continuing fascination with the manners of the aristocracy which the British stage took almost a century to outgrow.

Only one other play, a drama dealing with the Franco-Prussian conflict entitled

War, was presented during Robertson's lifetime: it was not well received and taken off very swiftly. News of its failure was brought to the dying dramatist. For some years he had known that he was suffering from heart trouble, and in the early part of 1870 the disease had taken a fatal hold. Completing *MP* under great physical distress, he was unable to attend the first night, and although he improved sufficiently to watch a later performance, his condition deteriorated as autumn 1870 wore on, and his appearance on 26 November at the opening of *Ours*, the second of his successes to be revived, spelt his last visit to the playhouse whose celebrity derived largely from his labours. On 3 February 1871 Robertson died at his home in Hampstead.

IV

For the remainder of the century Robertson's comedies continued to captivate spectators: the Bancrofts staged numerous immensely successful revivals of the four plays in the present volume, and after their retirement it fell to John Hare to re-present some of the old Prince of Wales's pieces at various London theatres including the Court and the Globe. Provincial tours of the plays, initiated during the playwright's lifetime, remained popular attractions for many years; French published the two-volume edition of the *Principal Dramatic Works* in 1889, and there followed Pemberton's eulogistic but informative biography of 1893 and Clement Scott's rose-coloured reminiscences of Robertson contained in *The Drama of Yesterday and To-Day* (1899). But though homage was still paid at the shrine, some discordant notes could be detected in the chorus of praise well before 1900, and as the twentieth century advanced, so the fanfares died away.

Even the earliest criticisms of his work had been far from universally approving, and it was hardly to be expected that the newer school of drama critics, most of them apostles of the naturalistic faith which exalted Ibsen, Hauptmann, and others, would be content to leave Robertson's reputation unassailed, particularly when they sensed that the public preference for 'cup-and-saucer' pieces was preventing Ibsen and the modernists from obtaining a fair hearing. Clement Scott revered Robertson and reviled Ibsen; therefore Robertson had to be toppled from his plinth. Yet there were others who blamed Robertson for starting the trend towards realism which had permitted *Ibsen* to write as he did! Robertson had steered a middle course: now he was shelled from both banks, by radicals who belittled his modest attempts at naturalism because they did not go far enough, and by conservatives who despised his brand of homely truth and still hankered after fire and passion.

Of those commentators who condemned the lack of incident and significant action in the plays, contending that the commonplace and everyday might at first stimulate a *frisson* occasioned by recognition, but rapidly became dull and trite, Thomas Purnell who wrote in the *Athenaeum* under the pseudonym of 'Q' is typical:

> In our day 'stagey' has become a word of reproach. An audience no longer enjoys the representation of what is beyond its reach. The present and the near now best satisfies it. In the drama, as in prose fiction, realism is wanted. Every man judges what is laid before him by his own experience. Truth to current existence is the criterion of merit he applies to a drama . . . Mr. Robertson is a realist; the artificial and the ideal he eschews. Just as another dramatist introduces on the stage the real cab in which he has ridden to the theatre, so Mr. Robertson gives us the real conversation he has heard at the 'Owl's Roost', or in the West End Square where people come out at night to enjoy the evening breeze under a weeping ash in front of their houses. I cannot say we do not want the commonplace artistically represented on the stage, for it finds an appreciative public; I can only express my surprise that people pay to hear other men say behind footlights what they hear in their own houses.[22]

Others were less charitable than Purnell: there were complaints about 'superficiality' and 'triviality', charges of a lack of robustness, dignity and even grandeur, from advocates of the old-fashioned modes Robertson had supplanted; Henry James deplored the concentration at the Prince of Wales's on 'little things . . . a great many chairs and tables, carpets, curtains and knickknacks', and took no pains to conceal his contempt for plays which 'seem addressed to the comprehension of infants'.[23] The stern William Archer, too, as early as 1882 found Robertson's work sadly behind the times, finding the construction of *Society* and *Caste* primitive, seeing *School* as both trifling and flimsy, and adding of the latter that 'it takes no hold on real life, it illustrates no point in dramatic art, except the possibility of keeping an audience of Britons amused for two hours with cleverly flippant and feebly sentimental small-talk'.[24] John Coleman accused the dramatist of deliberately pandering to the tastes of his patrons:

> The author knew what his public wanted, and he gave it them. Whenever he suffered his dramatic instincts to carry him away, whenever he was in sight of a great situation, he pulled up and reduced his art to the standard of his auditor's intelligence.[25]

Even more severe were those who felt that Robertson had not carried his revolution far enough towards full-blown naturalism: typical was the young Max Beerbohm who not only castigated John Hare for reviving Robertson's plays in modern dress and so exposing their antiquated character, but attacked the snobbery of *School*, the silliness of *Ours*, and the mental limitations revealed in all the works. For this critic the plays 'were, *as plays*, dead as door-nails, but might, properly produced, stimulate the archaeologist and touch the sentimentalist to the quick'.[26]

Others were swift to concur, yet there remained at least one notable critic prepared to give Robertson his fair measure of credit for his reforms, however much he might qualify his remarks.[27] Whether stimulated as an archaeologist or touched as a sentimentalist, George Bernard Shaw gave due recognition to his predecessor in a notice of *Caste* at the Court Theatre for the *Saturday Review* on 19 June 1897; Shaw's judicious generosity is evident in every line:

> I do not defend it. I see now clearly enough that the eagerness with which it was swallowed long ago was the eagerness with which an ocean castaway, sucking his bootlaces in an agony of thirst in a sublime desert of salt water, would pounce on a spoonful of flat salutaris and think it nectar. After years of sham heroics and superhuman balderdash, Caste delighted everyone by its freshness, its nature, its humanity. You will shriek and snort, O scornful young men, at this monstrous assertion. 'Nature! Freshness!' you will exclaim. 'In Heaven's name (if you are not too modern to have heard of Heaven), where is there a touch of nature in Caste?' I reply, 'In the windows, in the doors, in the walls, in the carpet, in the ceiling, in the kettle, in the fireplace, in the ham, in the tea, in the bread and butter, in the bassinet, in the hats and sticks and clothes, in the familiar phrases, the quiet, unpumped, everyday utterance: in short, the commonplaces that are now spurned because they are commonplaces, and were then inexpressibly welcome because they were the most unexpected of novelties.'

Immediately after this appreciative paragraph Shaw does admit that Robertson was anticipated by others, and that his characters were simply thinly humanised versions of the stock figures beloved of the older drama, whose natures he rendered more credible only by the implantation of redeeming traits. Yet modest as the alteration was, Shaw himself did not scorn to profit from it when he came to write *You Never Can Tell* where the former stereotypes of traditional farce are transformed very much on Robertsonian principles.

Of course, Shaw's artistic purposes went far beyond those of Tom Robertson; a faithful imitation of the surfaces of life was never his goal, and paradoxically he wished to restore to the stage that overt theatricality and bravura which in Robertson's work had been supplanted by 'toned-down' acting, drawing-room manners, and the creation of a partial illusion of actuality. Robertson's tentative innovations were to be brushed aside, not only by the floodtide of 'total' naturalism, but by those forces inimical to naturalism which were to contend with it for possession of the twentieth-century stage. Yet Robertson helped to blaze a trail: he challenged the cherished premises on which the drama of the past had been founded, and he replaced them with a new set of artistic principles which more daring creators were free to develop and eventually to outgrow. While he might undermine the old conventions, it was beyond his intellectual scope to question the attitudes and assumptions of his age, or to probe those social, economic, political, and moral realities underlying its surface appearance. His plays merely sketched the obvious features of everyday existence; they did not analyse its bases as Shaw was to do. But Robertson's assertion that drama could legitimately present, if not an exact transcription of men's daily lives, then at least an impression of events and behaviour consistent with normal experience, was timely and invaluable. It is surely an indication not only of Robertson's attraction but also his importance that the greatest and most gifted of Britain's 'Ibsenite' dramatists should pay reluctant tribute to his work, even as he sought to transcend it.

NOTES

1 Quoted in John Coleman, *Players and Playwrights I Have Known*, 2 vols (London, 1888), I. 304.
2 John Coleman, *Fifty Years of an Actor's Life*, 2 vols (London, 1904), I. 153–5.
3 Preface to *Lyrical Ballads* (1800).
4 Sybil Rosenfeld, *A Short History of Scene Design in Great Britain* (Oxford, 1973), p. 113.
5 H. Barton Baker, *Our Old Actors*, 2 vols (London, 1878), II. 367.
6 *The Life of Charles James Mathews*, ed. Charles Dickens, 2 vols (London, 1879), II. 75–6.
7 Quoted in T. Edgar Pemberton, *The Life and Writings of Thomas William Robertson* (London, 1893), p. 92.
8 Edward Stirling, *Old Drury Lane*, 2 vols (London, 1881), mentions a drinking club known as 'The Owls' held at the Falstaff Inn opposite the Drury Lane Theatre (I. 122).
9 Lady Ptarmigant may owe something to Madame Deschappelles in Bulwer-Lytton's historical melodrama, *The Lady of Lyons* (1838), but Ernest Reynolds's suggestion in *Early Victorian Drama* that all *Society*'s leading characters are based on Lytton's cannot be substantiated.
10 *Mr and Mrs Bancroft On and Off the Stage*, 2 vols (London, 1888; 1891 edn), p. 86.
11 22 April 1865, p. 383.
12 Bancroft was knighted in the Jubilee Honours List of 1897. He died in 1926.
13 Clement Scott, *The Drama of Yesterday and To-Day*, 2 vols (London, 1899), II. 485–6, 495.
14 *The Bancrofts: Recollections of Sixty Years* (London, 1909; 1911 edn), pp. 101–2.
15 Diana Howard, *London Theatres and Music Halls 1850–1900* (London, 1970), pp. 215–16, estimates the capacity as *c.* 600, but her breakdown (stalls 143; pit 85; gallery 134; boxes 142) suggests a figure nearer 500.
16 Dutton Cook, *Nights at the Play*, 2 vols (London, 1883), I. 96–9. Cf. J. Hain Friswell, *Modern Men of Letters Honestly Criticised* (London, 1870), p. 352: 'The style is simply that of the drawing-room; the theatre is so small and yet so elegant that it *looks* like a drawing-room . . . '
17 See Pat Hodgson, *Early War Photographs* (London, 1974), p. 42.
18 *Mr and Mrs Bancroft*, p. 110.
19 *Dame Madge Kendal by Herself* (London, 1933), pp. 10–11.
20 Ernest Reynolds, *Early Victorian Drama (1830–1870)* (Cambridge, 1936), p. 89, argues that Eccles is based on the 'Parlour Orator' in *Sketches by Boz*, and that Sam recalls Sam Wilkins in 'Miss Evans and the Eagle' in the same volume; attempts to link the characters of *Caste* with those of Thackeray's *Vanity Fair* are common.
21 Said to have been based on informal entertainments got up by the Bancrofts and their friends during holidays at Waterloo, near Liverpool, the previous summer.

22 'Q' [Thomas Purnell], *Dramatists of The Present Day* (London, 1871), pp. 80–1, 93.

23 Review of January 1881, repr. in Henry James, *The Scenic Art*, ed. Allan Wade (London, 1949), p. 147.

24 William Archer, *English Dramatists of Today* (London, 1882), p. 25.

25 John Coleman, *Players and Playwrights*, II. 159–60.

26 Review of 25 February 1899, repr. in Max Beerbohm, *More Theatres* (London, 1969), p. 116.

27 Another was J.T. Grein, whose reviews may be found in *Dramatic Criticism* (London, 1899), pp. 202–5; *ibid.* (1904), pp. 84–6.

BIOGRAPHICAL RECORD

9 January 1829	Thomas William Robertson born at Newark-on-Trent, Notts, eldest child of William Robertson (1798–1872) and Margharette Elisabetta Marinus, actors on the 'Lincoln circuit', then managed by TWR's uncle, Thomas.
13 June 1834	TWR's first appearance on stage, as Hamish in *Rob Roy* (adapted from Scott's novel), at Wisbech, Cambs.
1836–41	Attends Henry Young's Academy at Spalding, Lincs.
1841–3	Attends Moore's School, Whittlesey, Cambs.
1843–8	Returns to work for the Lincoln company in a variety of capacities. Adapts two of Dickens's short stories for stage at Boston, Lincs; two adaptations from French performed at the Princess's Theatre, London, 1845–6.
1848	Leaves for London to seek employment as actor, then goes to work briefly as English-speaking usher in school at Utrecht, Holland. Returns to family in Newark after six weeks.
1849–60	Works in London as freelance writer and journalist; also as stage manager or actor, notably with Samuel Phelps at Sadler's Wells. Friendship and collaboration with H.J. Byron.
25 August 1851	*A Night's Adventure* (based on Bulwer-Lytton's novel *Paul Clifford*) staged at the Olympic Theatre, London, for four nights.
[March 1854–March 1856. England involved in the Crimean War.]	
1854	Employed for a time as prompter at the Lyceum Theatre, London, at £3 a week.
19 April 1854	*Faust and Marguerite* (translated from French) presented at the Princess's Theatre by Charles Kean.
29 April 1854	*Castles in the Air* (three-act play) staged at the City of London Theatre, Bishopsgate, London.
1854–60	Writes several original farces, and adapts a number of French plays for Thomas Hailes Lacy, London theatrical publisher and bookseller.
1856–8	Marie Wilton (later Bancroft) establishes reputation in burlesque, notably at the Strand Theatre, London, where she opens as Pippo in H.J. Byron's *The Maid and the Magpie*, October 1858.
27 August 1856	TWR marries Elizabeth Taylor (stage name Burton), an actress, at Christ Church, Marylebone. Joint engagements in Dublin, Dundalk, and Belfast follow.

8 September 1856	*The Half-Caste; or, The Poisoned Pearl* staged at the Surrey Theatre, London.

[29 March 1857. The Indian Mutiny breaks out.]

1857–60	TWR continues to work as a writer, and acts in minor London and provincial theatres. Eventually (*c.* 1859) retires to devote self to writing, becoming a prolific contributor to newspapers and magazines, and dramatic critic of the *Illustrated Times*, to which he contributes a memorable series of articles, 'Theatrical Types'.
1858–61	E.A. Sothern scores great success as Lord Dundreary in Tom Taylor's *Our American Cousin*, first in New York, then London.
14 February 1861	*The Cantab* (one-act farce) staged at the Strand Theatre.
1863	TWR writes novel *David Garrick*, adapted from the play *Sullivan* by 'Mélesville' (pseudonym of Anne H.J. Duveyrier), seen at the St James's Theatre, London. (*David Garrick* published, March 1865.)
April 1864	Play version of *David Garrick* (written *c.* 1857) staged with E.A. Sothern as Garrick at the Prince of Wales's Theatre, Birmingham. Transfers to the Theatre Royal, Haymarket, London, 30 April 1864.
12 August 1864	TWR completes *Society*, intending Sothern to play Sidney Daryl.
23 January 1865	*Constance* (libretto by TWR, music by Frederick Clay), opens at the Covent Garden Theatre.
15 April 1865	Marie Wilton and H.J. Byron present their first programme at the Prince of Wales's Theatre, Tottenham Street, London (formerly the Queen's Theatre).
8 May 1865	*Society* opens at the Prince of Wales's Theatre, Liverpool, after rejection by several London managements.
14 August 1865	Death of Elizabeth, Robertson's first wife.
11 November 1865	*Society* presented at the Prince of Wales's by the Wilton–Byron management; cast includes John Hare, John Clarke, Squire Bancroft, and Marie Wilton. Runs for 150 performances.
23 August 1866	*Ours* staged at the Prince of Wales's Theatre, Liverpool, under TWR's personal supervision; cast includes Hare, Clarke Bancroft, and Wilton.
15 September 1866	*Ours* opens at the Prince of Wales's Theatre, London. 150 performances.
Autumn 1866	TWR contributes a short story, 'The Poor-Rate Unfolds A Tale', to *Rates and Taxes and How They Were Collected*,

	edited by Thomas Hood the Younger (other contributors include W.S. Gilbert and Clement Scott).
6 February 1867	*Shadow-Tree Shaft* (a drama) staged at the Princess's Theatre.
2 March 1867	*A Rapid Thaw* (adapted from Sardou) at the St James's Theatre.
6 April 1867	*Caste* presented at the Prince of Wales's; cast includes Hare, Bancroft, Wilton, Frederick Younge, George Honey, Lydia Foote. (Plot based on 'The Poor-Rate Unfolds A Tale'.) Runs for 156 performances.
5 October 1867	*For Love* staged at the Holborn Theatre, London.
17 October 1867	TWR marries Rosetta Feist at the English Consulate, Frankfurt-am-Main.
15 February 1868	*Play* produced at the Prince of Wales's; cast includes Hare, Bancroft, Wilton, and H.J. Montague. 106 performances.
21 September 1868	Revival of *Society* at the Prince of Wales's. (H.J. Montague as Daryl.) 100 performances.
28 October 1868	*Passion Flowers* (adapted from de Musset's *On Ne Badine Pas Avec L'Amour*) staged at the Theatre Royal, Hull, starring TWR's sister, Madge Robertson, later Kendal.
14 January 1869	*Home* (adapted from Augier) presented at the Theatre Royal, Haymarket, with E.A. Sothern.
16 January 1869	*School* (loosely based on Benedix's *Aschenbrödel*) opens at the Prince of Wales's; cast includes Hare, Montague, Bancroft, and Wilton. Runs for 381 performances.
22 February 1869	*My Lady Clara* presented at the Alexandra Theatre, Liverpool; restaged on 27 March 1869 at the Gaiety Theatre, London, as *Dreams.* (London cast includes Alfred Wigan and Madge Robertson.) 96 performances.
10 April 1869	*A Breach of Promise* ('An Extravagant Farce') staged at the Globe Theatre, London.
18 May 1869	*Dublin Bay* (a comedietta) performed at the Theatre Royal, Manchester.
18 September 1869	*Progress* (adapted from Sardou) presented at the Globe Theatre; cast includes Henry Neville and Lydia Foote.
15 January 1870	*The Nightingale* (a drama) staged at the Adelphi Theatre, London, starring Benjamin Webster.
	TWR diagnosed as suffering from heart disease.
23 April 1870	*MP* produced at the Prince of Wales's; cast includes Hare, Bancroft, and Wilton. Runs for 150 performances.
5 October 1870	*Birth* (a comedy) presented by E.A. Sothern at the Theatre Royal, Bristol, followed by a provincial tour.
26 November 1870	Revival of *Ours* at the Prince of Wales's; runs for 230 performances. TWR attends first night against medical advice.

29 December 1870	TWR travels to Torquay in vain attempt to recover health, but returns to London after a fortnight.
16 January 1871	*War* (a drama) staged at the St James's Theatre.
3 February 1871	TWR dies at his home, 6 Eton Road, Haverstock Hill, South Hampstead. Buried in Abney Park Cemetery.
16 September 1871	Revival of *Caste* at the Prince of Wales's. 195 performances.

THE TEXTS

The early printed texts of Robertson's plays, particularly those pirated in the United States of America, are highly unreliable, and as a basis for the present edition I have relied on the versions which appear in *The Principal Dramatic Works of Thomas William Robertson*, published in 1889, since this was, in the words of T.W. Robertson Junior, 'the first authorised edition of my father's works'. However, the 1889 texts (cited hereafter as PDW) are not always satisfactorily edited, notably with regard to punctuation and occasional ascriptions of speeches, while there are numerous instances of valuable stage directions and pieces of dialogue being omitted. I have therefore collated the PDW versions with the individual Licensing Copies in the collection of Lord Chamberlain's Plays in the Department of Manuscripts, British Library (cited hereafter as LCP), and with the unpublished acting editions of *Ours*, *Caste*, and *School* (cited hereafter as AE) bequeathed with others in one volume to the British Library by Robertson's sister, Dame Madge Kendal, in 1936 (shelfmark 11780 b. 43). This has enabled me to adopt a number of variant readings, albeit of a minor nature, for the texts presented here; I discuss below the most significant divergences from the 1889 versions.

Obvious errors in the 1889 texts have been corrected without comment; a few editorial additions and emendations, other than those accounted for in the preceding paragraph, are enclosed within square brackets, and have invariably been inserted to clarify what is happening on stage. In accordance with the general editorial policy of the British and American Playwrights series, stage directions which merely indicate the characters' positions or movements (e.g. 'Crosses R.', 'Moves to L.C.', 'Exit L. 1. E' etc.) have been suppressed or suitably adapted, as being primarily of antiquarian interest. Certain other changes of a trifling nature have also been made in the interests of consistency, as when, for example, the same character is indicated by two different speech headings.

Society

Perhaps the most striking aspect of both the versions of *Society* collated for this edition is the omission of a large number of roles from the cast lists prefacing the texts. One must add fifteen separate parts to the extant lists, together with groups of extras such as the guests at the ball, the 'roughs' at Springmead-le-Beau, and the crowd of 'Countrymen and Women' who hail Daryl at the finale. The most important of these characters are Sir Farintosh Fadileaf and Colonel Browser for whom dialogue is provided in PDW act II, scene 2, but who do not appear in LCP which sets act II, scene 2 at Lord Ptarmigant's house, and not Sir Farintosh's. Even PDW makes provision in its text for the omission of both Sir Farintosh and Browser; in fact, it would seem doubtful if the Bancrofts ever included them, since cast lists do not mention the characters or assign actors to the parts, and their inclusion would entail a further set. Yet without them the remaining action seems bald: they help to 'flesh out' the roles of Lady Ptarmigant and Tom Stylus, and add a further stratum to Robertson's portrait of 'society'. I have accordingly printed the fuller version from PDW, where the simpler variation may also be located.

The original version of the song 'Cock-a-doodle-doo' in the Owl's Roost scene in act II given in the LCP text was later altered; instead of the stanza entitled 'Commercial', LCP reads 'Journalistic', and the verse runs:

When papers speak with puff and praise
Of things and people nowadays
Of kings, quack medicines, railways – plays –
Old laws, inventions new
Alliterative words and fuss
Big adjectives, terms curious,
Sounds fury – what's all this to us
  But cock-a-doodle-doo etc.

Given the strong journalistic interest of the play, it is curious that the 'Commercial' verse was preferred for PDW, although, since it does glance at the Chodd mentality, I have retained it. LCP also preserves the original version of the last four lines of the 'Amatory' stanza, and reads thus:

She answers with a loving kiss
Swears your life's chiefest, highest bliss
And plights herself, – why, what's all this
  But cock-a-doodle-doo!

The only other variant worth comment is Sidney's speech in act II, scene 2 denouncing the marriage market, which begins 'Feeling! Why, man, this is a market . . . ' LCP contains a slightly stronger and more colourful version of this speech, and I have adopted it for that reason.

Ours

All the major changes from PDW adopted for this play occur in act III; for instance, on p. 122 I have preferred LCP's less circumstantial explanation of the ladies' appearance in the Crimea. For purposes of comparison, PDW's reading runs:

CHALCOT: (*aside*) She's looking very well. But you must have dropped from the clouds.

LADY SHEN: It was all done in a moment. Lady Llandudno felt that she must come over here to see her boy – you know he's her only one. She sent Lord Llandudno to Southampton, where his yacht was lying, to ask the captain if the 'Curlew' was big enough to make the voyage to the Crimea. The captain answered that it was, and that it could be ready in two days. During that time, Lady Llandudno called on me to bid me goodbye. I was seized with the desire to come out too. Lady Llandudno acceded to my wish. Blanche asked to accompany me: I acceded to her wish. I brought Miss Netley as a companion for Blanche; and here we are. Major Samprey brought us from Balaclava in a cart.

CHALCOT: I saw female figures entering our hut from the top of the hill, and hobbled on as fast as I could. I took you for *vivandières* . . .

By contrast, I have filled out from LCP a few details of the roly-poly pudding making, and Chalcot's offer to educate Sergeant Jones's twin boy on p. 134 is taken from the same source, since this exchange in my view contributes greatly to the image of the 'reformed' Hugh.

Caste

The most fundamental textual problem with this play also involves one of staging: in all extant versions of *Caste* there is presumed to be only a single exit from the stage for acts I and III, namely the 'door practicable up right' which leads in imagination to a passageway from which the street door at the rear may be gained. LCP, AE, and PDW all agree on this point, but in act III some uncertainty arises when, after the quarrel with the Marquise, Esther retires to lie down in her bedroom with the baby (p. 169). If she leaves (as she presumably must) by the door up right (as if on her way to *another* room off the passage outside), a director then has the puzzle of coping with George's attempts to enter Esther's bedroom from the stage, and with his efforts to apply his eye to the key-hole of the bedroom door in order to contemplate his sleeping wife (p. 178). Squire Bancroft's prompt-copy now in the British Theatre Museum throws no light on the problem, except in so far as it notes that for act III the door key of act I must be removed, the reason for which must surely be to enable George to peer plausibly through the key-hole! Bancroft's stage plan has no reference to any other door in the room.

Yet what is George assumed to be looking *at* when he tries the key-hole? Esther's bedroom can scarcely be immediately outside the door. It is possible that the room was taken to lie across the corridor from the living-room, and that the absurdity of George's action in trying to see his wife from the room opposite was attributed to natural elation. However, it is tempting to introduce a second door (say down stage right) leading to Esther's bedroom into which George attempts to peer: such temerity might certainly be forgiven a director trying to achieve an intelligible production of *Caste*, but it is not textually justifiable.[1]

The textual variations adopted are few: I have restored from LCP George's confession in act I that his 'thick tongue and lisping' make him seem more foolish than he is, since it reminds audiences and directors that George was not intended to be the conventional stage cavalryman, and also conforms with the description of

---

1 I am grateful to Don Roy who first drew my attention to the difficulties presented by the text.

Ensign Daubray in 'The Poor-Rate Unfolds A Tale' (see pp. 227–31 below). I have also included a small but attractive detail from AE in act III; when Polly returns after waking Esther (p. 179), her change of mood following George's safe return is signalled by the fact that she now wears 'a light-coloured dress'. Although this instruction was possibly not complied with in production, since it is certainly struck out in Bancroft's prompt-copy, a present-day director might well wish to adopt Robertson's original suggestion.

School

Although I have incorporated a few trivial details taken from LCP and AE, this text is substantially that of PDW. AE is marginally more precise in its stage directions, but I have been able to print the dialogue virtually as it appears in PDW.

SOCIETY

A comedy in three acts

First produced at the Prince of Wales's Theatre, Liverpool, on 8 May 1865; afterwards at the Prince of Wales's Theatre, London, on Saturday 11 November 1865, with the following cast:

LORD PTARMIGANT	Mr Hare
LORD CLOUDWRAYS, MP	Mr Trafford
SIDNEY DARYL, *a barrister*	Mr Bancroft
MR JOHN CHODD, SENIOR	Mr Ray
MR JOHN CHODD, JUNIOR	Mr J. Clarke
TOM STYLUS	Mr F. Dewar
O'SULLIVAN	Mr H.W. Montgomery
MacUSQUEBAUGH	Mr Hill
DR MAKVICZ	Mr Bennett
BRADLEY	Mr Parker
DR SCARGIL	Mr Lawson
SAM STUNNER, PR (alias the Smiffel Lamb)	Mr J. Tindale
SHAMHEART	Mr G. Odell
DODDLES	Mr Burnett
MOSES AARON, *a bailiff*	Mr G. Atkins
SHERIDAN TRODNON	Mr Macart
LADY PTARMIGANT	Miss Larkin
MAUD HETHERINGTON	Miss Marie Wilton
LITTLE MAUD	Miss George
MRS CHURTON	Miss Merton
SERVANT [at Lord Ptarmigant's?]	Miss Thompson

[AUTHOR
REPORTER
WAITER at the Owl's Roost
PRINTER'S BOY
SIR FARINTOSH FADILEAF
COLONEL BROWSER
SERVANT at Sir Farintosh's
WAITER at Springmead
COUNTRY BOY
NURSEMAID; CHILD; GUARDSMAN; GUESTS at ball; SIX or EIGHT ROUGHS; A GENTLEMAN; Election Committee; COUNTRYMEN and WOMEN, including a GIRL and a CHILD.]

SCENE FROM THE NEW COMEDY, "SOCIETY," AT THE PRINCE OF WALES'S THEATRE: THE OWLS' ROOST.

III Artist's impression of the Owl's Roost scene from *Society* (1865)

ACT I

SCENE 1. SIDNEY DARYL*'s Chambers in Lincoln's Inn; set doorpiece right and set doorpiece left (to double up and draw off); the room to present the appearance of belonging to a sporting literary barrister; books, pictures, whips; the mirror stuck full of cards; a table, chairs, etc. As the curtain rises a knock heard, and* DODDLES *discovered opening door.*

TOM: (*without*) Mr Daryl in?

DODDLES: (*an old clerk*) Not up yet.

(*Enter* TOM STYLUS, CHODD JUNIOR, *and* CHODD SENIOR.)

CHODD JUN: (*looking at watch*) Ten minutes to twelve, eh, guv?

TOM: Late into bed; up after he oughter; call out for brandy and sobering water.

SIDNEY: (*within*) Doddles.

DODDLES: Yes, sir!

SIDNEY: Brandy and soda.

DODDLES: Yes, sir! (*Takes bottle off.*)

TOM: I said so! Tell Mr Daryl two gentlemen wish to see him on particular business.

CHODD JUN: (*a supercilious, bad swell; glass in eye; hooked stick; vulgar and uneasy*) So this is an author's crib – is it? Don't think much of it, eh, guv? (*crossing behind*)

CHODD SEN: (*a common old man, with a dialect*) Seems comfortable enough to me, Johnny.

CHODD JUN: Don't call me Johnny! I hope he won't be long (*looking at watch*). Don't seem to me the right sort of thing, for two gentlemen to be kept waiting by a man they are going to employ.

CHODD SEN: Gently, Johnny. (CHODD JUNIOR *looks annoyed.*) I mean gently without the Johnny – Mister –

TOM: Daryl – Sidney Daryl!

CHODD SEN: – Daryl didn't know as we was coming!

CHODD JUN: (*rudely to* TOM) Why didn't you let him know?

TOM: (*fiercely*) How the devil could I? I didn't see you till last night. (CHODD JUNIOR *retires into himself.*) You'll find Sidney Daryl just the man for you; young – full of talent – what I was thirty years ago; I'm old now, and not full of talent, if ever I was; I've emptied myself; I've missed my tip. You see, I wasn't a swell – he is!

CHODD JUN: A swell – what, a man who writes for his living?

(DODDLES *enters.*)

DODDLES: Mr Daryl will be with you directly; will you please to sit down?

---

double up, etc.: hinged to fold flat for easier movement and storage.
bad swell: a 'swell' was someone dressed in high fashion, though often (as here) ostentatiously so. However, applied to Daryl a few lines later, the word indicates good breeding.
glass in eye: a monocle.
crib: 'berth' (cf. present-day 'pad'). Since the term can also mean 'hovel', Chodd's remark may be derogatory.
a dialect: an 'accent'.
missed my tip: failed in my aim.

(CHODD SENIOR *sits;* TOM *takes a chair left of table;* CHODD JUNIOR, *waiting to have one given to him, is annoyed that no one does so, and sits on table.* DODDLES *goes round to left.*)

CHODD JUN: Where is Mr Daryl?

DODDLES: In his bath!

CHODD JUN: (*jumping off table*) What! You don't mean to say he's keeping us here while he washes himself?

(*Enter* SIDNEY, *in morning jacket.*)

SIDNEY: Sorry to have detained you; how are you, Tom?

(TOM *and* CHODD SENIOR *rise;* CHODD JUNIOR *sits again on table and sucks cane.*)

CHODD SEN: Not at all!

CHODD JUN: (*with watch*) Fifteen minutes.

SIDNEY: (*crossing, handing chair to* CHODD JUNIOR) Take a chair!

CHODD JUN: This'll do.

SIDNEY: But you're sitting on the steel pens.

TOM: Dangerous things, pens! (CHODD JUNIOR *takes a chair.*)

SIDNEY: Yes! Loaded with ink, percussion powder's nothing to 'em.

CHODD JUN: We came here to talk business. (*to* DODDLES) Here, you, get out!

SIDNEY: (*surprised*) Doddles – I expect a lot of people this morning, be kind enough to take them into the library.

DODDLES: Yes, sir! (*aside, looking at* CHODD JUNIOR) Young rhinoceros! (*Exit.*)

SIDNEY: Now, gentlemen, I am – (*crossing behind table*)

TOM: Then I'll begin. First let me introduce Mr Sidney Daryl to Mr John Chodd, of Snoggerston, also to Mr John Chodd, Junior, of the same place; Mr John Chodd, of Snoggerston, is very rich – he made a fortune by –

CHODD SEN: No! – My brother Joe made the fortune in Australey, by gold digging and then spec'lating; which he then died, and left all to me.

CHODD JUN: (*aside*) Guv! Cut it!

CHODD SEN: I shan't – I ain't ashamed of what I was, nor what I am; it never was my way. Well, sir, I have lots of brass!

SIDNEY: Brass?

CHODD SEN: Money!

CHODD JUN: Heaps!

CHODD SEN: Heaps; but having begun by being a poor man, without education, and not being a gentleman –

CHODD JUN: (*aside*) Guv! – Cut it.

CHODD SEN: I shan't – I know I'm not, and I'm proud of it – that is, proud of knowing that I'm not, and I won't pretend to be. Johnny, don't put me out – I say I'm not a gentleman, but my son is.

SIDNEY: (*looking at him*) Evidently.

CHODD SEN: And I wish him to cut a figure in the world – get into Parliament.

SIDNEY: Very difficult.

CHODD SEN: To get a wife?

SIDNEY: Very easy.

CHODD SEN: And in short, to be a – a real gentleman.

SIDNEY: Very difficult.

CHODD SEN: }
CHODD JUN: } Eh?

SIDNEY: I mean very easy.

CHODD SEN: Now, as I'm anxious he should be an MP as soon as –

SIDNEY: As he can.

CHODD SEN: Just so, and as I have lots of capital unemployed, I mean to invest it in –

TOM: (*slapping* SIDNEY *on knee*) A new daily paper!

SIDNEY: By Jove!

CHODD SEN: A cheap daily paper, that could – that will – What will a cheap daily paper do?

SIDNEY: Bring the 'Court Circular' within the knowledge of the humblest.

TOM: Educate the masses – raise them morally, socially, politically, scientifically, geologically, and horizontally.

CHODD SEN: (*delighted*) That's it – that's it, only it looks better in print.

TOM: (*spouting*) Bring the glad and solemn tidings of the day to the labourer at his plough – the spinner at his wheel – the swart forger at his furnace – the sailor on the giddy mast – the lighthouse keeper as he trims his beacon lamp – the housewife at her pasteboard – the mother at her needle – the lowly lucifer seller, as he splashes his wet and weary way through the damp, dreary, steaming, stony streets, eh? – you know. (*Slapping* SIDNEY *on the knee – they both laugh.*)

CHODD SEN: (*to* CHODD JUNIOR) What are they a-laughing at?

TOM: So my old friend Johnny Prothero, who lives hard by Mr Chodd, knowing that I have started lots of papers, sent the two Mr Chodds, or the Messrs Chodd – which is it? – you're a great grammarian – to me. I can find them an efficient staff, and you are the first man we've called upon.

SIDNEY: Thanks, old fellow. When do you propose to start it?

CHODD SEN: At once.

SIDNEY: What is it to be called?

CHODD SEN: We don't know.

CHODD JUN: We leave that to the fellers we pay for their time and trouble.

SIDNEY: You want something –

CHODD SEN: Strong.

TOM: And sensational.

SIDNEY: I have it (*rising*).

TOM: }
CHODD SEN: } What?
CHODD JUN: }

SIDNEY: The *Morning Earthquake*!

TOM: (*rising*) Capital!

CHODD SEN: (*rising*) First-rate!

CHODD JUN: (*still seated*) Not so bad. (*Goes up stage during next speech.*)

SIDNEY: Don't you see? In place of the clock, a mass of houses, factories, and palaces tumbling one over the other; and then the prospectus! 'At a time when thrones are tottering, dynasties dissolving – while the old world is displacing to make room for the new – '

TOM: Bravo!

CHODD SEN: (*enthusiastically*) Hurray!

TOM: A second edition at four o'clock p.m., the *Evening Earthquake*, eh? Placard the walls. 'The *Evening Earthquake*', one note of admiration; 'The *Earthquake*', two notes of admiration; 'The *Earthquake*', three notes of admiration. Posters: 'The *Earthquake* delivered every morning with your hot rolls.' 'With coffee, toast, and eggs, enjoy your *Earthquake*!'

CHODD SEN: (*with pocket-book*) I've got your name and address.

CHODD JUN: (*who has been looking at cards stuck in glass*) Guv. (*Takes old* CHODD *up stage and whispers to him.*)

TOM: (*to* SIDNEY) Don't like this young man!

SIDNEY: No.

TOM: Cub.

SIDNEY: Cad.

TOM: Never mind. The old 'un's not a bad 'un. We're off to a printer's.

SIDNEY: Goodbye, Tom, and thank you.

TOM: How's the little girl?

SIDNEY: Quite well. I expect her here this morning.

CHODD SEN: Good morning.

SIDNEY: Good morning.

(*Exeunt* CHODD SENIOR *and* TOM.)

SIDNEY: (*filling pipe, etc.*) Have a pipe?

CHODD JUN: (*taking out a magnificent case*) I always smoke cigars.

SIDNEY: Gracious creature! Have some bitter beer? (*getting it from locker*)

CHODD JUN: I never drink anything in the morning.

SIDNEY: Oh!

CHODD JUN: But champagne.

SIDNEY: I haven't got any.

CHODD JUN: Then I'll take beer. (*They sit.*) Business is business – so I'd best begin at once. The present age is, as you are aware – a practical age. I come to the point – it's my way. Capital commands the world. The capitalist commands capital, therefore the capitalist commands the world.

SIDNEY: But you don't quite command the world, do you?

CHODD JUN: Practically, I do. I wish for the highest honours – I bring out my cheque-book. I want to go into the House of Commons – cheque-book. I want the best legal opinion in the House of Lords – cheque-book. The best house – cheque-book. The best turn-out – cheque-book. The best friends, the best wife, the best-trained children – cheque-book, cheque-book, and cheque-book.

SIDNEY: You mean to say with money you can purchase anything.

CHODD JUN: Exactly. This life is a matter of a bargain.

SIDNEY: But 'honour, love, obedience, troops of friends'?

---

note of admiration: exclamation mark.
turn-out: possibly outfit, or 'get-up', but more probably a carriage.
'honour, love', etc.: see *Macbeth* V. 3. 25.

CHODD JUN: Can buy 'em all, sir, in lots, as at an auction.

SIDNEY: Love, too?

CHODD JUN: Marriage means a union mutually advantageous. It is a civil contract, like a partnership.

SIDNEY: And the old-fashioned virtues of honour and chivalry?

CHODD JUN: Honour means not being a bankrupt. I know nothing at all about chivalry, and I don't want to.

SIDNEY: Well, yours is quite a new creed to me, and I confess I don't like it.

CHODD JUN: The currency, sir, converts the most hardened sceptic. I see by the cards on your glass that you go out a great deal.

SIDNEY: Go out?

CHODD JUN: Yes, to parties. (*looking at cards on the table*) There's my Lady this, and the Countess t'other, and Mrs somebody else. Now that's what I want to do.

SIDNEY: Go into society?

CHODD JUN: Just so. You had money once, hadn't you?

SIDNEY: Yes.

CHODD JUN: What did you do with it?

SIDNEY: Spent it.

CHODD JUN: And you've been in the army?

SIDNEY: Yes.

CHODD JUN: Infantry?

SIDNEY: Cavalry.

CHODD JUN: Dragoons?

SIDNEY: Lancers.

CHODD JUN: How did you get out?

SIDNEY: Sold out.

CHODD JUN: Then you were a first-rate fellow, till you tumbled down?

SIDNEY: Tumbled down?

CHODD JUN: Yes, to what you are.

(SIDNEY, *about to speak, is interrupted by* MOSES AARON, *without.*)

AARON: Tell you I musht shee him.

(*Enter* MOSES AARON *with* DODDLES.)

AARON: (*not seeing* CHODD JUNIOR, *going round behind table*) Sorry, Mister Daryl, but at the shoot of Brackersby and Co. (*Arrests him.*)

CHODD JUN: Je-hosophat! (*rising*)

SIDNEY: Confound Mr Brackersby! It hasn't been owing fifteen months! – How much?

AARON: With exes, fifty-four pun' two.

SIDNEY: I've got it in the next room. Have some beer?

AARON: Thank ye, shir. (SIDNEY *pours it out.*)

SIDNEY: Back directly. (*Exit.*)

CHODD JUN: This chap's in debt. Here, you!

Sold out: commissions in the armed services were still purchased and sold at this period.

AARON: Shir.
CHODD JUN: Mr Daryl – does he owe much?
AARON: Sphecks he does, shir, or I shouldn't know him.
CHODD JUN: Here's half a sov. Give me your address.
AARON: (*gives card*) 'Orders execooted with punctuality and despatch.'
CHODD JUN: If I don't get into society now, I'm a Dutchman.

(*Enter* SIDNEY.)

SIDNEY: Here you are – ten fives, two twos – and a half-crown for yourself.
AARON: Thank ye, shir. Good mornin', shir.
SIDNEY: Good morning.
AARON: (*to* CHODD JUNIOR) Good mornin', sshir.
CHODD JUN: Such familiarity from the lower orders. (*Exit* MOSES AARON.) You take it coolly (*sitting*).
SIDNEY: (*sitting*) I generally do.
CHODD JUN: (*looking round*) You've got lots of guns?
SIDNEY: I'm fond of shooting.
CHODD JUN: And rods?
SIDNEY: I'm fond of fishing.
CHODD JUN: And books?
SIDNEY: I like reading.
CHODD JUN: And whips?
SIDNEY: And riding.
CHODD JUN: Why, you seem fond of everything?
SIDNEY: (*looking at him*) No; not everything.

(DODDLES *enters, with card.*)

SIDNEY: (*reading*) 'Mr Sam Stunner, PR.'
CHODD JUN: 'PR'? What's PR mean? Afternoon's PM.
SIDNEY: Ask him in.

(*Exit* DODDLES.)

CHODD JUN: Is he an author? or does PR mean Pre-Raphaelite?
SIDNEY: No; he's a prize-fighter – the Smiffel Lamb. (*Enter the* SMIFFEL LAMB.) How are you, Lamb?
LAMB: Bleating, sir, bleating – thanks kindly.
CHODD JUN: (*aside to* SIDNEY) Do prize-fighters usually carry cards?
SIDNEY: The march of intellect. Education of the masses – the Jemmy Masseys. Have a glass of sherry?
LAMB: Not a drain, thankee, sir.
CHODD JUN: (*aside*) Offers that brute sherry, and makes me drink beer.
LAMB: I've just bin drinkin' with Lankey Joe, and the Dulwich Duffer, at Sam Shoulderblow's. I'm a-going into trainin' next week to fight Australian Harry, the Boundin' Kangaroo. I shall lick him, sir. I know I shall.
SIDNEY: I shall back you, Lamb.

Jemmy Masseys: Jem Mace (1831–1910), English heavyweight champion 1861–72. In 1870 he became world champion by defeating Tom Allen in New Orleans.

LAMB: Thankee, Mr Daryl. I knew you would. I always does my best for my backers, and to keep up the honour of the science; the Fancy, sir, should keep square. (*Looks at* CHODD JUNIOR, *hesitates, then walks to door, closes it, and walks sharply up to* SIDNEY DARYL, CHODD JUNIOR *leaping up in alarm, and retiring to back. Leaning on table and speaking close to* SIDNEY DARYL*'s ear*) I jist called in to give you the office, sir, as has always bin so kind to me, not to put any tin on the mill between the Chokin' Chummy and Slang's Novice. It's a cross, sir, a reg'lar barney!

SIDNEY: Is it? Thank ye.

LAMB: That's wot I called for, sir; and now I'm hoff. (*Goes to door – turning.*) Don't put a mag on it, sir; Chokin' Chummy's a cove as well as would sell his own mother; he once sold *me*, which is *wuss*. Good day, sir.

(*Exit* LAMB. CHODD JUNIOR *reseats himself.*)

CHODD JUN: As I was saying, you know lots of people at clubs, and in society.

SIDNEY: Yes.

CHODD JUN: Titles, and Honourables, and Captains, and that.

SIDNEY: Yes.

CHODD JUN: Tip-toppers. (*after a pause*) You're not well off?

SIDNEY: (*getting serious*) No.

CHODD JUN: I am. I've heaps of brass. Now I have what you haven't, and I haven't what you have. You've got what I want, and I've got what you want. That's logic, isn't it?

SIDNEY: (*gravely*) What of it?

CHODD JUN: This; suppose we exchange or barter. You help me to get into the company of men with titles, and women with titles; swells, you know, real 'uns, and all that.

SIDNEY: Yes.

CHODD JUN: And I'll write you a cheque for any reasonable sum you like to name.

(SIDNEY *rises indignantly; at the same moment* LITTLE MAUD *and* MRS CHURTON *enter.*)

LITTLE MAUD: (*running to* SIDNEY) Here I am, uncle; Mrs Churton says I've been such a good girl.

SIDNEY: (*kissing her*) My darling. How d'ye do, Mrs Churton. (*to* LITTLE MAUD) I've got a waggon, and a baa-lamb that squeaks, for you. (*then to* CHODD JUNIOR) Mr Chodd, I cannot entertain your very commercial proposition. My friends are my friends; they are not marketable commodities. I regret that I can be of no assistance to you. With your appearance, manners, and cheque-book, you are sure to make a circle of your own.

CHODD JUN: You refuse, then –

---

the Fancy: the prize-fighting fraternity, participants and supporters.
office: service or favour.
tin: money.
mill: fight.
cross: 'fix'.
barney: not a 'set-to' but a 'cheat'.
a mag: slang for a halfpenny.

SIDNEY: Absolutely. Good morning.

CHODD JUN: Good morning. (*aside*) And if I don't have my knife into you, my name's not John Chodd Junior.

(*Exeunt* SIDNEY, LITTLE MAUD, *and* MRS CHURTON, *door right*, CHODD JUNIOR *door left*.)

SCENE 2. *The interior of a square at the West End. Weeping ash over a rustic chair, trees, shrubs, walks, rails, gates, etc.; houses at back. Time: evening – effect of setting sun in windows of houses; lights in some of the windows, etc.; street lamps.* MAUD *discovered in rustic chair, reading; street band heard playing in the distance.*

MAUD: I can't see to read any more. Heigho! How lonely it is! And that band makes me so melancholy – sometimes music after dinner makes me feel – (*rising*) Heigho! I suppose I shall see nobody tonight; I must go home. (*Starts.*) Oh! (SIDNEY *appears at left gate.*) I think I can see to read a few more lines. (*Sits again and takes book.*)

SIDNEY: (*feeling pockets*) Confound it! I've left my key at home. (*Tries gate.*) How shall I get in! (*looking over rails*) I'll try the other. (*Goes round at back to opposite gate.*)

MAUD: Why, he's going! He doesn't know I'm here. (*Rises, calling*) Sid – No, I won't, the idea of his – (*Sees* SIDNEY *at gate right.*) Ah! (*Gives a sigh of relief, reseats herself and reads.*)

SIDNEY: (*at gate*) Shut too! (*trying gate*) Provoking! What shall I – (*Sees* NURSEMAID *approaching with* CHILD; *drops his hat into square.*) Will you kindly open this? I've forgotten my key. (NURSEMAID *opens gate.*) Thanks! (SIDNEY *enters square;* NURSEMAID *and* CHILD *go out at gate;* LIFE GUARDSMAN *enters, speaks to* NURSEMAID; *they exeunt.* SIDNEY *sighs on seeing* MAUD.) There she is! (*Seats himself by* MAUD.) Maud!

MAUD: (*starting*) Oh! Is that you? Who would have thought of seeing you here?

SIDNEY: Oh, some – don't I know that you walk here after dinner? And all day long I've been wishing it was half-past eight.

MAUD: (*coquetting*) I wonder, now, how often you've said that, this last week.

SIDNEY: Don't pretend to doubt me, that's unworthy of you. (*a pause*) Maud!

MAUD: Yes!

SIDNEY: Are you not going to speak?

MAUD: (*dreamily*) I don't know what to say.

SIDNEY: That's just my case. When I'm away from you, I feel I could talk to you for hours; but when I'm with you, somehow or other, it seems all to go away. (*getting closer to her, and taking her hand*) It is such happiness to be with you, that it makes me forget everything else. (*Takes off his gloves and puts them on seat.*) Ever since I was that high, in the jolly old days down at Springmead, my greatest pleasure has been to be near you. (*Looks at watch.*) Twenty to nine. When must you return?

MAUD: At nine.

SIDNEY: Twenty minutes. How's your aunt?

MAUD: As cross as ever.

SIDNEY: And her dress as old-fashioned?

MAUD: Older.

SIDNEY: And Lord Ptarmigant?

MAUD: As usual – asleep.

SIDNEY: Dear old man! How he does doze his time away. (*another pause*) Anything else to tell me?

MAUD: We had such a stupid dinner; such odd people.

SIDNEY: Who?

MAUD: Two men by the name of Chodd.

SIDNEY: (*uneasily*) Chodd?

MAUD: Isn't it a funny name? – Chodd.

SIDNEY: Yes, it's a Chodd name – I mean an odd name. Where were they picked up?

MAUD: I don't know. Aunty says they are both very rich.

SIDNEY: (*uneasily*) She thinks of nothing but money. (*Looks at watch.*) Fifteen to nine. (*Stage has grown gradually dark.*) Maud?

MAUD: (*in a whisper*) Yes.

SIDNEY: If I were rich – if you were rich – if we were rich –

MAUD: Sidney! (*drawing closer to him*)

SIDNEY: As it is, I almost feel it's a crime to love you.

MAUD: Oh, Sidney!

SIDNEY: You who might make such a splendid marriage.

MAUD: If you had – money – I couldn't care for you any more than I do now.

SIDNEY: My darling! (*Looks at watch.*) Ten minutes. I know you wouldn't. Sometimes I feel mad about you – mad when I know you are out and smiling upon others – and – and waltzing.

MAUD: I can't help waltzing when I'm asked.

SIDNEY: No, dear, no; but when I fancy you are spinning round with another's arm about your waist – (*his arm round her waist*) Oh! – I feel –

MAUD: Why, Sidney! (*smiling*) You are jealous!

SIDNEY: Yes, I am.

MAUD: Can't you trust me?

SIDNEY: Implicitly. But I like to be with you all the same.

MAUD: (*whispering*) So do I with you.

SIDNEY: My love! (*Kisses her, and looks at watch.*) Five minutes.

MAUD: Time to go?

SIDNEY: No! (MAUD, *in taking out her handkerchief, takes out a knot of ribbon.*) What's that?

MAUD: Some trimmings I'm making for our fancy fair.

SIDNEY: What colour is it? Scarlet?

MAUD: Magenta.

SIDNEY: Give it to me.

MAUD: What nonsense.

SIDNEY: Won't you?

MAUD: I've brought something else.

SIDNEY: For me?

MAUD: Yes.

SIDNEY: What?

MAUD: These (*producing small case, which* SIDNEY *opens*).

SIDNEY: Sleeve links!

MAUD: Now, which will you have, the links or the ribbon?

SIDNEY: (*after reflection*) Both.

MAUD: You avaricious creature!

SIDNEY: (*putting the ribbons near his heart*) It's not in the power of words to tell you how I love you. Do you care for me enough to trust your future with me? Will you be mine?

MAUD: Sidney!

SIDNEY: Mine, and none other's; no matter how brilliant the offer – how dazzling the position?

MAUD: (*in a whisper – leaning towards him*) Yours and yours only! (*Clock strikes nine.*)

SIDNEY: (*with watch*) Nine! Why doesn't time stop, and Big Ben refuse to toll the hour?

(LADY *and* LORD PTARMIGANT *appear and open gate right.*)

MAUD: (*frightened*) My aunt!

(SIDNEY *gets to back, round left of square.* LORD *and* LADY PTARMIGANT *advance.*)

LADY PTARM: (*a very grand acid old lady*) Maud!

MAUD: Aunty, I was just coming away.

LADY PTARM: No one in the square? Quite improper to be here alone. Ferdinand!

LORD PTARM: (*a little old gentleman*) My love!

LADY PTARM: What is the time?

LORD PTARM: Don't know – watch stopped – tired of going, I suppose, like me.

LADY PTARM: (*sitting on chair – throws down gloves left by* SIDNEY *with her dress*) What's that? (*picking them up*) Gloves?

MAUD: (*frightened*) Mine, aunty!

LADY PTARM: Yours? You've got yours on! (*looking at them*) These are Sidney Daryl's. I know his size – seven-and-a-half. I see why you are so fond of walking in the square; for shame! (*turning to* SIDNEY, *who has just got the right gate open, and is going out*) Sidney! (*fiercely*) I see you! There is no occasion to try and sneak away. Come here. (SIDNEY *advances. With ironical politeness*) You have left your gloves.

(*All are standing except* LORD PTARMIGANT, *who lies at full length on chair and goes to sleep.*)

SIDNEY: (*confused*) Thank you, Lady Ptarm–

LADY PTARM: You two fools have been making love. I've long suspected it. I'm shocked with both of you; a penniless scribbler, and a dependent orphan, without a shilling or an expectation. Do you (*to* SIDNEY) wish to drag my niece, born and bred a lady, to a back parlour, and bread and cheese? Or do you (*to* MAUD) wish to marry a shabby writer, who can neither feed himself

---

Sleeve links: cuff links.
Big Ben: cast in 1856, Big Ben was set in the Clock Tower of the Houses of Parliament and first rung in 1859.

nor you? I can leave you nothing, for I am as well bred a pauper as yourselves. (*to* MAUD) To keep appointments in a public square! Your conduct is disgraceful – worse – it is unladylike; and yours (*to* SIDNEY) is dishonourable, and unworthy, to fill the head of a foolish girl with sentiment and rubbish. (*loudly*) Ferdinand!

LORD PTARM: (*waking up*) Yes, dear.

LADY PTARM: Do keep awake; the Chodds will be here directly; they are to walk home with us, and I request you to make yourself agreeable to them.

LORD PTARM: Such canaille.

LADY PTARM: Such cash!

LORD PTARM: Such cads.

LADY PTARM: Such cash! Pray, Ferdinand, don't argue (*authoritatively*).

LORD PTARM: I never do. (*Goes to sleep again.*)

LADY PTARM: I wish for no *esclandre.* Let us have no discussion in the square. Mr Daryl, I shall be sorry if you compel me to forbid you my house. I have other views for Miss Hetherington. (SIDNEY *bows.*)

(*The two* CHODDS, *in evening dress, appear at gate right; they enter.*)

LADY PTARM: My dear Mr Chodd, Maud has been so impatient. (*The* CHODDS *do not see* SIDNEY – *to* CHODD SENIOR) I shall take your arm, Mr Chodd. (*very sweetly*) Maud dear, Mr John will escort you.

(*Street band heard playing 'Fra Poco' in distance;* MAUD *takes* CHODD JUNIOR*'s arm; the two couples go off right gate; as* MAUD *turns, she looks an adieu at* SIDNEY, *who waves the bunch of ribbon, and sits down on chair in a reverie, not perceiving* LORD PTARMIGANT*'s legs;* LORD PTARMIGANT *jumps up with pain;* SIDNEY *apologises. Curtain quick.*)

ACT II

SCENE 1. *Parlour at the Owl's Roost public house. Cushioned seats all round the apartment; gas lighted over tables; splint boxes, pipes, newspapers etc., on table; writing materials on table near door; gong-bell on left table; door of entrance centre; clock above door (hands set to half-past nine); hat pegs and hats on walls. In the chair at left table head is discovered* O'SULLIVAN; *also, in the following order,* MacUSQUEBAUGH, AUTHOR, *and* DR MAKVICZ; *also at right table,* TRODNON (*at head*), SHAMHEART, BRADLEY, SCARGIL; *the* REPORTER *of 'Belgravian Banner' is sitting outside the right table, near the head, and with his back turned to it, smoking a cigar. The characters are all discovered drinking and smoking, some reading, some with their hats on.*

---

canaille: common folk, rabblement.
esclandre: an incident to provoke scandal, a 'scene'.
'Fra Poco': 'Ere long'. 'Fra poco a me' is a popular aria from Donizetti's opera *Lucia di Lammermoor* (1835). Performances of H.J. Byron's burlesque version accompanied *Society* at its opening.
splint boxes: boxes of thin wooden spills for lighting pipes, etc.

OMNES: Bravo! Hear, hear! Bravo!

O'SULL: (*on his legs, a glass in one hand, and terminating a speech, half-drunk, and in the broadest Irish accent*) It is, therefore, gintlemen, with the most superlative felicitee, the most fraternal convivialitee, the warmest congenialitee, the most burning friendship, and ardent admiration, that I propose his health!

OMNES: Hear, hear! etc.

O'SULL: He is a man, in the words of the divine bard –

TROD: (*in a sepulchral voice*) Hear, hear!

O'SULL: Who, in 'suffering everything, has suffered nothing'.

TROD: Hear, hear!

O'SULL: I have known him when, in the days of his prosperitee, he rowled down to the House of Commons in his carriage.

TROD: 'Twasn't his own – 'Twas a job!

OMNES: Silence! Chair! Order!

O'SULL: I have known him when his last copper, and his last glass of punch, has been shared with the frind of his heart!

OMNES: Hear, hear!

O'SULL: And it is with feelings of no small pride that I inform ye that that frind of his heart was the humble individual who has now the honour to address ye!

OMNES: Hear, hear! etc.

O'SULL: But, prizeman at Trinity, mimber of the bar, sinator, classical scholar, or frind, Desmond MacUsquebaugh has always been the same – a gintleman and a scholar; and that highest type of that glorious union – an Irish gintleman and scholar. Gintlemen, I drink his health – Desmond, my long loved frind, bless ye! (*All rise solemnly and drink* – 'Mr MacUsquebaugh'.) Gintleman, my frind, Mr MacUsquebaugh will respond.

OMNES: Hear, hear!

(*Enter* WAITER *with glasses, tobacco, etc., and received orders; changes* O'SULLIVAN*'s glass and exits. Enter* TOM STYLUS *and* CHODD JUNIOR. TOM *has a greatcoat on, over evening dress. Rather outré.*)

CHODD JUN: Thank you; no, not anything.

TOM: Just a wet – an outrider – or advanced guard, to prepare the way for the champagne.

CHODD JUN: No.

(*As soon as the sitters see* TOM *they give him a friendly nod, looking inquiringly at* CHODD, *and whisper each to other.*)

TOM: You'd better. They are men worth knowing. (*pointing them out*) That is the celebrated Olinthus O'Sullivan, Doctor of Civil Laws.

(O'SULLIVAN *is at this moment reaching to the gaslight to light his pipe.*)

CHODD JUN: The gent with the long pipe?

'in suffering everything', etc.: cf. *Hamlet* III.2.71: 'As one, in suffering all, that suffers nothing.'
'Twasn't his own, etc.: I have given this speech to Trodnon, rather than PDW's MacUsquebaugh.
a job: hired for the purpose.
prizeman at Trinity: winner of prizes for academic achievement at Trinity College, Dublin.

TOM: Yes; one of the finest classical scholars in the world; might have sat upon the woolsack if he'd chosen, but he didn't. (O'SULLIVAN *is now tossing with* MacUSQUEBAUGH.) That is the famous Desmond MacUsquebaugh, late MP for Killcrackskullcoddy, County Galway, a great patriot and orator; might have been Chancellor of the Exchequer if he'd chosen, but he didn't. (SCARGIL *reaches to the gaslight to light his pipe.*) That's Bill Bradley (*pointing to* BRADLEY, *who is reading paper with double eye-glass*), author of the famous romance of 'Time and Opportunity'; ran through ten editions. He got two thousand pounds for it, which was his ruin.

CHODD JUN: How was he ruined by getting two thousand pounds?

TOM: He's never done anything since. We call him 'One book Bradley'. That gentleman fast asleep – (*looking towards* AUTHOR *at table left*) has made the fortune of three publishers, and the buttoned-up one with the shirt front of beard is Herr Makvicz, the great United German. Dr Scargil there discovered the mensuration of the motive power of the cerebral organs.

(SCARGIL *takes a pinch of snuff from a box on the table.*)

CHODD JUN: What's that?

TOM: How many million miles per minute thought can travel. He might have made his fortune if he'd chosen.

CHODD JUN: But he didn't. Who is that mild-looking party, with the pink complexion, and the white hair? (*looking towards* SHAMHEART)

TOM: Sam Shamheart, the professional philanthropist. He makes it his business and profit to love the whole human race. (SHAMHEART *puffs a huge cloud of smoke from his pipe.*) Smoke, sir; all smoke. A superficial observer would consider him only a pleasant oily humbug, but I, having known him two-and-twenty years, feel qualified to pronounce him one of the biggest villains untransported.

CHODD JUN: And that man asleep at the end of the table?

TOM: Trodnon, the eminent tragedian.

(TRODNON *raises himself from the table, yawns, stretches himself, and again drops head on table.*)

CHODD JUN: I never heard of him.

TOM: Nor anybody else. But he's a confirmed tippler, and here we consider drunkenness an infallible sign of genius – we make that a rule.

CHODD JUN: But if they are all such great men, why didn't they make money by their talents?

TOM: Make money? They'd scorn it! They wouldn't do it – that's another rule. That gentleman there (*looking towards* [REPORTER,] *a very seedy man with eye-glass in his eye*) does the evening parties on the *Belgravian Banner.*

CHODD JUN: (*with interest*) Does he? Will he put my name among the fashionables tonight?

TOM: Yes.

CHODD JUN: And that we may know who's there and everything about it – you're going with me?

TOM: Yes, I'm going into *society*; thanks to your getting me the invitation. I can dress up an account, not a mere list of names, but a picturesque report of the soirée, and show under what brilliant auspices you entered the *beau-monde.*

CHODD JUN: *Beau-monde.* What's that?

TOM: (*chaffing him*) Every man is called a cockney who is born within the sound of the *beau-monde.*

CHODD JUN: (*not seeing it*) Oh! Order me two hundred copies of the *Belgravian* – what's its name?

TOM: *Banner.*

CHODD JUN: The day my name's in it – and put me down as a regular subscriber. I like to encourage high-class literature. By the way, shall I ask the man what he'll take to drink?

TOM: No, no.

CHODD JUN: I'll pay for it. I'll stand, you know (*going to* REPORTER; TOM *stops him*).

TOM: No, no – he don't know you, and he'd be offended.

CHODD JUN: But, I suppose all these chaps are plaguy poor?

TOM: Yes, they're poor; but they are *gentlemen.*

CHODD JUN: (*grinning*) I like that notion – a *poor* gentleman – it tickles me.

TOM: (*crossing into left corner*) Metallic snob!

CHODD JUN: I'm off now. You'll come to my rooms and we'll go together in the brougham. I want to introduce you to my friends, Lady Ptarmigant and Lord Ptarmigant.

TOM: I must wait here for a proof I expect from the office.

CHODD JUN: How long shall you be?

TOM: (*looking at clock*) An hour.

CHODD JUN: Don't be later.

(*Exit* CHODD JUNIOR; *the* REPORTER *rises, gets paper from left table, and shows it to* SHAMHEART, *sitting next him.*)

O'SULL: Sit down, Tommy, my dear boy. Gintlemen, Mr Desmond MacUsquebaugh will respond (*tapping with hammer*).

(*Enter* WAITER, *and gives* BRADLEY *a glass of grog.*)

MacUSQ: (*rising*) Gintlemen. (TOM, *taking his coat off, shows evening dress.*)

TOM: A go of whisky.

WAITER: Scotch or Irish?

TOM: Irish.

(*Exit* WAITER. *All are astonished at* TOM*'s costume: they cry* 'By Jove! there's a swell' *etc.*)

O'SULL: Why, Tom, my dear friend – are ye going to be married tonight, that ye're got up so gorgeously?

MacUSQ: Tom, you're as handsome as an angel.

O'SULL: Or a duke's footman. Gintleman, rise and salute our illustrious brother.

(*All rise and make* TOM *mock bows.*)

BRADLEY: The gods preserve you, noble sir.

SHAMHEART: May the bill of your sublime highness's washerwoman be never the less.

MacUSQ: And may it be paid. (*A general laugh.*)

---

a go of whisky: a specific quantity or measure.

O'SULL: Have you come into a fortune?

MAKVICZ: Or married a widow?

SHAMHEART: Or buried a relation? (*A general laugh.*) By my soul, Tom, you look an honour to humanity!

O'SULL: And your laundress. (*A general laugh.*)

BRADLEY: Gentlemen, Mr Stylus's health and shirt front! (*A general laugh: all drink and sit.*)

TOM: Bless ye, my people, bless ye! (*Sits, and takes out a short pipe and smokes.*)

O'SULL: Gintlemen. (*rising*) My friend, Mr MacUsquebaugh, will respond.

OMNES: Hear, hear!

MacUSQ: (*rising*) Gintlemen –

(*Enter* SIDNEY, *in evening dress and wrapper. Enter* WAITER *with* TOM*'s grog.*)

OMNES: Hallo, Daryl!

SIDNEY: How are ye, boys? Doctor, how goes it? (*shaking hands*) Mac. How d'ye do, O'Sullivan? Tom, I want to speak to you.

O'SULL: Ah, Tom, this is the rale metal – the genuine thing; compared to him, you are a sort of Whitechapel would-if-I-could-be. (*to* SIDNEY) Sit down, my gorgeous one, and drink with me.

SIDNEY: No, thanks. (SIDNEY *and* TOM *sit at right table head.*)

O'SULL: Waiter, take Mr Daryl's order.

SIDNEY: Brandy cold. (*Exit* WAITER.)

MacUSQ: Take off your wrap, rascal, and show your fine feathers.

SIDNEY: No; I'm going out, and I shall smoke my coat.

(TOM *extinguishes his pipe, and puts it in his dresscoat pocket, then puts on his greatcoat with great solemnity.*)

O'SULL: Going?

TOM: No.

O'SULL: Got the rheumatism?

TOM: No; but I shall smoke my coat. (*General laugh.*)

(*Enter* WAITER. *He gives glass of brandy and water to* SIDNEY, *and glass of grog to* SHAMHEART.)

O'SULL: What news, Daryl?

SIDNEY: None, except that the Ministry is to be defeated. (O'SULLIVAN *pays* WAITER.)

OMNES: No!

SIDNEY: I say, yes. They're whipping up everybody to vote against Thunder's motion. Thunder is sure of a majority, and out they go. Capital brandy. (*coming forward*) Tom! (TOM *rises; they come down stage.*) I am off to a soirée.

TOM: (*aside*) So am I; but I won't tell him.

SIDNEY: I find I've nothing in my portmonnaie but notes. I want a trifle for a cab. Lend me five shillings.

---

wrapper: loose evening cloak.
smoke my coat: make my coat smell of smoke.
portmonnaie: a flat leather purse or pocket-book.

TOM: I haven't got it, but I can get it for you.

SIDNEY: There's a good fellow, do. (*Returns to seat.*)

TOM: (*to* MacUSQUEBAUGH, *after looking round*) Mac, (*whispering*) lend me five bob.

MacUSQ: My dear boy, I haven't got so much.

TOM: Then don't lend it.

MacUSQ: But I'll get it for you. (*Crosses to* BRADLEY – *whispers*) Bradley, lend me five shillings.

BRADLEY: I haven't it about me, but I'll get it for you. (*Crosses to* O'SULLIVAN – *whispers*) O'Sullivan, lend me five shillings.

O'SULL: I haven't got it, but I'll get it for you. (*Crossing to* SCARGIL – *whispers*) Scargil, lend me five shillings.

SCARGIL: I haven't got it, but I'll get it for you. (*Crossing to* MAKVICZ – *whispers*) Doctor, lend me five shillings.

MAKVICZ: I am waiting for a chaange vor a zoveren; I'll give it you when de waiter brings to me.

SCARGIL: All right! (*to* O'SULLIVAN) All right!

O'SULL: All right! (*to* BRADLEY) All right!

BRADLEY: All right! (*to* MacUSQUEBAUGH) All right!

MacUSQ: All right! (*to* TOM) All right!

TOM: (*to* SIDNEY) All right!

O'SULL: (*tapping*) Gintlemen, my friend, Mr MacUsquebaugh will respond to the toast that –

MacUSQ: Gintlemen –

SIDNEY: Oh, cut the speechifying, I hate it! You ancients are so fond of spouting; let's be jolly, I've only a few minutes more.

BRADLEY: Daryl, sing us 'Cock-a-doodle-doo'.

SIDNEY: I only know the first two verses.

TOM: I know the rest.

(*Enter* WAITER; *gives glass of grog to* MAKVICZ.)

SIDNEY: Then here goes. Waiter, shut the door, and don't open it till I've done. Now then, ready. (*Exit* WAITER. O'SULLIVAN *taps* [*for silence*].)

SIDNEY: (*giving out*) Political:–

(*Sings*) When Ministers in fear and doubt,
That they should be from place kicked out,
Get up 'gainst time and sense to spout
A long dull evening through,
What mean they then by party clique,
Mob orators and factions weak?
'Tis only would they truth then speak
    But cock-a-doodle-doo!
Cock-a-doodle, cock-a-doodle, cock-a-doodle-doo.

CHORUS: (*gravely and solemnly shaking their heads*) Cock-a-doodle, etc.

---

giving out: making an announcement.
When Ministers, etc.: for musical setting, see p. 84 below.

SIDNEY: (*speaking*) Commercial:–
(*Sings*) When companies, whose stock of cash
Directors spend to cut a dash,
Are formed to advertise and smash,
And bankruptcy go through,
When tradesfolk live in regal state,
The goods they sell adulterate,
And puff in print, why, what's their prate
But cock-a-doodle-doo?
Cock-a-doodle, cock-a-doodle, cock-a-doodle-doo.

CHORUS: (*as before*) Cock-a-doodle, etc.

(*Enter* WAITER.)

O'SULL: How dare you come in and interrupt the harmony!

WAITER: Beg pardon, sir, but there's somebody says as he must see Mr Stylus.

TOM: Is he a devil?

WAITER: No, sir, he's a juvenile. (*A general laugh.*)

TOM: Send in some whisky – Irish – and the devil.

WAITER: Hot, sir? (*A general laugh.*)

(TOM *nods to* WAITER, *who exits.*)

SIDNEY: Why can't you see your proofs at the office?

TOM: I'm in full fig, and can't stew in that atmosphere of steam and copperas.

(*Enter* PRINTER*'s* BOY; *he goes up to* TOM *at head of right table. Enter* WAITER *with tray, hot-water jug, etc.; he gives change in silver to* MAKVICZ, *who crosses to* SCARGIL. WAITER *puts hot-water jug and whisky before* TOM, *and exits.*)

MAKVICZ: Here! (*giving two half-crowns to* SCARGIL) Scargil!

SCARGIL: (*crossing in same manner to* O'SULLIVAN) Here, O'Sullivan.

O'SULL: (*crossing to* BRADLEY) Here, Bradley.

BRADLEY: (*crossing to* MacUSQUEBAUGH) Here, Mac.

MacUSQ: (*crossing to* TOM) Here, Tom.

PRINTER's BOY: (*to* TOM) Please sir, Mr Duval said would you add this to it? (*giving* TOM *a proof slip*)

TOM: All right – wait outside – I'll bring it to you. (*Exit* PRINTER*'s* BOY. TOM *draws writing pad towards him, takes his grog, and is about to pour hot water from pewter jug into it, when he burns his fingers, starts up and dances.*) Confound it!

OMNES: What's the matter?

TOM: I've scalded my fingers with the hot water.

SIDNEY: (*taking up pen*) Here, I'll correct it for you.

TOM: Thank you.

O'SULL: Gintlemen, proceed with the harmony. Mr Stylus –

Commercial: see p. 36 above.
devil: i.e. a printer's devil, the errand boy on a newspaper or in a printing house.
in full fig: dressed up smartly.
copperas: green copperas (ferrous sulphate), one of the constituents of printing ink.

TOM: One minute. (*to* SIDNEY) Just add this to it. (SIDNEY *sits down to write,* TOM *standing over him, reading slip.*) 'Fashionable Intelligence. – We hear a marriage is on the tapis between Mr John Chodd, Junior, son of the celebrated millionaire, and Miss Maud Hetherington, daughter of the late Colonel Hetherington.' (SIDNEY *starts.*)

TOM: What's the matter?

SIDNEY: Nothing! (*He goes on writing –* O'SULLIVAN *taps hammer.*)

TOM: (*speaking*) Amatory:–

(*Sings*) When woman, lovely woman, sighs,
You praise her form, her hair, her eyes;
Would link your heart by tend'rest ties,
And vow your vows are true,
She answers tenderly and low,
Though from her lips the words that flow,
So softly sweet, are nought we know
But cock-a-doodle-doo! etc. etc. etc.

(TOM *throws the five shillings to* SIDNEY, *which rattle on the table.* SIDNEY *gives him back the proof: his face is deadly pale; as his head falls on the table the* CHORUS *is singing* 'Cock-a-doodle-doo' etc. – *closed in.*)

SCENE 2. *A retiring room at* SIR FARINTOSH FADILEAF*'s; large archway or alcove left, with curtain drawn or doors leading to ballroom; small arch or alcove right, leading to supper-room, with drawn curtain; centre opening curtains drawn; the room is decorated for a ball; candelabra, flowers, etc.*

LADY PTARM: (*without*) Very pretty – very pretty indeed, Sir Farintosh; all very nice.

(LADY PTARMIGANT *enters from right, with* SIR FARINTOSH, LORD PTARMIGANT, *and* MAUD, *all in evening dress.*)

SIR FARIN: (*an old beau*) So kind of you, Cousin Ptarmigant, to take pity on a poor old widower, who has no womankind to receive for him, and all that.

LADY PTARM: Not at all – not at all; I am only too glad to be useful.

LORD PTARM: (*speaking off*) Bring chairs.

LADY PTARM: Ferdinand, you can't want to go to sleep again!

LORD PTARM: I know I can't, but I do.

(SERVANT *brings two chairs and a small table.*)

LADY PTARM: Besides, I don't want chairs here, young men get lolling about, and then they don't dance. (LORD PTARMIGANT *sits, and closes his eyes.*) Farintosh, (*Knocks heard.*) the arrivals are beginning.

SIR FARIN: But, Lady Ptarmigant, if –

LADY PTARM: Remember that the old Dowager Countess of McSwillumore has plenty of whisky toddy in a green glass, to make believe hock.

---

on the tapis: under discussion (literally 'on the table-cloth').
Amatory: see p. 36 above.
closed in: flats for the next scene are slid across to hide the Owl's Roost set from view.
SIR FARINTOSH FADILEAF's: see pp. 35–6 above.

SIR FARIN: But if –

LADY PTARM: Now go. Oh dear me! (*Almost forces* SIR FARINTOSH *off.*) Now, Maud, one word with you; you have been in disgrace all this last week about that writing fellow.

MAUD: (*indignant*) What writing fellow?

LADY PTARM: Don't echo me, if you please. You know who I mean – Daryl!

MAUD: Mr Daryl is a relation of your ladyship's – the son of the late Sir Percy Daryl, and brother of the present Baronet.

LADY PTARM: And when the present Baronet, that precious Percy, squandered everything at the gaming table, dipped the estates, and ruined himself, Sidney gave up the money left him by his mother, to reinstate a dissolute beggared brother, don't forget that.

MAUD: (*with exultation*) I do not forget it, I never shall. To give up all his fortune, to ruin his bright prospects to preserve his brother, and his brother's wife and children, to keep unsullied the honour of his name, was an act –

LADY PTARM: Of a noodle, and now he hasn't a penny save what he gets by scribbling – a pretty pass for a man of family to come to. You are my niece, and it is my solemn duty to get you married if I can. Don't thwart me, and I will. Leave sentiment to servant wenches who sweetheart the policemen; it's unworthy of a lady. I've a man in my eye – a rich one – young Chodd.

MAUD: (*with repugnance*) Such a commonplace person.

LADY PTARM: With a very uncommonplace purse. He will have eighteen thousand a year. I have desired him to pay you court, and I desire you to receive it.

MAUD: He is so vulgar.

LADY PTARM: He is so rich. When he is your husband put him in a back study, and don't show him.

MAUD: But I detest him.

LADY PTARM: What on earth has that to do with it? You wouldn't love a man before you were married to him, would you? Where are your principles? Ask my lord how I treated him before our marriage. (*hitting* LORD PTARMIGANT *with her fan*) Ferdinand!

LORD PTARM: (*waking up*) My love!

LADY PTARM: Do keep awake.

LORD PTARM: 'Pon my word you were making such a noise I thought I was in the House of Commons. (*with fond regret*) I used to be allowed to sleep so comfortably there.

LADY PTARM: Are you not of opinion that a match between Mr Chodd and Maud would be most desirable?

LORD PTARM: (*looking at* LADY PTARMIGANT) Am I not of opinion – my opinion – what is my opinion?

LADY PTARM: (*hitting him with fan*) Yes, of course.

LORD PTARM: Yes – of course – my opinion is yes, of course. (*aside, crossing to centre stage with chair*) Just as it used to be in the House. I always roused in time to vote as I was told to.

MAUD: But, uncle, one can't purchase happiness at shops in packets, like bon-bons. A thousand yards of lace cost so much, they can be got at the milliner's; but an hour of home or repose can only be had for love. Mere wealth –

LORD PTARM: My dear, wealth, if it does not bring happiness, brings the best imitation of it procurable for money. There are two things – wealth and poverty. The former makes the world a place to live in; the latter a place to – go to sleep in – as I do. (*Leans back in chair and dozes.*)

(*Enter* SIR FARINTOSH, COLONEL BROWSER, *and* LORD CLOUDWRAYS.)

SIR FARIN: Have you heard the news? The division is come off tonight. Many men won't be able to come. I must be off to vote. If the Ministry go out –

COLONEL B: They won't go out – there'll be a dissolution!

SIR FARIN: And I shall have to go down to be re-elected. Cloudwrays, will you come and vote?

LORD CLOUD: (*languidly*) No.

SIR FARIN: Why not?

LORD CLOUD: I'm dying for a weed.

SIR FARIN: You can smoke in the smoking-room!

LORD CLOUD: So I can – that didn't occur to me!

SIR FARIN: Ptarmigant, cousin, you do the honours for me. My country calls, you know, and all that. Come on, Cloudwrays; how slow you are. Hi, Tobacco!

(CLOUDWRAYS *rouses himself. Exeunt* SIR FARINTOSH *and* LORD CLOUDWRAYS. LORD PTARMIGANT *dozes.*)

COLONEL B: (*who has been talking to* LADY PTARMIGANT, *turns to* LORD PTARMIGANT) As I was saying to her ladyship –

LADY PTARM: Ferdinand, do wake up!

LORD PTARM: Hear, hear! (*waking*) My dear!

(*Enter* SERVANT.)

SERVANT: Mr Chodd, Mr John Chodd, and Mr Stylus.

(*Enter* CHODD JUNIOR, CHODD SENIOR, *and* TOM. *Exit* SERVANT.)

LADY PTARM: My dear Mr Chodd, how late you are! Maud dear, here is Mr Chodd. Do you know we were going to scold you, you naughty men!

CHODD SEN: (*astonished, aside*) Naughty men! Johnny, her ladyship says we're naughty men; we've done something wrong!

CHODD JUN: No, no – it's only her ladyship's patrician fun. Don't call me Johnny. I'm sure I hurried here on the wings of – (*crossing, falls over* LORD PTARMIGANT*'s feet, who rises and turns his chair the reverse way;* CHODD *seeing* MAUD *repellant*) – a brougham and pair. Lady Ptarmigant, let me introduce a friend of mine. Lady Ptarmigant – Mr Stylus, whom I took the liberty of –

LADY PTARM: Charmed to see any friend of yours!

(TOM *advances from back, abashed; as he is backing and bowing he falls over* LORD PTARMIGANT*'s legs;* LORD PTARMIGANT *rises with a look of annoyance; they bow;* LORD PTARMIGANT *again turns chair and sits.*)

LADY PTARM: Mr Chodd, take me to the ballroom. (CHODD SENIOR *offers his arm.*) You will look after Maud, I'm sure (*to* CHODD JUNIOR, *who smilingly offers his arm to* MAUD, *who, with a suppressed look of disgust, takes it*). Mr Si-len-us.

TOM: Stylus – ma'am – my lady.

LADY PTARM: Stylus – pardon me – will you be kind enough to keep my lord awake? (*significantly*) Maud! Now, dear Mr Chodd.

CHODD JUN: Guv!

(*Exeunt* LADY PTARMIGANT, MAUD, *and the* CHODDS.)

TOM: (*aside*) These are two funny old swells!

COLONEL B: Odd-looking fellow. (*to* TOM) Nice place this!

TOM: Very.

COLONEL B: And charming man, Fadileaf.

TOM: Very. I don't know him, but I should say he must be very jolly.

COLONEL B: (*laughing*) Bravo! Why, you're a wit!

TOM: Yes! (*aside*) What does he mean?

COLONEL B: (*offering box*) Snuff? Who's to win the Leger? Diadeste?

TOM: I don't know – not in my department.

COLONEL B: (*laughing*) Very good.

TOM: What is? (*innocently*)

COLONEL B: You are. Do you play whist?

TOM: Yes; cribbage, and all fours, likewise.

COLONEL B: We'll find another man, and make up a rubber.

TOM: (*pointing to* LORD PTARMIGANT *asleep*) He'll do for dummy.

COLONEL B: (*laughing*) Capital!

TOM: What a queer fellow this is – he laughs at everything I say. (*Dance music.*)

COLONEL B: They've begun.

TOM: (*waking up* LORD PTARMIGANT) My lady said I was to keep you awake.

LORD PTARM: Thank you.

COLONEL B: Come and have a rubber! Let's go and look up Chedbury.

LORD PTARM: Yes.

COLONEL B: (*to* TOM) You'll find us in the card-room.

(*Exeunt* LORD PTARMIGANT *and* COLONEL BROWSER).

TOM: Here I am in society and I think society is rather slow; it's much jollier at the Owl, and there's more to drink. If it were not wicked to say it, how I should enjoy a glass of gin and water!

(*Enter* LADY PTARMIGANT.)

LADY PTARM: Mr Si-len-us!

TOM: (*abashed*) Stylus, ma'am – my lady!

LADY PTARM: Stylus! I beg pardon. You're all alone.

TOM: With the exception of your ladyship!

LADY PTARM: All the members have gone down to the House to vote, and we are dreadfully in want of men – I mean dancers! You dance, of course?

TOM: Oh! Of course – I – (*abashed*)

Silenus: the fat, jolly, drunken attendant on Bacchus.
all fours: here a card-game for two, in which four points (High, Low, Jack, and Game) are at stake.

LADY PTARM: As it is Leap-year, I may claim the privilege of asking you to see me through a quadrille!

TOM: (*frightened*) My lady! I –

LADY PTARM: (*aside*) He's a friend of the Chodds, and it will please them. Come then. (*She takes his arm; sniffing.*) Dear me! What a dreadful smell of tobacco! (*sniffing*)

TOM: (*awfully self-conscious – sniffing*) Is there?

LADY PTARM: (*sniffing*) Some fellow must have been smoking.

TOM: (*sniffing*) I think some fellow must, or some fellow must have been where some other fellows have been smoking. (*aside*) It's that beastly parlour at the Owl. (*In taking out his pocket-handkerchief his pipe falls on floor.*)

LADY PTARM: What's that?

TOM: (*in torture*) What's what? (*turning about and looking through eye-glass at the air*)

LADY PTARM: (*pointing*) That!

TOM: (*as if in doubt*) I rather think – it – is – a pipe!

LADY PTARM: I'm sure of it. You'll join me in the ballroom (*going*).

TOM: Instantly, your ladyship. (*Exit* LADY PTARMIGANT. *Looking at pipe, he picks it up.*) If ever I bring you into society again – (*Drops it.*) Waiter! (*Enter* SERVANT.) Somebody's dropped something. Remove the Whatsoname. (*Quadrille music in ballroom;* SERVANT *goes off, and returns with tray and sugar tongs, with which he picks up pipe with an air of ineffable disgust and goes off.*) Now to spin round the old woman in the mazy waltz. (*Splits kid gloves in drawing them on.*) There goes one-and-nine.

(*Exit* TOM. *Enter* SIDNEY. *He is pale and excited; one of the gold links of his wrist-band is unfastened.*)

SIDNEY: I have seen her – she was smiling – dancing, but not with him. She looked so bright and happy. I won't think of her. How quiet it is here: so different to that hot room, with the crowd of fools and coquettes whirling round each other. I like to be alone – alone! I am now thoroughly – and to think it was but a week ago – one little week – But I'll forget her – forget, and hate her. Hate her – Oh, Maud, Maud, till now I never knew how much I loved you; loved you – loved you – gone; shattered; shivered; and for whom? For one of my own birth? For one of my own rank? No! For a common clown, who – confound this link – but he is rich – and – it won't hold (*trying to fasten it – his fingers trembling*). I've heard it all – always with her, at the Opera and the Park, attentive and obedient – and she accepts him. My head aches. (*louder*) I'll try a glass of champagne.

TOM: (*without*) Champagne – here you are! (*Draws curtain. Enter* TOM, *with a champagne glass, from supper-room; portion of supper-table seen in alcove. Seeing* SIDNEY) Sidney!

SIDNEY: Tom! You here!

TOM: Very much here. (*drinking*) I was brought by Mr Chodd.

LADY PTARM: What's that?: 'This incident is taken from M. Émile Augier's admirable comedy of "Les Effrontés".' (Robertson's note)

SIDNEY: Chodd!

TOM: Don't startle a fella. You look pale – aren't you well?

SIDNEY: (*rallying*) Jolly; never better.

TOM: Have some salmon.

SIDNEY: I'm not hungry.

TOM: Then try some jelly, it's no trouble to masticate and is emollient and agreeable to the throat and palate.

SIDNEY: No, Tom, champagne.

TOM: Here you are (*fetching bottle from table*).

SIDNEY: I'll meet her eye to eye. (*Drinks.*) Another, Tom – and be as smiling and indifferent. As for that heavy-metalled dog – thanks, Tom. (*Drinks.*) Another.

TOM: I've been dancing with old Lady Ptarmigant.

SIDNEY: Confound her.

TOM: I did. As I was twirling her round I sent my foot through her dress and tore her skirt out of the gathers.

SIDNEY: (*laughing hysterically*) Good! Good! Bravo, Tom! Did she row you?

TOM: Not a bit. She said it was of no consequence; but her looks were awful.

SIDNEY: Ha! Ha! Ha! Tom, you're a splendid fellow, not like these damned swells, all waistcoat and shirt front.

TOM: But I like the swells. I played a rubber with them and won three pounds, then I showed them some conjuring tricks – you know I'm a famous conjuror. (*taking a pack of cards out of his pocket*) By Jupiter! Look here, I've brought the pack away with me; I didn't know I had. I'll go and take it back.

SIDNEY: (*taking the cards from him absently*) No, never mind, stay with me, I don't want you to go.

TOM: I find high life most agreeable, everybody is so amiable, so thoughtful, so full of feeling.

SIDNEY: Feeling! Why, man, this is a market where the match-making mammas and chattering old chaperons – those women with the red cheeks and roman noses – have no more sense of feeling than cattle drovers driving their beasts to Smithfield – the girls no more sentiment than sheep, and the best man is the highest bidder; that is, the biggest fool with the longest purse.

TOM: Sidney, you're ill.

SIDNEY: You lie, Tom – never better – excellent high spirits – fill my glass again; confound this link!

(*Enter* LORD CLOUDWRAYS *and* SIR FARINTOSH.)

LORD CLOUD: }
SIR FARIN: } By Jove! Ha, Sidney, heard the news?

SIDNEY: News – there is no news! The times are bankrupt, and the assignees have sold off the events.

LORD CLOUD: }
SIR FARIN: } The Ministry is defeated.

TOM: No!

LORD CLOUD: }
SIR FARIN: } Yes; by a majority of forty-six.

SIDNEY: Serve them right.

LORD CLOUD:
SIR FARIN: } Why?

SIDNEY: I don't know. Why, what fellows you are to want reasons.

LORD CLOUD: Sidney!

SIDNEY: Hullo, Cloudwrays! My bright young British senator – my undeveloped Chatham, and mature Raleigh.

TOM: Will they resign?

SIDNEY: Of course they will: resignation is the duty of every man, or Minister, who can't do anything else.

TOM: Who will be sent for to form a Government?

SIDNEY: Cloudwrays.

LORD CLOUD: How you do chaff a man!

SIDNEY: Why not? Inaugurate a new policy – the policy of smoke – free trade in tobacco! Go in, not for principles, but for Principes – our hearths – our homes, and 'bacca boxes!

TOM: If there's a general election?

SIDNEY: Hurrah, for a general election! Eh, Cloudwrays? Eh, Farintosh? What speeches you'll make – what lies you'll tell, and how your constituents *won't* believe you!

LORD CLOUD:
SIR FARIN: } How odd you are.

LORD CLOUD: Aren't you well?

SIDNEY: Glorious! Only one thing annoys me.

LORD CLOUD:
SIR FARIN: } What's that?

SIDNEY: They won't give me any more champagne.

(*Enter* COLONEL BROWSER.)

LORD CLOUD: Lady Ptarmigant sent me here to say –

COLONEL B: Farintosh, the ladies want partners. (COLONEL BROWSER *and* SIR FARINTOSH *go off.*)

SIDNEY: Partners! Here are partners for them – long, tall, stout, fat, thin, poor, rich. Cloudwrays, you're the man! (*Enter* CHODD JUNIOR. SIDNEY *sees and points to him.*) No; this is the man!

CHODD JUN: (*aside*) Confound this fellow!

SIDNEY: This, sir, is the 'Young Lady's Best Companion', well-bound, Bramah-locked, and gilt at the edges – mind, gilt only at the edges. This link will *not* hold. (*Sees the pack of cards in his hand.*) Here, Chodd, take these – no, cut for a ten-pound note. (*Puts cards on small table.*)

CHODD JUN: (*quickly*) With pleasure. (*aside*) I'll punish this audacious pauper in the pocket (*crossing to table*).

LORD CLOUD: You mustn't gamble here.

SIDNEY: Only for a frolic!

CHODD JUN: I'm always lucky at cards!

Principes: a cigar size-mark, denoting a large impressive-looking example.
Bramah-locked: Joseph Bramah (1748–1814) invented a number of mechanical devices bearing his name, including the first efficient water-closet; his lock was patented in 1784.

SIDNEY: Yes, I know an old proverb about that.
CHODD JUN: Eh?
SIDNEY: Lucky at play, unlucky in – This link will not hold.
CHODD JUN: (*maliciously*) Shall we put the stakes down first?
SIDNEY: (*producing portmonnaie*) With pleasure!
LORD CLOUD: But I don't think it right – (*advancing* – CHODD JUNIOR *stays him with his arm.*)
TOM: Sidney!
SIDNEY: Nonsense! Hold your tongue, Cloudwrays, and I'll give you a Regalia. Let's make it for five-and-twenty!
CHODD JUN: Done!
SIDNEY: Lowest wins – that's in your favour.
CHODD JUN: Eh?
SIDNEY: Ace is lowest. (*They cut.*) Mine! Double the stakes?
CHODD JUN: Done! (*They cut.*)
SIDNEY: Mine again! Double again?
CHODD JUN: Done! (*They cut.*)
SIDNEY: You're done again! I'm in splendid play tonight. One hundred, I think?
CHODD JUN: I'd play again (*handing notes*) but I've no more with me.
SIDNEY: Your word's sufficient – you can send to my chambers – besides, you've got your cheque-book. A hundred again?
CHODD JUN: Yes. (*They cut.*)
SIDNEY: Huzzah! Fortune's a lady! Again? (CHODD JUNIOR *nods – they cut.*) Bravo! Again? (CHODD JUNIOR *nods – they cut.*) Mine again! Again? (CHODD JUNIOR *nods – they cut.*) Mine again! Again? (CHODD JUNIOR *nods – they cut.*) Same result! That makes five! Let's go in for a thousand?
CHODD JUN: Done!
LORD CLOUD: (*advancing*) No!
CHODD JUN: (*savagely*) Get out of the way! (LORD CLOUDWRAYS *looks at him through eye-glass in astonishment.*)
SIDNEY: Pooh! (*They cut.*) Mine! Double again?
CHODD JUN: Yes.
LORD CLOUD: (*going round to back of table and seizing the pack*) No; I can't suffer this to go on – Lady Ptarmigant would be awfully angry (*going off*).
SIDNEY: Here, Cloudwrays! What a fellow you are. (*Exit* LORD CLOUDWRAYS. *Turning to* CHODD JUNIOR) You owe me a thousand!
CHODD JUN: I shall not forget it.
SIDNEY: I don't suppose you will. Confound – (*trying to button sleeve link*) Oh, to jog your memory, take this. (*Gives him sleeve link, which he has been trying to button, and goes off after* LORD CLOUDWRAYS.)
CHODD JUN: And after I have paid you, I'll remember and clear off the old score.
TOM: (*taking his arm as he is going*) Going into the ballroom?
CHODD JUN: (*aghast at his intrusion*) Yes!
TOM: I'll go with you.

Regalia: a large top-quality cigar.

CHODD JUN: (*disengaging his arm*) I'm engaged! (*Exit* CHODD JUNIOR. *Music till end.*)

TOM: You've an engaging manner! I'm like a donkey between two bundles of hay. On one side woman – lovely woman! On the other wine and wittles. (*taking out a sovereign*) Heads, supper – tails, the ladies. (*Tosses at table.*) Supper! Sweet goddess Fortune, accept my thanks! (*Exit into supper-room. Enter* MAUD *and* CHODD JUNIOR.)

MAUD: This dreadful man follows me about everywhere.

CHODD JUN: My dear Miss Hetherington!

MAUD: I danced the last with you.

CHODD JUN: That was a quadrille. (*Enter* SIDNEY.) This is for a polka.

SIDNEY: (*advancing between them*) The lady is engaged to me.

CHODD JUN: (*aside*) This fellow's turned up again. (*to him*) I beg your pardon.

SIDNEY: I beg yours! I have a prior claim. (*bitterly*) Ask the lady – or perhaps I had better give her up to you.

MAUD: The next dance with you, Mr Chodd; this one –

CHODD JUN: Miss, your commands are Acts of Parliament. (*looking spitefully at* SIDNEY *as he crosses*) I'll go and see what Lady Ptarmigant has to say to this.

(*Exit* CHODD JUNIOR. *Music changes to a slow waltz.*)

SIDNEY: Listen to me for the last time. My life and being were centred in you. You have abandoned me for money! You accepted me; you now throw me off, for money! You gave your hand, you now retract, for money! You are about to wed – a knave, a brute, a fool, whom in your own heart you despise, for money!

MAUD: How dare you?

SIDNEY: Where falsehood is, shame cannot be. The last time we met (*producing ribbon*) you gave me this. See, 'tis the colour of a man's heart's blood. (*Curtains or doors at back draw apart.*) I give it back to you. (*casting the bunch of ribbon at her feet* – LORD CLOUDWRAYS, SIR FARINTOSH, COLONEL BROWSER, TOM, LORD PTARMIGANT, *and* LADY PTARMIGANT, CHODD JUNIOR *and* CHODD SENIOR, *appear at back.* GUESTS *seen in ballroom.*) And tell you, shameless girl, much as I once loved you, and adored, I now despise and hate you.

LADY PTARM: (*advancing, in a whisper to* SIDNEY) Leave the house, sir! How dare you – go!

SIDNEY: Yes; anywhere.

(*Crash of music.* MAUD *is nearly falling when* CHODD JUNIOR *appears near her; she is about to lean on his arm, but recognising him, retreats and staggers.* SIDNEY *is seen to reel through ballroom full of dancers. Drop.*)

---

wittles: i.e. victuals. The cockney habit of exchanging 'w' for 'v', with which Charles Dickens made great play, did not die out until the late nineteenth century.

Drop: a canvas cloth, rather than the front curtain, lowered at the end of an act.

ACT III

SCENE 1. *The Owl's Roost (same as scene 1, act II). Daylight; the room in order.* TOM *discovered writing at table right.* BOY *sitting on table left, and holding the placard on which is printed: 'Read the* Morning Earthquake *– a first-class daily paper' etc. On the other, 'The* Evening Earthquake [–] *a first-class daily paper – Latest intelligence' etc.*

TOM: Um! It'll look well on the walls, and at the railway stations. Take these back to the office (BOY *jumps down.*) – to Mr Piker, and tell him he must wait for the last leader – till it's written. (*Exit* BOY. TOM *walks to and fro, smoking long clay pipe.*) The ME – that is, the *Morning Earthquake*, shakes the world for the first time tomorrow morning, and everything seems to have gone wrong with it. It is a crude, unmanageable, ill-disciplined, ill-regulated earthquake. Heave the first – Old Chodd behaves badly to me. After organising him a first-rate earthquake, engaging him a brilliant staff, and stunning reporters, he doesn't even offer me the post of sub-editor – ungrateful old humbug! Heave the second, – no sooner is he engaged than our editor is laid up with the gout; and then Old Chodd asks me to be a literary warming-pan, and keep his place hot, till colchicum and cold water have done their work. I'll be even with Old Chodd, though! I'll teach him what it is to insult a man who has started eighteen daily and weekly papers – all of them failures. Heave the third – Sidney Daryl won't write the social leaders. (*Sits at the end of table.*) Poor Sidney! (*Takes out the magenta ribbon which he picked up at the ball.*) I shan't dare to give him this – I picked it up at the ball, at which I was one of the distinguished and illustrious guests. Love is an awful swindler – always drawing upon Hope, who never honours his drafts – a sort of whining beggar, continually moved on by the maternal police. But 'tis a weakness to which the wisest of us are subject – a kind of manly measles which this flesh is heir to, particularly when the flesh is heir to nothing else. Even I have felt the divine damnation – I mean emanation. But the lady united herself to another, which was a very good thing for me, and anything but misfortunate for her. Ah! happy days of youth! – Oh! flowing fields of Runnington-cum-Wapshot – where the yellow corn waved, our young loves ripened, and the new gaol now stands. Oh! Sally, when I think of you and the past, I feel that (*looking into his pot*) the pot's empty, and I could drink another pint. (*Putting the ribbon in his pocket.*) Poor Sidney – I'm afraid he's going to the bad. (*Enter* SIDNEY; *he strikes bell on left table and sits at the head, his appearance altered.*) Ha! Sid, is that you? Talk of the devil – how d'ye do?

SIDNEY: Quite well – how are you?

TOM: I'm suffering from an earthquake in my head, and a general printing office in my stomach. Have some beer? (*Enter* WAITER.)

SIDNEY: No thanks – brandy –

---

colchicum: a medicine based on meadow saffron (*Colchicum autumnale*), much used to relieve gout and rheumatism.

TOM: So early?

SIDNEY: And soda. I didn't sleep last night.

TOM: Brandy and soda, and beer again.

(*Exit* WAITER, *with pint pot off table.*)

SIDNEY: I never do sleep now – I can't sleep.

TOM: Work hard.

(*Enter* WAITER.)

SIDNEY: I do – it is my only comfort – my old pen goes driving along, at the rate of – (WAITER, *after placing pint of porter before* TOM, *places tray with brandy and soda before* SIDNEY.) That's right! (WAITER *uncorks and exits.*) What a splendid discovery was brandy. (*Drinks.*)

TOM: Yes, the man who invented it deserves a statue.

SIDNEY: That's the reason that he doesn't get one.

TOM: (*reading paper*) 'Election Intelligence'. There's the general election – why not go in for that?

SIDNEY: Election – pooh! What do I care for that?

TOM: Nothing, of course, but it's occupation.

SIDNEY: (*musing*) I wonder who'll put up for Springmead!

TOM: Your brother's seat, wasn't it?

SIDNEY: Yes, our family's for years. By the way, I'd a letter from Percy last mail; he's in trouble, poor fellow – his little boy is dead, and he himself is in such ill-health that they have given him sick leave. We are an unlucky race, we Daryls. Sometimes, Tom, I wish that I were dead.

TOM: Sidney!

SIDNEY: It's a bad wish, I know; but what to me is there worth living for?

TOM: What! Oh, lots of things. Why, there's the police reports – mining intelligence, hop districts – the tallow market – ambition –

SIDNEY: Ambition!

TOM: And society!

SIDNEY: (*heartily*) Damn society!

TOM: And you know, there are more women in the world than one.

SIDNEY: But only one a man can love.

TOM: I don't know about that; temperaments differ.

SIDNEY: (*pacing about and reciting*)

'As the husband, so the wife is.
Thou art mated to a clown:
    And the grossness of his nature
Shall have power to drag thee down;
    He will hold thee when his passion
Shall have spent its novel force,
    Something better than his dog, and
Little dearer than his horse.'

I'm ashamed of such a want of spirit – ashamed to be such a baby! And you,

---

'As the husband . . . Little dearer than his horse': slightly misquoted from lines 47–50 of Tennyson's *Locksley Hall* (1842). Robertson also divides Tennyson's couplets into quatrains.

Tom, are the only man in the world I'd show it to; but I – I can think of nothing else but her – and – and of the fate in store for her. (*Sobs and leans on table with his face in his hands.*)

TOM: Don't give way, Sid; there are plenty of things in this life to care for.

SIDNEY: Not for me – not for me.

TOM: Oh, yes! There's friendship; and – and – the little girl, you know!

SIDNEY: That reminds me, I wrote a week ago to Mrs Churton, asking her to meet me with Mau– with the little darling in the square. I always asked them to come from Hampstead to the square, that I might look up at her window as I passed. What a fool I've been – I can't meet them this morning! Will you go for me?

TOM: With pleasure.

SIDNEY: Give Mrs Churton this (*wrapping up money in paper from* TOM*'s case*). It's the last month's money. Tell her I'm engaged, and can't come – and – (*putting down money*) buy the baby a toy, bless her! What a pity to think she'll grow to be a woman!

(*Enter* MacUSQUEBAUGH, O'SULLIVAN, *and* MAKVICZ.)

MacUSQ: (*entering*) A three of whisky, hot!

O'SULL: The same for me – neat.

MAKVICZ: A pint of stoot. (*All sit.*)

O'SULL: Tom, mee boy, what news of the *Earthquake*?

(*Enter* WAITER *with orders, and gives* TOM *a note.*)

TOM: Heaving, sir – heaving. (TOM *opens note;* SIDNEY *sits abstracted.*) Who's going electioneering?

MAKVICZ: I am.

O'SULL: And I.

MacUSQ: And so am I.

TOM: Where?

MacUSQ: I don't know.

O'SULL: Somewhere – anywhere.

TOM: (*reading note*) From Chodd Senior – the old villain! (*Reads*) 'Dear Sir, Please meet me at Lady Ptarmigant's at two p.m.' (*suddenly*) Sidney!

SIDNEY: (*moodily*) What?

TOM: (*reading note*) 'I am off to Springmead-le-Beau by the train at two-fifty. My son, Mr John Chodd Junior, is the candidate for the seat for the borough.'

SIDNEY: (*rising*) What! – That hound! – That cur! – That digesting cheque-book – represent the town that my family have held their own for centuries! I'd sooner put up for it myself.

TOM: (*rising*) Why not, Daryl for Springmead – here's occupation – here's revenge!

SIDNEY: By heaven, I will! (*Crosses stage and returns.*)

TOM: Gentlemen, the health of Mr Daryl, MP for Springmead-le-Beau!

OMNES: (*rising and drinking*) Hurrah!

TOM: We'll canvass for you. (*aside*) And now, Mr Chodd Senior, I see the subject for the last leader. I'll fetter you with your own type.

A three of whisky: a measure, probably 'three fingers'.

SIDNEY: I'll do it! I'll do it! When does the next train start?

MacUSQ: (*taking 'Bradshaw' from table*) At two-fifty – the next at five.

SIDNEY: Huzzah! (*with excitement*) I'll rouse up the tenants – call on the tradesmen!

O'SULL: But the money?

SIDNEY: I'll fight him with the very thousand that I won of him. Besides, what need has a Daryl of money at Springmead?

TOM: We can write for you.

O'SULL: And fight for you.

SIDNEY: I feel so happy – Call cabs.

MacUSQ: How many?

SIDNEY: The whole rank! (*Goes up stage.*)

TOM: But, Sidney, what colours shall we fight under?

SIDNEY: What colours? (*Feels in his breast and appears dejected.* TOM *hands him the ribbons; he clutches them eagerly.*) What colours? Magenta!

OMNES: Huzzah! (*Closed in as they go up stage.*)

SCENE 2. *An apartment at* LORD PTARMIGANT*'s.*

LADY PTARM: (*without*) Goodbye, dear Mr Chodd. A pleasant ride, and all sorts of success. (*Enter* LADY PTARMIGANT.) Phew! There's the old man gone. Now to speak to that stupid Maud. (*looking off*) There she sits in the sulks – a fool! Ah, what wise folks the French were before the Revolution, when there was a Bastille or a convent in which to pop dangerous young men and obstinate young women. (*sweetly*) Maud dear! I'll marry her to young Chodd; I'm determined.

(*Enter* MAUD, *very pensive* [*carrying a letter*].)

LADY PTARM: Maud, I wish to speak to you.

MAUD: Upon what subject, aunt?

LADY PTARM: One that should be very agreeable to a girl of your age – marriage.

MAUD: Mr Chodd again?

LADY PTARM: Yes, Mr Chodd again.

MAUD: I hate him.

LADY PTARM: You wicked thing! How dare you use such expressions in speaking of a young gentleman so rich?

MAUD: Gentleman!

LADY PTARM: Yes, gentlemen! – At least he will be.

MAUD: Nothing can make Mr Chodd – what a name! – anything but what he is.

LADY PTARM: Money can do everything.

MAUD: Can it make me love a man I hate?

LADY PTARM: Yes; at least, if it don't it ought. I suppose you mean to marry somebody.

MAUD: No.

LADY PTARM: You audacious girl! How can you talk so wickedly? Where do you expect to go to?

Closed in: see note on p. 58 above.

MAUD: To needlework! Anything from this house; and from this persecution.

LADY PTARM: Miss Hetherington!

MAUD: Thank you, Lady Ptarmigant, for calling me by my name; it reminds me who I am, and of my dead father, 'Indian Hetherington', as he was called. It reminds me that the protection you have offered to his orphan daughter has been hourly embittered by the dreadful temper, which is an equal affliction to you as to those within your reach. It reminds me that the daughter of such a father should not stoop to a *mésalliance*.

LADY PTARM: *Mésalliance*! How dare you call Mr Chodd a *mésalliance*? And you hankering after that paltry, poverty-stricken, penny-a-liner!

MAUD: Lady Ptarmigant, you forget yourself; and you are untruthful. Mr Daryl is a gentleman by birth and breeding! I loved him – I acknowledge it – I love him still!

LADY PTARM: You shameless girl! And he without a penny! After the scene he made!

MAUD: He has dared to doubt me, and I have done with him for ever. For the moment he presumed to think that I could break my plighted word – that I could be false to the love I had acknowledged – the love that was my happiness and pride – all between us was over.

LADY PTARM: (*aside*) That's some comfort. (*aloud*) Then what do you intend to do?

MAUD: I intend to leave the house.

LADY PTARM: To go where?

MAUD: Anywhere from you!

LADY PTARM: Upon my word! (*aside*) She has more spirit than I gave her credit for. (*aloud*) And do you mean to tell me that that letter is not intended for that fellow Daryl?

MAUD: (*giving letter*) Read it.

LADY PTARM: (*opens it and reads*) 'To the Editor of *The Times*. Please insert the enclosed advertisement, for which I send stamps. Wanted: a situation as governess by – ' (*embracing* MAUD) Oh, my dear – dear girl! You couldn't think of such a thing – and you a lady, and my niece.

MAUD: (*disengaging herself*) Lady Ptarmigant, please don't!

LADY PTARM: (*thoroughly subdued*) But, my love, how could I think –

MAUD: What Lady Ptarmigant thinks is a matter of the most profound indifference to me.

LADY PTARM: (*aside*) Bless her! Exactly what I was at her age. (*aloud*) But, my dear Maud, what is to become of you?

MAUD: No matter what! Welcome poverty – humiliation – insult – the contempt of fools – welcome all but dependence! I will neither dress myself at the expense of a man I despise, control his household, owe him duty, or lead a life that is a daily lie – neither will I marry one I love, who has dared to doubt me, to drag him into deeper poverty.

(*Enter* SERVANT.)

SERVANT: My lady, there is a gentleman inquiring for Mr Chodd.

LADY PTARM: Perhaps some electioneering friend. Show him here. (*Exit* SERVANT.) Don't leave the room, Maud, dear.

MAUD: I was not going – why should I?

(SERVANT *shows in* TOM *with* LITTLE MAUD.)

LADY PTARM: It's the tobacco man!

TOM: (*to* LITTLE MAUD) Do I smell of smoke? I beg your ladyship's pardon, but Mr Chodd, the old gentleman, wished me to meet him here.

LADY PTARM: He has just driven off to the station.

TOM: I know I'm a few minutes behind time – here's the young lady. Good morning, Miss – Miss – I don't know what the rest of her – I – I – have been detained by the – this little girl.

LADY PTARM: A sweet little creature, Mr Silenus.

TOM: Stylus.

LADY PTARM: Stylus, pardon me.

TOM: (*aside*) This old lady will insist on calling me Silenus! She'd think me very rude if I called her Ariadne.

LADY PTARM: Sweet little thing! Come here, my dear! (LITTLE MAUD *crosses to her.*) Your child, Mr – Stylus?

TOM: No, my lady, this is Mr Sidney Daryl's *protégée*.

LADY PTARM: (*moving from* LITTLE MAUD) Whose?

TOM: Sidney Daryl's.

(MAUD *advances.*)

LADY PTARM: Nasty little wretch! How do you mean? Speak, quickly!

TOM: I mean that Sidney pays for her education, board, and all that. Oh, he's a splendid fellow – a heart of gold! (*aside*) I'll put in a good word for him, as his young woman's here. I'll make her repent!

MAUD: Come to me, child. (LITTLE MAUD *crosses to her.*) Who are you?

LITTLE MAUD: I'm Mrs Churton's little darling, and Mr Daryl's little girl. (*Crosses to* TOM, *as* MAUD *moves away.*)

LADY PTARM: His very image. (*Goes to* MAUD. MAUD *sinks on chair.*)

TOM: Bless her little tongue! I took her from the woman who takes care of her. She's going down with me to Springmead. I've bought her a new frock, all one colour, magenta. (*aside*) That was strong.

LADY PTARM: Did I tell you Mr Chodd had gone?

TOM: I'm one too many here. I'll vamose! Good morning, my lady.

LADY PTARM: Good morning, Mr – Bacchus.

TOM: Stylus – Stylus! [(*aside*)] I shall have to call her Ariadne. Um! They might have asked the child to have a bit of currant cake, or a glass of currant wine. Shabby devils! [(*aloud*)] Good morning, my lady.

(*Exeunt* TOM *and* LITTLE MAUD. *A pause.*)

LADY PTARM: (*aside*) Could anything have happened more delightfully?

MAUD: (*throwing herself into* LADY PTARMIGANT*'s arms*) Oh, aunty! Forgive me – I was wrong – I was ungrateful – forgive me! Kiss me, and forgive me! I'll marry Mr Chodd – anybody – do with me as you please.

Good morning: Tom has not yet eaten lunch.
Ariadne: married to Bacchus, the god of wine.
vamose: US slang (*c.* 1848) for 'clear off quickly'.

LADY PTARM: My dear niece! (*affected*) I – I – feel for you. I'm – I'm not so heartless as I seem. I know I'm a harsh, severe old woman, but I am a woman, and I can feel for you (*embracing her*).

MAUD: And to think that with the same breath he could swear that he loved me, while another – this child too! (*Bursts into a flood of tears.*) There, aunt, I won't cry. I'll dry my eyes – I'll do your bidding. You mean me well, while he – oh! (*Shudders.*) Tell Mr Chodd I'll bear his name, and bear it worthily (*sternly*).

LADY PTARM: (*embracing – kissing her at each stop*) Men are a set of brutes. I was jilted myself when I was twenty-three – and, oh, how I loved the fellow! But I asserted my dignity, and married Lord Ptarmigant, and *he*, and *he* only, can tell you how I have avenged my sex! Cheer up, my darling! Love, sentiment, and romance are humbug! – But wealth, position, jewels, balls, presentations, a country house, town mansion, society, power – that's true, solid happiness, and if it isn't, I don't know what is!

(*Exeunt.*)

SCENE 3. *The wells at Springmead-le-Beau. An avenue of elms, sloping off right; on left house with windows, etc., on to lawn; railings at back of stage. Garden seats, chairs, lounges, small tables, etc., discovered near house.* LORD PTARMIGANT *discovered asleep in garden chair against house, his feet resting on another. Enter* CHODD SENIOR *down avenue right.*

CHODD SEN: Oh, dear! Oh, dear! What a day this is! There's Johnny to be elected, and I'm expecting the first copy of the *Morning Earthquake* – my paper! my own paper! by the next train. Then here's Lady Ptarmigant saying that positively her niece will have Johnny for her wedded husband, and in one day my Johnny is to be a husband, an MP, and part-proprietor of a daily paper! Whew! how hot it is! It's lucky that the wells are so near the hustings – one can run under the shade and get a cooler. Here's my lord! (*waking him*) My Lord!

LORD PTARM: (*waking*) Oh! Oh! Mr Chodd – good morning! – How d'ye do?

CHODD SEN: (*sitting on stool*) Oh, flurried, and flustered, and worritted. You know today's the election.

LORD PTARM: Yes, I believe there is an election going on somewhere. (*calling*) A tumbler of the waters No. 2!

(*Enter* WAITER *from house, places a tumbler of water on the table, and exits.*)

CHODD SEN: Oh, what a blessing there is no opposition! If my boy is returned – (*rising*)

(*Enter* CHODD JUNIOR, *agitated, a placard in his hand.*)

CHODD JUN: Look here, guv! Look here!

CHODD SEN: What is it, my Johnny?

CHODD JUN: Don't call me Johnny! Look here! (*Shows electioneering placard, 'Vote for Daryl!'.*)

CHODD SEN: What?

---

lounges: sofas or easy-chairs for reclining on.

CHODD JUN: That vagabond has put up as candidate! His brother used to represent the borough.

CHODD SEN: Then the election will be contested?

CHODD JUN: Yes. (CHODD SENIOR *sinks on garden chair.*)

LORD PTARM: (*rising, and taking tumbler from table*) Don't annoy yourself, my dear Mr Chodd; these accidents will happen in the best regulated constituencies.

CHODD JUN: Guv, don't be a fool!

LORD PTARM: Try a glass of the waters.

(CHODD SENIOR *takes tumbler and drinks, and the next moment ejects the water with a grimace, stamping about.*)

CHODD SEN: Oh, what filth! O-o-o-o-o- oh!

LORD PTARM: It is an acquired taste. ([*calling*] *to* WAITER) Another tumbler of No. 2!

CHODD SEN: So, Johnny, there's to be a contest, and you won't be MP for Springmead after all.

CHODD JUN: I don't know that.

CHODD SEN: What d'ye mean?

CHODD JUN: Mr Sidney Daryl may lose, and, perhaps, Mr Sidney Daryl mayn't show. After that ball –

CHODD SEN: Where you lost that thousand pounds?

CHODD JUN: Don't keep bringing that up, guv'nor. After that I bought up all Mr Daryl's bills – entered up judgement, and left them with Aaron. I've telegraphed to London, and if Aaron don't nab him in town he'll catch him here.

CHODD SEN: But, Johnny, isn't that rather mean?

CHODD JUN: All's fair in love and Parliament.

(*Enter* COUNTRY BOY *with newspapers.*)

BOY: Mr Chodd?

CHODD SEN: }
CHODD JUN: } Here!

BOY: Just arrived.

CHODD JUN: The *Morning Earthquake.*

(*They both clutch at it eagerly; each secures a paper, and sits under tree.*)

CHODD SEN: (*reading*) Look at the leader. 'In the present aspect of European politics – '

CHODD JUN: 'Some minds seem singularly obtuse to the perception of an idea.'

CHODD SEN: Johnny!

CHODD JUN: Guv!

CHODD SEN: Do you see the last leader?

CHODD JUN: Yes.

CHODD SEN: (*reading*) 'The borough of Springmead-le-Beau has for centuries been represented by the house of Daryl.'

CHODD JUN: (*reading*) 'A worthy scion of that ancient race intends to offer himself as candidate at the forthcoming election, and, indeed, who will dare to oppose him?'

CHODD SEN: 'Surely not a Mister – '

CHODD JUN: 'Chodd.' (*They rise and come down stage.*)

CHODD SEN: 'Whoever he may be.'

CHODD JUN: 'What are the Choddian antecedents?'

CHODD SEN: 'Whoever heard of Chodd?'

CHODD JUN: 'To be sure, a young man of that name has recently been the cause of considerable laughter at the clubs on account of his absurd attempts to become a man of fashion.'

CHODD SEN: 'And to wriggle himself into society.'

CHODD JUN: Why, it's all in his favour (*in a rage*).

CHODD SEN: In our own paper, too! Oh, that villain Stylus!

CHODD JUN: There are no more of these in the town, are there?

BOY: Yes, sir. A man came down with two thousand; he's giving them away everywhere.

CHODD JUN: Confound you! (*Pushes him off – follows.*)

CHODD SEN: Oh, dear! Oh, dear! Oh, dear! Now, my lord, isn't that too bad? (*Sees him asleep.*) He's off again! (*waking him*) My lord, here's the *Earthquake*! (*half throwing him off his seat*)

LORD PTARM: Earthquake! Good gracious! I didn't feel anything (*rising*).

CHODD SEN: No, no, the paper.

LORD PTARM: Ah, most interesting. (*Drops paper, and leisurely reseats himself.*) My dear Mr Chodd, I congratulate you.

CHODD SEN: Congratulate me? (*Looks at watch.*) I must be off to the committee. (*Exit* CHODD SENIOR.)

LORD PTARM: Waiter! Am I to have that tumbler of No. 2?

(*Band heard playing 'Conquering Hero', and loud cheers as* LORD PTARMIGANT *goes into house, and enter* SIDNEY, O'SULLIVAN, MacUSQUEBAUGH, *and* DR MAKVICZ, SIDNEY *bowing off as he enters. Cheers.*)

SIDNEY: So far so good. I've seen lots of faces that I knew. I'll run this Dutch-metalled brute hard, and be in an honourable minority anyhow.

(*Enter* TOM *hastily.*)

TOM: Daryl!

SIDNEY: Yes.

TOM: Look out!

SIDNEY: What's the matter?

TOM: I met our friend Moses Aaron on the platform. He didn't see you, but what does he want here?

SIDNEY: Me, if anybody. (*musing*) This is a shaft from the bow of Mr John Chodd, Junior – I see his aim.

TOM: What's to be done? The voters are warm, but, despite the prestige of the family name, if you were not present –

Dutch-metalled: Dutch metal, an alloy made up of copper and zinc, was a cheap imitation of gold-leaf.

SIDNEY: Besides, I couldn't be returned from Cursitor Street, MP for the Queen's Bench. (*thinking*) Did the Lamb come down with us?

TOM: Yes – second class.

SIDNEY: Let him stop the bailiffs – Aaron is as timid as a girl. I'll go through here, and out by the grand entrance. Let in the Lamb, and –

TOM: I see.

SIDNEY: Quick! (*Exit* TOM.)

O'SULL: Daryl, is there any fighting to be done?

MacUSQ: Or any drinking?

MAKVICZ: If so, we shall be most happy.

SIDNEY: No, no, thanks. Come with me – I've a treat for you.

OMNES: What?

SIDNEY: (*laughing*) The chalybeate waters.

(*Exeunt* OMNES *into house. Enter* CHODD JUNIOR *and* AARON.)

CHODD JUN: You saw him go in – arrest him. The chaise is ready – take him to the next station, and all's right. I'll stay and see him captured (*in great triumph*).

AARON: Very good, shur – do it at vunsh.

(*Is going into the house, when the* LAMB *springs out;* AARON *staggers back; the* LAMB *stands in boxing attitude before the door;* TOM *and* SIX *or* EIGHT ROUGHS *enter by avenue.*)

LAMB: (*with back half turned to audience*) Now, then, where are *you* a-shovin' to?

AARON: I want to passh by.

LAMB: Then you can't.

AARON: Why not?

LAMB: (*doggedly*) 'Cos I'm doorkeeper, and you haven't got a check.

AARON: Now, Lamb, dooty'sh dooty, and –

LAMB: (*turning with face to audience, and bringing up the muscle in his right arm*) Feel that!

AARON: (*alarmed*) Yesh, shur. (*Feels it slightly.*)

LAMB: You can't come in.

CHODD JUN: (*crossing to* LAMB *fussily*) Why not?

LAMB: (*looks at him, half contemptuously, half comically*) 'Cos that sez I mustn't let you. Feel it! (*Taps muscle.*)

CHODD JUN: Thank you, some other time.

(*Crossing. The* ROUGHS *surround him, jeer, and prepare to justle him.* TOM *mounts seat.*)

TOM: Vote for Daryl!

LAMB: (*making up to* AARON *in sparring attitude, who retreats in terror*) Are yer movin'?

CHODD JUN: Do your duty (ROUGHS *laugh.*)

AARON: I can't – they are many, I am a few. (*Cheers without.*)

Cursitor Street: off Chancery Lane, it took its name from the clerks of the Court of Chancery, who made out and 'ran about' with writs.
Queen's Bench: the supreme court of Common Law.

CHODD JUN: (*losing his presence of mind*) Particular business requires me at the hustings. (*Goes off, midst jeers and laughter of* ROUGHS.)

LAMB: (*at same time advancing upon* AARON) Are yer movin'?

AARON: Yesh, Mr Lamb.

(*By this time he has backed close to* TOM, *perched upon the seat, who bonnets him.*)

TOM: Vote for Daryl!

(AARON *is hustled off, by* MOB, *followed leisurely by* LAMB.)

TOM: (*on chair*) Remember, gentlemen, the officers of the law – the officers of the sheriff – are only in the execution of their duty. (*Shouts and uproar without.*) Don't offer any violence. (*Shouts.*) Don't tear them limb from limb! (*Shouts, followed by a loud shriek.* TOM *leaps from chair, dances down stage, and exits. Enter* LADY PTARMIGANT *and* CHODD SENIOR. LADY PTARMIGANT *is dressed in mauve.* CHODD SENIOR *escorts her to house.*)

CHODD SEN: But if he is absent from his post?

LADY PTARM: His post must get on without him. Really, my dear Mr Chodd, you must allow me to direct absolutely. If you wish your son to marry Miss Hetherington, now is the time – now or never. (*Exit into house.* CHODD SENIOR *exits. Enter* CHODD JUNIOR, *and* MAUD *dressed in mauve.*)

CHODD JUN: Miss Hetherington, allow me to offer you a seat. (*She sits under tree; aside*) Devilish awkward! Lady Ptarmigant says, 'Strike while the iron's hot'; but I want to be at the hustings. I've made my speech to the electors, and now I must do my courting. She looks awfully proud. I wish I could pay some fellow to do this for me. Miss Hetherington, a – a – a – I got the speech I spoke just now off by heart. I wish I'd got this written for me, too. Miss Hetherington, I – I am emboldened by the – by what I have just been told by our esteemed correspondent, Lady Ptar – I mean by your amiable aunt. I – I – (*boldly*) I have a large fortune, and my prospects are bright and brilliant – bright and brilliant. I – I am of a respectable family, which has always paid its way. I have entered upon a political career, which always pays its way; and I mean some day to make my name famous. My lady has doubtless prepared you for the hon – I offer you my – my humble hand, and large – I may say colossal – fortune.

MAUD: Mr Chodd, I will be plain with you.

CHODD JUN: Impossible for Miss Hetherington to be plain.

MAUD: You offer me your hand; I will accept.

CHODD JUN: Oh, joy! Oh – (*endeavouring to take her hand*)

MAUD: Please hear me out. On these conditions.

CHODD JUN: Pin money no object. Settle as much on you as you like.

MAUD: I will be your true and faithful wife – I will bear your name worthily; but you must understand our union is a union of convenience.

CHODD JUN: Convenience!

---

bonnets him: pulls his hat down over his eyes.
Pin money: a cash allowance made to a wife for her personal use, often stipulated in the marriage settlement.

MAUD: Yes; that love has no part in it.

CHODD JUN: Miss Hetherington – may I say Maud? – I love you – I adore you with my whole heart and fortune. (*aside*) I wonder how they are getting on at the hustings.

MAUD: I was saying, Mr Chodd –

CHODD JUN: Call me John – your own John! (*Seizing her hand; she shudders, and withdraws it.*)

MAUD: (*struggling with herself*) I was saying that the affection which a wife should bring the man she has elected as – (*Cheers without.*)

SIDNEY: (*speaking without*) Electors of Springmead.

MAUD: We hardly know sufficient of each other to warrant –

SIDNEY: (*without*) I need not tell you who I am. (*Cheers.* MAUD *trembles.*)

MAUD: We are almost strangers.

SIDNEY: [(*without*)] Nor what principles I have been reared in.

CHODD JUN: The name of Chodd, if humble, is at least wealthy.

SIDNEY: [(*without*)] I am a Daryl; and my politics those of the Daryls. (*Cheers.*)

CHODD JUN: (*aside*) This is awkward. (*to* MAUD) As to our being strangers –

SIDNEY: [(*without*)] I am no stranger. (*Cheers.*) I have grown up to be a man among you. There are faces I see in the crowd I am addressing, men of my own age, whom I remember children. (*Cheers.*) There are faces among you who remember me when I was a boy. (*Cheers.*) In the political union between my family and Springmead, there is more than respect and sympathy, there is sentiment. (*Cheers.*)

CHODD JUN: Confound the fellow! Dearest Miss Hetherington – Dearest Maud – you have deigned to say you will be mine.

SIDNEY: (*without*) Why, if we continue to deserve your trust, plight your political faith to another?

MAUD: (*overcome*) Mr Chodd, I –

CHODD JUN: My own bright, particular Maud!

SIDNEY: [(*without*)] Who is my opponent?

TOM: (*without*) Nobody. (*A loud laugh.*)

SIDNEY: [(*without*)] What is he?

TOM: [(*without*)] Not much. (*A roar of laughter.*)

SIDNEY: [(*without*)] I have no doubt he is honest and trustworthy, but why turn away an old servant to hire one you don't know? (*Cheers.*) Why turn off an old love that you have tried and proved, for a new one? (*Cheers.*) I don't know what the gentleman's politics may be. (*Laugh.*) Or those of his family. (*Roar of laughter.*) I've tried to find out, but I can't. To paraphrase the ballad:-

I've searched through Hansard, journals,
Books, De Brett, and Burke, and Dodd,
And my head – my head is aching,

De Brett, and Burke, and Dodd: Debrett's *Peerage, Baronetage, Knightage and Companionage* first appeared in 1802, Burke's *Peerage, Baronetage, and Knightage* in 1826. Charles Roger Phipps Dod(d) followed his *Parliamentary Pocket Companion* (1832) with *The Peerage, Baronetage and Knightage of Great Britain and Ireland* in 1841. His *Electoral Facts from 1832 to 1852, Impartially Stated* came out in 1852.

To find out the name of Chodd.

(*Loud laughter and three cheers.* MAUD *near fainting.*)

CHODD JUN: I can't stand this; I must be off to the hustings, Miss Heth— Oh! She's fainting. What shall I do? Lady Ptarmigant! Oh, here she comes. Waiter, a tumbler of No. 2! (*Runs off.*)

SIDNEY: (*without*) And I confidently await the result which will place me at the head of the poll. (*Cheers.*)

(*Enter* LORD *and* LADY PTARMIGANT *from house.* LADY PTARMIGANT *attends to* MAUD.)

MAUD: 'Twas nothing – a slight faintness – an attack of –

LORD PTARM: An attack of Chodd, I think! (*aside*) What a dreadful person my lady is, to be sure. (*Sits.*)

LADY PTARM: (*to* MAUD) Have you done it?

MAUD: Yes.

LADY PTARM: And you are to be his wife?

MAUD: Yes. (*Cheers.*)

(*Enter* SIDNEY, O'SULLIVAN, MacUSQUEBAUGH, *and* DR MAKVICZ.)

SIDNEY: (*coming down stage*) Tom, I feel so excited – so delighted – so happy – so – (*Sees* MAUD, *stops; takes his hat off;* MAUD *bows coldly.*) In my adversary's colours!

LADY PTARM: That fellow, Sidney!

MAUD: (*aside*) It seems hard to see him there, and not to speak to him for the last time. (*Is about to advance when* TOM *brings on* LITTLE MAUD, *dressed in magenta.* MAUD *recedes.* LORD PTARMIGANT *goes to sleep in garden seat.*)

LADY PTARM: The tobacco man!

TOM: Ariadne!

(SIDNEY *kisses* LITTLE MAUD. *Enter* CHODD JUNIOR, *and comes down stage.*)

LADY PTARM: (*with a withering glance at* SIDNEY) Maud, my child, here's Mr Chodd.

(CHODD JUNIOR, *crossing, gives his arm to* MAUD. SIDNEY *stands with* LITTLE MAUD. *All go off, except* LADY PTARMIGANT, SIDNEY, LITTLE MAUD, TOM, *and* LORD PTARMIGANT.)

SIDNEY: On his arm! Well, I deserve it! I am poor!

LADY PTARM: Mr Daryl. (SIDNEY *bows.*)

TOM: Ariadne is about to express her feelings; I shall go! (*Exit.*)

SIDNEY: Lady Ptarmigant.

LADY PTARM: I cannot but express my opinion of your conduct. For a long time I have known you to be the associate of prize-fighters, betting men, race-horses, authors and other such low persons; but despite that, I thought you had some claims to be a gentleman.

SIDNEY: In what may I have forfeited Lady Ptarmigant's good opinion?

LADY PTARM: In what, sir? In daring to bring me, your kinswoman, and a lady – in daring to bring into the presence of the foolish girl you professed to love – that child – your illegitimate offspring! (LORD PTARMIGANT *awakes.*)

SIDNEY: (*stung*) Lady Ptarmigant, do you know who that child is?
LADY PTARM: Perfectly! (*with a sneer*)
SIDNEY: I think not. She is the lawful daughter of your dead and only son, Charles!
LADY PTARM: What?
SIDNEY: Two days before he sailed for the Crimea, he called at my chambers, and told me that he felt convinced he should never return. He told me, too, of his connection with a poor and humble girl, who would shortly become the mother of his child. I saw from his face that the bullet was cast that would destroy him, and I begged him to legitimise one who, though of his blood, might not bear his name. Like a brave fellow, a true gentleman, on the next day he married –
LADY PTARM: How disgraceful!
SIDNEY: Joined his regiment, and, as you know, fell at Balaclava.
LADY PTARM: My poor – poor boy.
SIDNEY: His death broke his wife's heart – she, too, died.
LADY PTARM: What a comfort!
SIDNEY: I placed the child with a good motherly woman, and I had intended, for the sake of my old friend, Charley, to educate her, and to bring her to you, and say, 'Take her, she is your lawful grandchild, and a lady *pur sang*; love her, and be proud of her, for the sake of the gallant son, who galloped to death in the service of his country.'
LADY PTARM: (*affected*) Sidney!
SIDNEY: I did not intend that you should know this for some time. I had some romantic notion of making it a reason for your consent to my marriage with – (LADY PTARMIGANT *takes* LITTLE MAUD.) – with Miss Hetherington – that is all over now. The ill opinion with which you have lately pursued me has forced this avowal from me.
LADY PTARM: (*to child*) My darling! Ah! My poor Charley's very image! My poor boy! My poor boy!
LORD PTARM: (*who has been listening, advancing*) Sidney, let my son Charley's father thank you. You have acted like a kinsman and a Daryl! (*affected*)
LITTLE MAUD: Uncle, have you given me a new father and mother, as well as a new dress?
LADY PTARM: Sidney, forgive me!
SIDNEY: Pray forget it, Lady Ptarm –
LADY PTARM: I will take care that Miss Hetherington shall know –
SIDNEY: (*hotly*) What! Did she, too, suspect! Lady Ptarmigant, it is my request – nay, if I have done anything to deserve your good opinion, my injunction – that Miss Hetherington is not informed of what has just passed. If she has

---

the Crimea: England and France joined the war between Russia and Turkey in March 1854; peace was signed at Paris in March 1856.
Balaclava: the battle of Balaclava, fought on 25 October 1854, featured the celebrated Charge of the Light Brigade under Lord Cardigan.
pur sang: thoroughbred.
galloped to death: the phrase suggests that Charles Ptarmigant was involved in the famous charge in which squadrons of Lancers, Dragoons, and Hussars participated.

thought that I could love another – she is free to her opinion! (*Goes up stage, and comes down with the child.*)

LORD PTARM: But *I* shall tell her.

LADY PTARM: (*astonished*) You! (*aside*) Don't you think, under the circumstances, it would be better –

LORD PTARM: I shall act as I think best.

LADY PTARM: Ferdinand! (*authoritatively*)

LORD PTARM: Lady Ptarmigant, it is not often I speak, goodness knows! But on a question that concerns my honour and yours, I shall *not* be silent.

LADY PTARM: Ferdinand! (*imploringly*)

LORD PTARM: Lady Ptarmigant, I am *awake*, and you will please follow my instructions. (*crossing*) What is my granddaughter's name?

LITTLE MAUD: Maud.

LORD PTARM: Maud, Maud – is it Maud? (*Playfully; lifts her in his arms, and is carrying her off.*)

LADY PTARM: My lord! Consider – people are looking!

LORD PTARM: Let 'em look – they'll know I'm a *grandfather*!

(*Exit* LORD PTARMIGANT, *with* LITTLE MAUD, *and* LADY PTARMIGANT, *up avenue.* TOM *runs on.*)

TOM: It's all right, Sid! Three of Chodd's committee have come over to us. They said that so long as a Daryl was not put up, they felt at liberty to support him, but now – (*seeing that* SIDNEY *is affected*) What's the matter?

SIDNEY: Nothing.

TOM: Ah, that means love! I hope to be able to persuade the majority of Chodd's committee to resign; and if they resign, he must too, and we shall walk over the course. (SIDNEY *goes up stage and sits. Aside*) Cupid's carriage stops the way again. Confound that nasty, naughty, naked little boy! I wonder if he'd do less mischief if they put him into knickerbockers. (*Exit.*)

SIDNEY: Mr Chodd shall not have Springmead.

(*Enter* MAUD, *leading* LITTLE MAUD *by the hand.* SIDNEY*'s face is buried in his hands on the table.*)

MAUD: (*kissing the child, then advancing slowly to* SIDNEY) Sidney!

SIDNEY: (*rising*) Maud – Miss Hetherington!

LITTLE MAUD: Uncle, this is my new aunt. She's my aunt and you're my uncle. You don't seem pleased to see each other, though – ain't you? Aunt, why don't you kiss uncle?

MAUD: (*after a pause*) Sidney, I have to beg your forgiveness for the – the – mistake which –

SIDNEY: Pray don't mention it, Maud – Miss Hetherington. It is not of the –

MAUD: It is so hard to think ill of those we have known.

SIDNEY: I think that it must be very easy! Let me take this opportunity of apologising personally, as I have already done by letter, for my misconduct at the ball. I had heard that you were about to – to –

MAUD: Marry! Then you were in error. Since then I have accepted Mr Chodd. (*pause*)

SIDNEY: I congratulate you. (*Turns his face aside.*)

MAUD: You believed me to be false – believed it without inquiry!

SIDNEY: As you believed of me!

MAUD: Our mutual poverty prevented.

SIDNEY: (*bursting out*) Oh, yes, we are poor! We are poor! We loved each other – but we were poor! We loved each other – but we couldn't take a house in a square! We loved each other – but we couldn't keep a carriage! We loved each other – but we had neither gold, purple, plate, nor mansion in the country! You were right to leave me, and to marry a *gentleman* – rich in all these assurances of happiness!

MAUD: Sidney, you are cruel.

SIDNEY: I loved you, Maud; loved you with my whole heart and soul since we played together as children, and you grew till I saw you a lovely blushing girl, and now – pshaw! This is folly, sentiment, raving madness! Let me wish you joy – let me hope you will be happy.

LITTLE MAUD: (*coming down stage*) Uncle, you mustn't make my new aunt cry. Go and make it up with her, and kiss her.

(LADY PTARMIGANT, LORD PTARMIGANT, *and* LORD CLOUDWRAYS *have entered during the last speech.*)

MAUD: Farewell, Sidney! (*holding out her hand*)

SIDNEY: Farewell!

LADY PTARM: (*advancing*) Farewell! What nonsense; two young people so fond of each other. Sidney – Maud, dear, you have my consent.

SIDNEY: (*astonished*) Lady Ptarmigant!

LADY PTARM: I always liked you, Sidney, though, I confess, I didn't always show it.

LORD PTARM: I can explain my lady's sudden conversion – at least, Cloudwrays can.

LORD CLOUD: Well, Sid, I'm sorry to be the bearer of good news – I mean of ill news; but your brother – poor Percy – he – a –

SIDNEY: Dead!

LORD CLOUD: The news came by the mail to the club, so as I'd nothing to do, I thought I'd come down to congratulate – I mean condole with you.

LORD PTARM: Bear up, Sidney, your brother's health was bad before he left us.

SIDNEY: First the son, and then the father.

MAUD: Sidney!

SIDNEY: (*catching her hand*) Maud!

MAUD: No, no – not now – you are rich, and I am promised.

LADY PTARM: Why, you wicked girl; you wouldn't marry a man you didn't love, would you? Where are your principles?

(LORD PTARMIGANT *sits on garden seat with* LITTLE MAUD.)

MAUD: But – but – Mr Chodd?

LADY PTARM: What on earth consequence is Mr Chodd?

(*Enter* CHODD SENIOR *and* CHODD JUNIOR *down avenue.*)

CHODD SEN: My lady, it's all right, Johnny has been accepted!

(MAUD *goes up stage and sits.* SIDNEY *and* LORD CLOUDWRAYS *also go up with her.*)

LADY PTARM: By whom?

CHODD SEN: By Miss Hetherington – by Maud!

LADY PTARM: Why, you must be dreaming, the election has turned your brain – my niece marry a Chodd!

CHODD SEN: } My lady!
CHODD JUN: }

LADY PTARM: Nothing of the sort; I was only joking, and thought you were, too. (*aside*) The impertinence of the lower classes in trying to ally themselves with us! (*going up stage*)

CHODD JUN: Guv.

CHODD SEN: Johnny!

CHODD JUN: We're done! (*Crosses stage.*)

(*Loud cheering. Enter* TOM, *who whispers and congratulates* SIDNEY. *Enter a* GENTLEMAN, *who whispers to* CHODD SENIOR *condolingly, and exits.*)

CHODD SEN: (*shouting*) Johnny!

CHODD JUN: Guv.

CODDD SEN: They say there's no hope, and advise us to withdraw from the contest.

(*All congratulate* SIDNEY, *up stage.*)

LADY PTARM: Sir Sidney Daryl MP, looks like old times. (*to* LORD PTARMIGANT) My lord, congratulate him.

LORD PTARM: (*waking and shaking* CHODD JUNIOR *by the hand*) Receive my congratulations.

LADY PTARM: Oh! It's the wrong man!

CHODD SEN: Mr Stylus, I may thank you for this.

TOM: And yourself, you may. I brought out your journal, engaged your staff, and you tried to throw me over. You've got your reward. Morning paper! (*Throws papers in the air.*)

(*Enter* AARON, *with hat broken and head bound up.*)

AARON: (*to* SIDNEY) Arresht you at the shoot of – (*The* CHODDS *rub their hands in triumph.*)

TOM: Too late! Too late! He's a member of Parliament.

(CHODD JUNIOR *and* CHODD SENIOR *turn into right and left corners.*)

SIDNEY: (*to* TOM) I haven't taken the seat or the oaths yet.

TOM: They don't know that.

SIDNEY: We can settle it another way. (*taking out pocket-book and looking at* CHODD JUNIOR) Some time ago I was fortunate enough to win a large sum of money; this way, if you please. (*Goes up stage with* AARON, *and gives money, notes, etc.*)

CHODD JUN: Pays his own bills, which I'd bought up, with my money.

CHODD SEN: (*crossing*) Then, Johnny, you won't get into society.

LADY PTARM: (*coming down*) Never mind, Mr Chodd, your son shall marry a lady.

CHODD JUN: } Eh!
CHODD SEN: }

LADY PTARM: I promise to introduce you to one of blue blood.

CHODD JUN: Blue blood – I'd rather have it the natural colour.

(*Cheers. Enter* O'SULLIVAN, MacUSQUEBAUGH, MAKVICZ, *and* COMMITTEE. *Stage full. Church bells heard.*)

O'SULL: Sir Sidney Daryl, we have heard the news. In our turn we have to inform you that your adversaries have retired from the contest, and you are member for Springmead. (*Cheers.*) We, your committee, come to weep with you for the loss of a brother, to joy with you on your accession to a title and your hereditary honours. Your committee most respectfully beg to be introduced to Lady Daryl (*with intention and Irish gallantry*).

(SIDNEY *shows* MAUD *the magenta ribbon; she places her hand in his.*)

SIDNEY: Gentlemen, I thank you; I cannot introduce you to Lady Daryl, for Lady Daryl does not yet exist. In the meantime I have permission to present you to Miss Hetherington.

TOM: (*leaping on chair, and waving handkerchief*) Three cheers for my lady!

(*All cheer. Church bells; band plays 'Conquering Hero'.* GIRL *at window of house waves handkerchief, and* CHILD *a stick with magenta streamer attached.* COUNTRYMEN, *etc., wave hats; band plays, etc.*)

CURTAIN

NOTE

According to T.W. Robertson Junior's memoir of his father attached to PDW (p. xlvii), 'Cock-a-doodle-doo' was sung in the original production of *Society* to Robertson's own adaptation of 'an old air' entitled 'As Mars and Minerva', found in Chappell's *Old English Melodies*. No doubt Daryl's song was influenced by a burlesque version describing the Battle of Waterloo, often sung at the Savage Club, with 'Cock-a-doodle-doo' as its refrain.

In fact, the melody, 'one of the common street ballad tunes of London' known as 'Under the Rose', appears in William Chappell, *Popular Music of the Olden Times*, 1855–9, parts XVI and XVII, p. 730. The words, said to date from about 1820, run:

As Mars and Minerva were viewing of some implements,
Bellona stept forward and asked the news;
Were they for repairing those war-like instruments,
That's now growing rusty for want to be used?
  The money is withdrawn, and our trade is diminishing,
  Mechanics are wand'ring without shoes or hose;
  Come, stir up the wars and our trade will be flourishing.
  This grand conversation was under the rose.

Only a certain amount of adaptation is required to tailor the tune as given for 'As Mars and Minerva' in Chappell, to fit the words of 'Cock-a-doodle-doo'.

---

intention: implied meaning.

OURS

An original comedy in three acts

First performed at the Prince of Wales's Theatre, Liverpool, on 23 August 1866, and at the Prince of Wales's Theatre, London, on Saturday 15 September 1866 with the following cast:

PRINCE PEROVSKY	Mr Hare
SIR ALEXANDER SHENDRYN, BART.	Mr J.W. Ray
CAPTAIN SAMPREY	Mr Trafford
ANGUS MacALISTER	Mr Bancroft
HUGH CHALCOT	Mr J. Clarke
SERGEANT JONES	Mr F. Younge
HOUGHTON [one of Sir Alexander's keepers]	Mr Tindale
LADY SHENDRYN	Miss Larkin
BLANCHE HAYE	{ Miss L. Moore Miss Lydia Foote
MARY NETLEY	Miss Marie Wilton

[SERVANT
JENNINGS, Lady Shendryn's maid
SOLDIER]

Period: Before, and during the Crimean War.

Ours: a common dialect term for a near relative or the speaker's house, 'ours' is used to indicate mutual membership of a military regiment in Charles Lever's *Tom Burke of 'Ours'* (1843).
Houghton: Houghton only appears by name once, at the beginning of the play, but a 'Keeper' enters with Sergeant Jones later during act I, and I have assumed that to Robertson this character and Houghton were the same man.
Lady Shendryn: Robertson also used the name for his heroine's great-aunt in his novel *David Garrick*, published in 1865.

IV Artist's impression of act III of *Ours* (1866)

ACT I

SCENE. *An avenue of trees in Shendryn Park; the avenue leading off up right. Seat round tree in foreground right. Stumps of trees left. The termination of the avenue out of sight. Throughout the act the autumn leaves fall from the trees.* CHALCOT *discovered asleep on ground under tree, a handkerchief over his face. Enter* SERGEANT JONES, *right, meeting* HOUGHTON, *who enters with gun, left.*

SERGEANT: Good morning.

HOUGHTON: Good morning. (SERGEANT *shakes* HOUGHTON*'s hand warmly.* HOUGHTON *surprised.*)

SERGEANT: (*warmly*) How are you?

HOUGHTON: Quite well; how are you?

SERGEANT: I'm – I'm as well as can be expected (*semi-important*).

HOUGHTON: What d'ye mean? (*with dialect*)

SERGEANT: (*with importance*) I mean that last night my missus – (*Whispers to* HOUGHTON.)

HOUGHTON: (*surprised*) Nay!

SERGEANT: Fact!

HOUGHTON: Two! (SERGEANT *nods.*) Twins? (SERGEANT *nods.*) Well, mate, it does you credit! (*Shakes hands condolingly.*) And I hope you'll soon get over it.

SERGEANT: Eh?

HOUGHTON: I mean I hope your missus 'ull soon get over it. Come and ha' some beer.

SERGEANT: I must go to the Hall first. I wish they'd been born in Malta.

HOUGHTON: Where?

SERGEANT: At Malta.

HOUGHTON: Malta! Be that where they make the best beer?

SERGEANT: No; it's 'furrin'. When a child's born in barracks there, it gets half a pound o' meat additional rations a day.

HOUGHTON: Child does?

SERGEANT: Its parents. Twins would ha' been a pound a day – pound o' meat you know. It's worth while being a father in Malta.

HOUGHTON: (*looking at* SERGEANT *admiringly and shouldering his gun*) Come and ha' some beer to drink to this here joyful double-barrelled event.

(*Exeunt* SERGEANT *and* HOUGHTON. CHALCOT *wakes up, lights his pipe, and looks round moodily; then rearranges the handkerchief over his face, and lies down again. Enter* BLANCHE *and* MARY, *both with baskets, through trees.*)

BLANCHE: Don't walk so fast, Mary. Lady Shendryn said she'd overtake us. Let us rest here. (*They sit on seat.*) It's charming under the trees. I mean to look after the little boy. That's for him. (*Puts portmonnaie into basket.*)

MARY: (*taking out portmonnaie*) And I mean to look after the little girl. This is for her. (*Puts portmonnaie into basket.*)

---

portmonnaie: a flat leather purse or pocket-book.

BLANCHE: But, Mary dear, can you afford it?

MARY: Yes; though I am poor, I must have some enjoyments. You rich people mustn't monopolise all the pleasures in the world.

BLANCHE: (*hurt*) My dear Mary, you know I didn't mean –

MARY: And *I* didn't mean; but I can't help being sensible. I know my place, and if I didn't Lady Shendryn and the world would make me. I haven't a penny, so I'm a companion, though I don't receive wages, which the cook does. But then she's respected – she's not in a false position. I wish I hadn't been born a lady.

BLANCHE: No, you don't.

MARY: Yes, I do. I should have kept a Berlin-wool shop, and been independent and happy. And you, Blanche – you could have rolled down in your carriage, and given your orders – 'Miss Netley, please send me home this – or that' – and so on (*with imitation*).

BLANCHE: Mary, do talk about something else.

MARY: Well, I will, dear, to please you; but it is annoying to be a companion. Not your companion, Blanche – that's charming – to know that you're kept in the room to save another woman from rising to ring a bell, or to hand her the scissors, or to play the piano when you're ordered. (*imitating*) 'Miss Netley – oh! – Yes, a very nice person; so useful about the house.' 'Useful' – oh! – There, I beg your pardon, Blanche; but really Lady Shendryn's temper does upset me – one minute she's so tender and sentimental, and the next – poor Sir Alick. Then there's Mr Chalcot – I detest him.

BLANCHE: Why?

MARY: Oh, for his gloomy air, and his misanthropic eye-glass. (*imitating*) Liking nothing, and dissatisfied with everything.

BLANCHE: Despite all that, he has a very good heart.

MARY: My gentleman is rich, and thinks that every girl he speaks to is dying for his ugly face, his stupid bank-notes, and his nasty brewhouse. When I look at him I feel that I could smack his face.

BLANCHE: For being rich?

MARY: Yes – perhaps. No, for being disagreeable.

BLANCHE: I'm rich; at least, they tell me so.

MARY: But you're not disagreeable.

BLANCHE: Do talk about something else.

MARY: Who – what?

BLANCHE: Anything – anybody.

MARY: Of the people staying at the Hall?

BLANCHE: Yes.

MARY: Prince Perovsky?

BLANCHE: If you like.

MARY: He means 'you'; I can see it in his eye. I know Sir Alick would say yes, and so would my lady. Blanche, what would you say?

BLANCHE: (*pensively*) I don't know.

Berlin-wool: a fine dyed wool.

MARY: That means 'yes'! A Russian prince – wealthy, urbane – quite the grand air, but dried up as a Normandy pippin. Will my Blanche be a princess?

BLANCHE: Prince Perovsky is a little old.

MARY: Not for a prince. Princes are never old.

BLANCHE: And I'm a little young.

MARY: Not too young for a princess. Princesses are never too young.

BLANCHE: Why, Mary, you're quite worldly.

MARY: Only on your account. I should like to see you a princess. You'd be charming as a princess.

BLANCHE: (*smilingly*) And if I were and had a court, what would you be?

MARY: (*rising*) Mistress of the Robes, and First High Gold Parasol in Waiting! Oh, my charming, darling Royal Highness. My Highest, Mightiest, Most Serene Transparentissima! (*Curtseying;* CHALCOT *wakes up, and looks about him.*)

BLANCHE: (*laughs*) How silly!

MARY: Who – me?

BLANCHE: Yes.

MARY: Then I renounce my allegiance – turn Radical, and dethrone you. I wish the Prince would ask me.

BLANCHE: Ask you what?

MARY: To be his wife.

CHALCOT: (*aside*) Devil doubt you!

BLANCHE: How would you answer?

MARY: I'd answer – No!

CHALCOT: (*aside*) Dreadful falsehood!

MARY: Though I'd like to be a princess – a Russian princess – and have slaves.

BLANCHE: Oh! I shouldn't like to have slaves.

MARY: I should, particularly if they were men.

CHALCOT: (*aside*) Nice girl that!

BLANCHE: Let's leave off talking Russian.

MARY: What shall we talk then? Scotch? (*Sits again.*)

BLANCHE: What a time Lady Shendryn is!

MARY: About Angus MacAlister? (*maliciously*)

BLANCHE: (*seeing* CHALCOT) Hush! (*rising and crossing left*)

MARY: What?

BLANCHE: There's a man.

CHALCOT: (*rising*) Don't be alarmed; I've heard nothing that I oughtn't to.

MARY: (*primly*) Impossible you should.

CHALCOT: I fell asleep under that tree.

MARY: Why did you wake up?

BLANCHE: Asleep, just after breakfast!

CHALCOT: Humph! There was nothing else to do.

MARY: You mean nothing else that *you* could do.

CHALCOT: I thought of climbing the tree; good notion, wasn't it?

MARY: Excellent – if you'd stayed up there!

CHALCOT: Eh?

MARY: I mean, if you hadn't come down. (*Guns fired without.* MARY *rises.*)

CHALCOT: Sir Alick might have brought me down.

BLANCHE: Mistaken you for a rook!
MARY: (*aside*) Or a scarecrow!
CHALCOT: (*pointing to basket*) What have you got there?
BLANCHE: Guess.
CHALCOT: Can't. Never could make out conundrums – or ladies.
MARY: Beyond your comprehension?
CHALCOT: Quite. (*annoyed*) Confound the girl! (*aloud*) But what's in the basket?
BLANCHE: (*holding up basket*) Fowls, jelly, sago, tapioca, wine!
MARY: (*repeating her words*) Wine, tapioca, sago, jelly, fowls!
CHALCOT: That's variety! Somebody ill? (MARY *sits.*)

(*Enter* LADY SHENDRYN, *who heard the last few words.*)

LADY SHEN: Ill – no! Nobody. They're all doing well.
CHALCOT: All! Who?
LADY SHEN: The twins!
CHALCOT: Twins! What twins?
LADY SHEN: Ours.
CHALCOT: Yours? Yours and Sir Al–
LADY SHEN: (*a languishing, sentimental, frisky person*) Mine and – no, no! What a man you are! When I say Ours, I mean Sergeant Jones's.
CHALCOT: Sergeant Jones's!
LADY SHEN: Of Ours – of Sir Alexander's regiment. Alexander is very fond of him; and I quite dote on Mrs Jones. You know that the barracks are not eight miles off, and the railway drops you close to it. (*turning*) Miss Netley, I'll sit down – (MARY *rises, and crosses to* BLANCHE. LADY SHENDRYN *sits.*) So I gave Mrs Jones the use of the Cottage – and it's – a most agreeable circumstance; isn't it?
CHALCOT: (*thoughtfully*) Very – for poor Jones!
MARY: (*aside to* BLANCHE) Make him give you something – subscription – you know.
CHALCOT: (*overhearing*) Make me! I should like to see anyone make me!
BLANCHE: (*rising, and crossing to* CHALCOT) By the way (*to* CHALCOT) I'm collecting for them. (*taking out pocket-book*) How much shall I put you down for?
CHALCOT: (*seeing* MARY*'s eyes on him*) Nothing.
MARY: Nothing!
LADY SHEN: Oh, Hugh!
BLANCHE: Oh, Mr Chalcot!
MARY: Oh, these men!
BLANCHE: Consider poor Mrs Jones!
LADY SHEN: And the twins!
CHALCOT: Twins! I don't think these sort of women ought to be encouraged.
MARY: (*aside*) And that's a man worth thousands!
BLANCHE: (*coaxingly*) Let me put you down for something!
MARY: A shilling!
CHALCOT: (*to* MARY) I'm not to be put down.
LADY SHEN: Miss Netley, pray don't interfere. (*Girls go up stage.*) How charming it is here, under the trees! – So poetical and leafy!

CHALCOT: (*throwing insect off her mantle*) And insecty! (LADY SHENDRYN *starts up.*)

(*Enter* PRINCE, *smoking a cigarette.* CHALCOT *crosses.* PRINCE *seeing ladies raises his hat, and throws cigarette on ground.*)

LADY SHEN: Ah, here's the Prince. How charming!

MARY: He'll give something.

BLANCHE: Prince, I'm begging – making a subscription.

PRINCE: Let me trust I may be permitted to become a subscriber.

BLANCHE: For any amount you please. How much? (*with pocket-book*)

PRINCE: I leave that to you.

LADY SHEN: Oh, Prince, you are so kind!

MARY: What a difference! (*to* CHALCOT) A noble nation, the Russians! (*Goes up stage.*)

BLANCHE: Will that do? (*writing, and showing him*)

PRINCE: If you think it sufficient. (BLANCHE *joins* MARY.)

LADY SHEN: Charmingly chivalric!

PRINCE: Shall I be indiscreet in asking the object of –

LADY SHEN: *Objects*! There are two!

PRINCE: Two objects!

CHALCOT: Yes – babies.

LADY SHEN: Twins.

CHALCOT: The Jones's gemini! (*Crosses up stage and sits under tree.*)

PRINCE: (*to* CHALCOT) Twins! Extraordinary people you English.

LADY SHEN: We're going to take these things to the Cottage for them. (*crossing*) Prince! will you come as far?

PRINCE: If I may be allowed to take part in so delicate a mission.

LADY SHEN: Blanche! The Prince will escort you.

PRINCE: (*crossing to* BLANCHE) May I carry the basket?

BLANCHE: Can I trust you?

PRINCE: With what?

BLANCHE: The sago.

(*Exeunt* PRINCE *and* BLANCHE.)

LADY SHEN: Miss Netley will be my cavalier.

MARY: What a treat!

LADY SHEN: Unless you, Mr Chalcot –

CHALCOT: (*eye to eye with* MARY) Thanks, no. I'll stay where I am.

LADY SHEN: We shall leave you all alone.

CHALCOT: I don't mind that.

MARY: That's just the sort of man who would pinch his wife on his wedding day.

(*Exeunt* LADY SHENDRYN *and* MARY.)

CHALCOT: That's a detestable girl! Whenever I meet her, she makes me thrill with dislike.

(SERGEANT *and* KEEPER *enter at end of avenue, carrying a large hamper, meeting* SIR ALEXANDER, *in shooting dress.* KEEPER *takes gun and exits with* SERGEANT.)

SIR ALEX: Ah, Hugh – that you?

CHALCOT: Yes. (*seated*)

SIR ALEX: What have you been doing here? (*Sits on stump.*)

CHALCOT: Sleeping. Shot anything?

SIR ALEX: A brace. I'm nervous. I've been annoyed this morning.

CHALCOT: I'm annoyed every morning – and evening, regularly.

SIR ALEX: I'd bad news by post – and then my lady – and I'm so horribly hard up.

CHALCOT: A little management –

SIR ALEX: I know; but I've other troubles, Hugh. You're an old friend, and so was your father before you. If you only knew what was on my mind. There's my lady – wrangling perpetually.

CHALCOT: People always quarrel when they're married – or single; and you must make allowances – her ladyship is much younger than you.

SIR ALEX: She might remember how long we have – But it isn't that – it isn't that.

CHALCOT: What then?

SIR ALEX: I mustn't tell – I wish I could.

CHALCOT: I'm open to receive a confession of early murder, or justifiable matricide.

SIR ALEX: It isn't my secret, or I'd tell it you. Oh! My lady is very wrong. The idea of her being jealous!

CHALCOT: I've heard that years ago you were a great killer.

SIR ALEX: (*not understanding*) Killer? Of what – birds?

CHALCOT: No. Ladies.

SIR ALEX: Oh! – Like other men.

CHALCOT: That's bad – that's very bad. But surely my lady knew that before marriage you were not a Joseph?

SIR ALEX: Not she.

CHALCOT: But she must have guessed –

SIR ALEX: Pooh! Pooh! You're talking like a bachelor.

CHALCOT: A bachelor may know –

SIR ALEX: A bachelor can know nothing. It is only after they're married that men begin to understand the purity of women – (*aside*) – or of their tempers.

CHALCOT: But do you mean to tell me – between men, you know – that Lady Shendryn has no cause for –

SIR ALEX: Has no cause? Certainly not – no cause whatever.

CHALCOT: *Had* no cause, then?

SIR ALEX: *Had*! Um – well – the slightest possible –

CHALCOT: Did she find it out?

SIR ALEX: Unfortunately she did.

CHALCOT: Ah! Nuisance that – being found out. Is the cause removed now?

SIR ALEX: The what?

CHALCOT: The cause – the slightest possible –

SIR ALEX: Oh yes – long ago. Gone entirely.

---

a Joseph: immune to sexual temptation, as Joseph proved in the house of Potiphar (see Genesis 39. 1–20).

CHALCOT: Dead?

SIR ALEX: No – married.

CHALCOT: Better still. Further removed than ever.

SIR ALEX: But my lady has never forgotten it. It was an absurd scrape; for I cared nothing about her.

CHALCOT: About my lady?

SIR ALEX: (*irritably*) No – the –

CHALCOT: Slightest possible – no, no.

SIR ALEX: Where is my lady? I haven't seen her since she did me the honour of upbraiding me two hours ago.

CHALCOT: She has gone to the Cottage to see the interesting little Joneses. The Prince went with her – and Blanche – and – that other girl.

SIR ALEX: Mary Netley! Charming girl that!

CHALCOT: Very.

SIR ALEX: She's the daughter of very dear old friends, who died without leaving her a penny.

CHALCOT: Very dear old friends always do.

SIR ALEX: What?

CHALCOT: Die without leaving pennies.

SIR ALEX: Poor little thing! I wish I could find her a husband.

CHALCOT: What a misanthropic sentiment!

SIR ALEX: Now there's Blanche; she's a fortune. She, like Mary, has no guardians but us – neither father nor mother.

CHALCOT: Splendid qualification that; but Blanche is much too nice a girl to have a mother.

SIR ALEX: She's another anxiety.

CHALCOT: All girls are anxieties.

SIR ALEX: You were wrong to let Blanche slip through your fingers.

CHALCOT: Me marry an heiress! Ugh! (*Shudders.*) There's Prince Perovsky, he is very particular in his attentions.

SIR ALEX: Yes; it would be a good match. He owns two-thirds of a Russian province.

CHALCOT: Poor devil! Isn't it rather awkward, his staying here? If war is to be declared – (*Rises and goes up stage looking off right.*)

SIR ALEX: He's off in a couple of days; besides, after all, Russia may not mean fighting.

CHALCOT: There's Angus, coming down the avenue!

SIR ALEX: (*rising*) Between you and me, Hugh, I wish he wouldn't come so often. He's too fond of teaching Blanche billiards. I'm always finding them with their heads closer together than is warranted by the rules of the game. When children, they saw a good deal of each other. Blanche is my ward, and an heiress; Angus, a distant cousin, poor as a rat – the Scotch branch of the family. I shouldn't like it to be thought that I threw them together.

If war is to be declared: Turkey declared war on Russia on 6 October 1853; England joined in on 28 March 1854.

CHALCOT: No, no.

SIR ALEX: I'll go and meet the people at the Cottage. I promised to join them in a game at bowls. (*taking letters from his pocket, selecting one*) I daren't take this into the house with me; eh – yes, I may this from Lady Llandudno. She's in a terrible fright about the prospect of war. You know her boy's in Ours. Asks me if I think the regiment will be ordered out. I may show my lady that. (*Replaces letter in pocket, then tears another into very small pieces. Sighs deeply.*) Heigho! It's not much use. It is sure to be found out at last. (CHALCOT *sits by stump, on ground.*)

(*Exit* SIR ALEXANDER. ANGUS MacALISTER *comes down the avenue.* CHALCOT *smokes incessantly; as soon as one cigar or pipe is out, he lights another.*)

CHALCOT: Well, Gus. Just got in?

ANGUS: Yes. Slept last night in barracks. Got leave again for today. (ANGUS *is grave and composed in manner; as he speaks, he looks about him, as if his thoughts were away.*)

CHALCOT: Bring down a paper with you?

ANGUS: Yes. (*Gives him newspaper, which* CHALCOT *looks over.*) Where are all the people gone? There's nobody in the Hall.

CHALCOT: Gone to the Cottage to try on a pair of new twins – born on the estate. My lady, Sir Alick, Miss Netley, the Prince, and Blanche.

ANGUS: Have they been gone long? (*Crosses to seat and puts right foot on it.*)

CHALCOT: No. I haven't quite made up my mind whether I like Prince Perovsky or not. Do you like him?

ANGUS: I never think about him.

CHALCOT: (*aside*) That's not true, Angus, my man. (*aloud*) I wonder if we shall have war with Russia? (*eyeing* ANGUS)

ANGUS: I don't know – I don't care – I wish we had!

CHALCOT: Out of sorts?

ANGUS: Yes.

CHALCOT: Have a weed. (*Handing cigar-case;* ANGUS *goes to* CHALCOT *and takes cigarette.*) Why want war? For the sake of change?

ANGUS: Yes.

CHALCOT: Change of scene?

ANGUS: Change of anything – change for anything – silver, copper – anything out of this! (*Goes to seat and sits.*)

CHALCOT: Out of what? (*puffing smoke*)

ANGUS: Out at elbows! If there's no war I shall go to India. What use is staying here – without a shilling or a friend? (*plucking leaf*) What chance is there?

CHALCOT: What chance! You mean what chances? Plenty. You're young – good family – marry a fortune.

ANGUS: Marry for money! That's not the way with the MacAlisters.

CHALCOT: Umph! Marriage is a mistake, but ready money's real enjoyment; at least, so people think who haven't got it. I suppose you've made your choice?

ANGUS: I have. Perhaps you're aware of that?

CHALCOT: Yes.

ANGUS: And who it is?

CHALCOT: Yes.

ANGUS: I'm a bad hand at concealment. I'm too proud of loving her I love to hide it. That's why I mean to go to India. (*Crosses to tree.*)

CHALCOT: Better stop here and smoke. I feel in a confidential humour. (ANGUS *sits again, or leans against tree.*) So you're in love with Blanche?

ANGUS: Yes.

CHALCOT: I saw that long ago. You know that I proposed to her? (*sitting on ground*)

ANGUS: Yes.

CHALCOT: But I'm proud to say she wouldn't have me. Ah! She's a sensible girl; and her spirited conduct in saying 'No!' on that occasion laid me under an obligation to her for life.

ANGUS: She declined?

CHALCOT: She declined very much. I only did it to please Sir Alick, who thought the two properties would go well together – never mind the two humans. Marriage means to sit opposite at table, and be civil to each other before company. Blanche Haye and Hugh Chalcot. Pooh! The service should have run: 'I, Brewhouses, Malt-kilns, Public houses, and Premises, take thee, Landed Property, grass and arable, farm houses, tenements, and Salmon Fisheries, to my wedded wife, to have and to hold for dinners and evening parties, for carriage and horse-back, for balls and presentations, to bore and to tolerate, till mutual aversion do us part'; but Land, grass and arable, farm houses, tenements, and Salmon Fisheries said 'no'; and Brewhouses is free. (*Strikes match.*)

ANGUS: At all events, you could offer her a fortune.

CHALCOT: And you're too proud to make her an offer because you're poor! (ANGUS *sighs.*) You're wrong. You're very wrong. I have more cause for complaint than you. I'm a great match. My father was senior partner in the brewery. When he died, he left me heaps. His brother, my uncle, died – left me more. My cousin went mad – bank-notes on the brain. His share fell to me; and, to crown my embarrassments, a grand-aunt, who lived in retirement in Cornwall on four hundred a year, with a faithful poodle and a treacherous companion, died too, leaving me the accumulated metallic refuse of misspent years. Mammas languished at me for their daughters, and daughters languished at me as their mammas told them. At last my time came. I fell in love – down, down, down, into an abyss where there was neither sense, nor patience, nor reason – nothing but love and hope. My heart flared with happiness as if it were lighted up with oxygen. She was eighteen – blue eyes – hair the colour of wheat, with a ripple on it like the corn as it bends to the breeze – fair as milk. She looked like china with a soul in it. Pa made much of me – Ma made much of me; so did her brothers and sisters, and uncles and aunts, and cousins and cousinettes, and cousinculings. How I hated 'em! One day I heard her speaking of me to a sister – she said – her voice said – that voice that, as I listened to it, ran up and down my arms, and gave me palpitation – she said 'I don't care much about him; but then he's so very rich!' (*His face falls.*) That cured me of marriage, and mutual affection, and the rest of the poetical lies. (*knocking ashes out of pipe*) You've youth, health, strength, and not a shilling – everything to hope for. Women can love *you* for *yourself* alone. Money doesn't poison your existence. You're not a prize pig tethered in a golden sty. What is left for me? Purchasable charms; every wish gratified; every aspiration anticipated, and the sight of the drays belonging to the firm rolling about London with my name on them, and a fat and happy drayman sitting on the shafts, whom I envy with all my heart. Pity the poor! Pity the rich; for they are bankrupts in friendship, and beggars in love.

ANGUS: (*crossing to* CHALCOT *and standing over him*) So, because one woman was selfish, you fall in love with poverty, and the humiliations and insults – insults you cannot resent – heaped on you daily by inferiors. Prudent mothers point you out as dangerous, and daughters regard you as an epidemic. You are a waiter upon fortune – a man on the look-out for a wife with money – a creature whose highest aim and noblest ambition is to sell himself and his name for good rations and luxurious quarters – a footman out of livery, known as the husband of Miss So-and-so, the heiress. You talk like a spoiled child! The rich man is to be envied. He can load her he loves with proofs of his affection – he can face her father and ask him for her hand – he can roll her in his carriage to his palace, and say, 'This is your home, and I am your servant!' ([*Goes*] *back to seat.*)

CHALCOT: You talk like a – man in love. Couldn't you face Sir Alick?

ANGUS: No. (*Sits.*)

CHALCOT: His marriage hasn't made him very happy. Poor Sir Alick! He never could have been happy with his weakness.

ANGUS: You mean Lady Shendryn?

CHALCOT: No; she's not a weakness – she's a power. No; Sir Alick's great regret in life is that he isn't tall. There's a skeleton everywhere; and his skeleton lacks a foot. He can't reach happiness by ten inches. He's a fine soldier, and an accomplished gentleman; his misery is that he is short. An odd sort of unhappiness, isn't it, from the point of view of men of our height?

ANGUS: What's that to do with the subject of money *versus* none?

CHALCOT: Nothing whatever – that's why I mentioned it.

ANGUS: Talking of money – you lent me £50. Here it is (*giving him note from pocket-book*). I got a note for fifty, because it was portable. (*Crosses to* CHALCOT.)

CHALCOT: (*taking it reluctantly*) If it shouldn't be quite convenient –

ANGUS: Oh, quite. (*Goes up stage, cutting at leaves of tree with cane.*)

CHALCOT: (*aside*) Now this would be of use to him; it's of none to me. I know he wants it – I don't; I didn't even remember that I'd lent it him. Confound it (*putting it in his pocket*). It's enough to make a man hate his kind, and build a hospital.

ANGUS: (*at top of avenue*) Coming in?

CHALCOT: No; I shall stay here. (*turning, and lying on ground*) The great comfort of the country is, one can enjoy peace and quiet. (*Turns to left. A large wooden ball is thrown from left. It falls near* CHALCOT*'s head. He starts up.*) Eh! (*Four more balls are thrown, each nearly hitting him.*) By Jove! (*Rises and goes right.*)

ANGUS: Here they are!

(*Enter* PRINCE, BLANCHE, LADY SHENDRYN, MARY, SIR ALEXANDER, *and* CAPTAIN SAMPREY.)

PRINCE: (*looking at balls. To* BLANCHE) Yours – that's ten. It's your first throw. Permit me. (*Picks up the ball.* ANGUS *comes down between them.*)

ANGUS: Good morning.

BLANCHE: Oh, Cousin Angus, how you made me start! (*As the* PRINCE *hands her the ball, she drops it with a start.*)

LADY SHEN: My dear child, my nerves! (*Leans against* SIR ALEXANDER.)

SIR ALEX: (*aside to her*) Don't be so affected. (LADY SHENDRYN *sits.*)

ANGUS: Good morning, Lady Shendryn; good morning, Miss Netley (*raising hat*). How are you, Samprey?

SAMPREY: How d'ye do, Mac?

(*The* PRINCE *and* BLANCHE *are a little up stage.* ANGUS *joins them.*)

CHALCOT: Who threw that ball? (*pointing to the first one thrown*)

MARY: I did.

CHALCOT: It only just missed falling on my head.

MARY: I'm very sorry.

CHALCOT: That it missed me?

MARY: No; that it fell so far off.

CHALCOT: My head?

MARY: No; that other wooden thing (*pointing to ball*).

(CHALCOT, *very wild, goes up right.* MARY *laughing to herself, goes up stage left.*)

ANGUS: May I join in the game?

SAMPREY: Take my hand, Mac (*giving him ball*).

LADY SHEN: (*getting between* BLANCHE *and* ANGUS) It's going to rain. We'd better get indoors.

BLANCHE: Oh no, it won't. It never rains when I wish it to be fine. Now, where shall I throw it?

PRINCE: I would suggest this side of the hillock.

ANGUS: I would advise the other. We couldn't see what became of it then.

BLANCHE: The other side. There! (*Throws ball off.*)

ANGUS: (*about to throw*) Now then!

(PRINCE *and* ANGUS *both go to throw and collide.*)

LADY SHEN: (*interposing*) It's for the Prince to throw first.

ANGUS: I beg your pardon.

PRINCE: No; after you. (ANGUS *refuses.* PRINCE *throws.*) There! (ANGUS *throws.*)

(PRINCE *goes to* BLANCHE *and then to* LADY SHENDRYN *as soon as* ANGUS *has thrown, who immediately returns to* BLANCHE. CHALCOT, *in looking after the throwing, is in* MARY*'s way when her turn arrives. She coughs and he turns suddenly.*)

CHALCOT: (*to* MARY) Are you going to throw now?

MARY: Yes; why do you ask?

CHALCOT: That I may get out of the way. (*Crosses, up stage.*)

(MARY *throws, then goes up stage, and sits on stump, looking at paper.*)

PRINCE: Now, Lady Shendryn.

LADY SHEN: Oh, I am so fatigued! My dear Prince, pray throw for me.

(PRINCE *throws.* LADY SHENDRYN *goes up stage.*)

SAMPREY: All thrown. Who's won? (PRINCE *and* ANGUS *start together, then stop.*)

ANGUS: I beg your pardon.

PRINCE: After you. (*They hesitate, each unwilling to precede the other.*)

BLANCHE: (*crossing*) Oh, do go! You can't stop to behave prettily across country.

(BLANCHE *exits right, followed by* ANGUS *and the* PRINCE, *then* SAMPREY.)

LADY SHEN: (*coming down, trying to take* SIR ALEXANDER*'s arm*) I'm so tired, Alexander.

SIR ALEX: (*avoiding her*) Do leave me alone. (*Exit.*)

LADY SHEN: Miss Netley, I must trouble you.

(MARY *is seated on stump,* LADY SHENDRYN *takes her arm.* LADY SHENDRYN *and* MARY *cross and exeunt,* MARY *and* CHALCOT *exchanging looks.*)

CHALCOT: (*alone*) Serves her right. Poor Angus Mac-Moth. He'll flutter round that beautiful flame till he singes his philabeg. (*The patter of rain heard upon the leaves.*) Lady Shendryn was right. It's coming down. That'll break up the skittle party. (*The* SERGEANT *enters, puts out his hand, feels the rain, and takes shelter under tree.*) There's the Sergeant. I must tip him something in consideration of his recent domestic – affliction. (*Takes out pocket-book.*) I'll give him a fiver – eh? Here's Angus's fifty, I'll give him that. (*pausing*) No; he'll go mentioning it, and it will get into the papers, and there'll be a paragraph about the singular munificence of Hugh Chalcot, Esq., the eminent brewer – eminent! – as if a brewer could be eminent! No; I daren't give him the fifty. (*Stands under tree, next to* SERGEANT. SERGEANT *touches his cap.*) Wet day, Sergeant (*turning up coat collar*).

SERGEANT: Yes, sir.

CHALCOT: Glad to hear that Mrs Jones is getting over her little difficulty – I should say difficulties – so well.

SERGEANT: Thank you, sir; she is as a person might say, sir, as well as can be expected (*with solemnity*).

(*During this scene the rain comes down more heavily, and the stage darkens.*)

CHALCOT: Have a pipe, Sergeant?

SERGEANT: Thank you, sir. (CHALCOT *gives him tobacco and fusee. They fill and light pipes.*) Thank you, sir.

CHALCOT: Sergeant, how many are you in family now?

SERGEANT: Eight, sir (*lighting pipe*).

CHALCOT: Eight! Good gracious! (*aside, looking at note*) If I were only sure he wouldn't mention it –

---

philabeg: actually 'filibeg', itself a corruption of the Gaelic, and meaning a kilt.
fusee: a type of large-headed match.

SERGEANT: Yes, sir. Six before, and two this morning – six and two are eight.

CHALCOT: Rather a large family. May I ask what your pay is?

SERGEANT: One-and-tenpence a day, sir.

CHALCOT: One-and-tenp– (*aside*) Perhaps he wouldn't mention it! (*aloud*) A small income for so large a family!

SERGEANT: Yes, sir; the family is larger than the income; but then there are other things, and Sir Alick is very kind, and so is my lady, and I hope for promotion – I may be colour-sergeant some day, and my eldest boy will soon be in the band; and so you see sir, it's not a bad look-out, take one thing with another.

CHALCOT: (*astonished; aside*) Happiness and hope, with a wife and eight children on one-and-tenpence a day! Oh, Contentment! In what strange, out-of-the-way holes do you hide yourself! If he wouldn't mention it! (*looking at note; aloud*) Twins! Both of the same sex?

SERGEANT: No, sir – one boy, one girl.

CHALCOT: Which is the elder?

SERGEANT: Don't know, sir. Don't think Mrs Jones knows. Don't think they know themselves. We never had a baby-girl before, sir. It's quite a new invention on Mrs Jones's part. We always have boys, 'cos they make the best soldiers. There's one thing as strikes me with regard to these twins as being odd.

CHALCOT: Odd! – you mean even. What's odd?

SERGEANT: I'm their father, and so the credit of them must be half mine; and yet everybody asks after Mrs Jones, and nobody asks after me.

CHALCOT: Oh, vanity! Vanity! Poor human vanity! (*Rain hard.*) By Jove, it is coming down. The skittle party must be broken up. (*crossing up stage*) Well, Sergeant, I wish the twins all sorts of good luck, and their mamma and papa likewise. Please buy 'em something for me (*giving note*). Good morning. (*Hurries up avenue, and goes off.*)

SERGEANT: Here's luck! (*looking at note*) Hey! Hullo! Here's some mistake! (*calling after* CHALCOT) Hi! Sir! Sir! (CHALCOT *re-enters.*) I beg your pardon, sir, for calling you back; but you've made a mistake; you meant to give me a five-pun' note – and many thanks, sir; but this here's for fifty.

CHALCOT: (*after a pause, with suppressed rage*) Thank you, – yes – my mistake. (*Takes bank-note, and gives* SERGEANT *the other, and goes off, biting his lips with fury.*)

SERGEANT: Five pounds. He's a trump! Who'd a thought it? – and him only a civilian. My twins is as good as promotion. I'll go and show Mrs Jones. (*Exit* SERGEANT. *Rain and wind.*)

(*Enter* BLANCHE *and* ANGUS. BLANCHE *carries the skirt of her dress over her head.*)

BLANCHE: How unfortunate, the rain coming on! (*under tree*)

ANGUS: Very.

BLANCHE: Where are all the other people gone?

ANGUS: I don't know. (*aside*) And I don't care. Your feet will get wet through on the grass. Better stand upon the seat. Allow me. (*Helps her to get on seat.*)

BLANCHE: You're very careful of me.

ANGUS: As careful of you as if you were old –

BLANCHE: As if I were old?

ANGUS: Old china. (*Gets up on seat, and stands by her side.*) This is more comfortable, isn't it?

BLANCHE: Infinitely.

(*Enter* LADY SHENDRYN *and* SIR ALEXANDER, *at end of avenue.*)

LADY SHEN: (*her skirt over her head*) I said it would rain.

SIR ALEX: I didn't contradict you.

LADY SHEN: No, but I understood your silence (*sitting on stump of tree*).

SIR ALEX: Now you're under shelter, I'll leave you.

LADY SHEN: Leave me by myself in the park?

SIR ALEX: Do you suppose you'll be attacked by freebooters? What are you afraid of?

LADY SHEN: Of – of the deer!

SIR ALEX: (*sitting down, back to back with* LADY SHENDRYN; *aside*) The deer! They're more likely to be afraid of you.

LADY SHEN: (*sentimentally*) Ah! You would have been glad to have sat with me beneath the shelter of this verdant canopy years ago!

SIR ALEX: Years ago I was a fool! (*Rain and wind.*)

ANGUS: Quite a storm! Your hair will be wet!

BLANCHE: It is already.

ANGUS: Take my hat. (*Takes off* BLANCHE*'s hat and puts his own on her head. Then hangs* BLANCHE*'s hat by ribbon on branch of tree above his head.*)

BLANCHE: How do I look in a man's hat?

ANGUS: Beautiful! Take this, too. (*Takes off his coat, and wraps it round her shoulders; puts his arms round her waist, and ties coat over her bosom by its sleeves.*) That's much better, isn't it?

BLANCHE: But you'll catch cold.

ANGUS: No; we're used to cold in Cantyre; besides, we're trained not to care for it. There's a special sort of drill that makes us almost mackintosh! You've seen troops marching in the wet?

BLANCHE: Often.

ANGUS: That was rain drill!

LADY SHEN: [*to* SIR ALEXANDER] If you walked to the Hall, you could send me an umbrella.

SIR ALEX: I'd rather you got wet. Just now you wished me to stay for fear of highwaymen.

LADY SHEN: I might catch cold.

SIR ALEX: I should be sorry for the cold that caught you.

LADY SHEN: It might be my death.

SIR ALEX: Lady Shendryn, the rain fertilises the earth, nourishes the crops, and makes the fish lively; but still it does not bring with it every blessing. You have no right to hold out agreeable expectations which you know you do not intend to realise.

Cantyre: presumably Angus's home in Scotland (cf. 'Kintyre').

(These conversations to be taken up as if they were continuous.)

ANGUS: What was that song you sang at the Sylvesters?

BLANCHE: Oh!

ANGUS: I wish you'd hum it to me now.

BLANCHE: Without music?

ANGUS: It won't be without music.

BLANCHE: You know the story: it is supposed to be sung by a very young man who is in love with a very haughty beauty, but dare not tell her of his love.

ANGUS: Of course he was poor.

BLANCHE: N – o.

ANGUS: What else could keep him silent?

BLANCHE: Want of – courage.

ANGUS: How does it go?

BLANCHE: (*Sings. Air, 'La Chanson de Fortunio' in Offenbach's 'Maître Fortunio'.*)

If my glances have betrayed me,
    Ask me no more,
For I dare not tell thee, Lady,
    Whom I adore.
She is young, and tall, and slender,
    Eyes of deep blue,
She is sweet, and fair, and tender,
    Like unto you.
Unless my lady will me,
    I'll not reveal,
Though the treasured secret kill me,
    The love I feel.

LADY SHEN: Advertising our poverty to the whole county; a filthy, old, rumbling thing, not fit for a washerwoman to ride in. I won't go out in it again!

SIR ALEX: Then stay at home.

LADY SHEN: Why not order a new carriage?

SIR ALEX: Can't afford it.

ANGUS: The air has haunted me ever since I heard you sing it. I've written some words to it myself.

BLANCHE: Oh, give them to me, I'll sing them.

ANGUS: Will you? (*Gives her verses, which he takes from pocket-book in coat pocket.*)

LADY SHEN: Oh! I feel so faint. I think it must be time for lunch.

SIR ALEX: I'm sure it is. (*looking at watch*) And I'm awfully hungry. Confound it!

BLANCHE: (*reading verses which* ANGUS *has given her*) They're very charming. (*Sighs.*)

ANGUS: You're faint. They'll lunch without us.

BLANCHE: Never mind.

ANGUS: You're not hungry?

'La Chanson de Fortunio': in fact the *title* of a one-act opera by Jacques Offenbach (1819–80), first performed in Paris, 5 January 1861.

BLANCHE: No; are you?
ANGUS: Not in the least.
BLANCHE: Cousin, do you know I rather like to see you getting wet. May I keep these?
LADY SHEN: Where does all your money go to then? And what is that Mr Kelsey, the lawyer, always coming down for?
SIR ALEX: You'd better not ask. You'd better not know.
BLANCHE: But tell me, cousin, have you ever been in love?
ANGUS: Yes.
BLANCHE: How many times?
ANGUS: Once.
BLANCHE: Only once?
ANGUS: Only once.
LADY SHEN: I know where the money goes to.
SIR ALEX: Do you? I wish I did. Where?
LADY SHEN: I know.
BLANCHE: I shouldn't like a husband who was too good, he'd become monotonous.
ANGUS: No husband would be too good for you; at least, I think not!
LADY SHEN: Isolating me from my family! Never letting me see my brother!
SIR ALEX: Your brother –
LADY SHEN: Poor Percy! Only twenty-two, and –
SIR ALEX: (*in a fury*) Don't mention his name to me! I won't hear of him! Infernal young villain, always in scrapes himself and dragging others into them! Don't mention his name!
LADY SHEN: I should not have been so treated if I'd married a man of decent height. What could I expect from a little fellow of five feet two?
SIR ALEX: Lady Shendryn! (*rising, out of temper*)
LADY SHEN: Such violence! 'Tis the same as when years ago I discovered your falsehood. I know why we live so near. You have too many establishments to provide for!
SIR ALEX: Madam!
LADY SHEN: I suppose that when that woman –
SIR ALEX: Lady Shendryn!
LADY SHEN: That Mrs –
SIR ALEX: Silence!

(*Distant thunder and lightning.*)

LADY SHEN: (*rising and clinging to* SIR ALEXANDER) Alexander!
SIR ALEX: Don't touch me! (*Exits quickly.*)
ANGUS: (*nearing her*) Blanche!
BLANCHE: Angus!

(*The* PRINCE *enters with umbrella up, followed by* SERVANT *with another, which he takes to* LADY SHENDRYN, *holding it over her as she exits.* (*The umbrellas to be wet.*) *The* PRINCE *goes down to*

---

near: meanly.

BLANCHE, *and takes her off under umbrella, leaving coat in* ANGUS*'s hands; at the same time,* CHALCOT *and* MARY *enter, wrangling, she saying* 'I never saw such a man! You want all the umbrella' *etc., snatches it away from him, and runs off.* ANGUS, *who is reaching* BLANCHE*'s hat from tree, drops coat over* CHALCOT*'s head,* ANGUS *puts* BLANCHE*'s hat on his head,* CHALCOT *pointing to it as drop descends.*)

ACT II

SCENE. *Drawing-room at* LADY SHENDRYN*'s, in the neighbourhood of Birdcage Walk. Centre opening with folding-doors leading into inner room, with bay window, looking on to balcony. Door left. Oval tea-table right, with afternoon tea laid and gong-bell. Ottoman centre down stage. Sofa left, with small round table at side, with cup of tea upon it. Chandelier and lamps lighted. In inner room, door left, piano right, music-stool and chair against window. Folding-doors to be closed at rise of curtain. Small chairs head and left of table right.* MARY *discovered presiding at tea-table.* BLANCHE *looking over book of engravings on ottoman.* LADY SHENDRYN *on sofa, reading letter.*

LADY SHEN: My dear Blanche, I must request your attention to the subject of this letter again.

BLANCHE: I'm listening.

LADY SHEN: Although I am all excitement at Sir Alexander's departure tonight, still, this affair must be settled, and at once; for not only Sir Alexander, but the Prince leaves town tonight. I'll read the Countess's letter again. (MARY *and* BLANCHE *exchange looks.*) The last side is all that I shall trouble you with. (*Reads*) 'It could easily be arranged, and though a formal contract could not be entered into, a mutual agreement might be ratified, and when the war is concluded – and I hear from the very *best* authority' – 'best' underlined, my dear – 'that it *cannot* last long' – 'cannot' underlined, my dear – 'the Prince could return to this country and renew his suit. This is *my* opinion' – 'my' underlined, Blanche – 'and it is also the opinion of the *Duchess*, with whom I have held council' – 'Duchess' underlined. 'It is *most desirable*' – 'most desirable' underlined – 'that the match should be *made*.' – 'Made' underlined. 'Ever your own Adelaide.' There, Blanche! now you know what the Countess thinks! And when the Prince comes here tonight to make his adieux, you can act in accordance with the views she has so feelingly, so very feelingly, expressed.

BLANCHE: (*rising, and putting down book*) But why should I be engaged to Prince Perovsky?

LADY SHEN: Because he's a great match.

BLANCHE: But to engage oneself to a Russian at the very time we're going to war with them!

LADY SHEN: But when the fighting is over, you can be married.

---

drop: see p. 66 above.

MARY: (*aside*) And then the fighting can begin again!

BLANCHE: And Sir Alick going away this very night!

LADY SHEN: (*with suppressed emotion*) It is my husband's duty to go.

MARY: (*aside*) And his pleasure.

LADY SHEN: And go he must.

MARY: (*aside*) And will!

BLANCHE: Poor Sir Alick! I am so sorry.

LADY SHEN: Duty, my child! Duty!

BLANCHE: (*to* MARY) But I don't want to get married at all!

MARY: (*to her*) Duty, my pet! Duty! And in this case duty ought to be a pleasure.

BLANCHE: Duty! The same as it is Sir Alick's duty to go and fight?

LADY SHEN: Precisely.

BLANCHE: And a girl must put on her wedding-gown for the same reason a soldier puts on his regimentals?

MARY: And seek the mutual conflict at the altar.

BLANCHE: Oh, Mary – conflict!

MARY: I repeat – conflict. And may the best man win.

LADY SHEN: Miss Netley, I think you talk too much.

BLANCHE: Why do girls get married?

MARY: (*aside*) That's a poser!

LADY SHEN: O–h. For the sake of society.

BLANCHE: That means for the sake of other people?

LADY SHEN: Naturally. If people didn't, there would be no – evening parties.

MARY: (*aside*) And what a dreadful thing that would be!

BLANCHE: But I don't want to get married.

LADY SHEN: Then you ought to do.

BLANCHE: Ought I, Mary?

MARY: I don't know – I never was married.

LADY SHEN: (*severely*) And never will be. With your views, Miss Netley, you don't deserve to be. Marriage is one of those – a – dear me – I want a word. Marriage is one of those –

MARY: Evils?

LADY SHEN: No (*angrily*).

BLANCHE: Blessings?

LADY SHEN: Blessings – yes – blessings, which cannot be avoided.

BLANCHE: What do you think, Mary?

MARY: It is woman's mission to marry.

BLANCHE: Why?

MARY: That she may subdue man.

LADY SHEN: Quite so.

MARY: The first step to man's subjugation is courtship. The second matrimony. Any more tea? (*They signify 'No'.*)

BLANCHE: (*in a pet, rising and going to* MARY, *sitting in chair left of table*) Don't talk about it any more. Think of poor Sir Alick!

---

in a pet: sulkily.

MARY: (*to* BLANCHE) And Angus MacAlister.
LADY SHEN: What's that? (*sharply*)
BLANCHE: Nothing! What's what? (*rising with* MARY *quickly*)
LADY SHEN: Didn't I hear the name of Angus MacAlister?
BLANCHE:
MARY: } Oh, no.
BLANCHE: [(*aside*)] She doesn't believe us.
MARY: [(*aside*)] She knows better.

(*Enter* SIR ALEXANDER, *door left, in regimentals.* BLANCHE *and* MARY *meet him, back of ottoman.*)

SIR ALEX: Well, girls, my time is up, and I've come to bid you goodbye.
BLANCHE:
MARY: } Oh, Sir Alexander!
SIR ALEX: You won't see me again till I come back – if ever I do come back. One word with my lady. (*The* GIRLS *sit at tea-table as before.* SIR ALEXANDER *goes down stage beside* LADY SHENDRYN *on sofa.*) Diana, you know the dispositions I have made, and how I have left you – in case any – in case anything should befall me. For ready money, there is £2,000 at Coutts's in your name.
LADY SHEN: (*dignified*) You are very kind – indeed, you are very liberal.
SIR ALEX: With every possible allowance for your temper, and customary misapprehension of my conduct, I cannot understand why you should meet me in this way.
LADY SHEN: £2,000! Where does the rest of the money go? I know your income. What have you done with it?
SIR ALEX: Is this the moment – when I am about to leave you – perhaps never to return – to quarrel about money?
LADY SHEN: Money! You know that I despise it. I only speak of the disappearance of these large sums as a proof –
SIR ALEX: Proof! – Proof of what?
LADY SHEN: (*with tears*) Of your faithlessness – your infidelity!
SIR ALEX: Consider the girls.
LADY SHEN: They cannot hear me.

(SIR ALEXANDER *back to audience.*)

BLANCHE: (*to* MARY) This is all very dreadful. I don't think I'll ever marry.
MARY: Yes, you will.
BLANCHE: To quarrel with my husband?
MARY: Think how pleasant it is to own a husband to quarrel with!
LADY SHEN: Such large sums unaccounted for!
SIR ALEX: I know it (*turning*).
LADY SHEN: Where do they go?

Coutts's: eminent and fashionable firm of London bankers, founded in 1692.

SIR ALEX: I cannot tell you. You are the last person in the world I would have know.

LADY SHEN: Doubtless!

SIR ALEX: Diana, you are wrong – very wrong!

LADY SHEN: Alexander Shendryn, you know how you have treated me. You know –

SIR ALEX: I know that at one time you had just cause of complaint. I confessed my fault, and entreated your forgiveness. Instead of pardoning, you have never forgotten my indiscretion; but have dinned – dinned – dinned it into my ears unceasingly.

LADY SHEN: And, pray, sir, what divine creature is a man, that he may be faithless to his wife with impunity? What are we women, that our lot should be that we must be deceived that we may forgive; that we may be deceived again that we may forgive again, to be deceived again? Sir Alexander, these expenses from home demand my scrutiny, and I insist on knowing why they are, and wherefore? But perhaps I am detaining you, and you have adieux to make elsewhere!

SIR ALEX: Diana, I shall lose all patience! (*Goes down stage to right corner.*)

(*Enter a* SERVANT.)

SERVANT: The orderly is below, Sir Alexander, and wishes to speak to you.

SIR ALEX: May he come up here?

LADY SHEN: If you wish it.

SIR ALEX: (*after motioning to* SERVANT, *who goes off, coming to* LADY SHENDRYN) Consider, £2,000 is a large sum – more than enough for your immediate requirements.

LADY SHEN: (*with exultation*) My requirements! All I ask is a cottage, and a loaf of bread – and all your secrets told to me!

(*Enter* SERGEANT.)

SIR ALEX: Now, Sergeant!

SERGEANT: (*saluting*) This letter, Colonel. Mr Kelsey, the lawyer, brought it himself.

LADY SHEN: Mr Kelsey?

SIR ALEX: To the barracks?

SERGEANT: Yes, Colonel; he said it was of the utmost consequence, and that you was to have it directly, and that he would be back in half an hour at your quarters to receive your instructions. (SIR ALEXANDER *goes into inner room, and reads.*)

LADY SHEN: Mrs Jones quite well, Sergeant?

SERGEANT: Middling, my lady, thank you.

BLANCHE: And the children?

SERGEANT: Quite well, thank you, miss; all but the twins. The twins has got the twinsey!

BLANCHE:
MARY: } The what?

SERGEANT: The twinsey, inside their throats – just here – under the stock.

MARY: You mean quinsey?

SERGEANT: Very like, miss. It's a regulation infant complaint.

BLANCHE: And what does Mrs Jones think of your going away to Varna?

SERGEANT: Well, mum, she don't like it much. She is a little cut up about it, and has made me an outfit – six new shirts complete. (*piqued*) The twins don't seem to care much – but children never seem to know when you've done enough for 'em!

MARY: And how do you like it?

SERGEANT: Well, miss, I'm sorry to leave the missus and the children – 'specially them twins, who wants more looking after than the others, bein' two; but I shouldn't like to stay behind. I don't think the company could get along without me.

SIR ALEX: (*coming down stage, violently agitated*) Good heavens!

LADY SHEN: What's the matter? (*All rise.*)

SIR ALEX: Nothing! (*pacing stage*)

LADY SHEN: Can I – (*offering to take letter*)

SIR ALEX: (*crushing letter in his hand; aside*) What's to be done? What's to be done? (*Looks at time-piece.*) Sergeant, take a cab, drive to the Garrick – the Garrick Club – as hard as you can go. Ask for Mr Chalcot; bring him here directly. He's dining there, I know. Lose no time, for I haven't a moment to spare. (*Exit* SERGEANT, *after saluting.*)

LADY SHEN: More mystery! (*Sits on sofa.*)

BLANCHE: (*together*) You quite frighten me.
MARY: (*together*) Can I be of any –

SIR ALEX: No, my dears – no. I must speak to your aunt again, but alone. Step into this room for a few minutes. (*Signifies to them to go into inner room.* MARY *and* BLANCHE *go in, exchanging glances.* SIR ALEXANDER *closes door after them.*)

LADY SHEN: What's coming now?

SIR ALEX: (*looking at letter, then advancing*) Diana, I grieve to tell you that I cannot leave you the £2,000 I spoke of.

LADY SHEN: What?

SIR ALEX: (*looking at letter*) I can only leave you £500.

LADY SHEN: This is that letter?

SIR ALEX: Yes.

LADY SHEN: From Mr Kelsey! Whenever that fellow shows his face, there is always trouble.

SIR ALEX: Don't wrong poor Kelsey. He is an excellent man.

LADY SHEN: £2,000! – £500! Why this sudden call for £1,500?

SIR ALEX: I dare not tell you.

LADY SHEN: Show me that letter.

SIR ALEX: Impossible.

LADY SHEN: Why not?

Varna: Bulgarian port on the Black Sea where British forces were quartered prior to the Crimean campaign.

Garrick Club: opened in 1831, its membership included many actors, writers and artists, as well as members of the armed forces and the legal profession.

SIR ALEX: I cannot tell you. I must ask you to have confidence.

LADY SHEN: Confidence! – In you?

SIR ALEX: I have sent for Chalcot to – to –

LADY SHEN: To borrow money of him?

SIR ALEX: Yes.

LADY SHEN: For me?

SIR ALEX: No.

LADY SHEN: And am I not to know the reason of this sudden call upon your purse?

SIR ALEX: You must not (*going right*).

LADY SHEN: (*rising*) I will! (*advancing*)

SIR ALEX: (*about to tell her*) Diana – no, no! You must not know!

LADY SHEN: (*trying to snatch letter*) That letter!

SIR ALEX: (*struggling*) Diana!

LADY SHEN: I am your wife. I will have it. I will know this woman's name. (*As she gets hold of the letter, it tears in half. She has the blank side. Enter* SERGEANT, *and* CHALCOT *in evening dress.* BLANCHE *and* MARY, *hearing the noise, enter from inner room, and go down stage right.*)

LADY SHEN: (*showing blank*) The blank side!

SIR ALEX: (*showing the written side*) Thank heaven!

CHALCOT: (*aside*) There's been a row.

SERGEANT: Colonel, I met Mr Chalcot as I was running to the cab-rank.

SIR ALEX: (*crossing*) Chalcot, a word! – Sergeant. (*Speaks to* SERGEANT, *who salutes.*) In this room, Chalcot.

CHALCOT: An awful row! (*aside*)

(SIR ALEXANDER *and* CHALCOT *go off through folding-doors.*)

LADY SHEN: (*after a pause, crossing and sitting*) Sergeant, I shall take care of your wife while you are away.

SERGEANT: Thank you, my lady.

BLANCHE: And the children.

SERGEANT: Thank you, miss.

MARY: And the twins.

LADY SHEN: }
BLANCHE: } Oh, the twins! Certainly.

SERGEANT: (*affected*) Thank you, ladies. It'll make me more comfortable to know that they will be cared for, if anything should – if anything – 'cos accidents will happen with – the best regulated enemies. She's waiting below to march with me to parade, so as to see the last of me. (*a pause*) Thank you, ladies. Good evening.

(*Exit* SERGEANT. *The* WOMEN *look sorrowfully and go up stage. Enter* SIR ALEXANDER *and* CHALCOT.)

SIR ALEX: You understand?

CHALCOT: Perfectly!

SIR ALEX: And you'll see that it's explained as I –

CHALCOT: Certainly.

SIR ALEX: Thanks. (*shaking hands*) You are a friend indeed. (*Sits on sofa,* LADY SHENDRYN *and* BLANCHE *sitting at table,* MARY *right of ottoman,* CHALCOT *on ottoman.*)

CHALCOT: This is a charming wind-up to a jolly evening. Parting with all my pals. I didn't know I cared at all about them; and now they're going, I find out I like them very much. Saw Sergeant Jones's wife crying in the hall. Why don't she stop at home and cry? Why does she come and cry where I am?

MARY: (*half crying, coming down stage.*) What a world this is!

CHALCOT: Sad hole, I confess.

MARY: And what villains men are!

CHALCOT: They are! – They are!

MARY: To quarrel and fight, and bring grief upon poor women – and what fools women are –

CHALCOT: They are! – They are!

MARY: (*impatiently*) I mean, to cry about the men! How stupid you are!

CHALCOT: I am! – I am! You're quite right. (*rising*) I agree with you entirely (*coming down stage*).

BLANCHE: You two don't often agree.

CHALCOT: No; but then we very seldom meet.

MARY: Thank goodness!

CHALCOT: Thank goodness!

MARY: At all events, Mr Chalcot does not deny that women are far superior to men.

CHALCOT: Pardon me. He does deny it – he denies it very much.

BLANCHE: (*right*) Which, then, are the better?

CHALCOT: Neither! – Both are worst.

BLANCHE:
MARY: } Oh!

CHALCOT: And, as a general axiom, this truth is manifest. Whatever is – is wrong!

SIR ALEX: (*advancing to* LADY SHENDRYN) And now there is no more to say, but goodbye, and God bless you! (*Holds out his hand.* LADY SHENDRYN *remains motionless. A pause*) Won't you bid me goodbye?

LADY SHEN: The letter!

SIR ALEX: Impossible! It would make you more miserable.

LADY SHEN: Doubtless.

SIR ALEX: Diana! (*holding out his hand*)

LADY SHEN: You are waited for elsewhere. Kiss and bid goodbye to those you love.

SIR ALEX: It may be for the last time.

LADY SHEN: The letter! (SIR ALEXANDER *dissents, and again holds out his hand.*) Your lady-love is waiting. Waste no more time with me.

SIR ALEX: (*aside*) Ah! I may find peace in the campaign – I cannot find it here. I can control a regiment, but not a wife. Better battle than a discontented woman. (CHALCOT *persuades him to go back. Aloud*) Goodbye, Chalcot – (*shaking hands*) – and remember! Goodbye, Blanche – Goodbye, Mary (*kissing them*).

BLANCHE:
MARY: } (*hanging about him*) Oh, Sir Alick!

(*They look appealingly at him, and then towards* LADY SHENDRYN, *who remains motionless.* SIR ALEXANDER *again goes to her, and offers his hand. She takes no notice of him. He bows and goes off hurriedly, followed by* BLANCHE, *crying.* MARY *turns at door to look at* LADY SHENDRYN, *and meeting* CHALCOT*'s eye, stamps at him, saying* 'Go away', *and slams the door.* CHALCOT *looks with contempt at* LADY SHENDRYN. *A carriage is heard to drive off.* LADY SHENDRYN *starts, and nearly falls.* CHALCOT *stops her fall.*)

LADY SHEN: Mr Chalcot – don't leave me! Ring for Jennings, my maid. Give me some air – the heat overpowers me. Open those doors.

(CHALCOT *opens folding-doors and rings gong-bell on table. Enter* LADY'S-MAID. LADY SHENDRYN *motions her down stage and takes her arm.*)

LADY SHEN: To my room – and – thank you, Mr Chalcot. I'm better now – much better. (*Is led off by* MAID, *nearly fainting.*)

CHALCOT: No better than you should be. Oh, temper – temper! And that's matrimony!

(BLANCHE *enters hurriedly through door in inner room, followed by* ANGUS *in regimentals. She sits at piano and begins playing the chanson of the first act.* ANGUS *leaning over her at top of piano. Immediately* CHALCOT *hears the music he gets over to down stage left noiselessly, shaking his head.*)

CHALCOT: How people with these before their eyes can fall in love? (*Exits on tip-toe.*)

(BLANCHE *sings the song of act 1. She breaks down at the last words with a sob, and lets her face and arms fall on piano. Pause.*)

ANGUS: Won't you sing the words I wrote?

BLANCHE: I can't sing tonight. I can't play. (*Rising, and coming forward; sits on ottoman.*)

ANGUS: I shall often think of that air, when I am far away (*standing by her side*).

(*This scene is to be broken by frequent pauses.*)

BLANCHE: I – I am very sorry you are going.

ANGUS: I have few reasons for wishing to remain – hardly any – only one.

BLANCHE: And that one is –

ANGUS: (*nearing her*) To be near you! (*kneeling on ottoman*)

BLANCHE: (*averting her eyes*) Oh, cousin!

ANGUS: In the old days a soldier wore a badge, bestowed on him by the lady he – he vowed was the fairest in the world! They were his own individual personal colours! Some say the days of chivalry are over! Never mind that! Give me a token, Blanche – cousin Blanche – a ribbon – anything that you have worn!

BLANCHE: (*trembling*) But, cousin, these exchanges are only made by those who are – engaged!

ANGUS: (*standing*) And if this war had not been declared, should you have been engaged to Prince Perovsky? Should you have exchanged tokens with him?

BLANCHE: (*troubled*) Oh! How can I tell?

ANGUS: I should like to know before I go.

BLANCHE: And when must that be? (*Rises.*)

ANGUS: (*looking at timepiece*) In five minutes!

BLANCHE: (*approaching him*) So soon! (*Pauses.*)

ANGUS: Have you nothing to say to me?

BLANCHE: I – I hardly know – what would you have me say?

ANGUS: Only one word – that you care what becomes of me!

BLANCHE: You know I do.

ANGUS: Care for me? (*Clasps her in his arms, she recoiling.*)

BLANCHE: Yes – no – Oh, cousin! You make me say things –

ANGUS: That you don't mean?

BLANCHE: No – yes! You confuse me so – I hardly know what I'm doing!

(*Bugle without, at distance. Roll on side drum, four beats on big drum, then military band play 'Annie Laurie' – the whole to be as if in the distance.* ANGUS *starts up, and goes to window.* BLANCHE *springs up, and stands before door left.* ANGUS *goes to door, embracing* BLANCHE. *They form Millais's picture of the 'Black Brunswicker'.*)

BLANCHE: Oh, Angus – dear cousin Angus!

ANGUS: (*faltering*) Blanche! You are rich – an heiress. I am but a poor Scotch cadet; but Scotch cadets ere now have cut their way to fame and fortune; and I have my chance. Say, Blanche, do you love me? Say, if at some future day I prove myself not unworthy of you, will you be mine?

BLANCHE: Oh, Angus!

ANGUS: Answer, love; for every moment is precious as a look from you. May I hope?

(*Handle of the door moves; they separate. Enter* SERVANT.)

SERVANT: Prince Perovsky!

(*Enter* PRINCE. *Exit* SERVANT. *A pause.*)

PRINCE: I fear that I arrive inopportunely?

BLANCHE: No, Prince; my cousin is just bidding us goodbye. He is about to sail for – he is about to leave England. (ANGUS *comes down stage to door.*)

PRINCE: (*smiling*) On service?

ANGUS: Yes, on service. I have the honour, Prince, to take my leave.

(*They bow – a momentary pause –* PRINCE *takes in situation and abruptly turns his back on* ANGUS *and* BLANCHE, *taking a pinch of snuff as the following business proceeds:* ANGUS *goes down stage left, turns to* BLANCHE, *calling her by name. She rushes to him, tearing the locket from her neck, and gives it to* ANGUS, *unperceived by* PRINCE. ANGUS *holds her in his arms, kisses her, and exits hurriedly. The music of the band ceases as* BLANCHE *sits on ottoman. Pause*)

PRINCE: (*turning slowly round*) Miss Haye, I am charmed to find you alone; for what I have to say could only be said *tête-à-tête*. (BLANCHE *rises.*) Pray

---

Millais's 'Black Brunswicker': John Everett Millais's picture of a young German soldier in uniform about to leave for the Napoleonic Wars and bidding his sweetheart farewell was the success of the Royal Academy Summer Exhibition 1860: the models were a private in the Life Guards, and Dickens's daughter Kate, who left an account of the sittings.

cadet: not here a military cadet, but a younger son without financial expectations.

don't rise. Both Sir Alexander and Lady Shendryn are aware of the object of my visit, and do me the honour of approving it. Have I the happiness of engaging your attention? (BLANCHE *assents.* PRINCE *sits by her side, taking chair from left of table right.*) I leave London for Paris tonight *en route* to Vienna. I mention that fact that it may excuse the apparent *brusquerie* of what is to follow. Have I your permission to go on? (BLANCHE *assents. He bows.*) My mission here was not, as many supposed, diplomatic, but matrimonial. I may say, as the man said when he was asked who he was, 'When I am at home, I am somebody.' I came to England in search of a wife – one who would be an ornament to her station and mine. I wished to take back with me, to present to my province and to my Imperial master, a princess.

BLANCHE: A princess?

PRINCE: Unhappily, this Ottoman difficulty has arisen. I thought that diplomacy would have smoothed it away. I was wrong – and so my mission, which was so eminently peaceful, must be postponed until the war is over.

BLANCHE: Until the war is over?

PRINCE: That will be in very few months.

BLANCHE: (*eagerly*) Why so?

PRINCE: Wars with Russia never last long.

BLANCHE: Why not?

PRINCE: Pardon me, if for a moment I am national and patriotic. Against Russian powers, prowess and resources are useless. The elements have declared on our side, and in them we have two irresistible allies.

BLANCHE: And they are –

PRINCE: Frost and fire! If cold fails, we try heat – that is, to warm the snow, we burn our Moscows. (BLANCHE *shivers.*) But, pardon me, you are thinking of those among your relatives who hold rank in the English army? (*significantly*)

BLANCHE: (*hesitating*) Yes; Sir Alexander.

PRINCE: Of course – Sir Alexander. As I alighted, I saw troops mustering outside – a pretty sight. Fine fellows! – Fine fellows! But I fear I am fatiguing you; for I am – *hélas*! too many, many years your senior to hope to interest you personally. (*rising with courtliness and dignity*) Miss Haye, with the permission of your guardians, I lay my name and fortune at your feet. Should you deign to accept me, at the end of the war I shall return to England for my bride.

BLANCHE: (*rising, confused*) Prince, I am sensible –

PRINCE: Should you honour me by favourable consideration of my demand, in return for the honour of your hand, I offer you rank and power. On our own lands we hold *levées* – indeed, you will be queen of the province – of 400,000 serfs – of your devoted slave – my queen!

---

brusquerie: abrupt manner.

BLANCHE: (*Sits on sofa.*) Queen! If I should prove a tyrant?
PRINCE: (*standing*) I am a true Russian, and love despotism!
BLANCHE: (*smiling*) And could you submit to slavery?
PRINCE: At your hands – willingly. (*Sits on her right.*) I assure you, slavery is not a bad thing!
BLANCHE: But freedom is a better! And you came to England, Prince, to seek a wife?
PRINCE: Not only to seek a wife – to find a princess!
BLANCHE: You can make a princess of anybody!
PRINCE: But I cannot make anybody a princess! Let me hope my offer is not entirely objectionable, despite the disparity of our years.

(*Music – 'British Grenadiers' – drum and fife heard outside.*)

CHALCOT: (*without*) I beg your pardon.
MARY: (*without*) Beg my pardon? Couldn't you see?
CHALCOT: (*without*) I didn't.
MARY: (*without*) I was right before your eyes. (*Enters.*)
CHALCOT: (*entering*) Perhaps that was the reason.
MARY: Tearing one's dress to pieces!
CHALCOT: Really, what with the troops, and the bands and the bother, I feel I must tear something!
MARY: Poor fellows – leaving their wives!
CHALCOT: They consider that one of the privileges of the profession. (*Music grows distant.*)
MARY: (*excitedly*) Oh, when I hear the clatter of their horses' hoofs, and see the gleam of the helmets, I – I wish I were a man! (*walking about in inner room*)
CHALCOT: I wish you were! (*standing centre, his glass in his eye*)
MARY: (*opening window at back*) We can see them from the balcony.

(*Music ceases. When she opens window, the moonlight, trees, gas [light], etc., are seen at back. Distant bugle.*)

MARY: There's Sir Alick on horseback. (*Distant cheers. On balcony*) Do you hear the shouts?
CHALCOT: Yes (*up at window*).
MARY: And the bands?
CHALCOT: (*on balcony*) And the chargers prancing.
MARY: And the bayonets gleaming.
CHALCOT: And the troops forming.
MARY: And the colours flying. Oh, if I were not a woman, I'd be a soldier.

(*Music ceases.*)

CHALCOT: So would I.
MARY: Why are you not?
CHALCOT: What! – A woman!
MARY: No – a soldier. Better be anything than nothing. Better be a soldier than anything. (*Goes up stage again. Tramp of troops marching heard in the distance. Cheers.*)
CHALCOT: (*catching* MARY*'s enthusiasm, and sitting on ottoman*) She's right! She's right! Why should a great hulking fellow like me skulk behind, lapped in comfort, ungrateful, uncomfortable, and inglorious? Fighting would be

something to live for. I've served in the militia – I know my drill – I'll buy a commission – I'll go! (*Rises.*)

MARY: (*meeting him, as he goes up stage*) That's right. I like you for that.

(*Music – 'The Girl I Left Behind Me'. Cheers and music.*)

CHALCOT: Do you? (*Distant cheers.*) Come and shout. (*to* MARY*; then to* PRINCE, *who is seated on sofa, with* BLANCHE) Come and shout. Oh, I beg your pardon!

PRINCE: Not at all – not at all! (*Rises, and goes to window, and looks out.*) In splendid condition. Fine fellows! Fine fellows! Poor fellows! (*taking snuff, and coming down left*) Won't you come and look at them, Miss Haye?

(*As* BLANCHE *rises,* LADY SHENDRYN *enters.* BLANCHE *sits again on sofa.* CHALCOT *and* MARY *at window.*)

LADY SHEN: My dear Prince, I did not know you were here!

PRINCE: I profited by your ladyship's absence to urge the suit of which you have been kind enough to approve.

LADY SHEN: And have you received an answer?

PRINCE: Not precisely. (*Music stops.*)

CHALCOT: (*at balcony*) There's Sir Alick! (*Cheers.*)

SIR ALEX: (*outside*) Battalion! Attention! Form fours, right! March off by companies, in succession from the front! Number one, by your left, quick march!

(*Music. Repeat, 'The Girl I Left Behind Me'.* LADY SHENDRYN *starts. Tramp loud.*)

CHALCOT: They're marching right past the window. Come here and see. There's the Sergeant. (*Command outside,* 'Number two, by your left, quick march.')

PRINCE: Miss Haye, may I be permitted to know if I may hope?

MARY: (*at window*) There's Angus! (BLANCHE *rushes up stage.*)

ANGUS: (*without*) Number three, by your left! Quick march!

(*Music forte. Band plays 'God Save the Queen'. Cheers. Tramp of soldiers. Excitement. Picture.* CHALCOT *and* MARY *waving handkerchiefs, and cheering at window.* PRINCE, *taking snuff.* LADY SHENDRYN *centre.* BLANCHE *totters down stage and falls fainting at her feet.*)

ACT III

SCENE. *Interior of a hut, built of boulders and mud, the roof built out, showing the snow and sky outside. The walls bare and rude, pistols, swords, guns, maps, newspapers, etc., suspended on them. Door right. Window in flat right centre, showing snow-covered country beyond; rude fireplace left; wood fire burning; overhanging chimney and shelf; small stove right, very rude, with chimney going through roof, which is covered with snow and icicles; straw and rags stuffed in crevices and littered about floor; a rope stretched across back of hut, with fur rugs and horse-cloths hanging up to divide the beds off; camp and rough makeshift*

---

the militia: non-professional soldiery, auxiliaries.

furniture; camp cooking utensils, etc.; arm-chair made of tub, etc. Cupboards round left, containing properties; hanging lamp, a rude piece of planking before fireplace, stool, tubs, pail, etc. Portmanteau left of table, rough chair, broken gun-barrel near fireplace, for poker, and stack of wood. Stage half dark, music 'Chanson', distant bugle and answer, as curtain rises. ANGUS *discovered, very shabby, high, muddy boots, beard, etc., seated at table, reading by light of candle letters which are lying on an open travelling-desk.*)

ANGUS: (*reading old note*) 'Dear Cousin Angus, – Lady Shendryn desires me to ask you to come and dine on Thursday. The usual hour. Do come. – Yours, Blanche. P.S. Which my lady does not see. Mary says that men ought not to be believed, for all they say is fable.' (*Smooths note, and folds it, puts it away, reads another.*) 'Dear Cousin Angus, – I shall not be at dinner, but I shall be in the drawing-room, for inspection as you call it. I don't believe a word that you said the night before last. You know. – Blanche.' – (*Folds it, and places it in a large envelope, with other letters, an old glove, a flower, which he kisses, and a ribbon, seals them up, leaving packet on top of desk.*) If the attack is ordered for the morning, Hops will find this on the table as I told him. (*taking letter from his pocket*) How much oftener shall I read this? It contains the last news of her. (*Reads*) 'Dear Mac, – London is terribly slow, no parties, no nothing' – um – um – um – 'All the news comes to the Rag; but of course you know that before we do.' (*Turns over.*) Here it is! 'I saw the fascinating party, the thought of whom occupies your leisure hours, yesterday; she was in a carriage with Lady Shendryn, and Dick Fanshawe sat opposite. Dick has been often seen at Lady Shendryn's lately. I keep you posted upon this subject, because you told me to. Dick's uncle, the old mining-man, died two months ago, and left him a pot of money. Such is luck! My uncles never die, and when they do, they leave me dressing-cases! Damn dressing-cases! Dick's name, and that of the divine party, have been coupled, *À propos d'amour*. I am awfully hard up. Little Lucy has left me. She bolted with a Frenchman in the cigar-trade, taking all she could with her.' (*rising*) Um – that's four months ago. What a fool I am! Fanshawe's very rich, and not a bad fellow – as well he as another. (*Sighs.*) The next six hours may lay me on the snow, as has been the fate of many a better fellow. Oh! When I think of her, I feel that I could charge into a troop of cavalry, sabreproof with love. (*pause*) This won't do – I'm getting maudlin! (*Looks at watch, and takes fur greatcoat and cap from arm-chair, buckles on sword, buttons up his coat, etc.*) Mustn't be maudlin here. There's work! (*smiling sadly, and taking up packet*) If I can't live to marry Blanche, and make her Lady MacAlister, wife of General Sir Angus MacAlister, I can, at least, die a decent soldier. So there, Master Hops! (*placing packet on table, and lighting pipe by candle, left. Exit, singing –*)

'Parti-t-en guerre, pour tuer l'ennemi,
Parti-t-en guerre, pour tuer l'ennemi;

---

the Rag: the nickname for the Army and Navy Club in Pall Mall.
'Parti-t-en guerre', etc.: untraced.

Revint de guerre, après six ans et demi,
Revint de guerre, après six ans et demi;
Que va-t-il faire? Le Sire de Framboissey –
Que va-t-il faire? Le Sire de Framboissey.'

(*All exits and entrances are made from door right. Wind is heard as door opens, and snow is driven in.*)

CHALCOT: (*sneezes, then sings behind curtain*) A-choo!

'In Liquorpond Street, London, a merchant did dwell,
Who had only one darter – an uncommon nice young gal;
Her name it was Dinah, just sixteen years old,
And she'd a very large fortin' in siliver and gold.
Ri – tiddle-um, etc.'

(*Drawing curtains, is discovered on a rude bed of straw, rough wrapping, etc., his appearance entirely altered, hair rough, long beard, face red and jolly, his whole manner alert and changed. He wears an old uniform coat; one leg is bandaged at the calf, the trouser being cut to the knee, and tied with strings and tape; he sits up in bed and yawns; rubbing his eyes and hitting his arms out with enjoyment.*)

CHALCOT: What a jolly good sleep I have had, to be sure! (*Takes flask from under pillow, and drinks.*) Ah! What a comfort it is that in the Crimea you can drink as much as you like without its hurting you! The doctor says it's the rarefaction of the atmosphere. Bravo, the rarefaction of the atmosphere! – Whatever it may be. I must turn out. (*Takes pillow, and addresses it in song.*) 'Kathleen Mavourneen, arouse from thy slumbers.' (*Hits pillow, and gets out of bed.*) *Gardez vous* the poor dumb leg. It's jolly cold! (*Goes to fireplace and warms his hands, then turns and holds them round the candle, whilst so doing sees letters.*) Oh, Gus has left his love-traps to my keeping in case he should be potted. (*Puts letters in cupboard.*) Now for my toilette. Where's the water? (*Goes across stage, finds bucket against barrel up stage right.*) Ice, as usual! Where's the hammer? (*As he comes down stage he strikes foot against old gun-barrel lying amongst the straw on stage; he winces from pain to leg. Breaks ice in bucket, and taking up tin basin from side of barrel, retires behind curtain. Business of pouring out water, washing, etc.; comes out, wiping hands and face with straw.*) If the water's cold, the straw's warm. What luxuries those fellows in London do enjoy to be sure, soap and towels everywhere, and coffee for ringing for it. The Sergeant left the coffee – good. (*Takes coffee-pot from stove, and pours out coffee. Drinking coffee, and shaking his head. Sings*)

'Oh, father, says Dinah, I am but a child,
And for to get married just yet don't feel not at all inclined;

'In Liquorpond Street', etc.: the opening lines of one version of 'Villikins and his Dinah', a popular cockney song, made famous first by Frederick Robson, and then by Sam Cowell, who both died in 1864.
Kathleen Mavourneen: one of the most popular and enduring of Victorian ballads, words by Mrs Julia Crawford, music by Frederick N. Crouch.

If you'll let me live single for a year or two more,
My werry large fortin' I freely will give o'er.'

(*getting biscuit from canister, left*) Oh! this poor dumb leg of mine! Just my luck! I obtain my commission all right – get into the same company as Angus – went into action – and was wounded in my first engagement. If it hadn't been for the Sergeant I should have been killed. He received cut number three meant by the Russian for me. Down went the Russian and up I got. (*Sits at head of table, on barrel.*) And while he was down, the brute ran his bayonet into the calf of my leg. A mean advantage to take – to stick me while he was down. However, I split his skull (*Cracks biscuit.*), so he didn't get the best of it; and here I am – lame for another month. The first fortnight's dressing did my leg no good, for that fool of a Sergeant, instead of putting on the ointment given him by the doctor, went and spread the bandages all over orange marmalade; and I should never have found it out if he hadn't served up the salve for breakfast along with the anchovies. (*eating and drinking*) Now I superintend the cookery department – when there's anything to cook. (*Knock at door.*) Who's there? If you're French, *Entrez*; if you're Sardinian, *Entre*; if you're Turkish, *Itcherree*; if you're Russian, *Vnutri*; and if you're English, Come in!

(*Enter* SERGEANT – *ragged greatcoat, long beard, his left arm in a sling, bundle slung over his right shoulder, straw bands on legs, snow on coat, boots, beard, etc. Wind heard as door opens, and snow driven in.*)

CHALCOT: Shut the door; shut the door – it's awfully cold.

SERGEANT: (*shutting the door by placing his back against it; saluting*) Good morning, sir. How's your leg this morning, sir?

CHALCOT: It feels the cold, Sergeant. How's your arm?

SERGEANT: Thank you, sir, it feels frosty too; but I can move it a little. (*Moves arm, and winces.*)

CHALCOT: Gently, Sergeant, gently. How about dinner?

SERGEANT: Here you are, sir. (*placing bundle on table*) Mutton, sir – for roasting.

CHALCOT: And vegetables?

SERGEANT: Under the meat, sir.

CHALCOT: (*lifting up meat*) Capital! The muddy, but floury potato; the dirty milky turnip, and the humble, blushing, but digestive carrot. Can you cook 'em? (*putting them near cupboard*)

SERGEANT: Not today, sir. I'm on hospital duty.

CHALCOT: Then I suppose I must.

SERGEANT: But I shall be able to look in, sir, now and then.

CHALCOT: Do; for your legs are indispensable. Any news outside?

SERGEANT: They say, sir, there's to be an attack shortly.

CHALCOT: Um!

SERGEANT: And the enemy was heard moving in the night.

CHALCOT: Oh!

SERGEANT: And that they're very strong in artillery.

CHALCOT: Oh! (*drinking*)

SERGEANT: Talking of artillery, sir, Captain Rawbold sent his compliments to you, sir, and would you oblige him with the loan of your frying-pan, a pot of anchovies, and a few rashers of bacon.

CHALCOT: (*annoyed*) Anything else?

SERGEANT: No, sir.

CHALCOT: Confound Captain Rawbold! – He's always borrowing something. Last week I lent him our own private and particular gridiron, and he sent it back with one of the bars broken. (*aside*) Confound those damned gunners! Borrowing one's *batterie-de-cuisine*. (*rising. Knock* [*at door*].)

SERGEANT: I dare say that is Captain Rawbold come himself to –

CHALCOT: Open the door. I'll just give him a bit of my mind about that gridiron. Well (*taking frying-pan*), you don't deserve it; but here's your frying-pan, and – (SERGEANT *opens door.* SIR ALEXANDER *enters.* CHALCOT *sees him.*) Eh! – Colonel!

(SERGEANT *salutes, shutting door with his back.* CHALCOT *puts frying-pan behind him. Wind heard as door opens. Snow.*)

SIR ALEX: Good morning, Chalcot. I want to speak to you. (*Goes to fire.*)

CHALCOT: Sergeant, my compliments – and frying-pan to the captain – and – and – (*aside to* SERGEANT) he mustn't do it again. (*Opening door for* SERGEANT; SERGEANT *salutes with frying-pan, and exits, holding it before his face. Wind heard as door opens.*) Did you meet MacAlister? (*Crosses to fireplace.*)

SIR ALEX: (*Sits on barrel at head of table.*) Yes; and that's what I came to speak to you about. He reminded me of the documents that I intended to entrust to your care – should anything befall me. (*Gives him packet, which* CHALCOT *places in portmanteau.*)

CHALCOT: Is there any news, then?

SIR ALEX: I think we shall be ordered to the front – and I believe there is to be a combined attack, which is likely to be decisive. Angus told me that he had made his last will and testament, and confided it to you. I have done the same.

CHALCOT: (*who is arranging a rude spit and string for suspending mutton before fire*) And while you're fighting, I shall have to stop in here, cooking – like a squaw in a wigwam.

SIR ALEX: I'm sorry you can't go with us.

CHALCOT: Just my luck! Where's the cookery book? (*Gets book from mantel-piece, and goes to table.*)

SIR ALEX: Hugh – you've been a good friend – a real friend! At that time, when Kelsey came with that terrible news just before we sailed –

CHALCOT: (*at table; reading, and feigning not to hear*) 'Roast' – 'boil' – 'bake' – 'fry' – 'stew' –

SIR ALEX: (*taking book from him*) Put that down and listen to me. You know the original cause of my quarrel – with my lady.

CHALCOT: The slightest possible – Oh, yes.

SIR ALEX: You know, too, how she has wronged me since by her suspicions. I wrote a long letter to her last night – here it is (*showing it*). If this general engagement should give promotion to our senior major, send it home at once. My lady will find – when it is too late – how far she has been mistaken. (*Gives him letter.*)

CHALCOT: (*endeavouring to hide his feelings, and looking at mutton on table*) You don't know how mutton is usually roasted, do you – I mean, which side up? (*taking it in his hands*)

SIR ALEX: I had more to say to you – but I must go. (*Rises.*)

CHALCOT: I'd hobble with you as far as the hill, if it wasn't for the mutton. (*Hangs mutton at fire.*)

SIR ALEX: And I could speak to you as we walked.

CHALCOT: (*warming himself at stove, putting on cloak, etc.*) The Sergeant will be back directly. I can leave it for a few minutes. I have it! (*Writes on a piece of paper, folds it, and sticks it on the point of a sword, then fixes sword in drawer of table, so that the point is upwards.*) He can't help seeing that. (*putting on cap and cloak*) I believe I've hung it wrong side up. Now, Sir Alick; since my wound, this will be my first walk (*taking stick*).

SIR ALEX: And perhaps my last.

(*Wind and snow, as door opens. Exeunt* SIR ALEXANDER *and* CHALCOT. *Bugle. A pause.* CAPTAIN SAMPREY, LADY SHENDRYN, BLANCHE *and* MARY, *and* SOLDIER, *pass window from left. Knocking heard* [*at door*]. *Knocking repeated.*)

SAMPREY: (*without*) Chalcot, MacAlister – nobody at home? (*Wind. Looks in, then enters.*) This way, we have the field to ourselves. (*Enter* BLANCHE, LADY SHENDRYN, *and* MARY, *and* SOLDIER *with whip.*) These are their quarters.

LADY SHEN: Oh, thank you, Major – so kind of you to have escorted us from Balaclava.

SAMPREY: So kind of you to have accepted my escort. They are out, but I should think they're sure to be back directly. In the meantime –

LADY SHEN: We'll stay here. I suppose we need be under no apprehension.

SAMPREY: My dear Lady Shendryn, let me reassure you. Sir Alexander is quite well – so is Chalcot – and so is MacAlister. I'll now go and seek Sir Alexander (*all this lively*) – and tell him who is here.

BLANCHE: Where are they?

SAMPREY: I don't know. Pray be under no alarm – nobody will come here. There's no fighting going on – nor is there likely to be. We've no employment here but to keep ourselves warm – and to go without our dinners.

(*Exit* SAMPREY *and* SOLDIER. *The* LADIES, *who are shivering with cold, run to fire.*)

BLANCHE: Mary, your nose is red.

MARY: So's your's.

BLANCHE: So's my lady's.

LADY SHEN: Blanche, how can you take such a liberty?

BLANCHE: It was the frost not me. Let us warm our noses.

(*They go on their knees, and warm their noses at fire, rub them with handkerchiefs, etc.*)

---

no fighting going on: Samprey is either deliberately hiding the news of the attack, or is ignorant of its imminence.

LADY SHEN: I wonder when Mr Chalcot will come back.

(BLANCHE *and* MARY *examine furniture, peep behind curtain, see bed, and drop curtain, exclaiming 'Oh!'*)

BLANCHE: (*at fire*) And this is a hut. And this is the Crimea which we have all heard about and read about so much. And neither Sir Alick, nor Mr Chalcot –

MARY: Nor Captain MacAlister –

BLANCHE: Expect us, and here we are. (*seeing sword*) What's that?

LADY SHEN: Looks like a sword, with a note at the top of it.

MARY: Perhaps that's the Crimean method of delivering letters.

BLANCHE: (*taking* MARY*'s hand sentimentally*) Perhaps, Mary, Chalcot –

MARY: Or MacAlister –

BLANCHE: Or some comrade, has left that letter containing his last request.

MARY: Or a letter to his wife.

LADY SHEN: More probably to his sweetheart.

BLANCHE: A few lines to his mother.

LADY SHEN: Or his children.

MARY: Or his tailor.

BLANCHE: I wonder what *is* in it! (*crossing to sword*) I declare I feel like Blue Beard's wife at the door of the blue chamber.

MARY: So do I.

LADY SHEN: What absurdity!

(BLANCHE, MARY, *on each side of table,* LADY SHENDRYN *at fire*)

MARY: There's no address on it.

BLANCHE: Then it's intended for anybody.

MARY: Or nobody.

LADY SHEN: Do you consider yourself nobody, Miss Netley?

MARY: Almost.

BLANCHE: My fingers tingle to know what's inside it.

LADY SHEN: Blanche, I'm surprised at you. Open a letter not addressed to you! Most unladylike.

MARY: (*whispering to* BLANCHE) Tell her you think it's in Sir Alick's handwriting.

BLANCHE: It's open at this end. I can read *T – h – e*, 'the'. I think it's Sir Alexander's handwriting.

LADY SHEN: (*rising*) Eh?

BLANCHE: But we mustn't open it, Mary; so whether it is Sir Alexander's or anybody else's –

LADY SHEN: My dear Blanche, if you insist on gratifying this childish whim –

BLANCHE: You'll let me?

LADY SHEN: To please you, my dear.

BLANCHE: [*to* MARY] You take it off.

MARY: No, you.

BLANCHE: No, you.

(*Pushing each other forward,* MARY *snatches letter, the sword falls to the ground. All frightened.*)

ALL: Oh!

BLANCHE: It's like the taking of Sebastopol.

MARY: Yes; only that we've got it. (*All come down stage.* MARY *opens letter, and reads*) 'Please to look after the mutton!'

ALL: Oh!

(LADY SHENDRYN *goes to stove.*)

LADY SHEN: Sir Alexander never wrote that; it's not his style. (*Takes off mantle and wrapper.*)

MARY: Such a stupid thing to say! Now put the sword and letter back.

BLANCHE: No; that would be mean. We'll look after the mutton ourselves. I feel so excited; I think it must be the air. (*twirling mutton*) Isn't it fun seeing it go round? (*standing with her back to the fire*) Upon my word, Mary, I think I should make as good an officer as any of the men. I could stand with my back to the fire, as they do (*imitating*).

MARY: But you couldn't face the fire, as they do.

BLANCHE: I don't know that. I could talk just as they do. (*imitating slow swell smoking, and taking cigars from case on mantelpiece*) Yaas, it's a very fine cigaw – but I know man – Bedfordshire man – who imports for his own smoking, very finest cigaws evaw smoked. Now, Mary, you go on.

MARY: (*sitting; imitating different sort of swell, with eye-glass, and hands in pockets*) Look here, old fella, if you talk of cigars – I know some cigars that are cigars – and such cigars as no other fella's got the like cigars.

BLANCHE: (*slow*) You don't say so (*smoking*).

MARY: (*quick*) Assure you – never saw such cigars before in all my life. (*rising*) Oh! Ain't they nasty? (*They put them down.*)

BLANCHE: Mary, let's play at soldiers (*snatching up sword that note was attached to*).

LADY SHEN: Oh! You stupid girls. (*Rises, and goes to fire.*)

MARY: Oh! It's such a silly game.

BLANCHE: No, it isn't. To please me! There, take one of those guns. (MARY *takes gun hesitatingly, from left of barrel.*)

MARY: D'ye think it'll go off?

BLANCHE: No; it is not loaded. Now, you be the soldier, and I'll be the officer.

MARY: No; I'll be the officer.

BLANCHE: No; I'll be the officer.

MARY: No; then I shan't play.

BLANCHE: We can't both be officers.

MARY: Yes, we can.

BLANCHE: Then who's to give the word of command?

MARY: Both.

BLANCHE: And who's to obey it?

MARY: Neither.

BLANCHE: Nonsense.

---

the taking of Sebastopol: after a gallant defence by the Russians lasting eleven months, the town of Sebastopol was occupied by the Allies on 9 September 1855.
swell: see note on p. 41 above, though the dominant characteristic here is obviously affectation.

MARY: It's going off, Blanche.

BLANCHE: (*in tone of command*) Hi! Ho! Ha! Attention! Form hollow square! Prepare to receive (*prancing over to right*) cavalry!

(BLANCHE *charges upon* MARY. MARY, *somewhat frightened, retreats to the corner. Door opens;* ANGUS *and* CHALCOT *enter.*)

CHALCOT: Lady Shendryn!

ANGUS: Blanche!

CHALCOT: Miss Netley!

LADY SHEN: How do you do, Hugh? (*general shaking of hands*) How are you, Angus?

BLANCHE: We're so glad to see you, Mr Chalcot. (*embarrassed*) And you too, Captain MacAlister.

MARY: How do you do, Captain? How do you do, Mr Chalcot? (*Places stock of gun in his hand. Goes up stage and disrobes.* CHALCOT *and* ANGUS *take off overcoats, etc.* ANGUS *helps* CHALCOT *off with coat. Puts his sword against barrel.*)

CHALCOT: (*aside*) She's looking very well. But you must have dropped from the clouds. I saw female figures entering our hut from the top of the hill, and hobbled on as fast as I could. I took you for *vivandières*.

(ANGUS *and* BLANCHE *never take their eyes off each other.*)

LADY SHEN:
BLANCHE:
MARY: } *Vivandières*!

BLANCHE: Do *vivandières* ever come here?

CHALCOT: (*exchanging glances with* ANGUS) No; but seeing petticoats – it seems a dream. How did you get here?

LADY SHEN: We came over in Lord Llandudno's yacht.

CHALCOT: The 'Curlew'?

LADY SHEN: Yes – Lady Llandudno was anxious to see her son.

CHALCOT: He's all right, and comfortable in hospital.

LADY SHEN: And so Lady Llandudno prevailed on us to accompany her. We landed yesterday – Major Samprey brought us here in a cart, and after great trouble we found you out and here we are.

CHALCOT: By Jove! If this were put in a play, people would say it was improbable. (ANGUS *and* LADY SHENDRYN *go up stage. Knocks his wounded leg against gun, and winces.*) Oh!

MARY:
BLANCHE: } What's the matter?

CHALCOT: I'm wounded.

BLANCHE:
MARY: } Wounded?

CHALCOT: Yes.

MARY: But how?

I saw female figures, etc.: see remarks on text (pp. 36–7 above).

vivandières: women who brought supplies to troops in the field.

CHALCOT: A Russian infantryman ran his bayonet in the calf of my leg.
MARY: Oh! How horrid! (*hiding her face*)
CHALCOT: I brought it away as a trophy.
BLANCHE: The leg?
CHALCOT: No – the bayonet. (*pointing to bayonet on wall*) That's the bayonet – this is the leg.
BLANCHE: What's the matter, Mary?
MARY: Nothing; but to find oneself close to the realities – to the horrors of war!
CHALCOT: Eh?
BLANCHE: (*laughing*) She says you're one of the horrors of war.
MARY: (*to* BLANCHE) Oh! Blanche! How can you!

(BLANCHE *and* MARY *go to* ANGUS *at table.*)

LADY SHEN: (*coming down; aside to* CHALCOT) Are Sir Alexander's quarters near here?
CHALCOT: No. (*aside*) If he only knew who was here! [(*aloud*)] At some distance.
LADY SHEN: Is he likely to come here?
CHALCOT: I think so – shortly – yes. (*aside*) This is awkward. (LADY SHENDRYN *returns to stove. With fashionable air; going up stage*) Well, ladies, happy to see you in the heart of luxury and civilisation; welcome to this baronial hall, which, by the way, we built ourselves. Chalcot *fundavit* – Chalcot *pinxit* – Chalcot *carpetavit*. This is the boudoir. Won't you come upon the Turkey carpet? (*standing upon a piece of planking, which rocks to and fro*)
ANGUS: (*bringing down rude arm-chair*) Allow me to offer your ladyship a chair. (ANGUS *goes to arm-chair, and then to right of table, facing* BLANCHE. MARY *sits at head of table, and* BLANCHE *at end, left.*)
CHALCOT: I made it myself; it's beautifully stuffed – put your feet on the hearth-rug. Dinner will be ready, when it's done. The *menu* is substantial, but not various. A *grand gigot de mouton rôti au naturel, pas de sauce*. In the mean-time, can we offer you any light refreshment – any lunch? We have an admirable tap of rum, and as for fruit, I can strongly recommend our raw onions. After dinner we can go to the Opera. (*Cannonade, distant.*)
LADY SHEN: What's that?
CHALCOT: (*looking at* ANGUS) The overture! May I offer you some coffee?

(LADY SHENDRYN *seated at stove,* MARY *at head of table, and* BLANCHE *at foot.*)

LADIES: Oh, yes.

(CHALCOT *hands coffee to* LADY SHENDRYN *and* MARY; ANGUS *to* BLANCHE, *fetching cups, etc., from cupboard, then a cup for himself; crossing to* BLANCHE, *stirring coffee with his eyes*

---

fundavit: laid the foundations (Latin).
pinxit: decorated (it) (Latin).
carpetavit: carpeted it (dog-Latin).

fixed on her; sees she has no spoon, gives her the fork he is using, squeezing her hand.)

ANGUS: (*conscious that* LADY SHENDRYN*'s eyes are upon him, to* BLANCHE) I hope I have the pleasure of seeing you quite well!

BLANCHE: Quite well; and you?

ANGUS: Quite well.

MARY: I want a spoon. (CHALCOT *gives her the wooden one.*)

CHALCOT: Our family plate. (*a pause. They sigh.*)

ANGUS: Any news in London when you left it?

BLANCHE: No; none. (*pause*)

ANGUS: No news?

BLANCHE: None; none whatever.

MARY: [(*to* CHALCOT)] It's so hot.

CHALCOT: Have some ice in?

BLANCHE: (*pause*) You remember Miss Featherstonhaugh?

ANGUS: No – yes. Oh – yes.

BLANCHE: The Admiral's second daughter, the one with the nice eyes; used to wear her hair in bands. Her favourite colour was pink?

(ANGUS *puts his cup to his lips, but does not drink.*)

ANGUS: Yes.

BLANCHE: She always wears green now.

ANGUS: Good gracious!

CHALCOT: Can I offer your ladyship the spoon?

ANGUS: (*not knowing what to say*) I heard that London had been very dull.

BLANCHE: Oh! Very dull.

ANGUS: Seen anything of our friends, the Fanshawes?

BLANCHE: No.

ANGUS: Not of *Mr* Fanshawe?

BLANCHE: Oh – Dick! He's married!

ANGUS: Married?

BLANCHE: Yes; to one of Sir George Trawley's girls.

ANGUS: (*with a sigh of relief*) Poor old Fanshawe! (*He empties cup at a draught; sees that* LADY SHENDRYN *is not looking, opens his coat, and taking out the locket shows it to* BLANCHE, *and whispers*) Do you remember the night we parted?

BLANCHE: Yes.

LADY SHEN: (*looking round*) Blanche, dear, are you not cold out there?

BLANCHE: No; quite warm, I assure you.

CHALCOT: Oh, they are quite warm – that's the warmest corner in the hut.

ANGUS: [(*to* BLANCHE)] You remember it?

BLANCHE: Yes.

(*Enter* SERGEANT *with order book, which he gives to* ANGUS. *He expresses surprise at seeing* LADIES. ANGUS *takes sword and belt from barrel.*)

LADY SHEN:
BLANCHE:
MARY: } Sergeant Jones!

ANGUS: (*aside to* CHALCOT) To the front! (*to* BLANCHE, *seeing that she has observed paper*) So Miss Featherstonhaugh wears green now, does she? (*buckling on sword*) I'm afraid that I must leave you.

BLANCHE: Must you?

ANGUS: Yes.

BLANCHE: On duty?

ANGUS: Yes.

BLANCHE: Shall you be back soon?

ANGUS: I hope so. Good day, Miss Netley. Good day, Lady Shendryn, for the present. (*pause; to* BLANCHE, *after shaking hands with* CHALCOT) I hope to have the pleasure of seeing you again.

(SERGEANT *opens door. Exit* ANGUS. *The 'Chanson' is playing as a march by band outside; it grows more and more distant. No snow or wind here*)

BLANCHE: What band is that playing? (*rising*)

SERGEANT: The band of 'Ours'.

BLANCHE: I think I've heard that march before.

SERGEANT: We call it Captain MacAlister's march. He had it arranged by the bandmaster. They often play it. (LADY SHENDRYN *speaks aside to* SERGEANT.)

CHALCOT: (*at fire, observing* BLANCHE, *sings*)

'And a cup of cold pisen lay close by her side,

(BLANCHE *crosses and sits, end of table.*)

'And a billy-dow, which said as how for Villikins she died.'

SERGEANT: Thank you, my lady – I'm glad to hear the missus is well, and the children – and the twins – and the new one which I haven't seen.

MARY: There's a letter I promised Mrs Jones to give you if I met you (*giving it*). I saw them all the day before we left. The twins have grown wonderfully.

SERGEANT: Have they now? Clever little things! Grown! – So like 'em – just the sort of thing they would do!

BLANCHE: (*rising, sighing*) Has Captain Mac – Has the regiment to go far?

SERGEANT: 'Ours', mum?

BLANCHE: Yes.

SERGEANT: We're going to the front, into –

CHALCOT: (*interrupting quickly*) To parade.

SERGEANT: (*catching his eye*) Yes; to parade.

LADY SHEN: (*advancing*) Will Sir Alexander be there?

SERGEANT: Yes, my lady. He wouldn't let the regiment go into –

CHALCOT: (*interrupting*) On parade.

SERGEANT: On parade – without him.

LADY SHEN: Can we see them? (*a pause.* CHALCOT *and* SERGEANT *look at each other embarrassed.*) I mean, can we not see the regiment parading? You can't escort us on account of your wound; but the Sergeant could conduct us to the top of the hill there where we could see them, could he not?

BLANCHE: Oh! – I should so like that!

---

billy-dow: *billet-doux*, a love letter.

CHALCOT: Well – if you insist – Sergeant, take the three ladies to the –

LADY SHEN: No. Miss Netley can remain here – she is such a bad walker.

MARY: No, I'm not (*pouting*).

LADY SHEN: We shall not be gone long.

(LADY SHENDRYN *and* BLANCHE *put on wraps,* MARY *assisting* LADY SHENDRYN.)

CHALCOT: You'll come back to dinner?

LADY SHEN: Yes. Miss Netley will perhaps be kind enough to assist in its preparation. We shall most likely be back before Sir Alexander or the Captain.

CHALCOT: Most likely. (*Opens door. Wind.*) It's not snowing, but you'd better stay here.

LADY SHEN: No, no.

BLANCHE: We've made up our minds.

CHALCOT: I understand female discipline too well to make another observation. (*Exeunt* LADY SHENDRYN *and* BLANCHE.) Sergeant, take the ladies to Flagstaff Hill. Goodbye, for the present; and (*aside to* SERGEANT) not a word about the action! (SERGEANT *exits.*)

CHALCOT: [(*aside*)] This is a singular *tête-à-tête* – shut up alone with this girl. I always hated her in England! Now I like her very much! Somehow, the air of the Crimea seems to improve everything. Everything has improved since I've had something to do – and a bayonet in the calf of my leg.

MARY: (*at fire.*) Now, Mr Chalcot, what are we to do for dinner?

CHALCOT: Dinner?

MARY: (*attending to fire*) Yes; of course I must obey Lady Shendryn's orders.

CHALCOT: Orders! (*aside*) Lady Shendryn behaves like a perfect brute to this girl. Such a charming girl, too – (*aloud*) About dinner – shall we have a set dinner?

MARY: If you like; I'm a capital cook.

CHALCOT: Are you?

MARY: Yes.

CHALCOT: What an accomplished creature it is!

MARY: In my poor father's time, I was housekeeper. He wasn't rich; but he always said his dinners were excellent; and he ought to know, for he was a clergyman.

CHALCOT: (*aside*) A housekeeper, too – ah! (*aloud*) Well now, for this dinner – this grand dinner; to begin at the beginning.

MARY: Soup?

CHALCOT: We've got no soup.

MARY: Fish?

CHALCOT: We're out of fish.

MARY: Entrées?

CHALCOT: I don't think we'll have any entrées today.

MARY: The joint?

CHALCOT: There we are strong. (*crossing to fire, singing 'Barcarole'* [*from*]

'Barcarole': the boating-song from *Masaniello*, an immensely popular opera by Daniel Auber (1782–1871), first performed in 1828.

'Masaniello') 'See the mutton brightly – brightly burning.' (MARY *crosses to right of table.*)

MARY: And the vegetables?

CHALCOT: *Pommes de terre au naturel, dans leur jackets* (*pointing to potatoes*).

MARY: Game?

CHALCOT: No game.

MARY: Sweets – ices?

CHALCOT: Lots of ice outside.

MARY: Puddings?

CHALCOT: Unheard-of luxuries.

MARY: Have you no flour?

CHALCOT: A barrelful (*pointing*).

MARY: Any preserves?

CHALCOT: Lots – pots!

MARY: I can make a pudding.

CHALCOT: (*lost in astonishment*) No!

MARY: I can – a roly-poly.

CHALCOT: A roly-poly pudding in the Crimea! It's a fairy-tale! (*They clear table.*)

MARY: I shall want a basin.

CHALCOT: There's one!

MARY: Now get the flour.

(*Turns up the sleeves of her dress.* CHALCOT, *waiting on her with wonder and admiration, gets flour from barrel.*)

MARY: I declare! Here's some paste ready-made; I shall want a paste-board. (*Takes up straw from floor and rubs table.*) That won't do. What have you there?

CHALCOT: The lid of the barrel?

MARY: That'll do. Now I shall want an apron.

CHALCOT: An apron? (*Looks round.*) I know. (*Crosses left.*) I've got an apron. This will do. It belonged to a pioneer of ours; he was shot at the Alma. (MARY *shrinks.*) But he didn't wear it that day. (*Helps her on with pioneer's apron. She mixes pudding.*)

MARY: Have you any butter, or suet, or lard?

CHALCOT: Here.

MARY: (*mixing pudding*) Oh! I forgot.

CHALCOT: What?

MARY: I shall want a rolling-pin.

CHALCOT: Rolling-pin? (*Looks about – then under table, sees small barrel – takes it up and rolls it up and down table.* MARY *laughs but rejects it – in putting it down again* CHALCOT *knocks three-legged stool over – after a little difficulty succeeds in pulling one of the legs out and brings it sharply down on pudding.* MARY *rolls pudding, etc.*) Beauty, accomplishments, amiability, no mother, and roly-poly pudding! (*approaching her*)

---

paste: dough.
pioneer: infantryman specialising in trench-digging, excavations, etc.
the Alma: the Allied victory at the River Alma was won on 20 September 1854.

MARY: My hands are all over flour! You mustn't talk to the cook. Now, the preserves!

CHALCOT: Here. (CHALCOT *gets preserves.*)

MARY: What's this?

CHALCOT: Strawberry.

MARY: Ah! I like strawberry. That'll do. (*Smells it.*) Take it away! Good gracious, what's that? (*Both smell it; knock heads together; business.*) Why, that's varnish!

CHALCOT: It's that damned ointment! (*Puts it in cupboard, gets another pot, breaks paper, smells it, tastes it.*) I think you'll find that right.

MARY: Now the spoon – the wonderful spoon.

CHALCOT: Our piece of family plate. (*producing spoon from pocket.* MARY *puts preserves in pudding.*)

CHALCOT: [(*aside*)] With such a woman as that to sweeten one's path through life – to put – metaphorically speaking – the preserves into one's pudding – that's woman's mission.

MARY: Oh – I forgot!

CHALCOT: What?

MARY: A pudding-cloth. What shall we do for a pudding-cloth?

CHALCOT: Won't the leather apron do? (MARY *shakes her head.*) Then I'm afraid our resources have broken down in the moment of victory! To think that a pudding – and such a pudding – should break down for the sake of a paltry pudding-cloth. (*after a pause*) I have it!

MARY: What?

CHALCOT: I received a packet of linen a month ago from England. I've never opened it. (*Opens portmanteau, and takes out towel.*) Eureka! I have found it! A towel! – And here have I been wiping my face with straw for the last three weeks!

MARY: Now I want a bit of string.

CHALCOT: (*getting string from cupboard*) Here you are.

MARY: Now get me a saucepan. (CHALCOT *gets saucepan and puts it on table.*) Does it boil?

CHALCOT: (*taking lid off and throwing it on floor*) Yes, I'll take my oath it boils.

MARY: (*Ties up the ends of pudding-cloth, puts it in saucepan.*) Now get the lid. (CHALCOT *gets lid from floor, puts it first on stool, then on table, and then on to saucepan.*)

MARY: Now then stand it on the fire, just there in the right-hand corner. (*pointing to fire with leg of stool.* CHALCOT *puts saucepan on fire.*)

MARY: The mutton's getting on beautifully. (*Pokes fire with leg of stool, and as she turns, hits* CHALCOT*'s leg.* CHALCOT *staggers to small barrel, left of table, down stage.*)

MARY: I have hurt your wound! – Pray, forgive me!

CHALCOT: It's nothing. Do it again. I like it.

MARY: I'm very, very sorry.

CHALCOT: Don't mention it – hurt me again! But speak in that tone – and look in that way again!

MARY: Shall I loosen the bandages? (*Kneels.*)

CHALCOT: If you like; but you can't fasten them up again.
MARY: I can.
CHALCOT: With what?
MARY: A hair-pin. (*Takes one from her hair and fastens bandages.*)
CHALCOT: Miss Netley – Mary – (*taking her hand*)
MARY: My hands are all over flour!
CHALCOT: Never mind – I like them all the better. You don't dislike me – do you, Mary?
MARY: Oh, Mr Chalcot!
CHALCOT: Not very much, I hope? I've always loved you even when we used to quarrel. May I trust that some day I may not be indifferent to you; and, if so, that I may make you my own – my wife! (*She turns away.*) Don't let me frighten you. I won't tell the Colonel – I mean Lady Shendryn! I know you can't love me now – but I'll try to deserve your love; and perhaps if I try hard – and I will – I may succeed. Sebastopol isn't taken in a day; and you'll let me try – won't you, Sebastopol? – I mean Mary? (*with great agitation*)
MARY: Mr Chalcot, you know I am a poor dependant.
CHALCOT: That's the very reason! I couldn't love a girl with money.
MARY: A man of your position – your property –
CHALCOT: For heaven's sake don't raise up the dismal spectre of my money. Mary! Don't let cash forbid the banns! If I am rich, don't reproach me with it. I don't deserve it – it isn't my fault! I never made a penny in my life – I never had the talent. Only say you will be mine! (*Bugle call without.*)
LADY SHEN: Mr Chalcot! (*outside*)

(*Enter* LADY SHENDRYN, *quickly.*)

CHALCOT: (*kissing* MARY, *who rises quickly, going up left; to* LADY SHENDRYN) All right. The mutton's doing beautifully.
LADY SHEN: They're fighting! – And my husband is in the action! I – I – I – Oh! I don't know what I'm doing! Give me your hand! (CHALCOT *supports her.*)

(*Enter* BLANCHE, *hurriedly.*)

BLANCHE: (*to* MARY) Mary – he's fighting! He's gone to battle – with two or three thousand others! I heard the officers who galloped by say there was an engagement! He's fighting! (CHALCOT *gathers things on table.*)
LADY SHEN: Who? – Sir Alexander?
BLANCHE: No; Angus.
LADY SHEN: Angus! What, then – do you love him?
BLANCHE: Yes, I do; and I don't care who knows it.
LADY SHEN: Well, my child, I don't blame you. We can't help these things. (*Kisses her.*)
BLANCHE: Perhaps, at this very moment – even now, as I speak – a bullet may have reached his heart.
LADY SHEN: Oh!

(*Both* WOMEN *horrified at the picture.* LADY SHENDRYN *and* BLANCHE *pull down* CHALCOT *to centre, and hurt his leg.* CHALCOT *has spoon in his hand.*)

LADY SHEN: Do you think he will come back?

BLANCHE: Will he return?

CHALCOT: Of course he will! No doubt of it! (*to* MARY) How the devil should I know?

LADY SHEN: }
BLANCHE: } If he should not!

CHALCOT: But he will – they will – they never do get killed in 'Ours'!

BLANCHE: Oh, Lady Shendryn! I'm so sorry for you (*crossing to her, and kissing her*).

LADY SHEN: And I for you (*kissing her*).

(CHALCOT *makes an offer to kiss* MARY. MARY *puts apron over* CHALCOT*'s head.*)

MARY: (*repulsing him*) I'm so glad you are not fighting!

CHALCOT: Are you? (*pointing to* LADY SHENDRYN *and* BLANCHE) It's wrong of me to be so happy, isn't it?

LADY SHEN: Think, dear; it's my husband!

BLANCHE: And the man I love!

LADY SHEN: And we parted in anger!

(*Distant cannon and bugle calls heard throughout following scene.*)

BLANCHE: And he never knew how much I loved him! Oh! If I could see him again!

(*Knock heard at door. All start.*)

BLANCHE: } (*together*) { Perhaps Angus.
LADY SHEN: } { If it is he!

(CHALCOT *opens door, and is met by* PRINCE PEROVSKY, *who wears full Russian uniform, orders, followed by* SAMPREY.)

BLANCHE: }
LADY SHEN: } Prince Perovsky!

PRINCE: (*entering*) Miss Haye! Lady Shendryn!

LADY SHEN: You here, Prince?

PRINCE: Yes – a prisoner – fortune of war.

(SAMPREY *enters* [*bearing* PEROVSKY*'s sword*]. CHALCOT *assists* PRINCE *to take off cloak.*)

SAMPREY: Pardon me, Lady Shendryn, I have the honour to be the Prince's escort. Knowing that you were acquainted, I took the liberty –

LADY SHEN: Sir Alexander –

BLANCHE: Captain MacAlister –

SAMPREY: (*very gravely*) Are in the engagement. I did not see their regiment – I could not for the smoke. Excuse me, I must go. Prince, you have given me your parole. (PRINCE *bows.*) I have the honour – (*presenting him with his sword.* PRINCE *bows, takes sword, and sheaths it. Exit* SAMPREY.)

(BLANCHE *sits, with her face on table,* CHALCOT, *with* LADY SHENDRYN *and* MARY.)

PRINCE: Pray, ladies, don't be alarmed; it is not a battle – a mere affair of outposts.

LADY SHEN: Oh, Prince, I am beyond comfort!

(LADY SHENDRYN *goes to fire.* MARY *sits by stove.* CHALCOT *talking to her, back to audience.* PRINCE *goes to* BLANCHE, *who is sitting at right corner of table.*)

PRINCE: (*to* BLANCHE) These are strange circumstances under which to meet. You see I am always a captive in your presence.

BLANCHE: Oh, Prince, to think that battle is raging so near us!

PRINCE: Be under no alarm; my presence –

BLANCHE: It is not that, but –

PRINCE: You fear for those dear to you?

BLANCHE: Yes.

PRINCE: Sir Alexander?

BLANCHE: Yes.

PRINCE: And perhaps for some other?

BLANCHE: Yes – my cousin Angus.

PRINCE: The young gentleman I met in London? (BLANCHE *assents.*)

BLANCHE: If he should be killed!

PRINCE: *Hélas*! Fortune of war!

BLANCHE: Or taken prisoner?

PRINCE: As I am. He would be treated with the respect and honour due to the sacred name of enemy. Reassure yourself, my dear Miss Haye; your young soldier is sheltered by your love. (BLANCHE *goes up to* MARY, LADY SHENDRYN *drops down to seat left of table.* CHALCOT *goes to fireplace.* [*Aside*]) Oh, Youth! Inestimable, priceless treasure! Lost for ever! To be a *sous-lieutenant*, and beloved as he is – psha! Am I a child, to cry for the moon? *Pas si bête*! (*Goes up stage to* BLANCHE.)

CHALCOT: (*coming down stage to* LADY SHENDRYN) If you see Sir Alexander again, of which I have but little doubt, I think what I am going to tell you will make you happy with him ever after. I am aware that you were jealous of him –

LADY SHEN: (*seated*) Not without cause. Even years ago I had cause.

CHALCOT: The slightest possible. Since then he has been true and faithful. I know, for I was in his confidence. Sir Alexander's money used to go mysteriously. Do you know where it went?

LADY SHEN: Yes; to some woman.

CHALCOT: No.

LADY SHEN: To whom then?

CHALCOT: To your brother Percy.

LADY SHEN: Percy!

CHALCOT: To save him – to save you and his family from dishonour. Five years ago Sir Alick discovered, by his banking account, that Percy had forged his name!

LADY SHEN: What!

CHALCOT: You remember the night that Sir Alick left England, when Kelsey, the lawyer, sent him a letter, and he sent for me?

LADY SHEN: And he withdrew £1,500 from my account.

CHALCOT: Yes; for fresh bills forged by Percy.

LADY SHEN: (*hiding her face*) And he concealed this from me?

Pas si bête: I'm not such a fool.

CHALCOT: Because he preferred to bear the brunt of your suspicions, rather than let you know the extent of your brother's – conduct. There is a letter, which in case of accidents, he gave to me for you; in it is contained the half of the letter you did not see, that Kelsey sent him. (MARY *goes up to back.*) You need not read it now. All that I tell you is true. Sir Alick is a gallant officer, and a noble gentleman, (*with emotion, then resuming his ordinary manner*) and come what may, he's sure to bring the regiment out of it creditably. So when you meet, learn to know him better.

LADY SHEN: When we meet – oh! This suspense is terrible. Any certainty – even of the worst!

(*Enter* SERGEANT.)

SERGEANT: If you please, sir – the Colonel – (LADY SHENDRYN *rises.*)

MARY: (*running between them*) Hush! (BLANCHE *rises.*)

LADY SHEN: You need not speak – I know all! – He is dead! (*a pause;* SERGEANT *astonished*)

BLANCHE: And Captain MacAlister?

SERGEANT: (*confounded*) Captain – (BLANCHE *covers her face with one hand.*)

BLANCHE: You may tell me – I can bear it.

(*Enter* ANGUS.)

ANGUS: Didn't I hear my name? (*going to* BLANCHE, *and throwing cap away*)

BLANCHE: (*rushing to him*) Oh! (*restraining herself*) I'm so glad to see you back!

CHALCOT: All right?

ANGUS: Quite.

BLANCHE: Unhurt?

ANGUS: Yes. (*a pause. They look sympathetically at* LADY SHENDRYN.)

CHALCOT: And Sir Alexander?

ANGUS: Came with me. He'll be here directly.

LADY SHEN: (*rising*) Here! Not killed?

ANGUS: No.

LADY SHEN: Alive?

ANGUS: Yes. (ALL *look at* SERGEANT.)

SERGEANT: That's just what I was going to say, only this young lady stopped me.

LADY SHEN: Oh – my husband! (SERGEANT *opens door;* SIR ALEXANDER *appears.*) If I could only see you, to kneel at your feet, and ask pardon for having wronged your noble nature! At the very time I reproached you for ruining your fortune for another, to have borne with me for the sake of the honour of my family!

SIR ALEX: (*advancing*) Diana! These expressions of affection –

LADY SHEN: Alexander. (*embracing; about to kneel, he prevents her*) I know all.

SIR ALEX: All what? (LADY SHENDRYN *shows him letter.*) Chalcot gave you this? (LADY SHENDRYN *assents.*) Hugh? What right had you to –

CHALCOT: (*coming down stage*) None whatever. That is why I did it. (*Goes up stage.*)

LADY SHEN: Forgive me!

SIR ALEX: Forget it, Diana, and – (*Staggers, and nearly falls.*)

LADY SHEN: What's the matter?

SIR ALEX: Nothing. I –

ANGUS: Nothing. Only a slight wound.

(LADY SHENDRYN *attends to* SIR ALEXANDER.)

MARY: (*to* SERGEANT) Why didn't you say that he was wounded?

SERGEANT: Just what I was going to do, miss, only you stopped me.

SIR ALEX: It is but a scratch – the affair was but a skirmish. The great event is postponed again. I came here to congratulate Angus.

CHALCOT: On what?

SIR ALEX: (*whispering, so that the* PRINCE *may not hear*) He has taken a Russian colour.

CHALCOT: Bravo, Angus! My luck, of course; I am out of all these good things. (*Goes up to* PRINCE.)

MARY: (*to* SERGEANT) Why didn't he mention his capturing the colours? (ALL *whispering*)

SERGEANT: We never do mention those sort of things in 'Ours'. (*Goes up stage, and takes off overcoat.*)

PRINCE: Sir Alexander, I trust that your hurt is but slight; wounded yourself, you will have more compassion upon others.

SIR ALEX: (*surprised*) Prince!

PRINCE: Permit me, in the hour of my adversity, to point out to you that those two young people love each other. Don't be surprised. Battle elevates as well as brutalises us. I withdraw my pretensions; I am too old.

BLANCHE: (*overhearing*) Prince!

SIR ALEX: But Angus is so poor.

PRINCE: No man is poor while he is young. Youth is wealth – inestimable and irretrievable.

SIR ALEX: } (*together*) { Well, but –
LADY SHEN: } { My dear Blanche –

BLANCHE: It's no use arguing, because I won't have anybody else; and if you don't consent, I'll wait till I'm twenty-one. You'll wait till I'm twenty-one, won't you, Angus?

SIR ALEX: Well – well – we'll see about it.

BLANCHE: When?

SIR ALEX: When? When the war is over.

(SIR ALEXANDER *and* LADY SHENDRYN *go up stage. He sits.*)

BLANCHE: What a horrid thing is war!

ANGUS: Prince, how can I express my deep sense of obligation?

PRINCE: By silence.

(ALL *go up stage.* SERGEANT *at fire, reading his letter. Tramp of soldiers heard without.*)

ANGUS: (*Turns left about and runs against* CHALCOT *who has lid of barrel* (*flour*) *in his hand.* CHALCOT *takes him to centre, and whispers*) You engaged to Mary? By what means?

CHALCOT: Roly-poly pudding – boiling in the pot. Tell you all about it.

(CHALCOT *and* ANGUS *go to barrel,* CHALCOT *puts flour pan and lid down and crosses to* MARY, ANGUS *to* BLANCHE.)

BLANCHE: (*aside to* MARY) You engaged to Chalcot? But he's such a little man.

MARY: You know I've no money – and I couldn't expect so big a husband as you.

CHALCOT: I feel awfully jolly – it must be the prospect of marriage – or the roly-poly pudding. Sergeant, what can I do for you?

SERGEANT: Nothing, sir – thank you.

CHALCOT: But I must – you saved my life.

SERGEANT: You gave me a five pound note.

CHALCOT: But you've only one life – I've many five-pound notes. I have it – your boy, the twin boy – how old is he?

SERGEANT: Nearly two, sir. Both on 'em is nearly two, sir.

(MARY, BLANCHE, *and* ANGUS *begin to lay cloth.*)

CHALCOT: I'll educate him, and when he's old enough, I'll buy him a commission. (*Goes up to* MARY.)

SERGEANT: (*affected*) My boy an officer! I'll have him taught reading and writing directly. If Mrs Jones and the twins could only come in this door now!

MARY: What a pleasant day! Capturing flags – and princes – and being engaged – it's delightful!

CHALCOT: I hope you'll find it so. You don't hate me now as you used to do.

MARY: I suppose you have been very wicked?

CHALCOT: Awful, but you don't dislike that, do you?

MARY: Um! I don't know. The Crimea has improved you wonderfully. (CHALCOT *helps her off with apron. They go up stage.*)

ANGUS: (*to* BLANCHE) The place is not the same now you are in it, and that you are to be mine. You illuminate it – you're a chandelier!

BLANCHE: Chandelier, indeed! A pretty compliment – all cut-glass and wire!

ANGUS: Lit up by love!

CHALCOT: (*at fire*) The mutton's done!

LADY SHEN: Prince, you'll dine with us?

BLANCHE: Oh, yes!

ANGUS: Let me add my solicitations.

(*General movement. They place seats, etc. All on the alert, as at a picnic. Each person, except* LADY SHENDRYN, SIR ALEXANDER *and* PRINCE, *has hold of either plates, or a chair, or a saucepan, etc.* CHALCOT *places mutton on table, which has been laid by* SERGEANT *and* MARY *and others.*)

CHALCOT: *Les reines sont servies.* (SERGEANT *waits at table.*)

(*The 'Chanson' march played, piano, without. Men heard marching. Cheers.* ANGUS *opens door.*)

LADY SHEN: What's that?

SIR ALEX: The Russian colours. (*whispering, and pointing to* ANGUS) 'Ours'!

MARY: What troops are those?

CHALCOT: (*sitting on floor*) 'Ours'!

BLANCHE: And what are we? (*to* ANGUS)

ANGUS: (*his hand in hers, leaning over her*) 'Ours'!

CURTAIN

CASTE

An original comedy in three acts

First produced at the Prince of Wales's Theatre, London, on Saturday 6 April 1867, with the following cast:

THE HON. GEORGE D'ALROY	Mr Frederick Younge
CAPTAIN HAWTREE	Mr Bancroft
ECCLES	Mr George Honey
SAM GERRIDGE	Mr Hare
DIXON [George's manservant]	Mr Hill
THE MARQUISE DE ST MAUR	Miss Larkin
ESTHER ECCLES	Miss Lydia Foote
POLLY ECCLES	Miss Marie Wilton

THE MARQUISE: there is some inconsistency in both LCP and PDW about the precise title of George's mother, who is often referred to as 'the Marchioness', but I have employed 'the Marquise' in all stage directions, which conforms to the cast list.

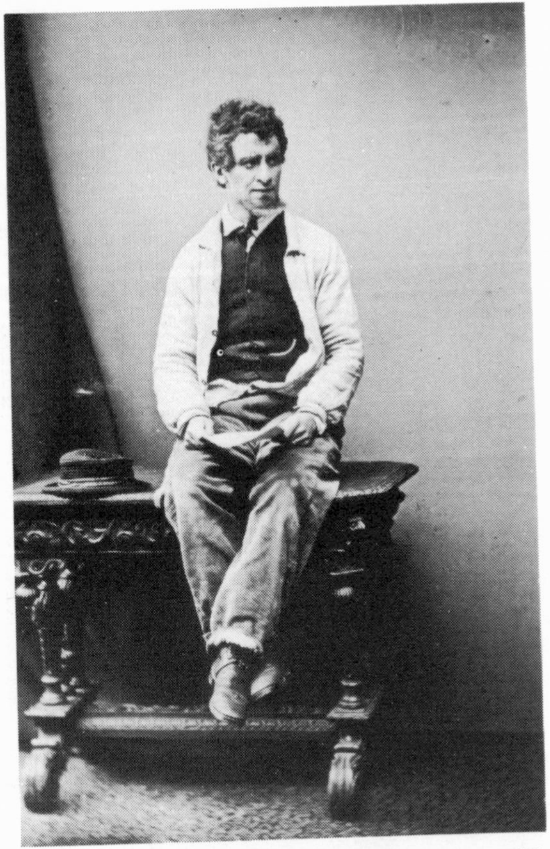

V a John Hare as Sam Gerridge in *Caste* (1867)

b George Honey as Eccles in *Caste* (1867)

ACT I

SCENE. *A plain set chamber, paper soiled. A window centre* [*back*] *with practicable blind; street backing and iron railings. Door practicable up right, when opened showing street door (practicable). Fireplace centre of left-hand piece; two-hinged gas-burners on each side of mantelpiece. Sideboard cupboard, cupboard in recess left, tea-things, teapot, tea-caddy, tea-tray, etc., on it. Long table before fire; old piece of carpet and rug down; plain chairs; bookshelf back left, a small table under it with ballet-shoe and skirt on it; bunch of benefit bills hanging under bookshelf. Theatrical printed portraits, framed, hanging about; chimney glass clock; box of lucifers and ornaments on mantelshelf; kettle on hob, and fire laid; doormats on the outside of door. Bureau centre of right-hand piece.* [*Door to bedroom?*] *Rapping heard at door, the handle is then shaken as curtain rises. The door is unlocked. Enter* GEORGE D'ALROY.

GEORGE: Told you so; the key was left under the mat in case I came. They're not back from rehearsal. (*Hangs hat on peg near door as* HAWTREE *enters.*) Confound rehearsal! (*Crosses to fireplace.*)

HAWTREE: (*back to audience, looking round*) And this is the fairy's bower!

GEORGE: Yes! And this is the fairy's fireplace; the fire is laid. I'll light it. (*Lights fire with lucifer from mantelpiece.*)

HAWTREE: (*turning to* GEORGE) And this is the abode rendered blessed by her abiding. It is here that she dwells, walks, talks – eats and drinks. Does she eat and drink?

GEORGE: Yes, heartily. I've seen her.

HAWTREE: And you are really spoons! – Case of true love – hit – dead.

GEORGE: Right through. Can't live away from her. (*With elbow on end of mantelpiece down stage.*)

HAWTREE: Poor old Dal! And you've brought me over the water to –

GEORGE: Stangate.

HAWTREE: Stangate – to see her for the same sort of reason that when a patient is in a dangerous state one doctor calls in another – for a consultation.

GEORGE: Yes. Then the patient dies.

HAWTREE: Tell us all about it – you know I've been away. (*Sits right of table, leg on a chair.*)

GEORGE: Well, then, eighteen months ago –

HAWTREE: Oh, cut that; you told me all about that. You went to a theatre, and saw a girl in a ballet, and you fell in love.

GEORGE: Yes. I found out that she was an amiable, good girl.

HAWTREE: Of course; cut that. We'll credit her with all the virtues and accomplishments.

---

chimney glass clock: clock under a glass dome.
lucifers: matches sold from 1829 onwards.
[*Door to bedroom*]: see remarks on texts (p. 37 above).
spoons: 'sweet on each other', originally slang for 'fools'.
Stangate: district of Lambeth immediately south of Westminster Bridge.

GEORGE: Who worked hard to support her drunken father.

HAWTREE: Oh! The father's a drunkard, is he? The father does not inherit the daughter's virtues?

GEORGE: No. I hate him.

HAWTREE: Naturally. Quite so! Quite so!

GEORGE: And she – that is, Esther – is very good to her younger sister.

HAWTREE: Younger sister also angelic, amiable, accomplished, etc., etc.

GEORGE: Um – good enough, but got a temper – large temper. Well, with some difficulty I got to speak to her. I mean to Esther. Then I was allowed to see her to her door here.

HAWTREE: I know – pastry-cooks – Richmond dinner – and all that.

GEORGE: You're too fast. Pastry-cooks – yes. Richmond – no. Your knowledge of the world, fifty yards round barracks, misleads you. I saw her nearly every day, and I kept on falling in love – falling and falling, till I thought I should never reach the bottom; then I met you.

HAWTREE: I remember the night when you told me; but I thought it was only an amourette. However, if the fire is a conflagration, subdue it; try dissipation.

GEORGE: I have.

HAWTREE: What success?

GEORGE: None; dissipation brought me bad health and self-contempt, a sick head and a sore heart.

HAWTREE: Foreign travel; absence makes the heart grow (*slight pause*) – stronger. Get leave and cut away.

GEORGE: I did get leave and I did cut away; and while away, I was miserable and a gone-er coon than ever.

HAWTREE: What's to be done? (*Sits cross-legged on chair, facing* GEORGE.)

GEORGE: Don't know. That's the reason I asked you to come over and see.

HAWTREE: Of course, Dal, you're not such a soft as to think of marriage. You know what your mother is. Either you are going to behave properly, with a proper regard for the world, and all that, you know; or you're going to do the other thing. Now, the question is, which do you mean to do? The girl is a nice girl, no doubt; but as to your making her Mrs D'Alroy, the thing is out of the question.

GEORGE: Why? What's to prevent me?

HAWTREE: Caste! – The inexorable law of caste! The social law, so becoming and so good, that commands like to mate with like, and forbids a giraffe to fall in love with a squirrel.

GEORGE: But my dear Bark –

HAWTREE: My dear Dal, all those marriages of people with common people are all very well in novels and in plays on the stage, because the real people don't exist, and have no relatives who exist, and no connections, and so no harm's done, and it's rather interesting to look at; but in real life with real relations,

---

pastry-cooks: cake-shops where food could be eaten, forerunners of the modern café.
coon: originally an abbreviation for the North American raccoon, much hunted for its fur; 'a gone coon' was someone on the verge of disaster, like a raccoon on the point of capture.

and real mothers, and so forth, it's absolute bosh. It's worse – it's utter social and personal annihilation and damnation.

GEORGE: As to my mother, I haven't thought about her. (*Sits, corner of table.*)

HAWTREE: Of course not. Lovers are so damned selfish; they never think of anybody but themselves.

GEORGE: My father died when I was three years old, and she married again before I was six, and married a Frenchman.

HAWTREE: A nobleman of the most ancient families of France, of equal blood to her own. She obeyed the duties imposed on her by her station and caste.

GEORGE: Still, it caused a separation and a division between us, and I never see my brother, because he lives abroad. Of course the Marquise de St Maur is my mother and I look upon her with a sort of superstitious awe. (*Moves chair with which he has been twisting about during speech from right of table to left corner.*)

HAWTREE: She's a grand Brahmin priestess.

GEORGE: Just so; and I know I'm a fool, and my having a thick tongue, and lisping makes me seem more foolish than I am. Now you're clever, Bark – a little too clever, I think. You're paying your *devoirs* – that's the correct word, isn't it – to Lady Florence Carberry, the daughter of a countess. She's above you – you've no title. Is she to forget *her* caste?

HAWTREE: That argument doesn't apply. A man can be no more than a gentleman.

GEORGE: 'True hearts are more than coronets,
And simple faith than Norman blood.'

HAWTREE: Now, George, if you're going to consider this question from the point of view of poetry, you're off to No Man's Land, where I won't follow you.

GEORGE: No gentleman can be ashamed of the woman he loves. No matter what her original station, once his wife he raises her to his rank.

HAWTREE: Yes, he raises her – *her*; but her connections – her relatives. How about them?

(ECCLES *enters* [*street door*].)

ECCLES: (*outside* [*room*]) Polly! Polly! (*Enters.*) Why the devil –

(GEORGE *crosses to* HAWTREE *who rises.* ECCLES *sees them, and assumes a deferential manner.*)

ECCLES: Oh, Mr De-Alroy! I didn't see you, sir. Good afternoon; the same to you, sir, and many on 'em. (*Puts hat on bureau and comes down stage.*)

HAWTREE: Who is this?

GEORGE: This is papa.

HAWTREE: Ah! (*Turns up to bookshelf, scanning* ECCLES *through eye-glass.*)

GEORGE: Miss Eccles and her sister not returned from rehearsal yet?

ECCLES: No, sir, they have not. I expect 'em in directly. I hope you've been quite well since I seen you last, sir?

GEORGE: Quite, thank you; and how have you been, Mr Eccles?

ECCLES: Well, sir, I have not been the thing at all. My 'elth, sir, and my spirits is both broke. I'm not the man I used to be. I am not accustomed to this sort of thing. I've seen better days, but they are gone – most like for ever. It is a

---

'True hearts', etc.: cf. Tennyson, 'Lady Clara Vere de Vere', lines 55–6.

melancholy thing, sir, for a man of my time of life to look back on better days that are gone most like for ever.

GEORGE: I dare say.

ECCLES: Once proud and prosperous, now poor and lowly. Once master of a shop, I am now, by the pressure of circumstances over which I have no control, driven to seek work and not to find it. Poverty is a dreadful thing, sir, for a man as has once been well off.

GEORGE: I dare say.

ECCLES: (*sighing*) Ah, sir, the poor and lowly is often 'ardly used. What chance has the working man?

HAWTREE: None (*aside*) when he don't work.

ECCLES: We are all equal in mind and feeling.

GEORGE: (*aside*) I hope not.

ECCLES: I am sorry, gentlemen, that I cannot offer you any refreshment; but luxury and me has long been strangers.

GEORGE: I am very sorry for your misfortunes, Mr Eccles. (*looking round at* HAWTREE, *who turns away*) May I hope that you will allow me to offer you this trifling loan? (*giving him a half-sovereign*)

ECCLES: Sir, you're a gentleman. One can always tell a real gentleman with half a sov – I mean with half an eye – a real gentleman understands the natural emotions of the working man. Pride, sir, is a thing as should be put down by the strong 'and of pecuniary necessity. There's a friend of mine round the corner as I promised to meet on a little matter of business; so, if you will excuse me, sir –

GEORGE: With pleasure.

ECCLES: (*going up stage*) Sorry to leave you, gentlemen, but –

GEORGE: } Don't stay on my account.
HAWTREE: } Don't mention it.

ECCLES: Business is business. (*Goes to door.*) The girls will be in directly. Good afternoon, gentlemen – good afternoon – (*going out*) – good afternoon!

(*Exit.* GEORGE *sits in chair, corner of table.*)

HAWTREE: Papa is not nice, but (*sitting on corner of table, down stage*) –
'True hearts are more than coronets,
And simple faith than Norman blood.'
Poor George! I wonder what your mamma – the Most Noble the Marquise de St Maur – would think of Papa Eccles. Come, Dal, allow that there is *something* in caste. Conceive that dirty ruffian – that rinsing of stale beer – that walking tap-room, for a father-in-law. Take a spin to Central America. Forget her.

GEORGE: Can't.

HAWTREE: You'll be wretched and miserable with her.

GEORGE: I'd rather be wretched with her, than miserable without her. (HAWTREE *takes out cigar case.*) Don't smoke here!

HAWTREE: Why not?

GEORGE: She'll be coming in directly.

HAWTREE: I don't think she'd mind.

GEORGE: I should. Do you smoke before Lady Florence Carberry?

HAWTREE: (*closing case*) Ha! You're suffering from a fit of the morals.

GEORGE: What's that?

HAWTREE: The morals is a disease like the measles, that attacks the young and innocent.

GEORGE: (*with temper*) You talk like Mephistopheles, without the cleverness. (*Goes up to window, and looks at watch.*)

HAWTREE: (*arranging cravat at glass*) I don't pretend to be a particularly good sort of fellow, nor a particularly bad sort of fellow. I suppose I'm about the average standard sort of thing, and I don't like to see a friend go down hill to the devil while I can put the drag on. (*turning, with back to fire*) Here is a girl of very humble station – poor, and all that, with a drunken father, who evidently doesn't care how he gets money so long as he don't work for it. Marriage! Pah! Couldn't the thing be arranged?

GEORGE: Hawtree, cut that! (*at window*) She's here! (*Goes to door and opens it.*)

(*Enter* ESTHER. GEORGE *receives her at the door.*)

GEORGE: (*flurried at the sight of her*) Good morning. I got here before you, you see.

ESTHER: Good morning. (*Sees* HAWTREE – *slight pause, in which* HAWTREE *has removed his hat.*)

GEORGE: I've taken the liberty – I hope you won't be angry – of asking you to let me present a friend of mine to you: Miss Eccles – Captain Hawtree.

(HAWTREE *advances and bows.* GEORGE *assists* ESTHER *in taking off bonnet and shawl.*)

HAWTREE: (*aside*) Pretty.

ESTHER: (*aside*) Thinks too much of himself.

GEORGE: (*Hangs up bonnet and shawl on pegs.*) You've had a late rehearsal. Where's Polly?

ESTHER: She stayed behind to buy something.

(*Enter* POLLY [*at street door*].)

POLLY: Hallo! (*head through door*) How de do, Mr D'Alroy? ([*Comes into room.*]) Oh! I'm tired to death. Kept at rehearsal by an old fool of a stage manager. But stage managers are always old fools – except when they're young. We shan't have time for any dinner – so I've brought something for tea.

ESTHER: What is it?

POLLY: Ham. (*showing ham in paper* – ESTHER *sits at window* – *seeing* HAWTREE Oh! I beg your pardon, sir. I didn't see you.

GEORGE: A friend of mine, Mary. Captain Hawtree – Miss Mary Eccles. (GEORGE *sits at window.*)

(POLLY *bows very low, one right, two left, three centre, half burlesquely, to* HAWTREE.)

HAWTREE: Charmed.

---

put the drag on: carriages were slowed down by some form of 'drag' such as an iron shoe acting as a brake.
Couldn't the thing be arranged?: i.e. that George should keep Esther as his mistress.

POLLY: (*aside*) What a swell! Got nice teeth, and he knows it. (*Hangs up her hat – a pause.*) How quiet we all are; let's talk about something. (*She crosses to fire, round table-front.* HAWTREE *crosses and places hat on bureau.*)

ESTHER: What can we talk about?

POLLY: Anything. Ham. Mr D'Alroy, do you like ham?

GEORGE: I adore her – (POLLY *titters.*) – I mean, I adore it.

POLLY: (*to* HAWTREE, *who has crossed to table, watching* POLLY *undo paper containing the ham. She turns the plate on top of the ham still in the paper, then throws the paper aside and triumphantly brings the plate under* HAWTREE*'s nose,* HAWTREE *giving a little start back.*) Do you like ham, sir? (*very tragically*)

HAWTREE: Yes.

POLLY: Now that is very strange. I should have thought you'd have been above ham (*getting tea-tray*).

HAWTREE: May one ask why?

POLLY: You look above it. You look quite equal to tongue – glazed (*laughing*). Mr D'Alroy is here so often that he knows our ways (*getting tea-things from sideboard and placing them on table*).

HAWTREE: I like everything that is piquante and fresh, and pretty and agreeable.

POLLY: (*laying table all the time for tea*) Ah! You mean that for me (*curtseying*). Oh! (*Sings*) Tra, la, la! la, la, la. (*Flourishes cup in his face; he retreats a step.*) Now I must put the kettle on. (GEORGE *and* ESTHER *are at window.*) Esther never does any work when Mr D'Alroy is here. They're spooning; ugly word spooning, isn't it? – Reminds one of red-currant jam. By-the-bye, love *is* very like red-currant jam – at the first taste sweet, and afterwards shuddery. Do you ever spoon?

HAWTREE: (*leaning across table*) I should like to do so at this moment.

POLLY: I dare say you would. No, you're too grand for me. You want taking down a peg – I mean a foot. Let's see – what are you – a corporal?

HAWTREE: Captain!

POLLY: I prefer a corporal. See here. Let's change about. You be Corporal – it'll do you good, and I'll be 'my lady'.

HAWTREE: Pleasure.

POLLY: You must call me 'my lady' though, or you shan't have any ham.

HAWTREE: Certainly, 'my lady'; but I cannot accept your hospitality, for I'm engaged to dine.

POLLY: At what time?

HAWTREE: Seven.

POLLY: Seven! Why, that's half-past tea-time. Now, Corporal, you must wait on me.

HAWTREE: As the pages did of old.

POLLY: 'My lady'.

HAWTREE: 'My lady'.

---

swell: see note on p. 41 above.

POLLY: Here's the kettle, Corporal. (*holding out kettle at arm's length.* HAWTREE *looks at it through eye-glass.*)

HAWTREE: Very nice kettle!

POLLY: Take it into the back kitchen.

HAWTREE: Eh!

POLLY: Oh! I'm coming too.

HAWTREE: Ah! That alters the case.

(*He takes out handkerchief and then takes hold of kettle – crosses as* GEORGE *rises and comes down, slapping* HAWTREE *on back.* HAWTREE *immediately places kettle on the floor.* POLLY *throws herself into chair by fireside up stage, and roars with laughter.* GEORGE *and* ESTHER *laugh.*)

GEORGE: What are you about?

HAWTREE: I'm about to fill the kettle.

ESTHER: (*going to* POLLY) Mind what you are doing, Polly! What will Sam say?

(POLLY *crosses to door.*)

POLLY: Whatever Sam chooses. What the sweetheart don't see, the husband can't grieve at. Now then – Corporal!

HAWTREE: 'My lady'! (*Takes up kettle.*)

POLLY: Attention! Forward! March! And mind the soot don't drop upon your trousers.

(*Exeunt* POLLY *and* HAWTREE, HAWTREE *first.*)

ESTHER: What a girl it is – all spirits! The worst is that it is so easy to mistake her.

GEORGE: And so easy to find out your mistake. (*They cross stage,* ESTHER *first.*) But why won't you let me present you with a piano? (*following* ESTHER)

ESTHER: I don't want one.

GEORGE: You said you were fond of playing.

ESTHER: We may be fond of many things without having them. (*leaning against end of table; taking out letter*) Now here is a gentleman says that he is attached to me.

GEORGE: (*jealous*) May I know his name?

ESTHER: What for? It would be useless, as his solicitations – (*Throws letter into fire.*)

GEORGE: I lit that fire.

ESTHER: Then burn these too. (GEORGE *crosses to fire.*) No, not that (*snatching one back*). I must keep that; burn the others.

(GEORGE *throws letter on fire, crosses to back of table quickly – takes hat from peg and goes to door as if leaving hurriedly.* ESTHER *takes chair right of table and goes centre stage with it, noticing* GEORGE*'s manner.* GEORGE *hesitates at door. Shuts it quickly, hangs his hat up again and comes down to back of chair in which* ESTHER *has seated herself.*)

GEORGE: Who is that from?

ESTHER: Why do you wish to know?

GEORGE: Because I love you, and I don't think you love me, and I fear a rival.

ESTHER: You have none.

GEORGE: I know you have so many admirers.
ESTHER: They're nothing to me.
GEORGE: Not one?
ESTHER: No. They're admirers, but there's not a husband among them.
GEORGE: Not the writer of that letter?
ESTHER: Oh, I like him very much (*coquettishly*).
GEORGE: Ah! (*sighing*)
ESTHER: And I'm very fond of this letter.
GEORGE: Then, Esther, you don't care for me.
ESTHER: Don't I! How do you know?
GEORGE: Because you won't let me read that letter.
ESTHER: It won't please you if you see it.
GEORGE: I dare say not. That's just the reason that I want to. You won't?
ESTHER: (*hesitates*) I will. There! (*giving it to him*)
GEORGE: (*reads*) 'Dear Madam'
ESTHER: That's tender, isn't it?
GEORGE: 'The terms are four pounds – your dresses to be found. For eight weeks certain, and longer if you should suit (*in astonishment*). I cannot close the engagement until the return of my partner. I expect him back today, and will write you as soon as I have seen him – Yours very' etc. Four pounds – find dresses. What does this mean?
ESTHER: It means that they want a Columbine for the pantomime at Manchester, and I think I shall get the engagement.
GEORGE: Manchester; then you'll leave London!
ESTHER: I must. (*pathetically*) You see this little house is on my shoulders. Polly only earns eighteen shillings a week, and father has been out of work a long, long time. I make the bread here, and it's hard to make sometimes. I've been mistress of this place, and forced to think ever since my mother died, and I was eight years old. Four pounds a week is a large sum, and I can save out of it. (*This speech is not to be spoken in a tone implying hardship.*)
GEORGE: But you'll go away, and I shan't see you.
ESTHER: P'raps it will be for the best. (*Rises and crosses stage.*) What future is there for us? You're a man of rank, and I am a poor girl who gets her living by dancing. It would have been better that we had never met.
GEORGE: No.
ESTHER: Yes, it would, for I'm afraid that –
GEORGE: You love me?
ESTHER: I don't know. I'm not sure; but I think I do. (*Stops and turns half-face to* GEORGE.)
GEORGE: (*trying to seize her hand*) Esther!
ESTHER: No. Think of the difference of our stations.
GEORGE: That's what Hawtree says. Caste! Caste! Curse caste! (*Goes up stage.*)
ESTHER: If I go to Manchester it will be for the best. We must both try to forget each other.
GEORGE: (*comes down stage*) Forget you! no, Esther; let me – (*seizing her hand*)
POLLY: (*without*) Mind what you're about. Oh dear! Oh dear! (GEORGE *and* ESTHER *retire up stage and sit in window seat.*)

(*Enter* POLLY *and* HAWTREE.)

POLLY: You nasty, great, clumsy Corporal, you've spilt the water all over my frock. Oh dear! (*coming down stage.* HAWTREE *puts kettle on ham on table.*) Take it off the ham! (HAWTREE *then places it on the mantelpiece.*) No, no; put it in the fireplace. (HAWTREE *does so.*) You've spoilt my frock (*sitting*).

HAWTREE: Allow me to offer you a new one.

POLLY: No, I won't. You'll be calling to see how it looks when it's on. Haven't you got a handkerchief?

HAWTREE: Yes!

POLLY: Then wipe it dry.

(HAWTREE *bends almost on one knee, and wipes dress. Enter* SAM, *whistling. Throws cap into* HAWTREE*'s hat on drawers.*)

SAM: (*sulkily*) Arternoon – I suppose yer didn't hear me knock! – The door was open. I'm afraid I intrude.

POLLY: No, you don't. We're glad to see you if you've got a handkerchief. Help to wipe this dry.

(SAM *pulls out handkerchief from slop, and dropping on one knee snatches skirt of dress from* HAWTREE, *who looks up surprised.*)

HAWTREE: I'm awfully sorry. (*rising*) I beg your pardon. (*Business;* SAM *stares* HAWTREE *out.*)

POLLY: It won't spoil it.

SAM: The stain won't come out (*rising*)

POLLY: It's only water!

SAM: (*to* ESTHER) Arternoon, Miss Eccles! (*to* GEORGE. POLLY *rises.*) Arternoon, sir! (*to* POLLY) Who's the other swell?

POLLY: I'll introduce you. Captain Hawtree – Mr Samuel Gerridge.

HAWTREE: Charmed, I'm sure. (*staring at* SAM *through eye-glass –* SAM *acknowledges* HAWTREE*'s recognition by a 'chuck' of the head over left shoulder – going up to* GEORGE) Who's this?

GEORGE: Polly's sweetheart.

HAWTREE: Oh! Now if I can be of no further assistance, I'll go.

POLLY: Going, Corporal?

HAWTREE: Yaas! (*Business: taking up hat and stick from bureau he sees* SAM*'s cap. He picks it out carefully, and coming down stage, examines it as a curiosity, drops it on the floor and pushes it away with his stick, at the same time moving backwards, causing him to bump against* SAM, *who turns round savagely.*) I beg your pardon! (*crossing up stage*) George, will you – (GEORGE *takes no notice.*) Will you –

GEORGE: What?

HAWTREE: Go with me?

GEORGE: Go? No!

HAWTREE: Then, Miss Eccles – I mean 'my lady'. (*Shaking hands and going; as he backs away bumps against* SAM, *and business repeated.* HAWTREE *close to door, keeping his eye on* SAM, *who has shown signs of anger.*)

---

slop: loose-fitting working-clothes, perhaps overalls.

POLLY: Goodbye, Corporal!

HAWTREE: (*at door*) Goodbye! Good afternoon, Mr – Mr – er – pardon me.

SAM: (*with constrained rage*) Gerridge, sir. Gerridge!

HAWTREE: (*as if remembering name*) Ah! Gerridge. Good day. (*Exit.*)

SAM: (*turning to* POLLY *in awful rage*) Who's that fool? Who's that long idiot?

POLLY: I told you, Captain Hawtree.

SAM: What's 'e want 'ere?

POLLY: He's a friend of Mr D'Alroy's.

SAM: Ugh! Isn't one of 'em enough?

POLLY: What do you mean?

SAM: For the neighbours to talk about. Who's he after?

POLLY: What do you mean by 'after'? You're forgetting yourself, I think.

SAM: No, I'm not forgetting myself – I'm remembering you. What can a long fool of a swell dressed up to the nines within an inch of his life want with two girls of your class? Look at the difference of your stations! 'E don't come 'ere after any good.

(*During the speech,* ESTHER *crosses to fire and sits before it in a low chair.* GEORGE *follows her, and sits on her left.*)

POLLY: Samuel!

SAM: I mean what I say. People should stick to their own class. Life's a railway journey, and Mankind's a passenger – first class, second class, third class. Any person found riding in a superior class to that for which he has taken his ticket will be removed at the first station stopped at, according to the bye-laws of the company.

POLLY: You're giving yourself nice airs! What business is it of yours who comes here? Who are you?

SAM: I'm a mechanic.

POLLY: That's evident.

SAM: I ain't ashamed of it. I'm not ashamed of my paper cap.

POLLY: Why should you be? I dare say Captain Hawtree isn't ashamed of his fourteen-and-sixpenny gossamer.

SAM: You think a deal of him 'cos he's a captain. Why did he call you 'my lady'?

POLLY: Because he treated me as one. I wish you'd make the same mistake.

SAM: Ugh!

(SAM *goes angrily to bureau.* POLLY *bounces up stage, and sits in window seat.*)

ESTHER: (*sitting with* GEORGE *tête-à-tête, by fire*) But we must listen to reason.

GEORGE: I hate reason!

ESTHER: I wonder what it means?

GEORGE: Everything disagreeable! When people insist in talking unpleasantly, they always say 'listen to reason'.

SAM: (*turning round*) What will the neighbours say?

POLLY: I don't care!

---

paper cap: a form of headgear commonly worn by Victorian workmen.
gossamer: a very light silk hat for men introduced in 1837.

SAM: What will the neighbours *think*?

POLLY: They can't think. They're just like you, they've not been educated up to it.

SAM: It all comes of your being on the stage (*going to* POLLY).

POLLY: It all comes to your not understanding the stage or anything else – but putty. Now, if you were a gentleman –

SAM: Why then, of course, I should make up to a lady!

POLLY: Ugh! (*Flings herself into chair.*)

GEORGE: Reason's an idiot! Two and two are four, and twelve are fifteen, and eight are twenty. That's reason!

SAM: (*turning to* POLLY) Painting your cheeks!

POLLY: (*rising*) Better paint our *cheeks* than paint *nasty old doors* as you do. How can you understand art? You're only a mechanic! You're not a professional. You're in trade. You are not of the same station that we are. When the manager speaks to you, you touch your hat, and say, 'Yes, sir', because he's your superior. (*Snaps fingers under* SAM*'s nose.*)

GEORGE: When people love there's no such thing as money – it don't exist.

ESTHER: Yes, it does.

GEORGE: Then it oughtn't to.

SAM: The manager employs me same as he does you. Payment is good everywhere and anywhere. Whatever's commercial, is right.

POLLY: Actors are not like mechanics. They wear cloth coats, and not fustian jackets.

SAM: I despise play actors (*sneeringly, in* POLLY*'s face*).

POLLY: And I despite mechanics. (POLLY *slaps his face.*)

GEORGE: I never think of anything else but you.

ESTHER: Really?

SAM: (*Goes to bureau, misses cap, looks around, sees it on floor, picks it up angrily and comes to* POLLY, *who is sitting right of table.*) I won't stay here to be insulted (*putting on cap*).

POLLY: Nobody wants you to stay. Go! Go! Go!

SAM: I will go. Goodbye, Miss Mary Eccles. (*Goes off and returns quickly.*) I shan't come here again! (*at door half-open*)

POLLY: Don't! Good riddance to bad rubbish.

SAM: (*rushing down stage to* POLLY) You can go to your *captain*!

POLLY: And you to your *putty*.

(*Throws his cap down and kicks it –* SAM *goes up stage and picks it up.* POLLY *turns and rises, leaning against table, facing him, crosses to door, and locks it.* SAM, *hearing the click of the lock, turns quickly.*)

ESTHER: And shall you always love me as you do now?

GEORGE: More.

POLLY: Now you *shan't* go. (*locking door, taking out key, which she pockets, and placing her back against door*) Nyer! Now I'll just show you my power. Nyer!

SAM: *Miss* Mary Eccles, let me out! (*advancing to door*)

Nyer!: There! (origin obscure).

POLLY: *Mr* Samuel Gerridge, I shan't. (SAM *turns away.*)

ESTHER: Now, you two. (*Postman's knock* [*at street door*].) The postman!

SAM: Now you must let me out. You must unlock the door.

POLLY: No, I needn't. (*Opens window, looking out.*) Here – postman. (*Takes letter from postman, at window.*) Thank you. (*Business; flicks* SAM *in the face with letter.*) For you, Esther!

ESTHER: (*rising*) For me?

POLLY: Yes. (*Gives it to her, and closes window, and returns to door triumphantly.* SAM *goes to window.*)

ESTHER: From Manchester!

GEORGE: Manchester?

ESTHER: (*reading*) I've got this engagement – four pounds a week.

GEORGE: (*placing his arm around her*) You shan't go. Esther – stay – be my wife!

ESTHER: But the world – your world?

GEORGE: Damn the world! You're my world. Stay with your husband, *Mrs George D'Alroy.*

(*During this* POLLY *has been dancing up and down in front of door.*)

SAM: I *will* go out! (*turning with sudden determination*)

POLLY: You can't, and you shan't!

SAM: I can – I will! (*Opens window, and jumps out.*)

POLLY: (*frightened*) He's hurt himself. (*running to window*) Sam – Sam, dear Sam! (SAM *appears at window.* POLLY *slaps his face and shuts window down violently.*) Nyer! (*During this* GEORGE *has kissed* ESTHER.)

GEORGE: *My wife!*

(*The handle of the door is heard to rattle, then the door is shaken violently.* ESTHER *crosses to door; finding it locked turns to* POLLY, *sitting in window seat, who gives her the key.* ESTHER *then opens the door.* ECCLES *reels in, very drunk, and clings to corner of bureau for support.* GEORGE *stands pulling his moustache.* ESTHER, *looking with shame, first at her father, then at* GEORGE. POLLY *sitting in window recess.*)

ACT DROP

(FOR CALL – GEORGE, *hat in hand, bidding* ESTHER *goodbye.* ECCLES *sitting in chair, nodding before fire.* SAM *again looks in at window.* POLLY *pulls the blind down violently.*)

ACT II

SCENE. D'ALROY*'s lodgings in Mayfair. A set chamber. Folding-doors* [*at rear*] *opening on to* [*dining-*] *room left in flat. Door,* [*to other room*] *right in flat.*

ACT DROP: a canvas cloth falls to mark the end of the act (see p. 66 above).

FOR CALL: It was common at this time to lower the curtain on a tableau, but the Bancrofts appear to have innovated the later practice of changing the picture 'to mark the natural progress of the story' with *Caste*.

Two windows, with muslin curtains, right. Loo-table. Sofa above piano. Two easy-chairs right and left of table. Dessert – claret in jug; two wine-glasses half full. Box of cigarettes, vase of flowers, embroidered slipper on canvas, and small basket of coloured wools, all on table. Footstool left of easy-chair. Ornamental gilt work-basket on stand in window. Easy-chair right. Piano left. Mahogany-stained easel with oil-painting of D'ALROY *in full Dragoon regimentals. Davenport, with vase of flowers on it, in window; a chair on each side; a watercolour drawing over it, and on each side of the room. Half moonlight through window.*

(ESTHER *and* GEORGE *discovered.* ESTHER *at window; when curtain has risen she comes down slowly to chair right of table, and* GEORGE *is sitting in easy-chair left of table.* GEORGE *has his uniform trousers and spurs on.*)

ESTHER: George, dear, you seem out of spirits.

GEORGE: (*smoking cigarette*) Not at all, dear, not at all (*rallying*).

ESTHER: Then why don't you talk?

GEORGE: I've nothing to say.

ESTHER: That's no reason.

GEORGE: I can't talk about nothing.

ESTHER: Yes, you can; you often do. (*crossing to* [*him*] *round back of table and caressing him*) You used to do before we were married.

GEORGE: No, I didn't. I talked about you, and my love for you. D'ye call that nothing?

ESTHER: (*sitting on stool left of* GEORGE) How long have we been married, dear? Let me see; six months yesterday. (*dreamily*) It hardly seems a week; it almost seems a dream.

GEORGE: (*putting his arm around her*) Awfully jolly dream. Don't let us wake up. (*aside and recovering himself*) How ever shall I tell her?

ESTHER: And when I married you I was twenty-two; wasn't I?

GEORGE: Yes, dear; but then, you know, you must have been some age or other.

ESTHER: No; but to think that I lived two-and-twenty years without knowing you!

GEORGE: What of it, dear?

ESTHER: It seems such a dreadful waste of time.

GEORGE: (*kissing her*) So it was – awful!

ESTHER: Do you remember our first meeting? Then I was in the ballet.

GEORGE: Yes; now you're in the Heavies.

ESTHER: Then I was in the front rank – now I am of high rank – the Honourable Mrs George D'Alroy. You promoted me to be your wife.

GEORGE: No, dear, you promoted me to be your husband.

ESTHER: And now I'm one of the aristocracy, ain't I?

GEORGE: Yes, dear; I suppose that we may consider ourselves –

ESTHER: Tell me, George; are you quite sure that you are proud of your poor little humble wife?

Loo-table: small round table, originally designed for the card-game Loo.
Davenport: a writing-desk with drawers.
the Heavies: George is punning on 'heavy' roles in the theatre, and a nickname applied to the heavy cavalry, especially to the Dragoon Guards whose members were heavier and taller than Hussars or Lancers.

GEORGE: Proud of you! Proud as the winner of the Derby.

ESTHER: Wouldn't you have loved me better if I'd been a lady?

GEORGE: You are a lady – you're my wife.

ESTHER: What will your mamma say when she knows of our marriage? I quite tremble at the thought of meeting her.

GEORGE: So do I. Luckily, she's in Rome.

ESTHER: Do you know, George, I should like to be married all over again.

GEORGE: Not to anybody else, I hope.

ESTHER: My darling!

GEORGE: But why over again? Why?

ESTHER: Our courtship was so beautiful. It was like a novel from the library, only better. You, a fine, rich, high-born gentleman, coming to our humble little house to court poor me. Do you remember the ballet you first saw me in? That was at Covent Garden. 'Jeanne la Folle; or, the Return of the Soldier'. (*Goes to piano.*) Don't you remember this dance? (*Plays a quick movement.*)

GEORGE: Esther, how came you to learn to play the piano? Did you teach yourself?

ESTHER: Yes. (*turning on music-stool*) So did Polly. We can only just touch the notes to amuse ourselves.

GEORGE: How was it?

ESTHER: I've told you so often. (*Rises and sits on stool at* GEORGE*'s feet.*)

GEORGE: Tell me again. I'm like the children – I like to hear what I know already.

ESTHER: Well, then, mother died when I was quite young. I can only just remember her. Polly was an infant; so I had to be Polly's mother. Father – who is a very eccentric man (GEORGE *sighs deeply* – ESTHER *notices it and goes on rapidly – all to be simultaneous in action.*) but a very good one when you know him – did not take much notice of us, and we got on as we could. We used to let the first floor, and a lodger took it – an old German – Herr Griffenhaagen. He was a ballet-master at the Opera. He took a fancy to me, and asked me if I should like to learn to dance, and I told him father couldn't afford to pay for my tuition; and he said that (*imitation*) he did not vant bayment, but dat he would teach me for noding, for he had taken a fancy to me, because I was like a leetle lady he had known long years ago in de far off land he came from. Then he got us an engagement at the theatre. That was how we first were in the ballet.

GEORGE: (*slapping his leg*) That fella was a great brick; I should like to ask him to dinner. What became of him?

ESTHER: I don't know. He left England. (GEORGE *fidgets and looks at watch.*) You are very restless, George. What's the matter?

GEORGE: Nothing.

ESTHER: Are you going out?

GEORGE: Yes. (*looking at his boots and spurs*) That's the reason I dined in –

ESTHER: To the barracks?

GEORGE: Yes.

Jeanne la Folle: a fictional ballet devised to effect the play's *dénouement*.

ESTHER: On duty?

GEORGE: (*hesitatingly*) On duty. (*rising*) And, of course, when a man is a soldier, he must go on duty when he's ordered, and where he's ordered, and – and – (*aside*) – why did I ever enter the service!

ESTHER: (*rises – crosses to* GEORGE – *and twining her arms round him*) George, if you must go out to your club, go; don't mind leaving me. Somehow or other, George, these last few days everything seems to have changed with me – I don't know why. Sometimes my eyes fill with tears, for no reason, and sometimes I feel so happy, for no reason. I don't mind being left by myself as I used to do. When you are a few minutes behind time I don't run and watch for you, and turn irritable. Not that I love you less – no, for I love you more; but often when you are away I don't feel that I am by myself. (*dropping her head on his breast*) I never feel alone. (*Goes to piano and turns over music.*)

GEORGE: (*watching* ESTHER) What angels women are! At least, this one is. I forget all about the others. (*Carriage-wheels heard off.*) If I'd known I could have been so happy, I'd have sold out when I married.

(*Knock at street door.*)

ESTHER: (*standing at table*) That for us, dear?

GEORGE: (*at first window*) Hawtree in a hansom. He's come for – (*aside*) me. I *must* tell her sooner or later. (*at door*) Come in, Hawtree.

(*Enter* HAWTREE *in regimentals.*)

HAWTREE: How do? Hope you're well, Mrs D'Alroy? George, are you coming to –

GEORGE: No, I've dined (*gives significant look*) – we dined early.

(ESTHER *plays scraps of music at piano.*)

HAWTREE: (*sotto voce*) Haven't you told her?

GEORGE: No, I daren't.

HAWTREE: But you must.

GEORGE: You know what an awful coward I am. You do it for me.

HAWTREE: Not for worlds. I've just had my own adieux to make.

GEORGE: Ah, yes – to Florence Carberry. How did she take it?

HAWTREE: Oh, (*slight pause*) very well.

GEORGE: Did she cry? (*earnestly*)

HAWTREE: No.

GEORGE: Nor exhibit any emotion whatever?

HAWTREE: No, not particularly.

GEORGE: Didn't you kiss her? (*surprisedly*)

HAWTREE: No; Lady Clardonax was in the room.

GEORGE: Didn't she squeeze your hand? (*wonderingly*)

HAWTREE: No.

GEORGE: Didn't she say anything? (*impressively*)

---

sold out: i.e. bought myself out of the army.
Lady Clardonax: the name borne by Ensign Daubray's mother in 'The Poor-Rate Unfolds a Tale' (see appendix I).

HAWTREE: No, except that she hoped to see me back again soon, and that India was a bad climate.

GEORGE: Umph! It seems to have been a tragic parting (*serio-comically*) – almost as tragic as parting – your back hair.

HAWTREE: Lady Florence is not the sort of person to make a scene.

GEORGE: To be sure; she's not your wife. I wish Esther would be as cool and comfortable. (*after a pause*) No, I don't – no, I don't. (*A rap at door.*)

(*Enter* DIXON.)

GEORGE: (*goes up to* DIXON) Oh, Dixon, lay out my –

DIXON: I have laid them out, sir; everything is ready.

GEORGE: (*coming down to* HAWTREE – *after a pause, irresolutely*) I must tell her – mustn't I?

HAWTREE: Better send for her sister. Let Dixon go for her in a cab.

GEORGE: Just so. I'll send him at once. Dixon! (*Goes up and talks to* DIXON.)

ESTHER: (*rising and going to back of chair left of table*) Do you want to have a talk with my husband? Shall I go into the dining-room?

HAWTREE: No, Mrs D'Alroy (*going to right of table and placing cap on it*).

GEORGE: No, dear. At once, Dixon. Tell the cabman to drive like – (*Exit* DIXON.) – like a – cornet just joined.

ESTHER: (*to* HAWTREE) Are you going to take him anywhere?

HAWTREE: (GEORGE *comes down right of* HAWTREE *and touches him quickly on the shoulder before he can speak.*) No. (*aside*) Yes – to India. (*to* GEORGE) Tell her now.

GEORGE: No, no. I'll wait till I've put on my uniform.

(*The door opens, and* POLLY *peeps in.*)

POLLY: How d'ye do, good people – quite well? (POLLY *gets to back of table – kisses* ESTHER.)

GEORGE: Eh? Didn't you meet Dixon?

POLLY: Who?

GEORGE: Dixon – my man.

POLLY: No.

GEORGE: Confound it! He'll have his ride for nothing. How d'ye do, Polly? (*Shakes hands.*)

POLLY: How d'ye do, George?

(ESTHER *takes* POLLY*'s things and places them up stage.* POLLY *places parasol on table.* ESTHER *returns left of* POLLY.)

POLLY: Bless you, my turtles. (*blessing them, ballet fashion*) George, kiss your mother. (*He kisses her.*) That's what I call an honourable brother-in-law's kiss. I'm not in the way, am I?

GEORGE: (*behind easy-chair right of table*) Not at all. I'm very glad you've come.

(ESTHER *shows* POLLY *the new music.* POLLY *sits at piano and plays comic tune.*)

HAWTREE: (*back to audience, and elbow on easy-chair; aside to* GEORGE) Under ordinary circumstances she's not a very eligible visitor.

---

cornet: a junior officer in a cavalry troop.

GEORGE: Caste again. I'll be back directly. (*Exit* GEORGE.)
HAWTREE: (*looking at watch, and crossing*) Mrs D'Alroy, I –
ESTHER: (*who is standing over* POLLY *at piano*) Going?
POLLY: (*rising*) Do I drive you away, Captain? (*taking her parasol from table*)
(ESTHER *gets to back of chair left of table.*)
HAWTREE: No.
POLLY: Yes, I do. I frighten you, I'm so ugly. I know I do. You frighten me.
HAWTREE: How so?
POLLY: You're so handsome. Particularly in those clothes, for all the world like an inspector of police.
ESTHER: (*half aside*) Polly!
POLLY: I will! I like to take him down a bit.
HAWTREE: (*aside*) This is rather a wild sort of thing in sisters-in-law.
POLLY: Any news, Captain?
HAWTREE: (*in a drawling tone*) No. Is there any news with you?
POLLY: Yaas (*imitating him*) we've got a new piece coming out at our theatre.
HAWTREE: (*interested*) What's it about?
POLLY: (*drawling*) I don't know. (*to* ESTHER) Had him there! (HAWTREE *drops his sword from his arm;* POLLY *turns round quickly, hearing the noise, and pretends to be frightened.*) Going to kill anybody today, that you've got your sword on?
HAWTREE: No.
POLLY: I thought not. (*Sings*)

'With a sabre on his brow,
And a helmet by his side,
The soldier sweethearts servant-maids,
And cuts cold meat besides.'

(*Laughs and walks about waving her parasol.*)
(*Enter* GEORGE *in uniform, carrying in his hand his sword, sword-belt, and cap.* ESTHER *takes them from him, and places them on sofa, then comes down stage.* GEORGE *goes down stage, by* HAWTREE.)

POLLY: (*clapping her hands*) Oh! Here's a beautiful brother-in-law. Why didn't you come in on horseback, as they do at Astley's? – gallop in and say (*imitating soldier on horseback and prancing up and down stage during the piece*) 'Soldiers of France! The eyes of Europe are a-looking at you! The Empire has confidence in you, and France expects that every man this day will do his – little utmost! The foe is before you – more's the pity – and you are before them – worse luck for you! Forward! Go and get killed; and to those who escape the Emperor will give a little bit of ribbon! Nineteens, about! Forward! Gallop! Charge! (*galloping to right, imitating bugle and*

'With a sabre', etc.: source unknown.
cuts cold meat: LCP; PDW has 'eats'.
Astley's: a London amphitheatre off Westminster Bridge Road, famous for its spectacular equestrian entertainments.

giving point with parasol. She nearly spears HAWTREE*'s nose.* HAWTREE *claps his hand upon his sword-hilt. She throws herself into chair, laughing and clapping* HAWTREE*'s cap (from table) upon her head. All laugh and applaud. Carriage-wheels heard without.*) Oh, what a funny little cap, it's got no peak. (*A peal of knocks heard at street door.*) What's that?

GEORGE: (*who has hastened to window*) A carriage! Good heavens – my mother!

HAWTREE: (*at window*) The Marchioness!

ESTHER: (*crossing to* GEORGE) Oh, George!

POLLY: (*crossing to window*) A Marchioness! A real, live Marchioness! Let me look! I never saw a real live Marchioness in all my life.

GEORGE: (*forcing her from the window*) No, no, no. She doesn't know I'm married. I must break it to her by degrees. What shall I do?

(*By this time* HAWTREE *is at door,* ESTHER *at [folding-] doors [up stage].*)

ESTHER: Let me go into the bedroom until –

HAWTREE: Too late! She's on the stairs.

ESTHER: Here then! (*At [folding-] doors, opens them.*)

POLLY: I want to see a real, live March–

(GEORGE *lifts her in his arms and places her within folding-doors with* ESTHER – *then shutting doors quickly, turns and faces* HAWTREE, *who, gathering up his sword, faces* GEORGE. *They then exchange places much in the fashion of soldiers 'mounting guard'. As* GEORGE *opens door, and admits the* MARQUISE, HAWTREE *drops down stage.*)

GEORGE: (*escorting her down stage, with great ceremony*) My dear mother, I saw you getting out of the carriage.

MARQ: My dear boy (*kissing his forehead*) I'm so glad I got to London before you embarked. (GEORGE *nervous.* HAWTREE *coming down stage*) Captain Hawtree, I think. How do you do?

HAWTREE: (*coming forward a little*) Quite well, I thank your ladyship. I trust you are –

MARQ: (*sitting in easy-chair*) Oh, quite, thanks. (*slight pause*) Do you still see the Countess and Lady Florence? (*looking at him through her glasses*)

HAWTREE: Yes.

MARQ: Please remember me to them – (HAWTREE *takes cap from table, and places sword under his arm.*) Are you going?

HAWTREE: Ya–a–s. Compelled. (*Bows, crossing round back of table. To* GEORGE, *who meets him*) I'll be at the door for you at seven. We must be at barracks by the quarter. (GEORGE *crosses to back of table.*) Poor devil! This comes of a man marrying beneath him!

(*Exit* HAWTREE. GEORGE *comes down stage to left of table.*)

MARQ: I'm not sorry that he's gone, for I wanted to talk to you alone. Strange that a woman of such good birth as the Countess should encourage the attentions of Captain Hawtree for her daughter Florence. (*During these lines* GEORGE *conceals* POLLY*'s hat and umbrella under table.*) Lady Clardonax was one of the old Carberrys of Hampshire – not the Norfolk Carberrys, but the direct line. And Mr Hawtree's grandfather was in trade – something in the

City – soap, I think, perhaps pickles – Stool, George! (*Points to stool.* GEORGE *brings it to her. She motions that he is to sit at her feet;* GEORGE *does so with a sigh.*) He's a very nice person, but *parvenu*, as one may see by his languor and his swagger. My boy (*kissing his forehead*), I am sure, will never make a *mésalliance*. He is a D'Alroy, and by his mother's side *Plantagenista.* The source of our life stream is royal.

GEORGE: How is the Marquis?

MARQ: Paralysed. I left him at Spa with three physicians. He always is paralysed at this time of year; it is in the family. The paralysis is not personal, but hereditary. I came over to see my steward; got to town last night.

GEORGE: How did you find me out here?

MARQ: I sent the footman to the barracks, and he saw your man Dixon in the street, and Dixon gave him this address. You're looking very well, and I dare say when mounted are quite a 'beau cavalier'. And so, my boy (*playing with his hair*), you are going abroad for the first time on active service.

GEORGE: (*aside*) Every word can be heard in the next room. If they've only gone upstairs!

MARQ: And now, my dear boy, before you go I want to give you some advice; and you mustn't despise it because I'm an old woman. We old women know a great deal more than people give us credit for. You are a soldier – so was your father – so was his father – so was mine – so was our royal founder; we were born to lead – to command – the common people expect it from us. It is our duty. Do you not remember in the Chronicles of Froissart? (*with great enjoyment*) I think I can quote it word for word; I've a wonderful memory for my age. (*with closed eyes*) It was in the fifth-ninth chapter – 'How Godefroy D'Alroy helde the towne of Saynte Amande, duryng the siege before Tournay. It said the towne was nat closed but with pales, and captayne ther was Sir Amory of Pauy, the Seneschall of Carcassoune – who had sayd yt was not able to holde agaynste an hooste – when one Godefroy D'Alroy sayd that rather than he wolde depart, he wolde keep it to the best of his power. Whereat the souldiers cheered and sayd, "Lead us on, Sir Godefroy" – and then begun a ferse assaut; and they within were chased and sought for shelter fro strete to strete. But Godefroy stood at the gate so valyantly that the souldiers helde the towne until the commynge of therle of Haynault with twelve thousande men.'

GEORGE: (*aside*) I wish she'd go. If she once gets on to Froissart, she'll never know when to stop.

MARQ: When my boy fights – and you will fight over there – he is sure to distinguish himself. It is his nature to – (*Toys with his hair.*) – he cannot forget his birth. And when you meet these Asiatic ruffians, who have dared to revolt, and to outrage humanity, you will strike as your ancestor, Sir Galtier

---

Froissart: the *Chroniques* of Jean Froissart (1338?–1410?) cover English and French history between c. 1332 and 1400. Robertson imitates the style of Lord Berners's English translation of 1523–5 in the two fictional extracts 'quoted'. I have selected readings from LCP and PDW to maintain the pastiche.

de Chevrault, struck at Poictiers. (*changing tone of voice as if remembering*) Froissart mentions it thus – 'Sir Galtier with his four Squires was in the front of that battell, and there did marvales in arms. And Sir Galtier rode up to the Prince and sayd to him – "Sir, take your horse and ryde forth, this journey is yours. God is this day in your hands. Gette us to the French kynge's batayle. I think verily by his valyantesse he wole not flye. Advance banner in the name of God and of Saynt George!" And Sir Galtier galloped forward to see his Kynge's victory, and meet his own death.'

GEORGE: (*aside*) If Esther hears all this!

MARQ: There is another subject about which I should have spoken to you before this; but an absurd prudery forbade me. I may never see you more. I am old – and you – are going into battle – (*kissing his forehead with emotion*) – and this may be our last meeting. (*A noise heard within folding-doors.*) What's that?

GEORGE: Nothing – my man Dixon in there.

MARQ: We may not meet again on this earth. I do not fear your conduct, my George, with men; but I know the temptations that beset a youth who is well born. But a true soldier, a true gentleman, should not only be without fear, but without reproach. It is easier to fight a furious man than to forgo the conquest of a love-sick girl. A thousand Sepoys slain in battle cannot redeem the honour of a man who has betrayed the confidence of a trusting woman. Think, George, what dishonour – what stain upon your manhood – to hurt a girl to shame and degradation! And what excuse for it? That she is plebeian? A man of real honour will spare the woman who has confessed her love for him, as he would give quarter to an enemy he had disarmed. (*taking his hands*) Let my boy avoid the snares so artfully spread; and when he asks his mother to welcome the woman he has chosen for his wife, let me take her to my arms and plant a motherly kiss upon the white brow of a lady. (*Noise of a fall heard within folding-doors; rising*) What's that?

GEORGE: Nothing (*rising*).

MARQ: I heard a cry. (*Goes up stage, and throws open folding-doors, discovering* ESTHER *lying on the floor with* POLLY *kneeling over her.*)

POLLY: George! George!

(GEORGE *goes up and* ESTHER *falls in his arms.* GEORGE *places* ESTHER *on sofa.*)

MARQ: (*coming down stage*) Who are these *women*?

POLLY: Women!

MARQ: George D'Alroy, these persons should have been sent away. How could you dare to risk your mother meeting women of their stamp?

POLLY: (*violently*) What does she mean? How dare she call me a woman? What's she, I'd like to know?

GEORGE: Silence, Polly! You mustn't insult my mother.

Sepoys: natives employed as soldiers in India by the European powers; a revolt of Sepoy troops in the Bengal army sparked off the Indian Mutiny in 1857.

MARQ: The insult is from you. I leave you, and I hope that time may induce me to forget this scene of degradation (*turning to go*).

GEORGE: Stay, mother. (MARQUISE *turns slightly away.*) Before you go (GEORGE *has raised* ESTHER *from sofa in both arms*) let me present you to Mrs George D'Alroy. *My wife!*

MARQ: Married!

GEORGE: Married.

(*The* MARQUISE *sinks into easy-chair.* GEORGE *replaces* ESTHER *on sofa, but still retains her hand. Three hesitating taps at door heard.* GEORGE *crosses to door, opens it, discovers* ECCLES, *who enters.* GEORGE *drops down stage to back of* MARQUISE*'s chair.*)

ECCLES: They told us to come up. When your man came Polly was out; so I thought I should do instead. (*calling at door*) Come up, Sam.

(*Enter* SAM *in his Sunday clothes, with short cane and smoking a cheroot. He nods and grins –* POLLY *points to* MARQUISE *–* SAM *takes cheroot from his mouth and quickly removes his hat.*)

ECCLES: Sam had just called; so we three – Sam and I, and your man, all came in the 'ansom cab together. Didn't we, Sam?

(ECCLES *and* SAM *go over to the girls, and* ECCLES *drops down stage to front of table – smilingly.*)

MARQ: (*with glasses up, to* GEORGE) Who is that?

GEORGE: (*coming to left of* MARQUISE) My wife's father.

MARQ: What is he?

GEORGE: A – nothing.

ECCLES: I am one of nature's noblemen. Happy to see you, my lady – (*turning to her*) – now, my daughters have told me who you are – (GEORGE *turns his back in an agony as* ECCLES *crosses to* MARQUISE.) – we old folk, fathers and mothers of the young couples, ought to make friends (*holding out his dirty hand*).

MARQ: (*shrinking back*) Go away! (ECCLES *goes back to table again, disgusted.*) What's his name?

GEORGE: Eccles.

MARQ: Eccles! Eccles! There never was an Eccles. He don't exist.

ECCLES: Don't he, though? What d'ye call this? (*Goes up to back of table as* SAM *drops down stage. He is just going to take a decanter when* SAM *stops him.*)

MARQ: No Eccles was ever born!

GEORGE: He takes the liberty of breathing though, for all that. (*aside*) And I wish he wouldn't!

MARQ: And who is the little man? Is he also Eccles?

(SAM *looks round.* POLLY *gets close up to him, and looks with defiant glance at the* MARQUISE.)

GEORGE: No.

MARQ: Thank goodness! What then?

GEORGE: His name is Gerridge.

MARQ: *Gerridge*! It breaks one's teeth. Why is he here?

GEORGE: He is making love to Polly, my wife's sister.

MARQ: And what is he?

GEORGE: A gasman.

MARQ: He looks it. (GEORGE *goes up to* ESTHER.) And what is she – the – the – the sister?

(ECCLES, *who has been casting longing eyes at the decanter on table, edges towards it, and when he thinks no one is noticing, fills wine-glass.*)

POLLY: (*asserting herself indignantly*) I'm in the ballet at the Theatre Royal, Lambeth. So was Esther. We're not ashamed of what we are! We have no cause to be.

SAM: That's right, Polly! Pitch into them swells! – Who are they?

(ECCLES *by this time has seized wine-glass, and turning his back is about to drink, when* HAWTREE *enters.* ECCLES *hides glass under his coat, and pretends to be looking up at picture.*)

HAWTREE: (*entering*) George! (*Stops suddenly, looking round.*) So, all's known!

MARQ: (*rising*) Captain Hawtree, see me to my carriage; I am broken-hearted! (*Takes* HAWTREE*'s arm, and is going up stage.*)

ECCLES: (*who has tasted the claret, spits it out with a grimace, exclaiming*) Rot!

(POLLY *goes to piano, sits on stool* – SAM *back to audience, leaning on piano* – ECCLES *exits through folding-doors.*)

GEORGE: (*to* MARQUISE) Don't go in anger. You may not see me again.

(ESTHER *rises in nervous excitement, clutching* GEORGE*'s hand.* MARQUISE *stops.* ESTHER *brings* GEORGE *down stage.*)

ESTHER: (*with arm round his neck*) Oh, George! Must you go? (*They come to front of table.*)

GEORGE: Yes.

ESTHER: I can't leave you! I'll go with you!

GEORGE: Impossible! The country is too unsettled.

ESTHER: May I come after you?

GEORGE: Yes.

ESTHER: (*with her head on his shoulder*) I may.

MARQ: (*coming down stage;* HAWTREE *at door*) It is his duty to go. His honour calls him. The honour of his family – *our* honour!

ESTHER: But I love him so! Pray don't be angry with me!

HAWTREE: (*looking at watch, and coming down stage*) George!

GEORGE: I must go, love! (HAWTREE *goes up to door again.*)

MARQ: (*advancing*) Let me arm you, George – let your mother, as in days of old. There is blood – and blood, my son. Let Radicals say what they will. See, your wife cries when she should be proud of you!

GEORGE: My Esther is all that is good and noble. No lady born to a coronet could be gentler or more true. Esther, my wife, fetch me my sword, and buckle my belt around me.

ESTHER: (*clinging to him*) No, no; I can't!

GEORGE: Try. (*Whispers to* ESTHER) To please my mother. (*to* MARQUISE) You shall see. (ESTHER *totters up stage,* POLLY *assisting her, and brings*

Theatre Royal, Lambeth: fictitious.

down his sword. As ESTHER *is trying to buckle his belt, he whispers*) I've left money for you, my darling. My lawyer will call on you tomorrow. Forgive me! I tried hard to tell you we were ordered for India; but when the time came, my heart failed me, and I –

(ESTHER, *before she can succeed in fastening his sword-belt, reels, and falls fainting in his arms.* POLLY *hurries to her.* SAM *standing at piano, looking frightened;* HAWTREE *with hand on handle of door;* MARQUISE *looking on.*)

ACT DROP

(FOR CALL – [MARQUISE,] GEORGE *and* HAWTREE *gone.* ESTHER *in chair, fainting;* POLLY *and* SAM *each side of her,* POLLY *holding her hands and* SAM *fanning her with his red handkerchief. The folding-doors thrown open, and* ECCLES *standing at back of table offering glass of claret.*)

ACT III

SCENE. *The room in Stangate* (*as in act I*). *Same furniture as in act I, with exception of piano, with roll of music tied up on it, in place of bureau, right. Map of India over mantelpiece. Sword with crape knot, spurs, and cap, craped, hanging over chimneypiece. Portrait of* D'ALROY (*large*) *on mantelpiece; berceaunette, and child, with coral, in it.* POLLY*'s bonnet and shawl hanging on peg, right. Small tin saucepan in fender, fire alight, and kettle on it. Two candles* (*tallow*) *in sticks, one of which is broken about three inches from the top and hangs over; sideboard up left. Slate and pencil on table. Jug on table, bandbox and ballet skirt on table.* (*At rise of curtain* POLLY *discovered seated at table, back of stage, comes down and places the skirt in bandbox. She is dressed in black.*)

POLLY: (*placing skirt in box, and leaning her chin upon her hand*) There – there's the dress for poor Esther in case she gets the engagement, which I don't suppose she will. It's too good luck, and good luck never comes to her, poor thing. (*Goes up to back of cradle.*) Baby's asleep still. How good he looks – as good as if he were dead, like his poor father; and alive too, at the same time like his dear self. Ah! Dear me; it's a strange world. (*Sits in chair right of table, feeling in pocket for money.*) Four and elevenpence. This must do for today and tomorrow. Esther is going to bring in the rusks for Georgy. (*Takes up slate.*) Three and five – eight, and four – twelve, one shilling – um – father can only have twopence. (*This all to be said on one breath.*) He must make do with that till Saturday, when I get my salary. If Esther gets the engagement, I shan't have many more salaries to take; I shall leave the stage and retire into private life. I wonder if I shall like private life, and if private life will like me.

---

crape knot: common funeral or memorial decoration of the period.
berceaunette: a trade refinement of 'bassinet', a hooded wickerwork cradle, with no etymological link with French 'berceau'.
coral: earlier believed to be a charm against sickness, a ring or necklace of coral was a favourite gift to a teething baby.

It will seem so strange being no longer Miss Mary Eccles – but Mrs Samuel Gerridge. (*Writes it on slate.*) 'Mrs Samuel Gerridge'. (*Laughs bashfully.*) La! To think of my being Mrs Anybody. How annoyed Susan Smith will be! (*writing on slate*) 'Mrs Samuel Gerridge presents her compliments to Miss Susan Smith, and Mrs Samuel Gerridge requests the favour of Miss Susan Smith's company to tea, on Tuesday evening next, at Mrs Samuel Gerridge's house.' (*pause*) Poor Susan! (*beginning again*) 'P.S. – Mrs Samuel Gerridge –' (*Knock heard at room door;* POLLY *starts.*)

SAM: (*without*) Polly, open the door.

POLLY: Sam! Come in.

SAM: (*without*) I can't.

POLLY: Why not?

SAM: I've got somethin' on my 'ead.

(POLLY *rises and opens door.* SAM *enters, carrying two rolls of wallpaper, one in each hand, and a small table on his head, which he deposits down stage, then puts rolls of paper on piano, as also his cap.* SAM *has a rule-pocket in corduroys.*)

POLLY: (*shuts door*) What's that?

SAM: (*pointing to table with pride*) Furniture. How are you, my Polly? (*kissing her*) You look handsomer than ever this morning. (*Dances and sings.*) 'Tiddle-di-tum-ti-di-do.'

POLLY: What's the matter, Sam? – are you mad?

SAM: No, 'appy – much the same thing.

POLLY: Where have you been these two days?

SAM: (*all excitement – throwing cap on piano*) That's just what I'm going to tell yer. Polly, my pet, my brightest batswing and most brilliant burner, what do yer think?

POLLY: Oh, do go on, Sam, or I'll slap your face.

SAM: Well, then, you've heard me speak of old Binks, the plumber, glazier, and gasfitter, who died six months ago?

POLLY: Yes.

SAM: (*sternly and deliberately*) I've bought 'is business.

POLLY: No!

SAM: (*excitedly*) Yes, of 'is widow, old Mrs Binks – so much down, and so much more at the end of the year. (*Dances and sings.*)

'Ri-ti-toodle,
Roodle-oodle,
Ri-ti-tooral-lay.'

POLLY: La, Sam!

SAM: (*pacing stage up and down*) Yes; I've bought the goodwill, fixtures, fittin's, stock, rolls of gas-pipe, and sheets of lead. (*Sits on table, quickly, facing* POLLY.) Yes, Polly, I'm a tradesman with a shop – a master tradesman.

---

batswing: one of the commonest forms of improved gas-burner introduced in the nineteenth century, the burner emitting the flame in the shape of a bat's wing.

(*coming to* POLLY *seriously*) All I want to complete the premises is a missus. (*Tries to kiss her. She pushes him away.*)

POLLY: Sam, don't be foolish!

SAM: (*arm round her waist*) Come and be Mrs Sam Gerridge, Polly, my patent-safety-day-and-night-light. You'll furnish me completely.

(POLLY *goes up stage,* SAM *watching her admiringly. He then sees slate, snatches it up and looks at it. She snatches it from him with a shriek, and rubs out writing, looking daggers at him,* SAM *laughing.*)

SAM: Only to think now (*putting arm round her waist,* POLLY *pouting*).

POLLY: Don't be a goose.

SAM: (*going towards table*) I spent the whole of yesterday lookin' up furniture. Now I bought that a bargain, and I brought it 'ere to show you for your approval. I've bought lots of other things, and I'll bring 'em all here to show yer for your approval.

POLLY: I couldn't think what had become of you (*seated right of table*).

SAM: Couldn't yer? Oh, I say, I want yer to choose the new paper for the little back parlour just behind the shop, you know. Now what d'yer think of this? (*fetching a pattern from piano and unrolling it*)

POLLY: (*standing*) No. I don't like that. (SAM *fetches the other, a flaming pattern.*) Ah! That's neat.

SAM: Yes, that's neat and quiet. I'll new-paper it, and new-paint it, and new-furnish it, and it shall all be bran-new. (*Puts paper on top of piano.*)

POLLY: But won't it cost a lot of money?

SAM: (*bravely*) I can work for it. With customers in the shop, and you in the back parlour, I can work like fifty men. (*Sits on table, beckons* POLLY *to him, she comes,* SAM *puts his arm round* POLLY; *sentimentally*) Only fancy, at night, when the shop's closed, and the shutters are up, counting out the till together! (*changing his manner*) Besides, that isn't all I've been doin'. I've been writin', and what I've written I've got printed.

POLLY: No!

SAM: True.

POLLY: You've been writing – about me? (*delighted*)

SAM: No – about the shop. (POLLY *disgusted*) Here it is. (*Takes roll of circulars from his canvas slop.*) You mustn't laugh – you know – it's my first attempt. I wrote it the night before last; and when I thought of you, Polly, the words seemed to flow like – red-hot solder. (*Reads*) Hem! 'Samuel Gerridge takes this opportunity of informin' the nobility, gentry, and inhabitants of the Borough-road – '

POLLY: The Borough-road?

SAM: Well, there ain't many of the nobility and gentry as lives in the Borough-road, but it pleases the inhabitants to make 'em believe yer think so (*resuming*) – 'of informin' the nobility, gentry, and inhabitants of the Borough-road, and its vicinity' – 'and its vicinity'. (*looking at her*) Now I think that's rather good, eh?

---

the Borough-road: the Borough lies immediately south of London Bridge; Borough Road leads from the Borough High Street to St George's Circus.

POLLY: Yes. (*doubtfully*) I've heard worse.

SAM: I first thought of saying neighbour'ood; but then vicinity sounds so much more genteel (*resuming*) – '*and* its vicinity, that 'e has entered upon the business of the late Mr Binks, 'is relict, the present Mrs B., 'avin' disposed to 'im of the same' – now listen, Polly, because it gets interestin' – 'S.G. – '

POLLY: S.G. Who's he?

SAM: (*looking at* POLLY *with surprise*) Why me. S.G. – Samuel Gerridge – me, us. We're S.G. Now don't interrupt me, or you'll cool my metal, and then I can't work. 'S.G. 'opes that, by a constant attention to business, and' – mark this – 'by supplyin' the best articles at the most reasonable prices, to merit a continuance of those favours which it will ever be 'is constant study to deserve.' There! (*turning on table, triumphantly*) Stop a bit – there's a little bit more yet. 'Bell-'angin', gas-fittin', plumbin', and glazin', as usual.' There! – It's all my own. (*Puts circular on mantelpiece, and crossing stage, contemplates it.*)

POLLY: Beautiful, Sam. It looks very attractive from here, don't it?

SAM: (*postman's knock* [*is heard*]) There's the postman. I'll go. I shall send some of these out by post. (*Goes off, and returns with letter.*)

POLLY: (*taking it*) Oh, for Esther. I know who it's from. (*Places letter on mantelpiece; at chair left of table.* SAM *sits corner of table, reading circular. Seriously*) Sam, who do you think was here last night?

SAM: Who?

POLLY: Captain Hawtree.

SAM: (*deprecatingly*) Oh, 'im! – Come back from India, I suppose.

POLLY: Yes; luckily, Esther was out.

SAM: I never liked that long swell. He was a uppish, conceited –

POLLY: (*sitting at end of table*) Oh, he's better than he used to be – he's a major now. He's only been in England a fortnight.

SAM: Did he tell yer anything about poor De Alroy?

POLLY: (*leaning against table end*) Yes; he said he was riding out not far from the cantonment, and was surrounded by a troop of Sepoy cavalry, which took him prisoner, and galloped off with him.

SAM: But about 'is death?

POLLY: Oh! (*hiding her face*) – that he said was believed to be too terrible to mention.

SAM: (*crossing to* POLLY) Did 'e tell yer anything else?

POLLY: No; he asked a lot of questions, and I told him everything. How poor Esther had taken her widowhood and what a dear, good baby the baby was, and what a comfort to us all, and how Esther had come back to live with us again.

SAM: (*sharply*) And the reason for it?

POLLY: (*looking down*) Yes.

SAM: How your father got all the money that 'e'd left for Esther.

---

relict: from Latin *relictus*, a widow.
cantonment: permanent military camp in India.

POLLY: (*sharply*) Don't say any more about that, Sam.

SAM: Oh! I only think Captain 'awtree ought to know where the money *did* go to, and you shouldn't try and screen your father, and let 'im suppose that you and Esther spent it all.

POLLY: I told him – I told him – I told him (*angrily*).

SAM: Did you tell 'im that your father was always at 'Armonic Meetin's at taverns, and 'ad arf cracked 'isself with drink, and was always singin' the songs and makin' the speeches 'e 'eard there, and was always goin' on about 'is wrongs as one of the workin' classes? 'E's a pretty one for one of the workin' classes, 'e is! 'Asn't done a stroke o' work these twenty year. Now, I *am* one of the workin' classes, but I *don't* 'owl about it. I work, I don't spout. (*Goes up stage, comes down again.*)

POLLY: Hold your tongue, Sam. I won't have you say any more against poor father. He has his faults, but he's a very clever man (*sighing*).

SAM: Ah! What else did Captain Hawtree say?

POLLY: He advised us to apply to Mr D'Alroy's mother.

SAM: What! The Marquissy? And what did you say to that?

POLLY: I said that Esther wouldn't hear of it. And so the Major said that he'd write to Esther, and I suppose this is the letter.

SAM: Now, Polly, come along and choose the paper for the little back parlour. (*Going towards table, and takes it up to wall behind door.*)

POLLY: (*rising*) Can't! Who's to mind baby?

SAM: The *baby*? Oh, I forgot all about 'im. (*Goes to cradle.*) I see yer! (*Goes to window casually.*) There's your father comin' down the street. Won't 'e mind him?

POLLY: (*going up stage*) I dare say he will. If I promise him an extra sixpence on Saturday. (SAM *opens window.*) Hi! Father! (POLLY *goes to cradle.*)

SAM: (*aside*) 'E looks down in the mouth, 'e does. I suppose 'e's 'ad no drink this mornin'. (*Goes to* POLLY.)

(*Enter* ECCLES *in shabby black. Pauses on entering, looks at* SAM, *turns away in disgust, takes off hat, places it on piano, and shambles across stage. Taking chair, places it and sits before fire.*)

POLLY: (*going to* ECCLES) Come in to stop a bit, father?

ECCLES: No; not for long. (SAM *comes down stage.*) Good morning, Samuel. Going back to work? That's right, my boy – stick to it. (*Pokes fire.*) Stick to it – nothing like it.

SAM: (*aside*) Now, isn't that too bad! (*aloud*) No, Mr Eccles. I've knocked off for the day.

ECCLES: (*waving poker*) That's bad! That's very bad! Nothing like work – for the young. I don't work so much as I used to, myself, but I like to (POLLY *sitting on corner of table*) see the young 'uns at it. It does me good and it does them good too. What does the poet say? (*rising impressively, and leaning on table*)

'Armonic Meetin's: many London taverns of the period featured concerts or Harmonic Meetings at which patrons could join in the singing; often such places eventually became music-halls. (Mr Eccles probably patronised the Bower Saloon in Stangate!)

'A carpenter said tho' that was well spoke,
It was better by far to defend it with hoak.
A currier, wiser than both put together,
Said "Say what you will, there is nothing like *labour*".
(*Sings*)
For a' that, an' a' that,
Your ribbon, gown, an' a' that,
The rank is but the guinea stamp,
The working man's the gold for a' that.'
(*Sits again, triumphantly wagging his head.*)

SAM: (*aside*) This is one of the public house loafers, that wants all the wages and none of the work, an idle old – (*Goes in disgust to piano, puts on cap, and takes rolls of paper under his arm.*)

POLLY: (*to* ECCLES) Esther will be in by-and-by. (*persuasive*) Do, father!

ECCLES: No, no. I tell you I won't!

POLLY: (*whispering, arm round his neck*) And I'll give you sixpence extra on Saturday.

(ECCLES*'s face relaxes into a broad grin.* POLLY *gets hat and cloak from peg.*)

ECCLES: Ah! You sly little puss, you know how to get over your poor old father.

SAM: (*aside*) Yes, with sixpence.

POLLY: (*putting on bonnet and cloak at door*) Give the cradle a rock if baby cries.

SAM: (*crossing to* ECCLES) If you should 'appen to want employment or amusement, Mr Eccles, just cast your eye over this. (*Puts circular on table, then joins* POLLY *at door.*) Stop a bit, I've forgot to give the baby one. (*Throws circular into cradle. Exeunt,* POLLY *first.*)

(ECCLES *takes out pipe from pocket, looks into it, then blows through it making a squeaking noise and finishes by tenderly placing it on the table. He then hunts in all his pockets for tobacco, finally finding a little paper packet containing a screw of tobacco in his right-hand waistcoat pocket, which he also places on table after turning up the corner of the tablecloth for the purpose of emptying the contents of his right-hand pocket of the few remnants of past screws of tobacco on to the bare table and mixing a little out of the packet with it and filling pipe. He then brushes all that remains on the table into the paper packet, pinches it up, and carefully replaces it in right-hand waistcoat pocket. Having put the pipe into his mouth, he looks about for a light, across his shoulder and under table, though never rising from the chair; seeing nothing his face assumes an expression of comic anguish. Turning to table he angrily replaces tablecloth and then notices* SAM*'s circular. His face relaxes into a smile, and picking it up, coolly tears the circular in half, makes a*

'A carpenter said', etc.: see appendix II.
currier: leather-dresser.
For a' that, etc.: see appendix II.

spill of it, and lighting it at fire, stands with his back to fireplace and smokes vigorously.)

ECCLES: Poor Esther! Nice market she's brought her pigs to – ugh! Mind the baby indeed! What good is he to me? That fool of a girl to throw away all her chances! – a *honourable-hess* – and her father not to have on him the price of a pint of early beer or a quartern of cool, refreshing gin! Stopping in here to rock a young honourable! Cuss him! (*Business – puffs smoke in baby's face, rocking it.*) Are we slaves, we working men? (*Sings savagely*)

'Britons never, never, never shall be – '

(*Nodding his head sagaciously, sits right of table.*) Howsoever, I won't stand this much longer. I've writ to the old cat – I mean to the Marquissy – to tell her that her daughter-in-law and her grandson is almost starving. That fool Esther's too proud to write to her for money. I hate pride – it's beastly! (*rising*) There's no beastly pride about me. (*Goes up left of table, smacking his lips.*) I'm as dry as a lime-kill. (*Takes up jug.*) Milk! – (*with disgust*) – for this young aristocratic pauper. Everybody in the house is sacrificed for him! (*at foot of cradle, with arms on chair back*) And to think that a *working man*, and a member of the Committee of the Banded Brothers for the Regeneration of Human Kind, by means of equal diffusion of intelligence and equal division of property, should be thusty, while this cub – (*Draws aside curtain, and looks at child. After a pause*) That there coral he's got round his neck is *gold*, real *gold*! (*with hand on knob at end of cradle*) Oh, Society! Oh, Gover'ments! Oh, Class Legislation! – *is this right*? Shall this mindless wretch enjoy himself, while sleeping, with a jewelled gawd, and his poor old grandfather want the price of half a pint? *No*! It shall not be! Rather than see it, I will myself resent this outrage on the rights of man! And in this holy crusade of class against class, of the weak and lowly against the *powerful and strong* – (*pointing to child*) – I will strike one blow for freedom! (*Goes to back of cradle.*) He's asleep. It will fetch ten bob round the corner; and if the Marquissy gives us anythink it can be got out with some o' that. (*Steals coral.*) Lie still, my darling! – It's grandfather a-watching over you –

'Who ran to catch me when I fell,
And kicked the place to make it well?
My grandfather!'

(*Rocking cradle with one hand; leaves it quickly, and as he takes hat off piano* ESTHER *enters. She is dressed as a widow, her face pale, and her manner quick and imperious. She carries a parcel and paper bag of rusks in her hand; she puts parcel on table, goes to cradle, kneels down and kisses child.*) My lovely had a nice walk? You should wrap yourself up well – you're so liable to catch cold!

ESTHER: My Georgy! – Where's his coral? (ECCLES *going to door, fumbles with*

---

quartern: a quarter of a pint.
lime-kill: old and now obsolete form of 'lime-kiln'.
got out: i.e. redeemed from the pawn-shop.
'Who ran to catch me', etc.: see appendix II.

the lock nervously, and is going out as ESTHER *speaks.*) Gone! – Father! (*Rising* – ECCLES *stops.*) – The child's coral – where is it?

ECCLES: (*confused*) Where's what, ducky?

ESTHER: The coral! You've got it – I know it! Give it me! – (*quickly and imperiously*) – *Give it me!* (ECCLES *takes coral from his pocket and gives it back.*) If you *dare* to touch *my* child – (*Goes to cradle.*)

ECCLES: Esther! (*going quickly to piano and banging his hat on it*) Am I not your father? – (ESTHER *gets round to front of cradle.*)

ESTHER: And I am his mother!

ECCLES: (*coming to her*) Do you bandy words with me, you pauper! You pauper!! You pauper!!! To whom I have given shelter – shelter to you and your brat! I've a good mind – (*raising his clenched fist*)

ESTHER: (*confronting him*) If you dare! I am no longer your little drudge – your frightened servant. When mother died – (ECCLES *changes countenance and cowers beneath her glance.*) – and I was so high, I tended you, and worked for you – and you beat me. That time is past. I am a woman – I am a wife – a widow – a *mother*! Do you think I will let you outrage *him*? (*pointing to cradle*) *Touch me if you dare!* (*advancing a step*)

ECCLES: (*bursting into tears and coming down stage*) And this is my own child, which I nussed when a babby, and sung 'Cootsicum Coo' to afore she could speak. (*Gets hat from piano, and returns a step or two.*) Hon. Mrs De Alroy (ESTHER *drops down stage behind chair right of table.*), I forgive you for all that you have done. In everything that I have done I have acted with the best intentions. May the babe in that cradle never treat you as you have this day *tret* a grey 'aired father. May he never cease to love and *h*onour you, as you have ceased to love and *h*onour me, after all that I have done for you, and the position to which I 'ave raised you by my own *industry*. (*Goes to door.*) May he never behave to you like the bad daughters of King Lear; and may you never live to feel how much more sharper than a serpent's (*slight pause as if remembering quotation*) scale it is to have a thankless child! (*Exit.*)

ESTHER: (*kneeling at back of cradle*) My darling! (*arranging bed and placing coral to the baby's lips, and then to her own*) Mamma's come back to her own. Did she stay away from him so long? (*Rises, and looks at the sabre, etc.*) My George! To think that you can never look upon his face or hear his voice. My brave, gallant, handsome husband! My lion and my love! (*Comes down stage, pacing the stage.*) Oh! To be a soldier, and to fight the wretches who destroyed him – who took my darling from me! (*action of cutting with sabre*) To gallop miles upon their upturned faces. (*Crossing with action – breaks down sobbing at mantelpiece – sees letter.*) What's this? – Captain Hawtree's hand. (*Sitting in chair, reads*) 'My dear Mrs D'Alroy, – I returned to England less than a fortnight ago. I have some papers and effects of my poor friend's, which I am anxious to deliver to you, and I beg of you to name a day when I can call with them and see you; at the same time let me express

---

how much more sharper: cf. *King Lear* I. 4. 311–13: '. . . that she may feel / How sharper than a serpent's tooth it is / To have a thankless child!'

my deepest sympathy with your affliction. Your husband's loss was mourned by every man in the regiment. (ESTHER *lays the letter on her heart, and then resumes reading.*) I have heard with great pain of the pecuniary embarrassments into which accident and the imprudence of others have plunged you. I trust you will not consider me, one of poor George's oldest comrades and friends, either intrusive or impertinent in sending the enclosed (*She takes out a cheque.*), and in hoping that, should any further difficulties arise, you will inform me of them, and remember that I am, dear Mrs D'Alroy, now, and always, your faithful and sincere friend, Arthur Hawtree.' (ESTHER *goes to cradle, and bends over it.*) Oh, *his* boy, if you could read it! (*Sobs, with head on head of cradle.*)

(*Enter* POLLY.)

POLLY: Father gone!

ESTHER: Polly, you look quite flurried. (*Goes [to her].*)

(POLLY *laughs, and whispers to* ESTHER.)

ESTHER: (*near head of table. Taking* POLLY *in her arms and kissing her*) So soon? Well – my darling, I hope you may be happy.

POLLY: Yes. Sam's going to speak to father about it this afternoon. (*Crosses round table, and putting rusks in saucepan.*) Did you see the agent, dear?

ESTHER: (*sits*) Yes; the manager didn't come – he broke his appointment again.

POLLY: (*sits*) Nasty, rude fellow!

ESTHER: The agent said it didn't matter, he thought I should get the engagement. He'll only give me thirty shillings a week, though.

POLLY: But you said that two pounds was the regular salary.

ESTHER: Yes, but they know I'm poor, and want the engagement, and so take advantage of me.

POLLY: Never mind, Esther. I put the dress in that bandbox. It looks almost as good as new.

ESTHER: I've had a letter from Captain Hawtree.

POLLY: I know, dear; he came here last night.

ESTHER: A dear, good letter – speaking of George, and enclosing me a cheque for thirty pounds.

POLLY: Oh, how kind! Don't you tell father. (*Noise of carriage-wheels without.*)

ESTHER: I shan't.

(ECCLES *enters, breathless.* ESTHER *rises and* POLLY *runs to window.*)

POLLY: Here's a carriage!

ECCLES: It's the Marquissy in her coach. (ESTHER *puts on the lid of bandbox.*) Now, girls, do be civil to her, and she may do something for us. (*Places hat on piano.*) I see the coach as I was coming out of the Rainbow. (*Hastily pulls an old comb out of his pocket, and puts his hair in order.*)

ESTHER: The Marquise!

(ESTHER *comes down stage to end of table,* POLLY *holding her hand.*)

ECCLES: (*at door*) This way, my lady – up them steps. They're rather awkward for the likes o' you; but them as is poor and lowly must do as best they can with steps and circumstances.

(*Enter* MARQUISE. *She surveys the place with aggressive astonishment.*)

MARQ: (*coming down stage, half aside*) What a hole! And to think that my grandson should breathe in such an atmosphere, and be contaminated by such associations! (*to* ECCLES) Which is the young woman who married my son?

ESTHER: I am Mrs George D'Alroy, widow of George D'Alroy. Who are you?

MARQ: I am his mother, the Marquise de Saint Maur.

ESTHER: (*with the grand air*) Be seated, I beg.

MARQ: (*rejecting chair offered servilely by* ECCLES, *and looking round*) The chairs are all dirty.

(SAM *enters with an easy-chair on his head, which he puts down, not seeing* MARQUISE, *who instantly sits down in it, concealing it completely.*)

SAM: (*astonished*) It's the Marquissy! (*looking at her*) My eye! These aristocrats are fine women – plenty of 'em – (*describing circle*) quality and quantity!

POLLY: Go away, Sam; you'd better come back in half an hour.

(ECCLES *nudges him, and bustles him towards the door. Exit* SAM. ECCLES *shuts door on him.*)

ECCLES: (*coming down rubbing his hands*) If we'd a-know'd your ladyship had bin a-coming, we'd a had the place cleaned up a bit. (*With hands on chair-back. He gets round behind* MARQUISE, *who turns the chair slightly from him.*)

POLLY: Hold your tongue, father! (ECCLES *crushed*)

MARQ: (*to* ESTHER) You remember me, do you not?

ESTHER: Perfectly, though I only saw you once. (*seating herself en grande dame*) May I ask what has procured me the honour of this visit?

MARQ: I was informed that you were in want, and I came to offer you assistance.

ESTHER: I thank you for your offer, and the delicate consideration for my feelings with which it is made. I need no assistance. (ECCLES *groans and leans on piano.*)

MARQ: A letter I received last night informed me that you did.

ESTHER: May I ask if that letter came from Captain Hawtree?

MARQ: No – from this person – your father, I think.

ESTHER: (*to* ECCLES) How dare you interfere in my affairs?

ECCLES: My lovey, I did it with the best intentions.

MARQ: Then you will not accept assistance from me?

ESTHER: No.

POLLY: (*aside to* ESTHER, *holding her hand*) Bless you, my darling! (POLLY *is standing beside her.*)

MARQ: But you have a child – a son – my grandson (*with emotion*).

ESTHER: Master D'Alroy wants for nothing.

POLLY: (*aside*) And never shall. (ECCLES *groans and turns on to piano.*)

MARQ: I came here to propose that my grandson should go back with me. (POLLY *rushes up to cradle.*)

ESTHER: (*rising defiantly*) What! Part with my boy! I'd sooner die!

---

en grande dame: like a great lady.

MARQ: You can see him when you wish. As for money, I –

ESTHER: Not for ten thousand million worlds – not for ten thousand million marchionesses!

ECCLES: Better do what the good lady asks you, my dear; she's advising you for your own good, and for the child's likewise.

MARQ: Surely you cannot intend to bring up my son's son in a place like this?

ESTHER: I do. (*Goes up stage, to cradle.*)

ECCLES: It *is* a poor place, and we are poor people, sure enough. We ought not to fly in the face of our pastors and masters – our pastresses and mistresses.

POLLY: (*aside*) Oh, hold your tongue, do! (*up stage at cradle*)

ESTHER: (*before cradle*) Master George D'Alroy will remain with his mother. The offer to take him from her is an insult to his dead father and to him.

ECCLES: (*aside*) He don't seem to feel it, stuck-up little beast!

MARQ: But you have no money – how can you rear him? – how can you educate him? – how can you live?

ESTHER: (*tearing dress from bandbox*) Turn Columbine – go on the stage again and dance!

MARQ: (*rising*) You are insolent – you forget that I am a lady.

ESTHER: You forget that I am a mother. (*Places dress in box.*) Do you dare to offer to buy my child – *his* breathing image, *his* living memory – with money? (*Crosses to door, and throws it open.*) There is the door – go! (*Picture.*)

ECCLES: (*to* MARQUISE, *who has risen, aside*) Very sorry, my lady, as you should be tret in this way, which was not my wishes.

MARQ: Silence! (ECCLES *retreats, putting back chair,* MARQUISE *goes up stage to door.*) Mrs D'Alroy, if anything could have increased my sorrow for the wretched marriage my poor son was *decoyed* into, it would be your conduct this day to his mother. (*Exit.*)

ESTHER: (*falling in* POLLY*'s arms*) Oh, Polly! Polly!

ECCLES: (*looking after* MARQUISE) To go away, and not to leave a sov. behind her! (*running up to open door*) Cat! Cat! Stingy old cat! (*Almost runs to fire, sits, and pokes it violently; carriage wheels heard without.*)

ESTHER: I'll go to my room and lie down. Let me have the baby, or that old woman may come back and steal him.

(*Exit* ESTHER, *and* POLLY *follows with the baby.*)

ECCLES: Well, women is the obstinatest devils as never wore horse-shoes. (*striking table*) Children? Beasts! Beasts!

(*Enter* SAM *and* POLLY.)

SAM: Come along, Polly, and let's get it over at once. (SAM *places cap on piano and goes to right of table.* POLLY *takes bandbox from table, and places it up stage.*) Now, Mr Eccles, (ECCLES *turns suddenly, facing* SAM.) since you've been talkin' on family matters, I'd like to 'ave a word with yer, so take this opportunity to –

ECCLES: (*waving his hand grandly*) Take what you like, and then order more.

---

go to my room: for the problems connected with this location, see p. 37 above.

(*rising, and leaning over table*) Samuel Gerridge, that hand is a hand that never turned its back on a friend, or a bottle to give him. (*Sings, front of table*)

'I'll stand by my friend,
I'll stand by my friend,
I'll stand by my friend,
If he'll stand to me' – me, genelmen!

SAM: Well, Mr Eccles, sir, it's this –

POLLY: (*aside, coming down*) Don't tell him too sudden, Sam – it might shock his feelings.

SAM: It's this: yer know that for the last four years I've been keepin' company with Mary – Polly (*turning to her and smiling*).

(ECCLES *drops into chair as if shot.*)

ECCLES: Go it! Go it! Strike home, young man! Strike on this grey head! (*Sings*) 'Britons, strike home!' Here (*tapping his chest*), to my heart! Don't spare me. Have a go at my grey hairs. Pull 'em – pull 'em out! A long pull, and a strong pull, and a pull all together! (*Cries, and drops his face on arm, upon table.*)

POLLY: There – I told you so. Oh, father! I wouldn't hurt your feelings for the world (*patting his head*).

SAM: No; Mr Eccles, I don't want to 'urt your feelin's, but I'm a-goin' to enter upon a business. Here's a circ'lar (*offering one*).

ECCLES: (*indignantly*) Circ'lars. What are circ'lars compared to a father's feelings?

SAM: And I want Polly to name the day, sir, and so I ask you –

ECCLES: This is 'ard, this is 'ard. One of my gals marries a soger. The other goes a-gasfitting.

SAM: (*annoyed*) The business which will enable me to maintain a wife is that of the late Mr Binks, plumber, glazier, etc.

ECCLES: (*Rising, sings. Air, 'Lost Rosabelle'.*)

'They have given thee to a plumber,
They have broken every vow,
They have given thee to a plumber,
And my heart, my heart is breaking now.'
(*Drops into chair again.*) Now, genelmen!

(SAM *thrusts circulars into his pocket, and turns away angrily.*)

POLLY: You know, father, you can come and see me. (*Leans over him.*)

SAM: (*sotto voce*) No, no. (*Motions to* POLLY.)

ECCLES: (*looking up*) So I can, and that's a comfort. (*shaking her hand*) And you can come and see me, and that's a comfort. I'll come and see you often – very often – every day (SAM *turns up stage in horror.*), and crack a fatherly bottle (*rising*) and shed a friendly tear. (*Wipes eyes with dirty pocket-handkerchief, which he pulls from breast pocket.*)

POLLY: Do, father, do. (*Goes up and gets tea-tray.*)

'I'll stand by my friend': see appendix II.
'Britons, strike home'; A long pull, etc.: see appendix II.
'Lost Rosabelle'; 'They have given thee' etc.: see appendix II.

SAM: (*with a gulp*) Yes, Mr Eccles, do. (*Goes to* POLLY *and gesticulates behind tray.*)

ECCLES: I will. And this it is to be a father. I would part with any of my children for their own good, readily – if I was paid for it. (*Sings*) 'For I know that the angels are whispering to me' – me, genelmen! (POLLY *gets tea-things.*)

SAM: I'll try and make Polly a good husband, and anything I can do to prove it (*lowering his voice*), in the way of spirituous liquors and tobacco (*slipping coin into his hand, unseen by* POLLY) shall be done.

ECCLES: (*lightening up and placing his left hand on* SAM*'s head*)

'Be kind to thy father,
Wherever you be,
For he is a blessing
And credit to thee' – thee, genelmen.

Well, my children – bless you, take the blessing of a grey 'air'd father. (POLLY *looking from one to the other*) Samuel Gerridge, she shall be thine (*mock heroically, looking at money*). You shall be his wife (*looking at* POLLY), and you (*looking at* SAM), shall be her husband – for for a husband I know no fitter – no 'gas fitter' man. (*Runs to piano and takes hat; goes to door, looks comically pathetic at* SAM *and* POLLY, *puts on hat and comes towards centre.*) I've a friend waiting for me round the corner, which I want to have a word with; and may you never know how much more sharper than a serpent's tooth it is to have a marriageable daughter. (*Sings*)

'When I heard she was married
    I breathed not a tone,
The h'eyes of all round me
    Was fixed on my h'own;
I flew to my chamber
    To hide my despair,
I tore the bright circlet
    Of gems from my hair.
When I heard she was married,
    When I heard she was married – '

(*Breaks down. Exit.*) (*without*) Married, genelmen!

POLLY: (*drying her eyes*) There, Sam. I always told you that though father had his faults, his heart was in the right place.

SAM: Poor Polly. (*Crosses to fireplace. Knock at door.*)

POLLY: (*top of table*) Come in!

(*Enter* HAWTREE.)

POLLY: Major Hawtree! (SAM *turns away as they shake hands.*)

'For I know that the angels', etc.: see appendix II.
'Be kind to thy father', etc.: see appendix II.
how much more sharper: cf. note on p. 166 above.
'When I heard she was married', etc.: see appendix II.
[*ECCLES*] *Exit*: 'This exit was afterwards abandoned with the author's permission, being somewhat of an anti-climax. The Exit is usually made at the words "marriageable daughter", Eccles breaking down in a comically hysterical manner and going out quickly' PDW.

HAWTREE: I met the Marquise's carriage on the bridge. Has she been here?

(SAM *at fire, with back to it.*)

POLLY: Yes.

HAWTREE: What happened?

POLLY: Oh, she wanted to take away the child.

SAM: In the coach. (POLLY *sets tea-things.*)

HAWTREE: And what did Mrs D'Alroy say to that?

SAM: Mrs D'Alroy said that she'd see her blow'd first! (POLLY *pushes* SAM.) – or words to that effect.

HAWTREE: I'm sorry to hear this; I had hoped – however that's over.

POLLY: (*sitting*) Yes, it's over; and I hope we shall hear no more about it. Want to take away the child, indeed – like her impudence! What next! (*getting ready tea-things*) Esther's gone to lie down. I shan't wake her up for tea, though she's had nothing to eat all day.

SAM: Shall I fetch some shrimps?

POLLY: No. What made you think of shrimps?

SAM: They're a relish, and consolin' – at least I always found 'em so. (*Check lights, gradually.*)

POLLY: (*sentimentally*) Sam, when we're married, what shall you give me to console me?

SAM: (*after reflection*) Winkles.

POLLY: Oh!

SAM: And I'd extract 'em for you myself.

(SAM *and* POLLY *sit at table.*)

POLLY: I won't ask you to take tea with us, Major – you're too grand.

(SAM *motions approbation to* POLLY, *not wanting* HAWTREE *to remain.*)

HAWTREE: (*placing hat on piano*) Not at all. I shall be most happy. (*aside*) 'Pon my word, these are very good sort of people. I'd no idea –

SAM: (*points to* HAWTREE) He's a-going to stop to tea – well, I ain't. (*Goes up to window and sits.* HAWTREE *crosses and sits right of table.*)

POLLY: Sam! Sam! (*pause – he says* 'Eh?') Pull down the blind and light the gas.

SAM: No, don't light up; I like this sort of dusk. It's unbusiness-like, but pleasant. (*Puts his arm around her waist.*)

(SAM *cuts enormous slice of bread, and hands it on point of knife to* HAWTREE. *Cuts small lump of butter, and hands it on point of knife to* HAWTREE, *who looks at it through eye-glass, then takes it.* SAM *then helps himself.* POLLY *meantime has poured out tea in two cups, and one saucer for* SAM, *sugars them, and then hands cup and saucer to* HAWTREE, *who has both hands full. He takes it awkwardly, and places it on table.* POLLY, *having only one spoon, tastes* SAM*'s tea, then stirs* HAWTREE*'s, attracting his attention by so doing. He looks into his teacup.* POLLY *stirs her own tea, and drops spoon into* HAWTREE*'s cup, causing it to spurt in his eye. He drops eye-glass and wipes his eyes.*)

POLLY: (*making tea*) Sugar, Sam! (SAM *takes tea and sits facing fire.*) Oh, there isn't any milk – it'll be here directly – it's just his time.

VOICE: (*outside; rattle of milk-pails*) Mia-oow!

POLLY: There he is. (*Knock at door.*) Oh, I know; I owe him fourpence. (*feeling her pockets*) Sam, have you got fourpence? (*Knock again, louder.*)

SAM: No (*his mouth full*) – I ain't got no fourpence.

POLLY: He's very impatient. Come in!

(*Enter* GEORGE, *his face bronzed, and in full health. He carries a milk-can in his hand, which, after putting his hat on the piano, he places on table.*)

GEORGE: A fella hung this on the railings, so I brought it in.

(POLLY *sees him, and gradually sinks down under the table. Then* SAM, *with his mouth full, and bread and butter in his hand, does the same.* HAWTREE *pushes himself back a space, in chair, remains motionless.* GEORGE *astonished. Picture.*)

GEORGE: What's the matter with you?

HAWTREE: (*rising*) George!

GEORGE: Hawtree! You here?

POLLY: (*under table*) O-o-o-o- oh! The ghost! – The ghost!

SAM: It shan't hurt you, Polly. Perhaps it's only indigestion.

HAWTREE: Then you're not dead?

GEORGE: Dead, no. Where's my wife?

HAWTREE: You were reported killed.

GEORGE: It wasn't true.

HAWTREE: Alive! My old friend alive!

GEORGE: And well. (*Shakes hands.*) Landed this morning. Where's my wife?

SAM: (*who has popped his head from under tablecloth*) He ain't dead, Poll – he's alive! (POLLY *rises from under table slowly.*)

POLLY: (*pause; approaches him, touches him, retreats*) George! (*He nods.*) George! George!

GEORGE: Yes! Yes!

POLLY: Alive! – My dear George! – Oh, my dear brother! (*looking at him intensely*) – Alive! – (*going to him*) Oh, my dear, dear, brother! – (*in his arms*) – How could you go and do so? (*Laughs hysterically.*)

(GEORGE *places* POLLY *in his arms.* SAM *goes to* POLLY. SAM *kisses* POLLY*'s hand violently.* HAWTREE *comes up, stares – business.* SAM *goes left with a stamp of his foot.*)

GEORGE: Where's Esther?

HAWTREE: Here – in this house.

GEORGE: Here! – Doesn't she know I'm back?

POLLY: No; how should she?

GEORGE: (*to* HAWTREE) Didn't you get my telegram?

HAWTREE: No; where from?

GEORGE: Southampton! I sent it to the club.

HAWTREE: I haven't been there these three days.

Mia-oow!: not (of course) a cat-imitation, but a rendering of 'Milk-o!'

POLLY: (*hysterically*) Oh, my dear, dear, dear dead-and-gone! – Come back all alive oh, brother George! (GEORGE *passes her down stage.*)

SAM: Glad to see yer, sir.

GEORGE: Thank you, Gerridge. (*Shakes hands.*) Same to you – but Esther?

POLLY: (*back to audience, handkerchief to eyes*) She's asleep in her room.

(GEORGE *is going to door;* POLLY *stops him.*)

POLLY: You mustn't see her!

GEORGE: Not see her! – After this long absence? – Why not?

HAWTREE: She's ill today. She has been greatly excited. The news of your death, which we all mourned, has shaken her terribly.

GEORGE: Poor girl! Poor girl!

POLLY: Oh, we all cried so when you died! – (*crying*) – And now you're alive again, I want to cry ever so much more! (*crying*)

HAWTREE: We must break the news to her gently and by degrees. (*Crosses to fire, taking his tea with him.*)

SAM: Yes. If you turn the tap on to full pressure, she'll explode!

(SAM *turns to* HAWTREE, *who is just raising cup to his lips and brings it down on saucer with a bang; both annoyed.*)

GEORGE: To return, and not to be able to see her – to love her – to kiss her! (*Stamps.*)

POLLY: Hush!

GEORGE: I forgot! I shall wake her!

POLLY: More than that – you'll wake the baby!

GEORGE: Baby! – What baby?

POLLY: Yours.

GEORGE: Mine? – Mine?

POLLY: Yes – yours and Esther's! Why, didn't you know there was a baby?

GEORGE: No!

POLLY: La! The ignorance of these men!

HAWTREE: Yes, George, you're a father (*at fireplace*).

GEORGE: Why wasn't I told of this? Why didn't you write?

POLLY: How could we when you were dead?

SAM: And 'adn't left your address. (*Looks at* HAWTREE, *who turns away quickly.*)

GEORGE: If I can't see Esther, I will see the child. The sight of me won't be too much for its nerves. Where is it?

POLLY: Sleeping in its mother's arms. (GEORGE *goes to door; she intercepts him.*) Please not! Please not!

GEORGE: I must. I will.

POLLY: It might kill her, and you wouldn't like to do that. I'll fetch the baby; but oh, please don't make a noise. You won't make a noise – you'll be as quiet as you can, won't you? Oh! I can't believe it. (*Exit* POLLY.)

(SAM *dances break-down and finishes up looking at* HAWTREE *who*

---

break-down: a vigorous dance popular at this period, performed in the presumed style of American negroes.

turns away astonished. SAM *is disconcerted; sits on chair.* GEORGE *at door.*)

GEORGE: My baby – my ba – It's a dream! You've seen it. (*to* SAM) What's it like?

SAM: Oh! It's like a – like a sort of – infant – white and – milky, and all that.

(*Enter* POLLY *with baby wrapped in shawls.* GEORGE *shuts door and meets her.*)

POLLY: Gently, gently – take care! (*giving child to him*) Esther will hardly have it touched. (SAM *rises and gets near to* GEORGE.)

GEORGE: But I'm its father!

POLLY: That don't matter. She's very particular.

GEORGE: Boy or girl?

POLLY: Guess.

GEORGE: Boy! (POLLY *nods.* GEORGE *proud.*) What's his name?

POLLY: Guess.

GEORGE: George? (POLLY *nods.*) Eustace? (POLLY *nods.*) Fairfax? Algernon? (POLLY *nods; pause*) My names!

SAM: (*to* GEORGE) You'd 'ardly think there was room enough in 'im to 'old so many names, would yer?

(HAWTREE *looks at him – turns to fire.* SAM *disconcerted again; sits.*)

GEORGE: To come back all the way from India to find that I'm dead, and that you're alive. To find my wife a widow with a new love aged – how old are you? I'll buy you a pony tomorrow, my brave little boy! What's his weight? I should say two pound nothing. My – baby – my – boy! (*Bends over him and kisses him.*) Take him away, Polly, for fear I should break him.

(POLLY *takes child, and places it in cradle.*)

HAWTREE: (*Crosses to piano. Passes* SAM *front – stares – business.* SAM *goes round to fireplace, flings down bread and butter in a rage and drinks his tea out of saucer.*) But tell us how it is you're back? – how you escaped? (*leaning up against piano*)

GEORGE: By-and-by. Too long a story just now. Tell *me* all about it. (POLLY *gives him chair.*) How is it Esther's living here?

POLLY: She came back after the baby was born, and the furniture was sold up.

GEORGE: Sold up? What furniture?

POLLY: That you bought for her.

HAWTREE: It couldn't be helped, George – Mrs D'Alroy was so poor.

GEORGE: Poor! But I left her £600 to put in the bank!

HAWTREE: We *must* tell you. She gave it to her father, who banked it in his own name.

SAM: And lost it in bettin' – every copper.

GEORGE: Then she's been in want?

Fairfax: Ensign Fairfax Daubray is the hero of 'The Poor-Rate Unfolds a Tale'.

POLLY: No – not in want. Friends lent her money.

GEORGE: (*seated*) What friends? (*pause; he looks at* POLLY, *who indicates* HAWTREE.) You?

POLLY: Yes.

GEORGE: (*rising, and shaking* HAWTREE*'s hand*) Thank you, old fella. (HAWTREE *droops his head.*)

SAM: (*aside*) Now who'd ha' thought that long swell 'ad it in 'im? 'E never mentioned it.

GEORGE: So Papa Eccles had the money? (*sitting again*)

SAM: And blued it! (*Sits on corner of table.*)

POLLY: (*pleadingly*) You see, father was very unlucky on the racecourse. He told us that if it hadn't been that all his calculations were upset by a horse winning who had no business to, he should have made our fortunes. Father's been unlucky, and he gets tipsy at times, but he's a very clever man, if you only give him scope enough.

SAM: I'd give 'im scope enough!

GEORGE: Where is he now?

SAM: Public house.

GEORGE: And how is he?

SAM: Drunk!

(POLLY *pushes him off table,* SAM *sits at fireplace.*)

GEORGE: (*to* HAWTREE) You were right. There is '*something*' in caste. (*aloud*) But tell us all about it. (*Sits.*)

POLLY: Well, you know, you went away; and then the baby was born. Oh! He was such a sweet little thing, just like – your eyes – your hair.

GEORGE: Cut that!

POLLY: Well, baby came; and when baby was six days old, your letter came, Major (*to* HAWTREE). I saw that it was from India, and that it wasn't in your hand (*to* GEORGE); I guessed what was inside it, so I opened it unknown to her, and I read there of your capture and death. I daren't tell her. I went to father to ask his advice, but he was too tipsy to understand me. Sam fetched the doctor. He told us that the news would kill her. When she woke up, she said she had dreamt there was a letter from you. I told her, No; and day after day she asked for a letter. So the doctor advised us to write one as if it came from you. So we did. Sam and I – and the doctor told her – told Esther, I mean, that her eyes were bad, and she mustn't read, and we read our letter to her; didn't we, Sam? But, bless you! She always knew it hadn't come from you! At last, when she was stronger, we told her all.

GEORGE: (*after a pause*) How did she take it?

POLLY: She pressed the baby in her arms, and turned her face to the wall. (*a pause*) Well, to make a long story short, when she got up, she found that father had lost all the money you left her. There was a dreadful scene between them. She told him he'd robbed her and her child, and father left the house, and swore he'd never come back again.

SAM: Don't be alarmed – 'e did come back (*sitting by fire*).

POLLY: Oh, yes; he was too good-hearted to stop long from his children. He has his faults, but his good points, when you find 'em, are wonderful!

SAM: Yes, when you find 'em! (*Rises, gets bread and butter from table, and sits left corner of table.*)

POLLY: So she had to come back here to us; and that's all.

GEORGE: Why didn't she write to my mother?

POLLY: Father wanted her – oh, he's full of thought for us – but she was too proud – she said she'd die first.

GEORGE: (*rising, to* HAWTREE) There's a woman! Caste's all humbug. (*Sees sword over mantelpiece.*) That's my sword, and a map of India, and that's the piano I bought her – I'll swear to the silk!

POLLY: Yes; that was bought in at the sale.

GEORGE: (*to* HAWTREE) Thank ye, old fella!

HAWTREE: Not by me; I was in India at the time.

GEORGE: By whom then?

POLLY: By Sam. (SAM *winks to her to discontinue.*) I shall! He knew Esther was breaking her heart about anyone else having it, so he took the money he's saved up for our wedding, and we're going to be married now – ain't we, Sam?

SAM: (*rushing to* GEORGE *and pulling out circulars from pocket*) And hope by constant attention to business to merit – (POLLY *pushes him away.*)

POLLY: She's never touched it since you died – it's been as silent as a coffin, but if I don't play it tonight, may I die an old maid! (*Goes up stage.*)

(GEORGE *crosses to* SAM, *and shakes his hand, then goes up stage, pulls up blind, and looks into street.* SAM *turns up and meets* POLLY *top of table.*)

HAWTREE: (*aside*) Now who'd have thought that little cad had it in him? He never mentioned it. (*aloud*) Apropos, George, your mother – I'll go to the square, and tell her of – (*Takes hat from piano.*)

GEORGE: Is she in town? (*at cradle*)

HAWTREE: Yes. Will you come with me?

GEORGE: And leave my wife? – and such a wife!

HAWTREE: I'll go at once. I shall catch her before dinner. Goodbye, old fellow. Seeing you back again, alive and well, makes me feel quite – that I quite feel – (*Shakes* GEORGE*'s hand. Goes to door, then crosses to* SAM, *who has turned* POLLY*'s tea into his saucer, and is just about to drink; seeing* HAWTREE, *he puts it down quickly, and turns his back.*) Mr Gerridge, I fear I have often made myself very offensive to you.

SAM: Well, sir, yer 'ave!

HAWTREE: (*at bottom of table*) I feared so. I didn't know you then. I beg your pardon. Let me ask you to shake hands – to forgive me, and forget it. (*offering his hand*)

SAM: (*taking it*) Say no more, sir; and if ever I've made myself offensive to you, forget it, and forgive me. (*They shake hands warmly; as* HAWTREE *crosses to door, recovering from* SAM*'s hearty shake of the hand,* SAM *runs to him.*) Hi, sir! When yer marry that young lady as I know you're engaged to, if you

---

the silk: the facing on the piano front.

should furnish a house, and require anything in my way – (*Bringing out circular; begins to read it.* POLLY *comes down stage, and pushes* SAM *away, against* HAWTREE. SAM *goes and sits in low chair by fireplace, down stage, disconcerted, cramming circulars into his pocket.*)

HAWTREE: Goodbye, George, for the present. (*at door*) 'Bye, Polly. (*Resumes his Pall Mall manner as he goes out.*) I'm off to the square. (*Exit.*)

GEORGE: (*at cradle*) But Esther?

POLLY: Oh, I forgot all about Esther. I'll tell her all about it.

GEORGE: How? (*by door*)

POLLY: I don't know; but it will come. Providence will send it to me, as it has sent you, my dear brother. (*embracing him*) You don't know how glad I am to see you back again! You must go. (*pushing him.* GEORGE *takes hat off piano.*) Esther will be getting up directly. (*at door with* GEORGE, *who looks through keyhole*) It's no use looking there; it's dark.

GEORGE: (*at door*) It isn't often a man can see his own widow.

POLLY: And it isn't often that he wants to! Now, you must go (*pushing him off*).

GEORGE: I shall stop outside.

SAM: And I'll whistle for you when you may come in.

POLLY: Now – hush!

GEORGE: (*opening door wide*) Oh, my Esther, when you know I'm alive! I'll marry you all over again, and we'll have a second honeymoon, my darling. (*Exit.*)

POLLY: Oh, Sam! Sam! (*Commences to sing and dance.* SAM *also dances; they meet in centre of stage, join hands, and dance around two or three times.*) Oh, Sam, I'm so excited. I don't know what to do. What shall I do – what shall I do?

SAM: (*taking up* HAWTREE*'s bread and butter*) 'Ave a bit of bread and butter, Polly.

POLLY: Now, Sam, light the gas; I'm going to wake her up. (*opening door*) Oh, my darling, if I dare tell you! (*whispering*) He's come back! He's come back! He's come back! Alive! Alive! Alive! Sam, kiss me! (SAM *rushes to* POLLY, *kisses her, and she jumps off,* SAM *shutting the door.*)

SAM: (*dances shutter dance.*) I'm glad the swells are gone; now I can open my safety valve and let my feelin's escape. To think of 'is comin' back alive from India, just as I am goin' to open my shop. Perhaps he'll get me the patronage of the Royal Family. It would look stunnin' over the door, a lion and a unicorn a-standin' on their 'ind legs, doin' nothin' furiously, with a lozenge between 'em – thus. (*Seizes plate on table, puts his left foot on chair right of table, and imitates the picture of the Royal arms.*) Polly said I was to light up, and whatever Polly says must be done. (*Lights brackets over mantelpiece, then candles; as he lights the broken one, says*) Why, this one is for all the world like old Eccles! (*Places candles on piano, and sits on music-stool.*) Poor

---

Pall Mall manner: i.e. a very 'correct' and dignified bearing.
shutter dance: appears to correspond to the 'cellar flap' dance, performed for greater resonance over the trap-door in a public house.

Esther! To think of my knowin' 'er when she was in the ballet line – then in the 'onourable line; then a mother – no, *h*onourables is 'mammas' – then a widow, and then in the ballet line again! – And 'im to come back (*growing affected*) – and find a baby, with all 'is furniture and fittin's ready for immediate use (*Crossing back of table during last few lines, sits in chair left of table.*) – and she, poor thing, lyin' asleep, with 'er eye-lids 'ot and swollen, not knowin' that that great, big, 'eavy, 'ulking, overgrown dragoon is prowlin' outside, ready to fly at 'er lips, and strangle 'er in 'is strong, lovin' arms – it – it – it – (*Breaks down and sobs with his head upon the table.*)

(*Enter* POLLY *with a light-coloured dress on.*)

POLLY: Why, Sam! What's the matter?

SAM: (*rises and crosses*) I dunno. The water's got in my meter.

POLLY: Hush! Here's Esther.

(*Enter* ESTHER. *They stop suddenly.*)

ESTHER: Is tea ready?

SAM: (*singing and dancing*) Tiddy-ti-tum', etc.

ESTHER: (*sitting near fire, left of head of table, taking up costume and beginning to work*) Sam, you seem in high spirits tonight?

SAM: Yes; yer see Polly and I are goin' to be married – and – and 'opes by bestowing a merit – to continue the favour –

POLLY: (*who has kissed* ESTHER *two or three times*) What are you talking about?

SAM: I don't know – I'm off my burner. (*Brings music-stool centre,* POLLY *goes round to chair facing* ESTHER.)

ESTHER: What's the matter with you tonight, dear? (*to* POLLY) I can see something in your eyes.

SAM: P'r'aps it's the new furniture! (*Sits on music-stool.*)

ESTHER: Will you help me with the dress, Polly?

(*They sit,* ESTHER *upper end, back of table,* POLLY *facing her, at lower end.*)

POLLY: It was a pretty dress when it was new – not unlike the one Mademoiselle Delphine used to wear. (*suddenly clapping her hands*) Oh!

ESTHER: What's the matter?

POLLY: A needle! (*Crosses to* SAM, *who examines* [*her*] *finger. Aside*) I've got it!

SAM: What – the needle – in your finger?

POLLY: No; an idea in my head!

SAM: (*still looking at finger*) Does it 'urt?

POLLY: Stupid! (SAM *still sitting on stool. Aloud*) Do you recollect Mademoiselle Delphine, Esther?

ESTHER: Yes.

POLLY: Do you recollect her in that ballet that old Herr Griffenhaagen arranged? – 'Jeanne la Folle, or, the Return of the Soldier'?

ESTHER: Yes; will you do the fresh hem?

---

with a light-coloured dress on: this significant detail occurs only in AE (see p. 38 above).
off my burner: an image taken from Sam's trade, as a gasman.

POLLY: What's the use? Let me see – how did it go? How well I remember the scene! – The cottage was on that side, the bridge at the back – then ballet of villagers, and the entrance of Delphine as Jeanne, the bride, – tra-lal-lala-lala-la-la. (*Sings and pantomimes,* SAM *imitating her.*) Then the entrance of Claude, the bridegroom – (*to* SAM, *imitating swell*) How-de-do, how-de-do?

SAM: (*rising*) 'Ow are yer? (*imitating* POLLY, *then sitting again*)

POLLY: There was the procession to church – the march of the soldiers over the bridge – (*Sings and pantomimes.*) – arrest of Claude, who is drawn for the conscription (*Business;* ESTHER *looks dreamily.*), and is torn from the arms of his bride, at the church porch. *Omnes* broken-hearted. This is *Omnes* broken-hearted. (*Pantomimes.*)

ESTHER: Polly, I don't like this; it brings back memories.

POLLY: (*going to table, and leaning her hands on it, looks over at* ESTHER) Oh, fuss about memories! – One can't mourn for ever. (ESTHER *surprised*) Everything in this world isn't sad. There's bad news, and – and there's good news sometimes – when we least expect it.

ESTHER: Ah! Not for me.

POLLY: Why not?

ESTHER: (*anxiously*) Polly!

POLLY: Second act! (*This to be said quickly, startling* SAM, *who has been looking on the ground during the last four or five lines.*) Winter – the Village Pump. This is the village pump. (*pointing to* SAM, *seated by piano, on music-stool.* SAM *turns round on music-stool, disgusted.*) Entrance of Jeanne – now called Jeanne la Folle, because she has gone mad. This is Jeanne gone mad. (*Pantomimes.*) Gone mad on account of the supposed loss of her husband.

SAM: The supposed loss?

POLLY: The supposed loss!

ESTHER: (*dropping costume*) Polly!

SAM: Mind! (*aside to* POLLY)

POLLY: Can't stop now! Entrance of Claude, *who isn't dead*, in a captain's uniform – a cloak thrown over his shoulders.

ESTHER: Not dead?

POLLY: Don't you remember the ballet? Jeanne is mad, and can't recognise her husband; and don't, till he shows her the ribbon she gave him when they were betrothed! A bit of ribbon! Sam, have you got a bit of ribbon? Oh, that crape sword-knot, that will do! (SAM *astonished*)

ESTHER: Touch that! (*rising, and coming down stage*)

POLLY: Why not? – It's no use *now*!

ESTHER: (*slowly, looking into* POLLY*'s eyes*) You have heard of George – I know you have – I see it in your eyes. You may tell me – I can bear it – I can indeed – indeed I can. Tell me – he is not dead? (*violently agitated*)

POLLY: No!

ESTHER: No?

POLLY: No!

ESTHER: (*whispers*) Thank heaven! (SAM *turns on stool, back to audience.*) You've seen him – I see you have! – I know it! – I feel it! I had a bright and happy dream – I saw him as I slept! Oh, let me know if he is near! Give me some sign – some sound – (POLLY *opens piano.*) – some token of his life and presence!

(SAM *touches* POLLY *on the shoulder, takes hat, and exits. All to be done very quickly.* POLLY *sits immediately at piano and plays air softly – the same air played by* ESTHER *act II, on the treble only.*)

ESTHER: (*in an ecstasy*) Oh, my husband! Come to me! For I know that you are near! Let me feel your arms clasp round me! – Do not fear for me! – I can bear the sight of you! – (*Door opens showing* SAM *keeping* GEORGE *back.*) – It will not kill me! – George – love – husband – come, oh, come to me!

(GEORGE *breaks away from* SAM, *and coming down behind* ESTHER *places his hands over her eyes; she gives a faint scream, and turning, falls in his arms.* POLLY *plays the bass as well as the treble of the air, forte, then fortissimo. She then plays at random, endeavouring to hide her tears. At last strikes piano wildly, and goes off into a fit of hysterical laughter, to the alarm of* SAM, *who, rushing down as* POLLY *cries 'Sam! Sam!' falls on his knees in front of her. They embrace,* POLLY *pushing him contemptuously away afterwards.* GEORGE *gets chair, sits, and* ESTHER *kneels at his feet – he snatches off* ESTHER*'s cap and throws it up stage.* POLLY *goes left of* GEORGE, SAM *brings music-stool, and she sits.*)

ESTHER: To see you here again – to feel your warm breath upon my cheek – is it real, or am I dreaming?

SAM: (*rubbing his head*) No; it's real.

ESTHER: (*embracing* GEORGE) My darling!

SAM: My darling! (POLLY *on music-stool, which* SAM *has placed for her.* SAM, *kneeling by her, imitates* ESTHER – POLLY *scornfully pushes him away.*)

ESTHER: But tell us – tell us how you escaped.

GEORGE: It's a long story; but I'll condense it. I was riding out, and suddenly found myself surrounded and taken prisoner. One of the troop that took me was a fella who had been my servant, and to whom I had done some little kindness. He helped me to escape, and hid me in a sort of cave, and for a long time used to bring me food. Unfortunately, he was ordered away; so he brought another Sepoy to look after me. I felt from the first this man meant to betray me, and I watched him like a lynx during the one day he was with me. As evening drew on, a Sepoy picket was passing. I could tell by the look in the fella's eyes, he meant to call out as soon as they were near enough; so I seized him by the throat, and shook the life out of him.

ESTHER: You strangled him?

GEORGE: Yes.

ESTHER: Killed him – dead?

GEORGE: He didn't get up again. (*Embraces* ESTHER.)

POLLY: (*to* SAM) You never go and kill Sepoys. (*Pushes him over.*)

SAM: No! I pay rates and taxes.

Esther's cap: as worn by widows of the period.

GEORGE: The day after, Havelock and his Scotchmen marched through the village, and I turned out to meet them. I was too done up to join, so I was sent straight on to Calcutta. I got leave, took a berth on the P and O boat; the passage restored me. I landed this morning, came on here, and brought in the milk.

(*Enter the* MARQUISE, *she rushes to embrace* GEORGE. *All rise,* SAM *putting piano-stool back.*)

MARQ: My dear boy! – My dear, dear boy!

POLLY: Why, see, she's crying! She's glad to see him alive, and back again.

SAM: (*profoundly*) Well! There's always some good in women, even when they're ladies. (*Goes to window.*)

(POLLY *puts dress in box, and goes to cradle, then beside* SAM.)

MARQ: (*crossing to* ESTHER) My dear daughter, we must forget our little differences. (*kissing her*) Won't you? and you'll let me present this hood and mantle to my darling grandson, won't you? How history repeats itself! You will find a similar and as unexpected a return mentioned by Froissart in the chapter that treats of Philip Dartnell –

GEORGE: Yes, mother – I remember. (*Kisses her.*)

MARQ: (*to* GEORGE, *aside*) We must take her abroad, and make a lady of her.

GEORGE: Can't, mamma – she's ready-made. Nature has done it to our hands.

MARQ: (*aside, to* GEORGE) But I won't have the man who smells of putty (SAM *business at back. He is listening, and at the word 'putty' throws his cap irritably on table.* POLLY *pacifies him, and makes him sit down beside her on window seat.*) nor the man who smells of beer. (*Goes to* ESTHER, *who offers her chair, and sits in chair opposite to her.* MARQUISE *back to audience,* ESTHER *facing audience.*)

(*Enter* HAWTREE, *pale.*)

HAWTREE: George! Oh, the Marchioness is here.

GEORGE: What's the matter?

HAWTREE: Oh, nothing. Yes, there is. I don't mind telling you. I've been thrown. I called at my chambers as I came along and found this. (*Gives* GEORGE *a note; sits on music-stool.*)

GEORGE: From the Countess, Lady Florence's mother. (*Reads*) 'Dear Major Hawtree, – I hasten to inform you that my daughter Florence is about to enter into an alliance with Lord Saxeby, the eldest son of the Marquis of Loamshire. Under these circumstances, should you think fit to call here again, I feel assured – ' Well, perhaps it's for the best. (*returning letter*) Caste! You know. Caste! And a marquis is a bigger swell than a major.

Havelock: General Sir Henry Havelock (1795–1857), active in suppressing the Indian Mutiny, entered and held Lucknow until the arrival of Lord Colin Campbell on 6 November 1857, dying fifteen days later.

P and O: the Peninsular and Oriental Steam Navigation Company, owners of the famous and extensive fleet of passenger liners plying between Britain and the East.

HAWTREE: Yes, best to marry in your own rank of life.

GEORGE: If you can find *the* girl. But if ever you find *the* girl, marry her. As to her station –

'True hearts are more than coronets,
And simple faith than Norman blood.'

HAWTREE: Ya–as. But a gentleman should hardly ally himself to a nobody.

GEORGE: My dear fella, Nobody's a mistake – he don't exist. Nobody's nobody! Everybody's somebody.

HAWTREE: Yes. But still – caste.

GEORGE: Oh, caste's all right. Caste is a good thing if it's not carried too far. It shuts the door on the pretentious and the vulgar: but it should open the door very wide for exceptional merit. Let brains break through its barriers, and what brains can break through love may leap over.

HAWTREE: Yes. Why George, you're quite inspired – quite an orator. What makes you so brilliant? Your captivity? The voyage? What then?

GEORGE: I'm in love with my wife!

(*Enter* ECCLES, *drunk, a bottle of gin in his hand.*)

ECCLES: (*crossing to centre*) Bless this 'appy company. May we 'ave in our arms what we love in our 'earts. (*Goes to head of table.* ESTHER *goes to cradle, back to audience.* POLLY *and* SAM *half amused, half angry.* MARQUISE *still sitting in chair, back to audience.* HAWTREE *facing* ECCLES. GEORGE *up stage leaning on piano in disgust.*) Polly, fetch wine-glasses – a tumbler will do for me. Let us drink a toast. Mr Chairman, (*to* MARQUISE) ladies, and gentlemen – I beg to propose the 'elth of our newly returned warrior, *my son-in-law.* (MARQUISE *shivers.*) The Right Honourable George De Alroy. Get glasses, Polly, and send for a bottle of sherry wine for my ladyship. *My* ladyship! My ladyship! M'lad'ship. (*She half turns to him.*) You and me'll have a drain together on the quiet. So delighted to see you under these altered circum – circum – circum – stangate.

(POLLY, *who has shaken her head at him to desist, in vain, very distressed.*)

SAM: Shove 'is 'ead in a bucket! (*Exit, in disgust.*)

HAWTREE: (*aside to* GEORGE) I think I can abate this nuisance – at least, I can remove it. (*Rises and crosses to* ECCLES, *who has got round to right side of table, leaning on it. He taps* ECCLES *with his stick, first on right shoulder, then on left, and finally sharply on right.* ECCLES *turns round and falls on point of stick –* HAWTREE *steadying him.* GEORGE *crosses behind, to* MARQUISE, *who has gone to cradle – puts his arm round* ESTHER *and takes her to mantelpiece.*) Mr Eccles, don't you think that, with your talent for liquor, if you had an allowance of about two pounds a week, and went to Jersey, where spirits are cheap, that you could drink yourself to death in a year?

ECCLES: I think I could – I'm sure I'll try. (*Goes up left of table, steadying himself by it, and sits in chair by fire, with the bottle of gin.*)

(HAWTREE *standing by fire.* ESTHER *and* POLLY *stand embracing. As they turn away from each other –*)

ESTHER: (*aside*) And she will live in a back room, behind a shop. Well – I hope she will be happy.

POLLY: (*aside*) And she will live in a fine house – and have a carriage – and be a lady. Well – I hope she will be happy.

GEORGE: (*coming across with* ESTHER) Come and play me that air that used to ring in my ears as I lay awake, night after night, captive in the cave – you know. (*He hands* ESTHER *to the piano. She plays the air.*)

MARQ: (*bending over the cradle*) My grandson!

(ECCLES *falls off the chair in the last stage of drunkenness, bottle in hand.* HAWTREE, *leaning one foot on chair from which* ECCLES *has fallen, looks at him through eye-glass.* SAM *enters, and goes to* POLLY, *behind cradle, and, producing wedding-ring from several papers, holds it up before her eyes.* ESTHER *plays until curtain drops.*)

ESTHER: (aside) . . . POLLY: (aside): these speeches only occur in AE, where Robertson's note reads: 'These last two speeches of ESTHER and POLLY were omitted in representation. For what reason on earth – or behind the footlights – the author cannot imagine.'

SCHOOL

A comedy in four acts

First performed at the Prince of Wales's Theatre, London, Saturday 16 January 1869, with the following cast:

LORD BEAUFOY	Mr H.J. Montague
DR SUTCLIFFE	Mr Addison
BEAU FARINTOSH	Mr Hare
JACK POYNTZ	Mr Bancroft
MR KRUX	Mr F. Glover
VAUGHAN	Mr Hill
MRS SUTCLIFFE	Mrs B. White
BELLA	Miss Carlotta Addison
NAOMI TIGHE	Miss Marie Wilton
TILLY	Miss Augusta Wilton
MILLY	Miss George
LAURA	Miss Phillips
CLARA	Miss Unah
KITTY	Miss Hutton
HETTY	Miss Atkins
[LITTLE GIRL	
TIGER, *a manservant*	
Two KEEPERS	
Two SERVANTS	
Two FOOTMEN]	

Scene: In and near Cedar Grove House. *Time:* The present.

Between the first and second acts eight days are supposed to elapse.
Between the second and third, two hours.
Between the third and fourth, six weeks.

VI The Prince of Wales's Theatre, Tottenham Street

ACT I

Music from 'La Cenerentola' before the curtain rises.

SCENE. *A glade.* [*A rustic platform left centre.*] *All the* GIRLS *discovered in various positions,* BELLA *standing.* NAOMI TIGHE *has a long string of wild flowers in her lap, which she is engaged in weaving together; other girls have ivy, etc.* BELLA *has a small branch, which she uses as a wand.*

BELLA: And her two haughty sisters stepped into a beautiful carriage and drove towards the palace, and when they were out of sight, Cinderella sat down in a corner and began to cry. Her godmother asked her what ailed her. 'I wish – I wish – ', said Cinderella, but she sobbed so she couldn't say another word. The godmother said, 'You wish to go to the ball.' (*imitation of godmother*) Now this godmother was a fairy.

NAOMI: I wish my godmother had been a fairy.

GIRLS: Hush! Silence!

NAOMI: Girls without fathers or mothers ought to have fairies for godmothers, to make up for the loss.

BELLA: Be a good girl,' said the fairy godmother, 'and you shall go.' 'But,' said poor Cinderella, 'I can't go, for I've no things fit to go in.'

GIRLS: Poor girl! (*with deep sympathy*)

NAOMI: If I hadn't nice dresses I should die.

GIRLS: Hush!

BELLA: 'Run into the garden,' said the fairy godmother, 'and bring me a pumpkin.' Cinderella brought a pumpkin, and her godmother scooped out the inside.

HETTY: (*eagerly*) Was it nice?

BELLA: The godmother scooped out the inside, leaving nothing but the rind. She then touched it with her wand, and the pumpkin instantly turned into a fine coach, gilded all over with gold.

NAOMI: Bravo, pumpkin.

GIRLS: Hush! Go on, Bella.

BELLA: Then Cinderella looked into the mousetrap, where she found six mice all alive and kicking.

NAOMI: (*with a shudder*) I hate mice. (*All shudder slightly.*)

LAURA: (*waking up*) Whenever I think of mice they make me feel quite – sleepy. (*Goes to sleep.*)

BELLA: Cinderella lifted the trap very gently and the fairy godmother touched the mice, and they turned into beautiful horses of a fine dapple-grey mouse-colour.

GIRLS: Oh!

BELLA: Then the fairy turned two rats into postillions.

GIRLS: Oh!

BELLA: And six lizards into six footmen.

'La Cenerentola': an opera by Rossini, first staged in 1817, telling the story of Cinderella, though without the glass slipper.
postillions: mounted riders in a team of carriage horses.

GIRLS: Six! My!

BELLA: 'There,' said the godmother, 'there is an equipage.' 'Yes,' said Cinderella, crying and pointing to her nasty ugly grey dress, 'but I cannot go in these filthy rags.' Then the godmother touched her with her wand, and her rags instantly became the most magnificent ball-dress that ever was seen.

GIRLS: Oh!

BELLA: Covered with the most costly jewels.

GIRLS: Oh!

NAOMI: I should like to be godmothered in that way.

BELLA: To these were added a beautiful pair of glass slippers. Then Cinderella, seated in her beautiful coach, drove off to the palace.

NAOMI: Gee up, gee oh! (*Sings 'Post Horn Galop'.*)

BELLA: As soon as she arrived, the king's son –

GIRLS: The king's son?

BELLA: A most beautiful young man –

KITTY: This is interesting.

BELLA: Presented himself at the door of her carriage, and helped her to alight.

HETTY: I should like to be helped twice to king's son.

GIRLS: Silence!

BELLA: The prince then conducted her to the place of honour and soon after took her out to dance with him.

GIRLS: Oh!

CLARA: Think of that – a prince.

NAOMI: Hetty would like to eat a prince, wouldn't you?

TILLY: So should I.

CLARA: So should we all.

BELLA: The prince fell in love with her.

GIRLS: Oh!

TILLY: Why shouldn't he? I suppose princes fall in love the same as common people.

KITTY: But they don't do it in the same way.

NAOMI: Go on Bella. (*repeating*) The prince fell in love –

CLARA: What is love?

MILLY: You silly thing!

TILLY: Such ignorance!

KITTY: That stupid Clara!

CLARA: I don't believe any of you know, not even you big girls.

TILLY: Everybody knows what love is!

CLARA: Then what is it?

NAOMI: Who's got a dictionary? – You're sure to find it there.

TILLY: My eldest sister says it's the only place in which you can find it.

KITTY: Then she's been jilted!

MILLY: My pa says love is moonshine.

'Post Horn Galop': composed by Herr Koenig, a celebrated cornet-player of the nineteenth century, it remains a favourite band composition.

NAOMI: Then how sweet and mellow it must be!
MILLY: Particularly when the moon is at the full!
NAOMI: And there is no eclipse!
TILLY: It seems that nobody knows what love is.
KITTY: I despise such ignorance!
CLARA: Then why don't they teach it us? We've a music-master to teach music, why not a love-master to teach love?
NAOMI: You don't suppose love is to be taught like geography or the use of globes, do you? No, love is an extra.
TILLY: Perhaps it comes naturally. Ask Laura what love is.
CLARA: (*rousing* LAURA, *who is asleep*) Laura, what is love?
LAURA: (*waking suddenly*) *J'aime*, I love; *tu aimes*, we lovest; *il aime*, they love; *nous aimons* – (*All laugh.*)
BELLA: Hush, here's Governess.

(*Enter* MRS SUTCLIFFE. *All rise, curtsey to* MRS SUTCLIFFE, *and surround her, except* LAURA.)

MRS S: Well, young ladies, what is the cause of your merriment? What is the subject under discussion?
NAOMI: Governess, we wish you to tell us something.
MRS S: What is it, dear?
GIRLS: What is love?
LITTLE GIRL: Yes, what is love?
MRS S: (*dumbfounded*) What is love? I – I – here is the Doctor!

(*Enter* DR SUTCLIFFE. GIRLS *curtsey to the* DOCTOR. MRS SUTCLIFFE *a woman of sixty; the* DOCTOR *a man over sixty-five years of age – scholastic, genial, and a cross of the clergyman in his manner.*)

MRS S: Doctor, I have just had a most extraordinary question proposed to me.
DR S: Indeed, dear?
MRS S: Yes, Doctor – What is love?
NAOMI *and* GIRLS: Yes, Doctor – What is love?
LITTLE GIRL: Yes, Doctor – What is love?
DR S: (*for a moment puzzled*) What is love? The cuneiform inscriptions on the Babylonian marbles have only been recently deciphered, so I will answer according to the comparatively modern notions of the Greeks. By them love was called Eros, but there were three separate Erotes. There was the Eros of the ancient cosmogonies. Hesiod, the earliest author who mentions him, calls him the cosmogonic Eros. In Plato's 'Symposium' he is described as the eldest of the gods. Then there was the Eros of the philosophers, and, lastly, the Eros of the later degenerate Greek poets, who said, erroneously, that he was the youngest of the gods. The parentage of Eros or Cupid is doubtful. It is generally assumed that he was the son of Zeus, that is Jupiter, and of Aphrodite, that is Venus – (MRS SUTCLIFFE *coughs.*) – so that he was both the son and grandson of – (MRS SUTCLIFFE *coughs, and arranges her dress. The*

---

cosmogonies: theories as to how the universe came into being.

DOCTOR *takes the hint.*) That is love! I mention these facts because I am about to say no more upon the subject.

NAOMI: I know what love is.

MRS S: (*aside*) Goodness forbid!

DR S: How forward the child is!

NAOMI: (*fondling* BELLA) I love Bella – and Bella loves me; don't you, Bella?

(BELLA *afraid and constrained before* MRS SUTCLIFFE.)

DR S: (*taking* BELLA*'s hand*) We all love Bella. It is impossible to know her without loving her. Goodness and amiability must command affection and esteem.

NAOMI: [*aside*] He talks just like a copy-book, don't he?

DR S: And I suppose, Bella, my child – (MRS SUTCLIFFE *coughs and arranges her dress.*) – that you are going to aid the young ladies in their botanical researches?

MRS S: Yes; young ladies, if you have sufficiently reposed yourselves from your walk across the meadow, you can resume your self-imposed labours.

(*All the* GIRLS *go off singing,* BELLA *standing on platform until all are off except* NAOMI, *who crosses behind* MRS SUTCLIFFE *to* LAURA *and wakes her – they follow the others.*)

GIRLS: 'Through the wood, through the wood, follow and find me,
Search every hollow, and dingle, and dell,
I leave not the print of a footstep behind me,
So they who would search for must look for me well.'

(*which dies away in the distance*)

MRS S: It is an extraordinary thing, Doctor, that, despite all my remonstrances, you will constantly show your too obvious preference for that girl Bella. It has a most injurious effect upon the other pupils.

DR S: My dear, she is an orphan, without friends or protectors, dependent entirely on us; that sad social anomaly, a pupil-teacher, less self-reliant than a servant, and only half a lady. Then, poor Bella is so pretty, and so young.

MRS S: Ah! – (*Sits on branch of tree, under large tree.* DOCTOR *sits on her right.*) There it is – so young (*nearly weeping*). Cruel Theodore, to remind me of my lost youth.

DR S: Amanthis, my love, that was far from my intention. You are too sensitive.

MRS S: Your thoughts are ever fixed on the fleeting and unsubstantial charms of youth and beauty.

DR S: No, no, no, no!

MRS S: Yes, yes, yes, yes! Do you not remember five-and-thirty years ago?

DR S: Amanthis! To recall that error of my youth.

MRS S: It is always present to my mind.

DR S: My love, I only danced with her three times, and it is five-and-thirty years ago.

MRS S: I remember! We had scarcely been married seven years.

---

copy-book: a book of 'improving' maxims to be copied out by school-pupils.
'Through the wood': 'Through the Wood' or 'The Forest Fairy's Song', a Cavatina, words by W.H. Bellamy, music by Charles Edward Horn, was published in 1830.

DR S: Since then you have been constantly reproaching me.

MRS S: It seems but as yesterday.

DR S: It seems to me much longer.

MRS S: Ah, Theodore, unfeeling.

DR S: No, no, Amanthis. I did not mean that. I meant that thirty-five years' conjugal serenity ought to compensate for dancing with a young lady three times at a ball; where, from the fault of hosts too hospitable, the negus had been made too strong. Come, Amanthis, don't be hard on Theodore. Think what Jason says: 'Credula res amor est.'

MRS S: 'Utinam temeraria dicar
Criminibus falsis insimula visse.'

(*Enter* KRUX. *He is reading a book.*)

DR S: (*correcting her*) 'Insimulasse virum'. The contraction for the pentameter. (*They join hands.* KRUX *comes down stage,* DOCTOR *rises.*) Ah! Mr Krux! Enjoying this beautiful day?

KRUX: No, sir; I was enjoying this beautiful book.

MRS S: (*rises*) What is it?

KRUX: Hervey's 'Meditations among the Tombs'.

DR S: Rather a serious work.

KRUX: Not to my taste, sir. This splendid sky, the plashing brook, the verdant meadow, these rustling trees and sweetly singing birds – all turn my thoughts unto the grave.

MRS S: Good gracious!

DR S: (*indignant*) It turns my thoughts to nothing of the sort. On the contrary, it send them back to years when –

MRS S: (*aside to him*) Not thirty-five years, Theodore.

DR S: No, Amanthis, not thirty-five; to thirty-four or thirty-six, but not to thirty-five. Come, let us join the pupils (*taking her arm*). For the present, Mr Krux. (*Bows; aside*) Prig! I can't bear prigs, particularly young prigs.

(*Exeunt* DOCTOR *and* MRS SUTCLIFFE.)

KRUX: Upstarts! I hate those people. But then, I hate most people; I think I hate most things – (*crushing beetle with his foot*) – except Bella, and when I look at her, I feel that I could bite her. Here she is. (*Enter* BELLA, *reading a book.*) Bella, where are you going?

BELLA: Mrs Sutcliffe has sent me to fetch her galoshes.

KRUX: Stay one moment. Sit down (*seating himself on large branch, under tree*).

BELLA: Mrs Sutcliffe told me I was not to loiter.

KRUX: What are you reading?

BELLA: A fairy tale. What are you reading?

KRUX: Hervey's 'Meditations'. A different sort of literature. Do sit down.

---

negus: sweetened mixture of port or sherry with hot water, flavoured with lemon and spice.
Credula res amor, etc.: an elegiac couplet from Ovid's *Heroides* VI. 21–2. 'Love is too ready to believe; may it prove that I have rashly brought groundless charges against my husband!' The speaker is not Jason but Hypsipele, whom he deserted.
Hervey's 'Meditations': James Hervey (1714–58) published his popular work in 1746 and 1747.

(BELLA *sits on branch of tree.*)

BELLA: (*reading*) 'The king's son, the handsome young prince, was continually by her side, and said to her the most obliging things imaginable.'

KRUX: What a beastly world this is, Bella, isn't it? Attend to me for a short time. I want to speak to you particularly.

BELLA: Be quick, then.

KRUX: Dr and Mrs Sutcliffe are getting very old.

BELLA: They are not *getting* old; they *are* old.

KRUX: And, therefore, must soon die.

BELLA: (*shocked*) Oh, Mr Krux, what a dreadful notion.

KRUX: We are all worms; particularly Dr and Mrs Sutcliffe. All men must die some time, the Doctor and Mrs Sutcliffe included.

BELLA: Mrs Sutcliffe isn't a man.

KRUX: She ought to have been. But as I was saying, Bella, when they are dead and buried –

BELLA: Mr Krux!

KRUX: They will be no longer able to keep on the school, will they? Then who is to keep on the school, eh?

BELLA: I don't know; I don't like to think of such things.

KRUX: I do. I repeat, who is to keep on the school? I am the only resident master; I am known to all the pupils.

BELLA: Alas, yes!

KRUX: I am known and, I hope, loved.

BELLA: No; feared.

KRUX: It's the same thing in a school. Bella, you're a very good scholar.

BELLA: No, I'm not.

KRUX: Yes, you are; and you understand all about the kitchen – pies, and coals, and vegetables, and the like. You're an orphan.

BELLA: Yes (*sighing*).

KRUX: So am I. You have no relations?

BELLA: No.

KRUX: Nor friends?

BELLA: Oh, yes; Dr and Mrs Sutcliffe, and the school, and the people in the village.

KRUX: I don't count them. I have no friends.

BELLA: No, not one.

KRUX: When the Sutcliffes – (BELLA *looks at him.*) – go – why shouldn't we keep on the school?

BELLA: (*astonished*) We?

KRUX: Yes, you and I; we are quite capable; I am clever, so are you; we could enlarge the connection. You could manage the girls, I could manage the boys. Think how pleasant to make money – take in pupils, teach them and correct them. I should like to correct them, particularly the boys. We should get on, Bella, if we got married –

BELLA: Got married! – Who got married?

KRUX: You to me – me to you! Mr and Mrs Krux, of Cedar Grove House. I love you, Bella.

BELLA: (*rises suddenly, drops her book, and hides her face in her hands*) Oh, don't; on such a nice day as this.

KRUX: Eh?

BELLA: Poor dear Dr and Mrs Sutcliffe, to think of their dying, it makes me cry – (*crying*) – so kind as they've been to me.

KRUX: She's a fool – (*Rises.*) – Bella.

BELLA: Go away, you bad man, do – to think of death and marriage, and such dreadful things.

KRUX: You won't tell the Sutcliffes, Bella, will you? I proposed it all for your good, and because I love you – (BELLA *shudders.*) – you won't tell 'em, will you, dear, and get me into trouble? Promise me you won't tell 'em! (*carneying*) Promise me; do, do!

BELLA: I won't tell 'em, if you'll promise me never to mention such subjects again.

KRUX: I won't – I'll take my oath I won't. Take your oath you won't tell them of me, Bella; take your oath, dear, will you?

BELLA: No – I give you my word. To think of our kind benefactors dying. You wicked man, I wonder that something doesn't happen to you. I wonder – (*Two shots heard without.*) Oh! (KRUX *frightened*) I won't stay any longer.

KRUX: Where are you going?

BELLA: To fetch the galoshes. (*Exit* BELLA.)

KRUX: A bad girl! A bad girl! A bad girl! She'll come to no good, if I can help it; an ungrateful beast – after the offer I made her. What is she? A nobody, a foundling, a pauper – (*Enter* LORD BEAUFOY *and* JACK POYNTZ, *in shooting dress, followed by two* KEEPERS.) – brought up on charity. Oh, if she were a man, I'd –

(LORD BEAUFOY *comes down on* KRUX*'s left, and touches him with gun, before he speaks.*)

LORD B: Have you seen anybody pass this way?

KRUX: A young girl, sir, (*meekly*) with a book?

LORD B: No – an old gentleman and two servants.

KRUX: No, sir.

JACK: (*aside*) What a mangy looking cur!

KRUX: (*aside*) Two young puppies.

LORD B: (*to* KEEPERS) Are you sure this was the place where lunch was to meet us?

JACK: (*looking off*) Yes – for here it comes.

(*Enter* TIGER, *carrying two small folding chairs; two* SERVANTS, *one with picnic case, with lunch plates, knives and forks. The other has a tray-stand and butler's tray, which he places centre. They spread the lunch during the dialogue, which follows their entrance.*)

JACK: (*seeing* KRUX) Good morning.

KRUX: (*servilely*) Good morning, sir. (*aside*) Upstart beasts! (*Exit* KRUX.)

(*Enter* BEAU FARINTOSH, *led on by* VAUGHAN, *who carries a camp stool which he places at table for the* BEAU; FARINTOSH *is a*

(carneying): coaxing, wheedling.

thin old man of seventy, dressed in the latest fashion, wigged, dyed, padded, eye-glassed, a would-be young man, blind as a bat – peering into everything. During the following SERVANTS *lay lunch, and* LORD BEAUFOY *and* JACK *eat and drink.*)

FARIN: (*shaking hands with* JACK) My dear boy – my dear boy, how d'ye do? The very image of my poor sister – so glad to see you.

JACK: Thank you, Mr Farintosh, but my mamma had not the happiness of being your sister. That is Lord Beaufoy.

FARIN: Ten thousand pardons, but my eyes are so – so – so – which is him, where is he? (*going to and shaking hands with* LORD BEAUFOY) My dear Arthur, quite well, eh? Strong, yes – you look so – very image of my poor sister.

LORD B: I'm quite well, Beau; you, too, I hope.

FARIN: Never better – never better – strong, active, fine condition – fine condition. (*striking himself on chest*) Bellows to mend, eh – bellows to mend – Ha! Ha! Ha! Sit down.

LORD B: Let me introduce my friend – Mr Poyntz – Mr Percy Farintosh.

FARIN: Poyntz! Worcestershire Poyntzes?

JACK: Worcestershire Poyntzes!

FARIN: Knew your grandfather. I mean your father – well – he was my second in Paris just after the battle of – no – no – sit down. (*They sit.*)

LORD B: May I – (*helping lunch*) You may go (*to* SERVANTS, *who exeunt*).

FARIN: Nothing before dinner, thanks.

LORD B: When we arrived at your place last night, you had gone to bed.

FARIN: Yes, early to bed – late up, my way.

LORD B: And your man gave us your message; told us to shoot this morning – and that you –

FARIN: Would meet you here to lunch, if fine. Pleasant in the open air. (*to* JACK) You appear to have a good appetite, Mr –

LORD B: Poyntz.

JACK: Yes – I'm quite a celebrity that way. It is my principal talent.

FARIN: Ah! A very enviable one.

JACK: It is convenient at dinner time.

LORD B: Your last letter said that you had some business?

FARIN: Yes, yes, yes!

JACK: Shall I and the lunch retire, and amuse ourselves together?

LORD B: No, no – Jack is an old friend. I presume it is on the old subject?

JACK: (*eating*) Ah, debt!

LORD B: No; marriage!

JACK: Oh, family troubles – shall I –

FARIN: No, no, no, Mr –

LORD: Poyntz.

FARIN: Mr Poyntz, my nephew and I are at loggerheads. You shall judge between us.

JACK: Most happy.

FARIN: I wish him to marry.

JACK: Hard, very; but some uncles are like that.

FARIN: Have you ever been married?

JACK: Never; but once I was in quarantine ten days off Malta.

FARIN: (*downcast*) I have been married.

JACK: There I have the advantage of you – I am the singlest young person possible; open to competition, and to be influenced only by money.

LORD B: (*in answer to a look from* FARINTOSH) You mustn't mind Jack; it's his humour to talk in that way.

FARIN: My poor wife died early; had she lived I should have been a different man – a different man.

JACK: (*aside*) Ah – dead most likely.

LORD B: It's a melancholy story, Jack, and I shall get over it quicker than the Beau. My uncle's wife died, leaving a son; this son married –

FARIN: Against my wishes.

LORD B: And he died –

FARIN: Without seeing me, that I might ask his pardon and forgive him.

LORD B: He, too, left a child; of this child and her mother, my uncle has been unable to find the least trace.

FARIN: I would give thousands to find them.

JACK: Try the second column of *The Times*. If you were to put in an advertisement, 'Wanted, a young person to adopt, by a gentleman of fortune', you'd have lots of applicants. Indeed, why go further than this present spot? Here am I, ready to be adopted. I should like to be adopted by any gentleman or lady of means. Here you are, a strong, healthy, useful orphan, with good appetite and expensive habits all ready laid on; no objection to travel, or to go in single or double harness.

FARIN: Your friend has a very singular humour.

LORD B: Yes, and it sometimes runs away with him.

JACK: And sometimes puts me down when I least expect it. Pray forgive me.

FARIN: But *revenons à nos – fleurs d'oranges.* I want Arthur to marry.

JACK: But Arthur would rather not.

LORD B: I won't marry.

FARIN: Did you ever hear such infatuation? It's tremendous. What was man invented for, but to marry?

LORD B: My tastes are so singular; I should want such a singular wife.

JACK: What sort? Give particulars – name your age, weight, and colour.

LORD B: My wife must be a woman.

JACK: Plenty about.

LORD B: Aye, but I mean a real woman.

JACK: That's difficult.

LORD B: Not a regulation doll of the same pattern as the other dolls – the same absence of thought, the same simper, the same stupid dove-like look out of the eyes. (*imitating*) 'I love papa, I love mamma. I go to church on Sunday; I

---

revenons à, etc.: the usual phrase 'revenons à nos moutons' (i.e. 'let's get back to the subject') occurs in the medieval French farce *Maître Pierre Pathelin*.
fleurs d'oranges: orange-blossom.

can walk, and talk, and play. *Je suis une jolie poupée et je veux bien un bon petit mari pour m'acheter des toilettes et me faire promener au bois.*'

FARIN: Did you ever hear? It's profane – quite profane.

JACK: (*lighting cigar*) Do you? (*offering him*)

FARIN: I don't smoke. (*taking snuff*) Do you? (*offering him*)

JACK: I do everything (*taking snuff*).

FARIN: How you must enjoy life!

JACK: (*smoking hard*) Sir, for sensual enjoyment I would give Caligula six, and distance him. It's a great comfort having no intellect.

FARIN: Many people find it so. Your language, Arthur, is blasphemy, perfect blasphemy, against the loveliest portion of creation.

LORD B: What is loveliness? Something to be bought in bottles and put on with a brush?

FARIN: You don't dislike beauty?

LORD B: No; but I hate paint.

FARIN: Paint?

LORD B: Paint! Shall I promise to love and cherish a plaister cast? Shall I promise to cleave only unto a living fresco, decked out in dead hair? I want a young wife, not an old master; I want charms that won't rub off on my coat sleeve if I touch them before they're dry. Pigments and spices are for Egyptian mummies; not for breathing flesh and blood. Can I exchange words of love with one who, before she has spoken, is a built-up falsehood? I choose men friends who don't tell lies; I choose women who don't look them.

JACK: Which means that when you're eighty you'll marry your cook, because she doesn't use pearl powder when on active service.

LORD B: The charms of my love must be warranted to wash.

JACK: You mean not to wash off.

FARIN: Arthur, I'm shocked; your opinions are – are – atheistic.

LORD B: It's not only cosmetics I do battle with. Some women would kill gallantry and chivalry by something called equality with men. What is equality with men? Having their clothes made by a he-tailor instead of a she-milliner. How pleasant for man and wife to be measured together; or, at an election, for him to walk arm-in-arm to the hustings with a wretched half-mad, whole-mannish creature, who votes for the candidate you wish to exclude.

JACK: I agree with you there; if women were admitted to electoral privileges, they'd sell them for the price of a new chignon; man, as the nobler animal, has the exclusive right to sell his vote – for beer!

LORD B: Give me simplicity. I'm one of the old school.

FARIN: (*rising*) And I'm one of the new. Give me chignons, cosmetics, perfumes –

Je suis, etc.: 'I am a pretty doll and I should very much like a good little husband to buy me dresses and to take me for walks in the woods.'

Caligula: Emperor of Rome AD 37–41, whose insane acts of debauchery and cruelty are proverbial.

pearl powder: for whitening the skin.

chignon: a coil of hair (often false) worn on the back of the head, which returned to fashion *c.* 1865.

in short, civilisation. I do not see why beings endowed with immortal souls should not repair the ravages of time by the appliances of art. As you say, it all depends upon the school one has been reared in. (*Sits.*)

JACK: What does it matter? Indeed, in this world, what does anything matter – after dinner?

FARIN [(*to* BEAUFOY)] Your sentiments are revolting, and remind me of the works of Burke and Hare, and Tom Paine and Voltaire, and other persons out of the social pale. Knowing your singular views, I had prepared a splendid *parti* for you, an heiress.

LORD B: I don't want money.

JACK: Not want money! You should be photographed. The man who don't want money deserves to be put into an album, and kept there.

FARIN: Miss Naomi Tighe – a West Indian heiress, without father or mother.

JACK: No father and no mother, and an heiress. It's a gorgeous thing in matrimonies. But why offer it to Arthur? He don't want it. I do.

FARIN: She's at school close by here, with some old friends of mine. I was asked to go and see the preliminary examination of the young ladies before the holidays. I thought it would be an excellent thing to take you with me, that you might see Miss Tighe, and, as I hoped, approve of her, for her guardians are also my oldest friends.

LORD B: I'd rather not go. (*Rises and beckons on* SERVANTS. *Enter* KEEPERS *and* VAUGHAN. *They remove table etc.*)

FARIN: The examination is today week.

LORD B: I'll go, uncle, to please you.

FARIN: Will your friend accompany us?

JACK: Thanks, I'll go to please myself.

FARIN: Here's Vaughan to take me home. I always sleep before I dress for dinner. Till then –

(JACK *sees something in the bushes. Motions* KEEPER *for a gun.* KEEPER *gives it him.*)

JACK: No; the rifle.

(KEEPER *gives* JACK *breech-loader, which* JACK *loads, and goes off.*)

FARIN: What's he doing?

LORD B: He's going to kill a bird with a bullet. He's a wonderful shot.

FARIN: Now give me your arm. (*taking* VAUGHAN*'s arm*) Ah, there you are; till dinner, Arthur –

(*Exeunt* FARINTOSH, VAUGHAN, *and* KEEPERS.)

LORD B: Marry me to a young lady, all bread and butter and boarding-school. Time enough for marriage when I'm forty-five, and wear a waist-belt.

Burke and Hare: Farintosh is confusing the political orator and writer Edmund Burke (1729–97) with one of the notorious Edinburgh murderers Burke and Hare, who sold their victims' bodies for dissection. (Hare having turned king's evidence, Burke was hanged in 1829.) Kipling in *Kim* (1900) makes his Hurree Chunder guilty of the same slip.

West Indian heiress: many families made their fortunes from the sugar plantations.

waist belt: worn to disguise increasing corpulence.

Marriage! Tut – a pile of boxes when you travel. Female friends to tell your wife what happened or what didn't happen before she was your wife. Hysteria when she's contradicted. Tears when you're cruel – that is, when you won't let her have her own way. Mild accents of mother-in-law. 'Is this the lot, sir, you have prepared for my dear child? Come home, love, come home.' By Jove, she might go home for me; there's always something the matter – a pain here or there, a sinking, or a swimming, or a floating, or a darting, or a shooting. (*Turns up stage. Shot heard within.* BELLA *runs across stage, frightened, and loses her shoe. Exits.* LORD BEAUFOY *does not see her.*) Then the brothers! What a horror is the brother of the girl you're spooning, particularly if he is like her; the thought will come that she might have been him, or he might have been her. No; love is a species of lunacy, of which marriage is the strait waistcoat. (*Kicks against shoe left by* BELLA.) What's this? Shoe! Child's shoe? No! Woman's shoe? No! Girl's shoe? (*Picks it up.*) Pretty little shoe; must belong to a pretty little foot, very pretty little foot. Now, why on earth could any young girl come into this wood for the purpose of losing her shoe? I should like to know who it belongs to. I feel quite a curiosity to – (NAOMI *screams outside.*) Eh, perhaps this is the fair and shoeless owner.

(NAOMI *runs on right, and* BELLA *from left. She runs to* NAOMI.)

BELLA: Oh, my darling, there you are. (*They embrace.*)

NAOMI: Oh! I thought we were both killed – that dreadful cow!

LORD B: Quite girls, both. Now to which does this belong? It is the very tiniest shoe. (*loudly*) Ahem! (*Comes down stage to back of them.*)

NAOMI: Oh, it's the gentleman who shot him. Oh, sir, so many, many, many thanks.

BELLA: Sir, you saved our lives; pray accept our gratitude.

LORD B: Gratitude for what? (*aside*) Surely not for finding –

BELLA: I was walking across the meadow.

NAOMI: And I saw her, and ran to meet her, when a great big ugly cow –

BELLA: Ran at us, and wanted to trample us to death –

NAOMI: When you shot him.

LORD B: I shot him!

NAOMI: And we ran away.

BELLA: We might have lost our lives.

LORD B: Haven't you lost anything else?

BELLA: (*together*) } No!
NAOMI: (*feeling her chignon*) } No!

LORD B: Not – ?

BELLA: } (*together*) { No.
NAOMI: } (*together*) { Nothing. (NAOMI *runs across to* BELLA.)

---

go home for me: go home as far as I was concerned.
spooning: courting (see note, p. 137 above).

LORD B: I thought you had (*disappointed*).

(*Enter* JACK POYNTZ, *with gun.* NAOMI *and* BELLA *go up stage.*)

LORD B: Jack, was it you who fired just now?

JACK: Yes.

LORD B: What have you got there – birds?

JACK: No; boots (*producing a pair of galoshes*).

LORD B: Good gracious! Does it rain boots about here? (*producing shoe*)

JACK: Just now I was going to pot a bird, when I saw two girls running away like mad from – what the newspapers call an infuriated animal; so I sighted him, and hit him just between the horns; out of compliment to my shooting he fell down dead, and the two girls ran away; I walked up to the scene of slaughter, and at first I thought that these (*showing galoshes*) belonged to the defunct, but of course that was quite impossi*bull*.

NAOMI: (*crossing to* JACK) Then, sir, it was you who shot the cow?

JACK: Yes; I shot the cow. The cow was a bull; but that is a detail.

NAOMI: It was you, and not this gentleman!

JACK: If a bull is shot, what does it matter who shot him, particularly to the bull!

LORD B: (*aside*) I wish I'd shot him. Confound that Jack, what luck he has.

JACK: May I ask if you know the owner of these (*showing galoshes*) trophies from the field of battle?

BELLA: (*advancing*) Oh, they're mine!

LORD B: (*astounded*) Yours?

BELLA: Yes; at least, I was carrying them to Mrs Sutcliffe.

LORD B: Mrs Sutcliffe! (*relieved*)

NAOMI: Yes; our governess! (BELLA *takes galoshes.*)

LORD B: (*to* BELLA) Then, I presume, that these belong to Mrs Sutcliffe.

BELLA: Yes.

LORD B: Then Mrs Sutcliffe's foot is somewhat large; and who does this belong to?

BELLA: (*seeing her foot is unshod*) Oh, that's mine.

LORD B: (*relieved*) I'm so glad.

BELLA: I didn't know I'd lost it, I was so frightened. (*taking it*) Thank you so much, sir, for saving my – shoe. (*Goes up stage, and puts it on.*)

JACK: May I know who I have the pleasure of addressing?

NAOMI: My name is Naomi Tighe.

JACK: (*aside*) The heiress –

LORD B: And your name? (*to* BELLA)

BELLA: Bella!

LORD B: Bella?

NAOMI: We're both pupils at Mrs Sutcliffe's.

BELLA: That is, I'm not quite a pupil – I'm only a pupil-teacher.

JACK: (*pointing to the red portion of* NAOMI*'s dress*) It was this attracted the bull.

NAOMI: Oh, don't look at me. I can't bear to be looked at. (*Puts her handkerchief over her face.*)

I thought you had: though the long skirts of the period would prevent Beaufoy from noticing that Bella had lost her shoe, it seems odd that Bella herself should be unaware of it!

JACK: How singular. (*to* LORD BEAUFOY) This is the very girl your uncle spoke of.

LORD B: Yes; do you think her handsome?

JACK: Not bad for an heiress. And the other?

LORD B: Charming.

BELLA: If you please, gentlemen, don't mention to Mrs Sutcliffe that we have been attacked. She is so nervous; it would make her ill.

(GIRLS *without, singing 'Through the Wood'.*)

NAOMI: Here's Governess.

LORD B: Let us go; our staying may embarrass.

JACK: No; let's stop and see them take their gallops.

(*The school passes across the stage, singing 'Through the Wood' etc.; the* DOCTOR *and* MRS SUTCLIFFE *last.* BELLA *offers* MRS SUTCLIFFE *her galoshes.* NAOMI *is on platform when* DOCTOR *appears, waving handkerchief to* JACK *and laughing. The* DOCTOR *touches her on the shoulder; the expression on her face alters suddenly, and she runs off, followed by* DOCTOR. MRS SUTCLIFFE *signifies to* BELLA *to retain galoshes, and exits, followed by* BELLA, *who looks at* LORD BEAUFOY. *As soon as she is off,* JACK *runs on to platform and waves his cap on his gun,* LORD BEAUFOY *watching* BELLA *from below.*)

(*Song –*)

'When the red sun sets at eve you may hear me,
Singing farewell to his rays as they fade;
But as soon as the step of a mortal is near me,
I take to my wings and fly off to the shade.'

(*Dies in the distance, as curtain falls quickly.*)

ACT II

SCENE. *The schoolroom. Shelves with books. Scene enclosed. Windows* [*at rear*]. *Door right. Desks, desk for master, etc. Maps. Music from 'La Cenerentola' as drop rises.* BELLA *discovered, seated at small table near open window, shelling peas.*

BELLA: (*humming*) 'Said the prince unto the maiden,
"There is none I love but thee";
"Let me hence, then," said the maiden,
"You are not of my degree."
"Love can raise thee to a lady,
Say, my princess wilt thou be?"
Faster, faster flew the maiden,
Faster, faster followed he.'

(NAOMI, *in a hat and shawl, appears outside window; she touches* BELLA *on the shoulder.*)

'Said the prince unto the maiden': unidentified.

BELLA: Nummy, is that you?

NAOMI: Yes, dear; what are you doing?

BELLA: Shelling peas, and –

NAOMI: Yes.

BELLA: And thinking –

NAOMI: (*in a whisper*) About the galoshes? (BELLA *nods.*)

BELLA: But only a little – only a little.

NAOMI: Bella, dear, I dreamt last night, and this morning I feel as if something were going to happen; that is, I feel quite hysterical, as if I should like somebody to hug or to scratch at. I dressed myself quickly, on purpose that I might come out into the garden and have a good think. It is so nice to think in the shrubbery.

BELLA: I'm afraid we are too young to have a right to think upon such subjects.

NAOMI: Not a bit: one is always old enough for a sweetheart. I'm eighteen. How old are you?

BELLA: I don't know.

NAOMI: Then perhaps you're twenty. I knew two girls who were married before they were nineteen; but then some people have such luck! Ain't you going to dress yourself for this examination, like the other girls?

BELLA: This is my Sunday frock.

NAOMI: But you can have my pink, my darling; you can wear anything of mine. (*Kisses* BELLA *through the window, and steals peas and eats them.*)

BELLA: You mustn't eat the peas, dear.

NAOMI: Why not?

BELLA: They're not nice.

NAOMI: Yes, they are, if you eat them when nobody's looking.

(*Enter* MRS SUTCLIFFE, *dressed for dinner.* NAOMI *darts from window.*)

MRS S: Bella, what are you doing there?

BELLA: Shelling peas, ma'am.

MRS S: Shelling peas in the schoolroom!

BELLA: They are so busy, and so pushed for room in the kitchen with the dinner, that I brought them here; I can take them back (*rising and taking basin*).

MRS S: (*looking at watch*) It is nearly time that Mr Farintosh and his friend should be here. Bella, if the young ladies are dressed, you can tell them that I will inspect them in this apartment. (*Door opens.*)

BELLA: Here are the young ladies.

MRS S: Good!

(BELLA *resumes her pea-shelling. Enter all the* GIRLS (*dressed for the examination*) *one by one, in the following order:* – MILLY, TILLY, CLARA, HETTY, KITTY, LITTLE GIRL. MRS SUTCLIFFE *turns them round, signifying approval or the reverse; they take their respective seats at the desks* – NAOMI *last but one.*)

MRS S: (*to* LITTLE GIRL) You shall be examined with the others to please you. What are you going to answer?

LITTLE GIRL: They condemned him to shoot –

MRS S: Yes, yes, that's right. (CHILD *goes to her seat.*) Why, Naomi my dear, you've been crying.

NAOMI: No, I haven't.

MRS S: Miss Tighe! Miss Tighe! You should say I was mistaken.

NAOMI: Then you are; and if I have been crying it's only a few tears. (*Goes to her seat.*)

TILLY: (*to* GIRLS) What could you cry but tears! You couldn't cry cucumbers, could you?

(*Enter* LAURA, *sleepy, her dress badly put on.*)

MRS S: Now then, Laura, you're last again.

LAURA: Somebody must be last. (*Goes to her place.*)

(BELLA *goes off with peas, and returns immediately.*)

MRS S: The Doctor will put you through an examination on the arrival of our friends. It will be an excellent bit of practice for the grand examination at the end of the half-year. The musical examination will take place in the drawing-room after dinner. Mr Farintosh brings a friend with him, Lord Beaufoy (*excitement of* GIRLS), the owner of half a county.

TILLY: Half a county? Which half?

CLARA: And which county?

NAOMI: Is he a real lord?

MRS S: Real? Yes.

NAOMI: But I mean a real, real, lord. When I get near him I'll pinch him, and see if he is flesh and blood, like other people.

TILLY: Oh, I daresay lords are very flesh.

NAOMI: And very blood – very good blood, I mean. (*Gate-bell.*)

MRS S: Hush! (*Awful silence.*) They are here.

NAOMI: Oh, I feel so nervous. I should like to scream.

MRS S: Young ladies, I have only time to say that I rely on you with every confidence.

(GIRLS *rise, curtsey, and seat themselves. Enter* DR SUTCLIFFE, *followed by* BEAU FARINTOSH, LORD BEAUFOY, *and* JACK POYNTZ, *dressed for dinner* (*not evening dress*). *The* GIRLS *all rise.* BEAU FARINTOSH *and* LORD BEAUFOY *speak to* DR *and* MRS SUTCLIFFE. JACK POYNTZ *wanders down row of desks until he comes to* NAOMI.)

NAOMI: (*recognising* JACK) It's the cow. (*Sinks on chair, blushing and giggling; then rises again, trying to restrain herself.*)

JACK: (*seeing her*) It's the little thing in red, who had the attack of bullock – the heiress (*to* LORD BEAUFOY).

MRS S: Young ladies, let me have the honour – Lord Beaufoy.

BELLA: (*at back*) He Lord Beaufoy!

(MRS SUTCLIFFE *presenting them;* GIRLS *curtsey.*)

MRS S: Mr Percy Farintosh, Mr –

(NAOMI *giggles again, and is silenced by a look from* MRS SUTCLIFFE.)

LORD B: Poyntz.

MRS S: Mr Poyntz.

NAOMI: (*whispering to herself, and writing it on slate*) Poyntz, Poyntz, Poyntz, Poyntz!

FARIN: A friend who was staying with me, and whom I have taken the liberty –

MRS S: Charmed.
DR S: Delighted. } (*shaking hands with* JACK)

FARIN: (*going towards desks*) My dear young ladies, permit me to say how highly I feel honoured by being permitted, by the kindness of my friends, Mrs Sutcliffe and – and Theodore – and the Doctor, to be present at this charming a – a –

LORD B: Inspection!
JACK: Review! } (*together*)

FARIN: Inspection – review – whatever it may be.

DR S: Examination.

FARIN: Examination. Indeed, this is one of the proudest privileges of my life.

MRS S: My dear Mr Farintosh!

DR S: Percy, my old friend.

FARIN: (*fumbling for his eye-glass*) To see so much grace and beauty, 'tis like gazing on a parterre of beautiful flowers, whose colours are audible and whose perfume is melody.

DR S: Bravo! Very elegant.

MRS S: Flowing.

LORD B: Like Tom Moore.

JACK: Broken-winded.

MRS S: The old school.

FARIN: *Vieille école*! *Bonne école*!

JACK: Good show of girls.

FARIN: That is new school – short, pithy, ungraceful –

JACK: And meaning that it says.

(*They talk in group.* BELLA, *who during this has been unobserved, crosses to door.* LORD BEAUFOY *turns and recognises her.*)

LORD B: My fairy in the wood.

NAOMI: (*aside to* BELLA) It's the shoe-horn.

DR S: Bella, my dear, you are not going?

BELLA: I – I – (*Faltering; comes down stage.*)

MRS S: Miss Tighe, let me introduce you to Mr Percy Farintosh.

FARIN: (*mistaking* BELLA *for* NAOMI) Miss Tighe, I knew your guardians intimately. I have –

MRS S: That is not Miss Tighe; that is Bella. (BELLA *and* BEAU FARINTOSH *scrutinise each other. During this* GIRLS *whisper.*) A little thing I took in out of charity. Makes herself very useful about the house.

DR S: (*coming down to* BELLA) The best scholar we can boast of; the pupil of whom I am most proud. Take your accustomed place, Bella, at the head of the class.

---

parterre: a level garden devoted to ornamental arrangements of flowerbeds.
Tom Moore: Irish poet and song-writer (1779–1852).

(BELLA *goes to her place, followed by* DR SUTCLIFFE.)

NAOMI: Bravo!

MRS S: (*looks at* NAOMI) Pray be seated (*to* GENTLEMEN, *who sit*, BEAU FARINTOSH *placing* MRS SUTCLIFFE*'s chair for her*).

NAOMI: (*looking at* JACK) I can't answer a single question if he looks at me.

LORD B: Handsome girls!

FARIN: Delightful! Can't see a single feature. (*Fumbles for his eye-glass, which is at his back.* BEAUFOY *finds it for him. All seated.* NAOMI *makes eyes at* JACK, *who has been gazing at her steadfastly, and then laughs.*)

MRS S: Hush, hush! Miss Tighe.

DR S: (*standing at desk*) The ancient Romans –

MRS S: (*coughs*) Doctor, as we are rather late and dinner will be punctual, if you would kindly make the preliminaries to the examination as short as possible.

DR S: I will so, my dear. We will begin with Roman history. (*As he asks the question, he indicates with a rule the* GIRL *he means, who rises as she answers.*) There were different forms of government in Rome. Please to inform me in what order those forms of government ruled the Roman people.

TILLY: First the regal power, that is the kings; next the consuls, until the first dictator was chosen; then the power of the *decemviri*; consular government again; imperial dictatorship; then the emperors.

FARIN: My dear Mrs Sutcliffe, let me congratulate you on your fair charges.

JACK: How the *propria quae maribus* they can remember it I can't make out.

LORD B: I suppose it's cram.

DR S: After Romulus had appointed the lictors, what other royal or civic guard did he appoint?

MILLY: The celeres.

DR S: Who were they?

MILLY: A guard of young men, numbering three hundred, who accompanied Romulus for the purpose of defending him.

LORD B: Sort of Life Guards?

JACK: Yes, without boots or breeches.

LORD B: Cool to fight in.

JACK: And convenient for fording rivers.

DR S: Name the reign and date rendered illustrious by Belisarius.

NAOMI: The reign of Justinian, in the year 561.

DR S: Who was Belisarius?

TILLY: Belisarius was a Roman general, who rendered the highest service to his country.

DR S: How was he rewarded?

CLARA: They deprived him of his dignities, and put his eyes out.

---

decemviri: from 451–49 BC a body of ten officials superseded the ordinary magistrates and governed Rome.

propria quae maribus: literally 'appropriate to, or characteristic of, males', perhaps a reference to male sex organs, emphasising Jack's incredulity. This interpretation seems slightly at odds with the Prince of Wales's Theatre's image of respectability: did Robertson risk that few would understand the allusion?

JACK: That must have been done by a Committee of the period! (MRS SUTCLIFFE *coughs.*)

DR S: Now for English history. With regard, now, to the ancient Druids. In what garments were the ancient Druids clothed when they offered – (MRS SUTCLIFFE *coughs; all the* GIRLS *hide their heads behind their slates or on the desks.* FARINTOSH, BEAUFOY, *and* JACK *laugh among themselves, and the* DOCTOR *mops his forehead. General discomfiture.*) I should say – ahem – In what reign was the ceremony of marriage first solemnised in churches?

ALL THE GIRLS: (*all rising*) In the reign of Henry III.

JACK: They all know that.

FARIN: Wonderful, wonderful; and all single girls, too.

DR S: What is the difference between the political parties, Whig and Tory?

TILLY: None whatever.

DR S: By whom were the Britons first conquered?

NAOMI: (*with fire*) They never were conquered – they'd sooner die.

JACK: Girl of spirit, by Jove!

DR S: In what reign was the famous Gunpowder Plot discovered?

CLARA: In the reign of November the fifth.

FARIN: Wonderful! My dear Mrs Sutcliffe – (LORD BEAUFOY *nudges* FARINTOSH.)

BELLA: In the reign of James the First.

DR S: Who was the instigator, criminal, and author of that atrocious plot?

CLARA: Oliver Cromwell.

TILLY: Guy Fawkes.

DR S: How was Guy Fawkes punished?

LITTLE GIRL: They condemned him to shoot an apple off the head of his own son.

DR S: Hum! Astronomy. How far distant is the moon from the earth?

NAOMI: (*after a pause*) It depends on the weather. I knew I couldn't do it.

DR S: Bella, dear.

BELLA: The mean distance of the moon from the earth is 236,847 miles.

JACK: Good gracious!

FARIN: Wonderful!

DR S: I told you Bella was our best pupil. And the diameter of the moon?

BELLA: Its apparent diameter is variable according to her distance from the earth. Her real diameter is 2,144 miles.

NAOMI: (*whispering*) What do they call the moon 'her' for?

TILLY: Because the moon's a lady.

NAOMI: The more shame for her to be out so late at night. What would they say if we did it?

TILLY: Consider her age.

DR S: And the magnitude of the moon?

BELLA: About one-fiftieth of the magnitude of the earth.

---

the ancient Druids: the reaction suggests a belief that the Druids sacrificed naked, but there is no evidence for this among ancient or modern historians.

FARIN: Tremendous! In astronomical knowledge that young lady is a perfect Sir Isaac – Davy.

(*Enter* KRUX, *dressed for dinner.*)

KRUX: (*to* MRS SUTCLIFFE) Pardon my interruption, but the servant didn't like to mention that dinner was ready, and –

MRS S: Oh, thank you. (*rising*) I fear we cannot proceed with the examination further. (*All rise except* GIRLS.) Mr Krux, as Mr Farintosh has brought two friends, one more than expected, I fear there will not be room for you at table; so – if you wouldn't mind excusing –

KRUX: (*mortified*) Oh, never mind me, Mrs Sutcliffe; I'm of no consequence.

MRS S: Oh, thank you; so kind of you.

FARIN: (*mistaking* KRUX *for* DR SUTCLIFFE) My dear Doctor, so many thanks. I shall be able to tell you all my admiration during dinner.

(DOCTOR *taps* FARINTOSH *on shoulder, who acknowledges mistake.*)

MRS S: Ladies (GIRLS *rise.*), then, until after dinner, when we will resume our studies.

(GIRLS *curtsey,* KRUX *goes and leans against desk at back,* FARINTOSH *offers* MRS SUTCLIFFE *his arm, and they go off.* JACK *goes towards* NAOMI, *nodding and laughing and backing towards door at same time, finally knocking up against* KRUX, *who is annoyed.* BEAUFOY*'s attention is rivetted on* BELLA. DOCTOR *at door coughs.* BEAUFOY *bows, goes to door, looks back and exits; followed by* DOCTOR. *All exeunt. As soon as they are off,* GIRLS *sit down, chatter, talk, and laugh loudly, taking no notice of* KRUX*'s authority.*)

KRUX: And they dine without me, and I'd kept such a good appetite, because I knew the dinner was nice. Silence, ladies! Oh, those upstarts – and the guests are as bad as the hosts. Ladies! That old fool and those two young idiots, I don't suppose they could conjugate a verb between them. (KRUX *has a white mark on his left shoulder, as if he had rubbed against a whitewashed wall.*) Ladies! Ladies!! Ladies!!! (*rapping desk*) I must request your attention. Miss Hetty, take your arms off the desk. Miss Laura, heads up! (*The* GIRLS *eat apples, write on slips of paper, draw on slates, etc. They see, as he turns, the white mark on his back, and laugh.*) Silence, if you please.

NAOMI: He's been powdering himself for dinner. (*Laugh.*)

TILLY: It's not powder, it's flour – he's been kissing the cook.

NAOMI: Oh, how I pity the cook. (*Laugh.*)

KRUX: Silence, ladies; we will resume our studies in geography. Miss Laura, will you tell me in what country we left off yesterday?

LAURA: (*half asleep*) In bed.

KRUX: Nowhere near it – we left off in South America. Miss Amelia?

MILLY: We left off in the mountains.

KRUX: What mountains?

MILLY: The Alps.

KRUX: Wrong.

KITTY: The Appenines.

KRUX: Wrong.

TILLY: The Pyrenees.

KRUX: Wrong.

CLARA: The Tiber.

KRUX: No – the Chimborazo. Where are the Chimborazo mountains, miss?

LITTLE GIRL: Wherever you please, sir.

KRUX: That's a nice child – she's respectful, though she's stupid. What is the height of the Chimborazo, Miss Naomi?

NAOMI: I don't know.

KRUX: Answer me, miss.

NAOMI: I can't.

KRUX: Why not?

NAOMI: Because I can't. I feel as if I could cry my eyes out.

KRUX: You're hysterical, and should go outside and have your head pumped on; but to resume – (*Turns up stage and shows white on coat again – laugh.*) – what are you laughing at? There is nothing to laugh at in me, I should think.

TILLY: You've got your coat all over white. (*Laugh.*)

KRUX: Oh, Bella, fetch me a brush. (BELLA *pauses.* GIRLS *look indignant, and* NAOMI *slaps book on desk.* KRUX *looking triumphant*) Didn't you hear me? – Fetch me a brush. (BELLA *goes off.*) What is the height of the Chimborazo mountains?

CLARA: Four hundred miles – (*Laugh.*) – no, I mean four hundred yards. I made a mistake.

KRUX: Wrong again – mountains of that height do not exist. The height of the Chimborazo is about one mile.

(BELLA *returns with brush, which she offers to* KRUX.)

KRUX: Oh, brush me! (*A pause* – BELLA *stands motionless.*) Did you hear me? Brush me!

(BELLA *crosses up stage, and places the brush on desk.*)

BELLA: (*facing him*) I can't do that.

GIRLS: (*murmur*) What a shame.

KRUX: (*savagely*) Silence in the class! (*to* BELLA) Do you know who I am?

BELLA: I'm not a servant.

KRUX: (*with a sneer*) Not a servant. If you shell peas you can brush coats. Then, pray, what am I?

NAOMI: (*who has endeavoured to restrain herself but failed*) You're a beast! Bella is here to teach ladies, not to brush blackguards. Insulting our Bella! Girls, don't stand it. (*Throws book at him; all the other girls rise and are about to throw books etc., at* KRUX, *as enter* DR SUTCLIFFE *holding up his hands,* MRS SUTCLIFFE, LORD BEAUFOY *and* JACK POYNTZ. FARINTOSH *at door with napkin round his neck.* GIRLS *resume their seats as if studying.* NAOMI *hides her head behind slate which has a comic drawing in chalk of* KRUX *upon it, and* BELLA *kneels at feet of* DR SUTCLIFFE. *Picture. Act drop quickly.*)

Act drop: see p. 66 above.

ACT III

SCENE. *The grounds of Cedar Grove House. Evening. Stage half dark.* LORD BEAUFOY *discovered, seated on garden chair* [*close to a swing*]. *Piano heard playing in house, and a joyful shout of laughter from the* GIRLS *as curtain rises.* [*There is a dwarf wall about seven feet high running across the stage, with a door in it; the house has a french window and a balcony with steps to the ground; the shrubbery lies off left, opposite the house.*]

LORD B: 'Pon my word, this is a very pretty place; so secluded, rustic, and all that. People seem to pass their lives so innocently, so different from Paris, or Vienna, or any big city. After all, big cities are only agglomerations of brick and mortar, while the country is made up of trees, and fields, and flowers, and birds, and mushrooms, and truffles, and the rest of it. There's better shooting in the country, too. The dinner was very good, and (*meditating, looking up*) it's eighty-something miles from here to the moon – eighty – something, I forget the odd thousands and hundreds. (*Rises, and wanders right.*) Singular little girl, that – fresh as nature and artless as moss. (*plucking a piece of moss from wall of steps; dreamily*) I wonder who she is, in her nice quiet grey dress, so different from those young persons in Paris, and the tremendous tame tiger lilies one meets in town. (*Leans against swing.*) Ah! Simplicity – beautiful simplicity! How you are neglected in this nineteenth century! She doesn't seem to be a boarder like the other girls. I don't care for that Miss Tighe. Poor Uncle Beau, he'll be disappointed in that match again. Jack's got my cigar-case (*feeling in his pocket*). I must find him. (*Enter* BELLA, *a large jug in her hand.*) I beg your pardon (*nearly running over her*).

BELLA: Oh! My lord, you nearly made me drop the jug.

LORD B: I'm very sorry.

BELLA: It's of no consequence. (*Crosses up stage.*)

LORD B: May I ask where you are going? (*following her*)

BELLA: I'm going for some milk, my lord.

LORD B: Alone?

BELLA: Yes.

LORD B: But do you feel equal to the task of going for milk without an escort?

BELLA: Oh, yes! Cook has used more milk than they expected; and so –

LORD B: The deficiency has to be supplied. (*leaning on back of chair facing* BELLA) But it seems so odd that you should have to go for milk. I thought that in the country they always carried milk about in cows. I mean that they had it on the premises, and drew it up in a bucket from a well.

BELLA: Drew milk from a well!

LORD B: No, no; of course – not milk, that's water; though sometimes the two things do get mixed up in one another. But couldn't they send a servant?

BELLA: They're all busy, and I'd nothing else to do.

LORD B: Very amiable of you; but perhaps you find it amusing.

BELLA: No, my lord; but I'm not a boarder here.

LORD B: No?

BELLA: No! Mrs Sutcliffe took me into the house out of charity.

LORD B: (*aside*) God bless Mrs Sutcliffe.

BELLA: And to please the Doctor.

LORD B: Ah! I meant God bless the Doctor.

BELLA: So, of course, I try to make myself as useful as I can, my lord, in return for their kindness.

LORD B: And your father and mother, do they approve?

(*The piano is again heard playing in the house.*)

BELLA: I have neither father nor mother.

LORD B: An orphan?

BELLA: Yes.

LORD B: What an interesting girl!

BELLA: I never knew my parents. My mother died in the village close by, when I was quite a baby, and then the poor woman where I was left, Mrs Marks, brought me up till I was nine years old.

(*The moon shines brightly from this time from behind the house.*)

LORD B: Is that Mrs Marks still living?

BELLA: No, my lord; she died two years ago.

LORD B: (*aside*) Confound these good folks, they always die; but I suppose it is to make room for the bad ones.

BELLA: It was my first sorrow. Then I came here and –

LORD B: You are an excellent scholar –

BELLA: I have tried to improve myself in order that when I am older I may no longer be a burden.

LORD B: And who in the school is your most particular friend?

BELLA: Nummy.

LORD B: Nummy! – What a singular name.

BELLA: I mean Naomi – Miss Tighe – we're the best friends in the school.

LORD B: She's very rich – is she not?

BELLA: Very; indeed she's as rich as she's good, so you may fancy what a lot of money she has. She, too, is an orphan like me; perhaps that's the reason we're so fond of one another; though we're very different in some respects – for she is wealthy and I am – not.

LORD B: Not wealthy. (*aside*) How these great natures misunderstand themselves.

BELLA: But I'm forgetting my errand. (*Runs up and opens door in wall.*)

LORD B: Oh, never mind the milk; let it bring itself. (BELLA *comes down stage again.*) I mean – is it far to the moon?

BELLA: Eh?

LORD B: I mean is it far to the milk?

BELLA: Only across the field.

LORD B: That's a pity. (*after a pause*) May I be allowed to accompany you?

BELLA: Oh, my lord, so much trouble.

LORD B: No trouble. The milk here is so pure it's a pleasure to walk with it. What a lovely night, so bright and – How far did you say it was from this grass plat to the moon?

BELLA: Two hundred and thirty-six thousand eight hundred and forty-seven miles.

---

grass plat: i.e. grass plot, a small patch of lawn.

LORD B: It's a long way.

BELLA: It's very kind of the moon to shine down here such a distance.

LORD B: Not at all – the grass plat is so soft and pleasant the moon can't help it. May I carry the jug?

BELLA: Oh! My lord –

LORD B: I should like it above all things. (*Takes jug.*) Thanks. Will you take my arm?

(*Church clock strikes eight very distinctly.*)

BELLA: My lord, I don't like to –

LORD B: You shouldn't take dislikes so suddenly.

BELLA: (*taking his arm*) Oh, it isn't that.

(*The piano stops playing.*)

LORD B: What long shadows the moonlight flings. See – there I am.

BELLA: But so tall – so high.

LORD B: And there are you.

BELLA: But not so tall as you are.

LORD B: And yet you're nearer the skies – see! (*moving*) Now we're far apart.

(*The moonlight throws long shadows from right to left.*)

BELLA: And now – (*moving*) – we're joined together. Wonderful things, shadows, are they not?

LORD B: Yes, when they lie before us.

BELLA: I often wonder what they're for – what they mean?

LORD B: No one can tell, except poets, and painters, and lovers; and they know all things, and what they don't know they feel. See, we are divided again.

BELLA: No. (*placing her hand on the jug*) The jug unites us.

LORD B: Only for a moment – (*Piano music again; the plaintive character of which is changed at their exit to a lively tune, to bring on* JACK.) only for a moment.

(*Exeunt through door in wall. Enter* JACK, *smoking; goes to swing, and sits in it.*)

JACK: (*after swinging*) Very nice girls these, particularly that Miss Tighe. Girl of spirit; pitched into that infernal teacher; quite right. (*The music stops.*) She's rather pretty, too; I wonder if she's clever; the two things don't often go together. When Nature makes a pretty woman, she puts all the goods into the shop-window. I wonder where she is. They were all walking about just now. My short day in these female infantry barracks has quite impressed me. Seeing a lot of pretty girls accidentally makes one feel like – going to church when you're not used to it. Let me see, what's the quotation? – Oh – 'Those who went to cough remained to pray.' (*Enter* NAOMI, *her dress, lined with white, over her head, so that she looks like the traditional ghost. She stands motionless.*) Here's a ghost; now really this is pleasant. I'm fond of ghosts, particularly ghosts in petticoats. If you are the departed spirit of any late

---

'Those who went to cough', etc.: cf. *The Deserted Village* by Oliver Goldsmith, line 180: 'And fools, who came to scoff, remained to pray.'

friend, come back to earth to tell me that you've left me money, please mention it at once.

NAOMI: (*lowering her dress from her face*) Weren't you frightened?

JACK: Awful! I'm a very timid man.

NAOMI: I've been in the shrubbery, frightening the girls, but it's very slow work; I'd rather talk to you.

JACK: I feel flattered in the highest degree.

NAOMI: Now don't go on like that; if you do, I shall run away. (*She goes out at door in wall, and shuts it; then opens it a little way, peeping in.*) You mustn't come after me.

JACK: Not for worlds.

NAOMI: (*going, then returning*) I can't understand you at all.

JACK: Why not?

NAOMI: You talk so oddly. You seem to tell truths as if they were not true, and fibs as if they were truths; but I like to hear you.

JACK: To hear me tell fibs or the truth?

NAOMI: Both. Go on; tell me something.

JACK: What about?

NAOMI: About yourself.

JACK: Really, the subject is so barren.

NAOMI: What are you?

JACK: Nothing; it's the occupation I'm most fitted for.

NAOMI: But you must be something.

JACK: No; I'm only myself.

NAOMI: Were you ever anything before you were what you are now?

JACK: Eh?

NAOMI: I mean – what used you to be?

JACK: I used to be – a little boy, but I got nothing for it – not even the birch.

NAOMI: Lord Beaufoy said you'd been in the army. (*looking at him admiringly*) Were you a horse soldier or a foot soldier?

JACK: Foot – a very foot soldier.

NAOMI: And he said you were in the Crimea.

JACK: Yes; I was there.

NAOMI: Were you at the Battle of Inkerman?

JACK: Yes.

NAOMI: Then why didn't you mention it?

JACK: Hardly worth while; so many other fellows were there!

NAOMI: Did you fight?

JACK: I was forced to.

NAOMI: Did you like it?

JACK: No; detested it.

NAOMI: Then why did you do it?

JACK: I was hired for the purpose; besides, I hadn't pluck enough to run away.

Battle of Inkerman: fought on 5 November 1854. The British forces decisively repulsed a Russian attack.

NAOMI: Did they give you much money for fighting?

JACK: Not much; but if they gave me very little money, I did very little fighting, so I was quite even with them in that respect.

NAOMI: I wish I was a man!

JACK: I don't.

NAOMI: Why not? (*turning on him sharply*)

JACK: You're so much nicer as you are.

NAOMI: If you say that I'll run away.

JACK: Then I won't say it. I'll keep on not saying it. (*aside*) Jolly girl for an heiress!

NAOMI: (*aside*) He's beautiful; he's lovely, perfectly lovely. (*aloud*) Are you fond of reading?

JACK: Um – yes – middling.

NAOMI: I am. Did you ever read 'Othello'?

JACK: Yes; I don't consider it nice reading for young ladies.

NAOMI: Othello used to tell Desdemona of all the dangers he had passed, and the battles he had won.

JACK: Othello was a nigger, and didn't mind bragging.

NAOMI: Still it must have been very pleasant for Desdemona.

JACK: A black man!

NAOMI: Yes; it must have been like looking at your husband through a piece of smoked glass.

JACK: As if he were a planet.

NAOMI: A heavenly body!

JACK: More like an eclipse. Shall we walk? May I be allowed? (*offering his arm*)

NAOMI: I don't like to.

JACK: You'll find it go very easy. (*Music of piano in house.*) Am I too tall? (*as she takes his arm*)

NAOMI: No; I like to look up. (*going*) And you've never been anything at all?

JACK: Never!

NAOMI: Not even married?

JACK: Not even married. Melancholy waste of time, isn't it?

NAOMI: (*looking up*) I know what could be made of you.

JACK: What?

NAOMI: You'd make a capital belfry.

JACK: Am I so deserving of a rope? Then you should be the bells.

NAOMI: Yes; I'd be the belle, and my tongue should go ding dong.

JACK: Yes; you should be a ding dong; a *dindon*, a *dindon truffé*.

(*Exeunt into shrubbery. The door in the wall opens, and* LORD BEAUFOY *and* BELLA *appear.* LORD BEAUFOY *with the jug.*)

BELLA: We're soon back.

LORD B: I'm sorry to say we are.

BELLA: So, if your lordship will give me the jug –

LORD B: Must you leave me?

BELLA: I must take the milk to the kitchen.

---

dindon truffé: turkey stuffed with truffles.

(*Enter* KRUX *from behind house. The music stops.*)

LORD B: Just as she was beginning to be so charming. (*Sees* KRUX *who comes down stage.*) Oh, here, you'll do. (*offering* KRUX *jug*) Take this to the kitchen, will you?

BELLA: Oh, no!

KRUX: (*indignant*) Me – me – milk – me?

BELLA: I'll take it, my lord. (*Takes jug.* LORD BEAUFOY *turns.*) I shall be back directly.

LORD B: (*aside to her*) I shall wait here.

(*Exit* BELLA, KRUX *following her.* BEAUFOY *goes to swing.* KRUX *then crosses to* BEAUFOY *with mock deference.*)

KRUX: My lord! Such invidious distinctions –

LORD B: Pardon me, Mr –

KRUX: Krux, my lord.

LORD B: Krux, I mistook you in the dark for –

KRUX: One of the female servants – very natural, my lord. Beautiful evening!

LORD B: Beautiful! Good night!

KRUX: Good night, my lord! (*aside*) Ahum – aha! (*Retires, and pretends to go off behind house. Enter* BELLA, *running; she stops short on seeing* LORD BEAUFOY – *she is out of breath.*)

LORD B: I'm so glad you've come back.

BELLA: I made all the haste I could.

LORD B: The shrubbery runs nearly round the whole garden, does it not?

BELLA: Yes, my lord.

LORD B: (*offers his arm, which she takes. Pause*) You're sure that when I go away tonight you won't quite forget me.

BELLA: Oh, yes! On a first acquaintance, and in so short a time, I never –

LORD B: Never –

BELLA: Liked to hear anybody talk so much. You're the first lord I ever saw.

LORD B: And you're the first little lady I ever took a liking to. (*walking towards the left*) And I shall be so sad at leaving you.

BELLA: Sad, my lord!

LORD B: Really.

BELLA: Why?

(*They walk off into the shrubbery. Enter* KRUX *from behind house.*)

KRUX: Where's Mrs Sutcliffe? Where's Mrs Sutcliffe? (*going and peering into the darkness*) So you wouldn't brush me, Miss Bella, wouldn't you, and my lord takes me for a female servant! Very good – we'll see – we'll see.

(*Exit* KRUX. *Enter* SCHOOLGIRLS *from different entrances.*)

MILLY: Where is that Naomi?

CLARA: And Mr Poyntz? The little flirt!

KITTY: To keep him to herself!

MILLY: I hate such selfishness!

HETTY: So do I. When one gets hold of a lord, one ought to divide him fairly, like a cake!

(*Enter* TILLY *from shrubbery.*)

TILLY: Girls! Girls!

GIRLS: What?

(TILLY *points, and* GIRLS *retire into shadow.* LORD BEAUFOY *and* BELLA *cross – his arm round her waist. They walk slowly, and are quite silent. Clock strikes nine very distant.*)

TILLY: (*after a pause*) Well!
MILLY: There!
KITTY: I never!
CLARA: Nor I; but I should like to –
LAURA: So should I.
MILLY: What?
LAURA: To go to sleep.
TILLY: That artful Bella!
MILLY: Hush!

(KRUX *appears at the entrance of the shrubbery,* JACK *appears from the same entrance with* NAOMI, *and pushes* KRUX *on one side.*)

JACK: Take care – thank you. (JACK *crosses with* NAOMI, *and exits.*)
TILLY: Ah!
MILLY: Oh!
ALL THE GIRLS: Well!
MILLY: Oh, those two!
CLARA: You mean those four.
LAURA: (*sleepy*) Twice two are four.

(*Enter* FARINTOSH *agitated – a letter in his hand,* DR *and* MRS SUTCLIFFE [, *and* VAUGHAN.])

MRS S: } (*together*) { Only another hour!
DR S: } { A glass of sherry or a sandwich –
FARIN: } { My dear friends, excuse me –

This letter, which my man has just brought me, is most important. If I drive home immediately, he can put my things together, and we can catch the next night train to town.

MRS S: But –
FARIN: Forgive me, I entreat, and let me thank you for a most charming and instructive day – instructive day, but this is imperative – imperative; the – the – search of a life, of my whole life, indeed; the news has so agitated me that I – I feel quite – quite agitated. Where is Arthur?

(*During this* JACK *and* NAOMI *have entered, and also* LORD BEAUFOY *and* BELLA – KRUX *following.*)

FARIN: (*mistaking* JACK *for* ARTHUR) Oh, Arthur, here you are; important business takes me to town tonight, so I shall take the carriage; you and your friend can walk home – the night's very fine, very fine; and apropos of your friend Mr Poyntz, the girls tell me that he's been seen paying too strong attentions to Miss Tighe, whom I had hoped you would have shown some, some – and I consider your friend's conduct very reprehensible, very reprehensible. (*Shakes his hand.*) God bless you!
JACK: So many thanks – a charming day!
NAOMI: And a most charming evening!

MRS S: Delighted to see you at any time, Mr Poyntz.

FARIN: Poyntz. (*crossing to* LORD BEAUFOY *and mistaking him for* JACK) Of course, Mr Poyntz, I need not say that my box is at your disposal so long as you choose to remain to shoot here – to shoot here. One word – these schoolgirls have wonderful eyes; they see everything, like me; and they tell me that Arthur has paid not the slightest attention to any one of them, except a Miss Bella something; now he shouldn't have done that, should he? Very wrong of him, very wrong. (*Goes up stage.*) So, once more, (*to* DR *and* MRS SUTCLIFFE) my dear friends, adieu! And wish me good luck in my search. (*Brings* DR SUTCLIFFE *down stage, mistaking him for* MRS SUTCLIFFE.) My dear Mrs Sutcliffe, I must tell you one thing – but not a word to Theodore, not a word to Theodore – poor Theodore, I think he is looking very ill – very ill indeed. I notice at dinner, too, that he drank too much, much too much; digestion going – poor Theodore, digestion going; take great care of him or you'll lose him, you'll lose him. Young ladies, good-night, and – and – and bless you all, very much. Receive the thanks of a man old enough to be – to be the father of anyone here, my dear friends, the Doctor and Mrs Sutcliffe excepted; and I feel as if I were their child, I do indeed. (MRS SUTCLIFFE *indignant*) Now – (*taking* KRUX*'s arm, mistaking him for* VAUGHAN) – to the carriage, and home quickly. I beg your pardon. (VAUGHAN *offers his arm.*) Oh, thank you – thank you – Goodnight! Goodnight!

(*They go off, centre door.* DOCTOR *and* MRS SUTCLIFFE *and* KRUX *exeunt.* JACK *and* LORD BEAUFOY *take their leaves of* BELLA *and* NAOMI, *and go up stage, and the other* GIRLS *cross over to the right and converse together.*)

JACK: Arthur, you've been paying too much attention to that little girl – I'm surprised at you!

LORD B: Not more than you've been paying to the little heiress!

JACK: But heiresses are heiresses; and, of course, to heiresses one's attentions are always the correctest thing possible.

LORD B: Give me a cigar and a light. (*They light cigars from each other's cigars.*) Do you think I've behaved badly?

JACK: Very: walking her about and spooning her; I shall keep my eye upon you; you belong to the old Satanic school.

LORD B: And you to the modern cynical.

JACK: Poor little thing, like Faust and Marguerite.

LORD B: And you're the Mephistopheles.

JACK: Mephistopheles be –

LORD B: Unnecessary; he is already. (*to* GIRLS) Once more, ladies, goodnight! (*looking at* BELLA) I trust I may say, *au revoir*.

(JACK *and* NAOMI *exchange glances. Exeunt* JACK *and* LORD BEAUFOY, *at gate.* NAOMI *and* BELLA *watch them out.*)

ALL THE GIRLS: (*cross to and attack* NAOMI *and* BELLA) Well, I'm sure, I –

(*Enter* MRS SUTCLIFFE, DR SUTCLIFFE, *and* KRUX. GIRLS *stop suddenly.*)

MRS S: Oh, Mr Krux – (*agitated*) – if it should be true – (*Sinks on garden seat, almost fainting* – BELLA *takes her hand; she repulses her.*) Don't touch me – how dare you? You, whom I have reared out of charity, how have you behaved this night? Your conduct towards Lord Beaufoy is known to me – touch me with your hand – or, rather, yes – give it me. (*Takes* BELLA*'s hand.*) Where did you get that ring?

BELLA: (*trembling*) Lord Beaufoy gave it me.

GIRLS: Lord Beaufoy!

KRUX: I told you – I told you –

MRS S: You have been watched, you wicked creature!

KRUX: (*aside*) Yes, I did that (*proudly*).

MRS S: Walking alone, and talking to Lord Beaufoy.

NAOMI: But there's no harm in that – I was walking and talking with Jack.

GIRLS: Oh!

NAOMI: Mr Poyntz! Mr Poyntz, and I'm sure –

MRS S: Silence, Miss Tighe. Little did I think when I took you into my house I was nourishing a serpent in my bosom.

DR S: My dear!

MRS S: Silence, Theodore! Young ladies, to your dormitories.

(GIRLS *cross stage silently.* NAOMI, *trying to get a word with* BELLA, *is prevented by* MRS SUTCLIFFE.)

BELLA: (*to* GIRLS) Goodnight! Wish me goodnight!

MRS S: Don't stir! You abandoned girl, do not dare to address any of the young ladies. (*Motions to* GIRLS *to go. Exeunt* GIRLS.)

NAOMI: I will! (*Kisses* BELLA, *and as she goes off, turns and makes a grimace at* KRUX.)

KRUX: Hussy! Too proud to brush her betters.

MRS S: You leave this house tomorrow morning. The man can drive you to the station, and, in London, you can go, for one month only, to my friend Mrs Stanton. By that time you may find some situation. You to dare, under my very eyes, to cast out lures to my guests. You –

DR S: My love!

MRS S: (*violently*) Theodore, silence!

DR S: (*in a subdued passion*) Amanthis, hold your tongue! (MRS SUTCLIFFE *dumbfounded*) The pupils are not here now, and I will speak. (*Crosses to* BELLA.) Tell me, Bella, did Lord Beaufoy give you that ring?

BELLA: Yes.

DR S: And why did he give it you?

BELLA: I must not tell you that.

KRUX: There!

DR S: (*turning and raising his stick*) Out of my sight, or I shall strike you! (*Exit* KRUX *hastily.*) Did Lord Beaufoy tell you that he loved you?

BELLA: Yes.

MRS S: I said so.

DR S: Good heavens! What harm is there in that? – Perhaps he spoke the truth. 'Tis easy to love Bella – I love her!

BELLA: (*gratefully*) Oh, Doctor!

MRS S: Take me into the house, or I shall faint.

DR S: You are harsh and cruel.

MRS S: (*weeping*) Oh, Theodore, you no longer love me.

DR S: No, dear – I mean – yes – I –

MRS S: Go, go, leave me – the same as thirty-five years ago! (*Exit.*)

DR S: (*following her*) My love – Amanthis! (*Exit.*)

BELLA: Was I so wrong to listen to him? Is it so wicked to wear the ring he gave me? If I thought so, I'd – (*About to throw it off, retains it.*) – No, it seems to comfort me. And tomorrow I must go. Must I leave you, my dear home? – The only home I ever knew – and my companions, and the old servants who have been so kind to me? What will become of me – how can I face the world alone? (*sobbing, sinking on her knees*) I am thrust forth – alone – alone – alone!

(*During the last few words* NAOMI *has opened the window and appeared on balcony.*)

NAOMI: Not alone, dear – I'm here, and I'll go with you. Here's my jewels – (*Throws down small parcel on stage.*) – and my purse. There's more than fourteen pounds in it – (*Descends staircase.*) – and we'll go together; and never, never will we be separated in this world, until death do us part.

(*The two* GIRLS *embrace each other, and sob as they kneel upon the ground.*)

BELLA: No, no, Naomi.

NAOMI: I will – I will – I will! (*fondling*)

(LORD BEAUFOY *appears on wall,* JACK *watching him. Tableau.*)

ACT IV

SCENE. *Same as act III. Morning. Discovered –* GIRLS *at play; skipping rope, battledore, hoops, etc.* NAOMI TIGHE *sitting apart on steps of house, pale and melancholy.*

MILLY: Naomi, will you play?

NAOMI: I've got a headache.

TILLY: Thinking of Bella?

NAOMI: Yes; thinking of Bella.

CLARA: Poor Bella!

NAOMI: I wonder where he is!

GIRLS: *He* is?

NAOMI: I mean *she* is – how could Bella be a *he*?

MILLY: You've never been well since she went away.

TILLY: And that's just six weeks ago.

NAOMI: Six weeks today. (*Sighs. All the* GIRLS *mimic and laugh.*) You're an unfeeling set of brutes; and, if you tease me, I'll slap your faces.

TILLY: (*crosses to* NAOMI) Really, Miss Tighe, you should remember that you are with white young ladies, and not among your blackamoor negroes, now. I should like to see you slap my face.

NAOMI: I shall feel me do it in a minute! Oh, I wish Bella was here.

TILLY: Bella was a servant.

NAOMI: She was not.

TILLY: She was.
NAOMI: She wasn't.
TILLY: She was.
NAOMI: She wasn't.
TILLY: Sighing about a little kitchen girl, because she was useful to you. Girls, did you like Bella?
GIRMS: U – m. N – o!
MILLY: She hadn't spirit enough for me.
KITTY: She was so stupid.
CLARA: She was too clever for me.
LAURA: I didn't care much for her, because she was so terribly wide awake.
HETTY: (*in swing*) I liked her.
GIRLS: Why?
HETTY: Because she used to give me her bread and butter. (*Laugh – school-bell rings.*) Oh, there's breakfast (GIRLS *going*).
NAOMI: I shan't go in to breakfast. Mrs Sutcliffe said that when I had my headaches I might stop out here for the fresh air. (*Laugh.*)
TILLY: Fresh air! Fresh – (*pretending to see* BELLA) Oh, here's Bella!
NAOMI: (*turning*) Eh! (GIRLS *laugh, and exeunt.*)
HETTY: (*going. Returns and kisses* NAOMI.) Never mind the sneerers. There's an acid drop. (*Gives her one, and goes.*)
NAOMI: I wish I'd been a boy! I don't see what use girls are – boys are so much more manly. (*Rises, looks round to see if she is unobserved – sits on garden seat, then draws letter from her bosom, and reads.*) 'My dear, dear Naomi!' (*Laughs, blushes, and hides her face in her hands.*) – 'My dear, dear Naomi!' – (*Business repeated.*) 'My dear, dear Naomi!' I read that so often that I hardly ever get to the rest of the letter – 'Though I have no business to write to you,' – such nonsense– 'I cannot refrain from sending you these few lines, to tell you what I have been about since my last. You see, my love' – (*Laughs again.*) – 'You see, my love' – how well he does express himself, to be sure. He's quite an author – 'You see, my love, I thought it necessary to see your guardians before I renewed my correspondence with you, because you are so young.' – I hate that; Jack's always flinging that in my face. People can't be born grown up, can they? No! I wish I was as old as Mrs Sutcliffe; then people couldn't say I was too young – 'However, Mr Farintosh was so ill that he couldn't see anybody. The poor old fellow had a sudden attack, and for three days his life was despaired of. However, he is now better. I saw him yesterday; he could hardly speak, but, as good fortune would have it, one of your guardians was with him, so I was introduced; and I am to dine with him tomorrow.' I wish I was my guardian, to have my Jack to dine with him; but I daresay he won't appreciate him; it requires great intellect and good taste to understand Jack – 'I have not heard a word of your friend, Bella, beyond what I have told you; she arrived safely at Mrs Stanton's, where Mrs Sutcliffe sent her, and three days after she disappeared. Mrs Stanton is of opinion that she has not gone to any situation. I have again tried to find Lord Beaufoy, but without success. So, dearest,' – oh, that's beautiful – 'So, dearest, wish me luck tomorrow at dinner, where I will feign all the interest in the money

market, and the tallow ditto, and in hides, cochineal, indigo, and grey shirtings, which these interesting topics are calculated to inspire' – he spells 'cochineal' with two e's, but affection is superior to orthography, and I love him all the better for his bad spelling – 'And now, dearest Naomi, to talk about ourselves. When I first saw you I looked at you with curiosity, because I had heard that you were very rich; but when I left you that evening I felt that I was in love,' – ah (*Sighs.*) – 'and since I left you I am as unhappy as a sailor without a ship. You know that I am poor;' now he's going to talk rubbish again – what has that to do with it? £10,000 couldn't look, and walk, and talk as he does. £10,000 couldn't have been fighting in the Crimea. £10,000 couldn't put its arm round your waist and squeeze you, could it? (*fiercely, then subsiding into gentleness*) No! – 'but I love you, fondly, truly, and devotedly (*beginning to cry*); and if I am happy enough, through old Farintosh's intercession, to please your guardians, the conduct of my life shall prove the truth of your affectionate and faithful Jack.' – (*crying*) – that's real poetry – 'Your affectionate and faithful Jack.' (*Cries in her pocket-handkerchief.*)

(JACK *looks over wall.*)

JACK: (*whispering*) Naomi. (NAOMI *starts.*)

NAOMI: Is it you? (*Hiding letter,* NAOMI *opens door. Enter* JACK, *with muddy boots, etc.; they come down stage and look at each other. A long pause*) Well, what have you to tell me?

JACK: Loads; but now I see you I forget it.

NAOMI: When did you come?

JACK: By the night train. I walked from the station here, over the fields.

NAOMI: Then you haven't been in bed all night?

JACK: No.

NAOMI: (*aside*) What devotion. (*Sits. Another pause*) Why did you come so suddenly, without letting me know?

JACK: (*fetching chair and sitting*) I called yesterday at old Farintosh's, and the servant told me that he was so much better that he had started for his box here; so I came on by the night train, because I knew, Naomi, that he would bring me with him, and that I should see you; so I wandered about, waiting for him, for I know he'll be here shortly; but I couldn't resist looking over the wall, and –

NAOMI: Here I was. (*another pause*) Are you quite well?

JACK: Quite; are you?

NAOMI: Yes, thank you. (*another pause*) When sweethearts meet after a long absence their conversation is so interesting, isn't it? Then you've had no breakfast?

JACK: No.

NAOMI: Neither have I. What sympathy! But what can old Farintosh want so particularly with the Sutcliffes?

JACK: I don't know; but tell me what has happened here since –

NAOMI: Since Bella left? Oh, Mrs Sutcliffe's been very ill, and the Doctor has been very cross. (*whispering*) The other day I overheard him talking about Mr Krux, and he said, D – a – m – n. Damn!

JACK: Tremendous!

NAOMI: But my guardians – what did they seem to think of you?

JACK: They're both City men, and they can't think. By the way, do you know how old you are?

NAOMI: Yes. Eighteen.

JACK: No; you're nearly twenty-one. Your guardians told me that you were so forward, and they didn't know where to send you, so they deceived you on the point of age intentionally.

NAOMI: What a shame, swindling a girl out of three years in that way. And Bella –

JACK: Poor girl!

NAOMI: I loved her so much, and she's never written a word to me. I think it pays best to put all your love upon a man – girls are so deceitful, and men are quite the contrary.

JACK: Some men. There are men, and – individuals.

NAOMI: Will you always be good to me?

JACK: I'll try.

NAOMI: I should like you to be bad, though, sometimes.

JACK: Why?

NAOMI: Because then I should have the pleasure of forgiving you.

JACK: (*rising and putting chair back*) I think I shall be able to accommodate you, as far as that goes.

NAOMI: Jack, when a girl's in love, why do they call her spoons?

JACK: Because she's so often carried to the lips.

(JACK *is about to kiss* NAOMI *as* KRUX *enters.* NAOMI *crosses stage.*)

KRUX: Miss Tighe. How do you do – I hope I have the pleasure of seeing you in health?

JACK: Quite.

KRUX: I'm quite well, thank you.

JACK: I didn't ask the question.

KRUX: I did not know that you were here.

NAOMI: That's not the only thing he don't know.

JACK: I came to tell the Doctor that Mr Farintosh is expected at the lodge, and seeing the gate open –

KRUX: The gate open! Tut, tut, tut. Now who could have opened the gate?

NAOMI: The cat.

KRUX: The cat – what cat?

NAOMI: (*crossing to* KRUX) A cat I keep to scratch spies' eyes out. (*to* JACK) You've been in the army – tell me, would it be wrong to kill Mr Krux?

JACK: By no means.

KRUX: Mrs Sutcliffe sent me to tell you that Mr Farintosh has arrived.

JACK: }
NAOMI: } Arrived!

KRUX: Yes, and here he is.

JACK: (*to* NAOMI) You'll hardly know the beau again. Since his recovery, he no longer dresses himself in the latest mode, but goes about like any other old gentleman, and looks much the better for it.

(*Enter* DR *and* MRS SUTCLIFFE, *both very grave.*)

JACK: My dear Doctor and Mrs Sutcliffe, so glad to see you. I got here before Mr Farintosh, and was just going –

MRS S: (*saluting* JACK – *seeing* NAOMI *about to go*) You may remain, Miss Tighe; Mr Farintosh wishes to see you.

(NAOMI *delighted. Enter* FARINTOSH, *his appearance entirely altered – silver hair, whiskers, and his dress appropriate to his age.*)

FARIN: My dear Miss Tighe, your guardians send you their love. Eh, Poyntz, you here! – How's that? How's that?

JACK: I came down by the train, because I heard you had come on here.

FARIN: Very kind, very kind.

JACK: And while I was waiting about –

KRUX: The garden gate was opened by the cat!

DR S: Eh?
MRS S: What? (*together*)

JACK: I – I – I saw the cat outside waiting to come in, so I opened the gate for him or her!

KRUX: From the outside?

JACK: No; I was lifting the animal over the wall, when seeing Miss Tighe in the garden –

NAOMI: I opened the gate; Mr Krux, you can shut it.

(KRUX *shuts door, and then comes down stage.*)

MRS S: (*who is very pale*) Mr Poyntz, let us thank you for the efforts you have made to find that poor girl.

FARIN: Yes, yes; a sad affair – a sad affair.

DR S: A child I was so much attached to!

KRUX: So was I! (*sighing*)

(DOCTOR *gives* MRS SUTCLIFFE *chair.* DOCTOR *sits between her and* FARINTOSH, *who sits on chair which* JACK *takes from* KRUX, *who was about to sit on it close by swing.*)

DR S: We have only just broken the news to our old friend.

FARIN: (*to* JACK, *slily*) It appears that the young lady went off with somebody who was not a young lady. These things happen – girls are but girls; we must not expect them to be angels.

KRUX: (*shaking his head*) If you do you'll be disappointed – continually disappointed.

FARIN: However, my dear friends, the news I bring will, I am sure, give you pleasure even in the midst of your grief. You know, Theodore, that my poor son (*with emotion*) died without my forgiveness – my boy died leaving a wife and child. For years I have been in search of them, but owing to the frequent names assumed by poor Fred for the sake of avoiding creditors, and to his having been some time abroad, I could find no traces either of my daughter-in-law or my grandchild. At last they are found.

DR S: My dear old friend, receive my congratulations.

MRS S: And mine.

NAOMI: (*crossing to* FARINTOSH) Oh, I am so glad, it must be so beautiful to have a father!

FARIN: (*taking* NAOMI*'s hand*) My dear child, you shall soon see our meeting. As I said, my lawyer has traced them out; my daughter-in-law, poor Fred's wife, is dead.

KRUX: I congrat– (JACK *stops* KRUX.)

FARIN: But her child lives – lives – lives! – My dear friends, lives to be a central object of my affections – lives to be a solace and a comfort to the few years yet remaining to me; for I have been a foolish, vain old fellow, and tried to pass for a young fop, when I was really an old fool. I thought of all this, night and day, as I lay in bed, when they told me I was dying, and the hardest part of all was that I should not live long enough to see my grandchild – but I recovered; I was never better – never so thankful – or so well.

DR S: We are so pleased.

MRS S: Your happiness compensates us for our grief.

FARIN: My dear friends, if you had children, or if you ever have – but I suppose that is almost past hope now – you could imagine my joy. You shall witness it. I invited you on purpose, for my grandchild is here.

JACK: Here!

FARIN: Yes.

NAOMI: Here! Is it Milly, or Tilly, or Laura, or Clara, or Hetty, or Kitty?

MRS S: Did you bring her with you?

FARIN: What! Didn't I tell you? What a stupid old man I am. Now comes the tremendous and delightful surprise. My poor boy's last *alias* was Mountain – his wife's maiden name. Pursued everywhere by his creditors, she retained the name after his death. Mrs Mountain, as she called herself, died in the village here close by. Her child was left to an old woman named Marks, who brought her up, till you – you adopted her – you best of men and women. You, my old college chum – (*shaking* DR SUTCLIFFE*'s hand*) – and you, my old sweetheart (*kissing her hand*). She is known here by the name of Bella Marks. I suppose I saw her when I was here a month ago, but I did not remember her among so many. Perhaps – ah, me! – I did not notice her. Now, where is she? This is the supreme moment of my life. Give her to me! I can contain myself no longer! My heart is hungry for her! Call Bella – my grandchild – call her – give her to me! (*all aghast; a pause*) What is the matter with you? Isn't she at home? Is she out on a visit? If so, never mind, send for her! (NAOMI *bursts out sobbing.*) My child! (*a pause*) She's not – dead! (NAOMI *gives him her hand.*) No! No! Thank heaven! Well, then – what – what – what – what – (*getting alarmed*) Tell me – tell me –

(*A pause.*)

KRUX: (*with concealed triumph*) Sir, if no one else will tell you, I will.

FARIN: Go on.

KRUX: Your grandchild left here six weeks ago. It seems that, in mentioning to you the fact of a pupil who was missing in London, Mrs Sutcliffe has not mentioned her name. (MRS SUTCLIFFE *indicates that she has not.*) The girl whom she has told you of, who eloped clandestinely, was Bella Marks – I should say, is Bella Farintosh, your granddaughter.

FARIN: (*seizing him by the collar*) You lie! I'll throttle you! I'll kill you! (JACK *releases* KRUX *from* FARINTOSH, *twisting* KRUX *into left-hand corner.*)

It's not true! Theodore, my friend, say it's not true! Jack Poyntz! (*to* NAOMI) My child! Speak! Speak!

(DOCTOR *and* MRS SUTCLIFFE *take his hands. He sinks into a chair. They surround him.*)

KRUX: (*frightened*) It is quite true – upon my honour as a gentleman.

DR S: My dear friend!

FARIN: To find her, but to find her – lost!

DR S: It may not be so bad as we suppose.

MRS S: My husband went to London to seek out –

FARIN: And the name of – of the man – she was supposed to accompany? (*another pause*) His name? You may tell me – I can bear it now. His name, I say?

KRUX: Lord Beaufoy.

FARIN: (*his hands hiding his face*) My nephew!

(*A ring heard at the door.* KRUX *opens it.*)

KRUX: Lord Beaufoy!

(*Enter* LORD BEAUFOY. KRUX *shuts door.*)

KRUX: Lord Beaufoy.

LORD B: (*radiant*) My dear uncle, Doctor, Mrs Sutcliffe, Jack! (*smiling and affable; pause*) Why, what's the matter?

DR S: (*rising*) My Lord Beaufoy, we believe that you, and you only, can tell us the hiding-place of Bella Marks.

NAOMI: (*crying*) My dear Bella!

KRUX: A most improper young person.

LORD B: The hiding-place of Bella Marks! Yes, I admit I know it – what then?

DR S: What then! (*calming himself*) But I forgot, Lord Beaufoy – you are ignorant that –

FARIN: (*rising*) Let me tell him, Theodore. You are ignorant that Bella is my granddaughter and your cousin.

LORD B: No; two days ago my lawyer, who, as you know, is also yours, informed me of the fact.

FARIN: And fearing that I should alter the disposition of my property, you accomplished this ruin for revenge.

LORD B: Not so; when Miss Farintosh left Mrs Stanton's, I believed her to be only Bella Marks.

FARIN: (*advancing*) Then all may be repaired. Arthur – my nephew – you – you know I'm very rich; my granddaughter shall inherit all I have – I can't last long. Let me implore you, marry her.

LORD B: Marry her? Impossible!

FARIN: Impossible?

LORD B: Yes; I cannot.

FARIN: Why not?

LORD B: I am already married.

JACK: }
FARIN: } Married?

FARIN: Secretly?

LORD B: Yes, secretly. (FARINTOSH *sinks again into chair.*)

FARIN: My punishment! My punishment!

LORD B: And apropos, Jack –

(*All in consternation.* LORD BEAUFOY *turns to* JACK.)

JACK: Lord Beaufoy, understand that from this time we are strangers. My contempt for you is too deep for utterance.

LORD B: You shall apologise to me for those words.

JACK: Apologise?

LORD B: And be sorry that you used them. Your (*to* JACK) indignant virtue amuses me; and so does yours (*to* DR SUTCLIFFE) and (*to* FARINTOSH) yours. (*to* JACK) I thought you were a cynic; you used to profess that no occurrence on this earth could be of the slightest consequence. Was your cynicism only a sham? If so, how do you defend it? If mock virtue be a bad sort of hypocrisy, what is mock vice? For you – (*turning*) – how can you reproach me? Bella is contented and happy. (*to* MRS SUTCLIFFE) She does not fetch or carry like a servant. She rings bells – she does not answer them. (*to* FARINTOSH) Your paternal interest is a somewhat sudden spasm of affection. You lived the last eighteen years happily without her – whence this new-born feeling? Am I to suppose it is compensation, or too late remorse? Or a desire to be attended by a nurse who takes no wages? Why has this neglected child become so suddenly an object of such tenderness? Not because she has been poor, unloved, and unprotected, but because she is the grandchild of a rich, proud gentleman, who has forgotten his duty to her for twenty years, to remember it during his seventy-first.

DR S: (*crossing to him, and speaking in a whisper*) Lord Beaufoy, ladies are present; I am an old man; if you do not instantly quit this place, by heaven! I'll conduct you by the collar.

(*Enter all the* GIRLS, *hats on, as from their morning walk.*)

MILLY: Oh, Mrs Sutcliffe, we saw such a lovely carriage and footmen, coming towards the school.

(GIRLS *indicate they see* LORD BEAUFOY *and* JACK.)

LORD B: (*his hand on the handle of the door, to* DOCTOR) I will go without assistance – but before I go, Mrs Sutcliffe, let me present you to – Lady Beaufoy! (*opening door, and discovering* BELLA, *dressed as a bride; two footmen attending her.* LORD BEAUFOY *brings her down stage.*) My wife and your grandchild.

(*Picture; music.*)

FARIN: My child – my dear – dear grandchild! (*Embraces her.*)

MRS S: (BELLA *goes to* MRS SUTCLIFFE.) My favourite pupil! (*kissing* BELLA)

NAOMI: (*hysterical*) Please pass her round! I want to kiss her, too! (BELLA *crosses to* NAOMI, *embracing her.*) Oh, my darling – my darling, my true, real lady!

(FARINTOSH, *in his excitement, kisses* MRS SUTCLIFFE. *Everybody astonished.*)

DR S: My dear, for thirty-five years –

FARIN: But, my dear Arthur, how could you be so cruel?

LORD B: My dear uncle, how could you be so suspicious? Knowing that you wished me to marry, in what conventional cant calls my own rank, I prevailed on Bella, who reluctantly consented to become my wife; knowing that once married not even an archbishop could unmarry us; imagine my delight when, on our return to town, my lawyer informed me that, unknowingly, I had married my own cousin.

NAOMI: Of course, you're cousins – it isn't unlawful for – no – cousins can marry. That's a real comfort, isn't it?

LORD B: We went to your house; were told that you had flown here; came after you. I wished to present my lady to her friends in proper form, and really your reception was such that I resolved to punish you.

(*Music, 'La Cenerentola', piano.*)

BELLA: (*to* FARINTOSH, *who has resumed seat*) You will not be ashamed of your grandchild, because she has not been brought up amid the luxury to which she will try to grow accustomed?

FARIN: Ashamed! My – my – happiness is only too great.

BELLA: (*to* DOCTOR *and* MRS SUTCLIFFE) And you, my dear, kind friends, to whom I owe everything, will forgive me for the suspense I have caused you? I would have written, but my lord –

LORD B: (*correcting her*) Arthur.

BELLA: Arthur wished me to keep silent, and –

DR S: *Finis coronat opus*!

MRS S: My sweet darling, I had no apprehensions; I always knew that your destiny would be a high one.

BELLA: (*to* NAOMI) And you'll come and pass your holidays with me?

NAOMI: Yes, dear; and you shall show me all your new things.

DR S: (*to* LORD BEAUFOY) I have to ask your lordship's pardon.

FARIN: Forgive me, Arthur.

JACK: I could bite my tongue off, Arthur, for what I said just now.

LORD B: Not another word; you were all quite right. I told you, Jack, you would be sorry. (*Music ceases.*)

BELLA: Mr Krux, I am sure you wish me every happiness.

KRUX: Every happiness, Miss Bella.

NAOMI: (*angrily*) Lady Beaufoy. Do you know who you are talking to? Lady Beaufoy.

DR S: Mr Krux, if you would like to take your usual walk, don't let regard for us prevent you.

KRUX: Thank you, Dr Sutcliffe, I – (*Bows to characters right and left, then going up stage bows to the two* FOOTMEN, *who are standing on either side of the door, and goes off by door.*)

NAOMI: (*quickly*) Jack, do you love me?

JACK: Naomi!

NAOMI: Then run after Mr Krux, and give him a good thrashing. You won't mind, will you?

JACK: It will be a pleasure.

Finis coronat opus: 'the end crowns the work' PDW translates this common Latin motto, but I have let Dr Sutcliffe retain his final tag, as in LCP.

(*Exit* JACK *after* KRUX. *Immediately after,* KRUX*'s hat comes flying over the wall.*)

TILLY: (*who has been reading book*) 'Cinderella was then conducted to the prince, who asked her to accept his hand. The marriage ceremony took place in a few days; and Cinderella gave her sisters magnificent apartments in the palace.'

MILLY: 'And a short time after married them to two great lords of the court.'

ALL THE GIRLS: (*cross stage surrounding* BELLA, *who is sitting by the swing*) Oh, my lady!

NAOMI: It's just like the story – (*looking off*) – prince, carriages, footmen, and all. (*taking up pumpkin*) And to think that this should ever grow into that (*pointing to* FOOTMEN, *and placing pumpkin at the feet of* FOOTMAN).

FARIN: And, in this fairy story, what am I?

NAOMI: You? – You're the godmother.

LORD B: (*taking parcel from* FOOTMAN) Knowing my wife's talent for narrative, I have here something I could only offer to her on the spot.

BELLA: Another present!

LORD B: (*opening case*) A pair of glass slippers.

GIRLS: Oh!

(*They surround him. Re-enter* JACK *through door in wall,* NAOMI *meeting him.*)

NAOMI: Did you do it?

JACK: Yes.

NAOMI: Did you hurt him much?

JACK: He said I did; and I believe he spoke the truth.

FARIN: (*taking the hands of* DOCTOR *and* MRS SUTCLIFFE) See, my friends, how a good deed germinates into a great one. Your past kindness to a friendless orphan girl is the cause of our all-present happiness.

DR S: No, no, not so; your nephew's nature is an exceptionally fine one. He is in the highest sense of the word a gentleman; and there is no sight under the sun finer than a true gentleman.

FARIN: Except one.

DR S: Eh?

FARIN: A true lady!

DR S: So many things are required for the composition of the real thing. One wants nobility of feeling.

FARIN: A kind heart.

DR S: A noble mind.

FARIN: Modesty.

DR S: Gentleness.

FARIN: Courage.

DR S: Truthfulness.

FARIN: Birth.

DR S: Breeding.

MRS S: And, above all – School!

(*As* LORD BEAUFOY *stoops to fit on slipper,* NAOMI *having taken off* BELLA*'s satin shoe, laughing, the curtain falls. Music.*)

APPENDIX I The source of *Caste*

It is of considerable interest to study the original short story from which Robertson took the basic elements for what was to prove his most successful play. 'The Poor-Rate Unfolds a Tale' was contributed to a collection of similar stories gathered together and published under the title *Rates and Taxes and How They Were Collected*, which appeared around Christmas 1866. The work was the production of a group of mutual friends, all amateur or professional writers, the denizens of a world not unlike that depicted in the Owl's Roost scene of *Society*. Their leader was Thomas Hood the Younger, whose name appears as principal editor of the volume; son of the prolific humorist and versatile poet of the same name, 'Tom' Hood was at this time editor of *Fun*, the only true rival to *Punch* as the best comic magazine of the day. H.J. Byron, one of Robertson's staunchest friends and earliest London acquaintances, was a former editor, and the circle of *Fun*'s regular contributors included W.S. Gilbert (then a briefless barrister in whose chambers in South Square, Gray's Inn, the group often used to congregate), the young Clement Scott (later the trenchant drama critic of *The Daily Telegraph* and as such the champion of Robertson and arch-enemy of the Ibsenites), W.J. ('Jeff') Prowse, C.G. Leland (creator of the 'Hans Breitmann' ballads), Thomas Archer, Henry S. Leigh, and a number of other budding artists, critics, and journalists, among them Tom Robertson.

In 1865, the year in which the Prince of Wales's staged *Society* and laid the foundations of Robertson's reputation, the group produced in volume-form a collection of six tales under the title *A Bunch of Keys. Where They Were Found, and What They Might Have Unlocked.* The authors were Robertson, Archer, Gilbert, Hood, Prowse, and Scott, and the formula employed – that of a number of disparate stories linked loosely to a connecting narrative – appears to have been sufficiently popular to warrant the compilation of a second miscellany on similar lines. The result was *Rates and Taxes*, its title deriving from the framework devised, possibly by Thomas Archer, to provide the fictional tellers with an excuse for recounting their tales. Archer's opening narrative describes how the various tax-collectors for the parish of 'Squashleigh' in London came to hold a weekly social club at the 'Greyhound' public house, the main contents of the book representing stories supposedly told by several of the collectors during the first meetings.

The first story, 'Like Will to Like. A Story Told by the Water-Rate', is by Prowse; next comes Hood's offering which purports to come from the 'Dog-Tax' under the title 'The True Story of Caesar and Brutus', and forms the longest story in the volume. There follows Robertson's item, the shortest tale in the book; Gilbert's contribution, 'Maxwell and I', told by the Income-Tax succeeds it, while the final tale, 'Three Chapters of a Policeman's MS' read by the Police-Rate, is from Clement Scott. A brief conclusion by Thomas Archer, which ties up the background narrative, completes *Rates and Taxes and How They Were Collected.*

Robertson's story only occupies twenty-seven pages of the original volume, but it contains many of the salient characters and incidents, and some of the dialogue, which were to go towards the creation of *Caste*. The tale begins with the same discussion of misalliances, between the love-smitten Ensign Fairfax Daubray and his friend Captain Swynton, which reappears at the opening of *Caste* conducted by George and Captain Hawtree; Daubray like George has a formidably aristocratic mother in the shape of Lady Clardonax while like Hawtree's Swynton's military hauteur is compromised by a slight suggestion of the parvenu.

Daubray's *inamorata* is, in fact, called Polly, and like Esther Eccles she is on the stage; not so Jenny who corresponds to *Caste*'s Polly Eccles and whom Robertson describes as 'the plainest of the sisters'. In the story there are in fact a whole bevy of sisters presided over by the drunken Eccles, Robertson being wise enough to scale down the household to Esther, Polly, and their father when he came to convert his tale for the theatre. However, the central crisis of the plot is engineered in much the same fashion in both play and story: Daubray marries in secret; his regiment is ordered to the Crimea, where he dies a reckless but gallant death in battle; the money left for the relief of widow and newly-born child is squandered on drink by old Eccles; Lady Clardonax's subsequent offer of charity is indignantly refused by the proud mother.

Here, however, the finale to Robertson's short story deviates significantly from that of *Caste*, suggesting perhaps that theatre audiences were not as prepared to accept harsh truths on the stage as they were in narrative fiction. At all events Ensign Daubray, unlike George D'Alroy, is truly dead, so there can be no touching reunion with wife and child. Indeed, after Daubray's death is reported, Polly herself soon falls mortally sick, and in the fullness of time her orphan son has to be brought up by his grandmother with the assistance of Swynton whose military exploits have by now deprived him of an arm (a detail which the Bancrofts considered adopting for Hawtree in act III of *Caste*). By these means Robertson gives his tale a poignant conclusion, and although humour is by no means lacking from it, the final effect of 'The Poor-Rate Unfolds a Tale' is to endorse the view that Daubray's marriage was imprudent, and that the couple's deaths offered the kindest way out of the problems posed by a blatant *mésalliance.* In fact the story insists on values which *Caste* sentimentally and humorously subverts. Furthermore, neither Swynton nor Daubray's mother is presented in a semi-satirical light; Jenny Eccles has little of Polly's sparkling high spirits, and while Eccles may be nearly as engaging in fiction as he is in the theatre, one misses the presence of a Sam Gerridge to act as a foil to the military swell, Swynton.

To enable readers to make some comparisons between source and play, extracts from the original edition of *Rates and Taxes and How They Were Collected* (London: Groombridge & Sons, 1866) are appended. 'The Poor-Rate Unfolds a Tale' appears on pages 157–84, and it is to these pages that the references apply.

'The fact is, my poor dear old Daubray, you're spoons – case of true love – dead!

'But what would you have me do?' spluttered Daubray.

'Do? get leave and cut away', was the reply.

'But I have got leave, and I *have* cut away – and while I was away I was miserable, and when I came back I was a gone-er coon than ever!' . . .

'Of course, Dib, you're not such a soft as to think of marriage?' said the captain eyeing his friend keenly.

The ensign made no reply.

'That is out of the question,' continued Swynton; 'you know what your mother is.'

Ensign Daubray sighed and nodded as if he knew what his mother was but too well.

Captain Swynton rose from his arm-chair, stirred the fire, and looking down upon his young friend like a benevolent Mephistopheles, said,

'Couldn't the thing be arranged?'

'Swynton,' said Ensign Daubray, rising and helping himself to a cigar, 'cut that.'

'Look here, Dib, if you're going to mount a moral hobby, and ride – in an argumentative sense – to the Devil, I shall cut the discussion altogether. Either you are going to behave properly – with a proper regard to the world and all that you know – or you are going to do the other thing. Now the question is, which do you mean to do? The girl is a very nice girl. I've seen nicer, but still she *is* a nice girl – but as to your making her Mrs Daubray – the thing won't hold water. All those marriages of people with common people are all very well in novels, and stories on the stage – because the real people don't exist, and have no relatives who exist, and no connections, and so no harm's done – and it's rather interesting – to look at; but in *real* life, with real social relations, and so on – real connections – and mothers, and so forth – it's absolutely' – Captain Swynton described a circle with his cigar. 'I don't pretend to be a particularly good fellow, or a particularly bad fellow; I suppose I'm a sort of average – regular standard kind of man – I'm not particularly worldly. I gave up the girl I was attached to – we'd neither of us any money – and I preferred that we should have enough and be apart, rather than be hard up together. You've heaps of money, but you can't marry a woman you can't present everywhere. Out of the question, Dib, and you know it. The world's the world, and you and I didn't make it – very good thing for the world we didn't . . . (pp. 157–9)

His [Daubray's] father was dead, and his mother, who had been a great beauty, and was in her age hook-nosed, majestic, and terrible, had married a second time, and she ruled Lord Clardonax as tightly as she had ruled Fairfax Daubray . . . He [Fairfax Daubray Junior] had a vacant expression of face, which fact, joined to the possession of a tongue either too broad or too thick for his mouth, made him seem stupid. He . . . had been reared to regard his lady-mother with a superstitious sort of awe . . .

There was a suspicion of trade in the family of the gallant captain [Swynton] . . .
[Fairfax visits Polly's home]

At Westminster Bridge Fairfax Daubray dismissed his cab, turned to the left, and walked till he came to Stangate . . . (pp. 160–1)

. . . Polly was the eldest, the darkest eyed, and the prettiest of the sisters; demure, quiet, and self-possessed.

. . . Jenny was the plainest of the sisters, and had acquired a sort of family celebrity for housekeeping and repartee. (p. 163)

Mr Eccles had been a mechanic of some sort or other. Mr Eccles was either overproud, or possessed of mental attributes too high for his station in life – for he would not work. As all men of active minds must find some occupation to interest and amuse them, Mr Eccles took to drinking – a pursuit which he varied at tolerably regular intervals by beating his wife.

. . . Polly, who was barely nine years of age, took after her mother, and nursed her baby sister, and washed and combed her other little sisters, and waited on her father, and was abused and beaten by him. It was a horrid thing, as Mr Eccles often remarked, to have ungrateful children.

. . . a young Frenchman, a watch-maker, took a room in the house. This young Frenchman was visited by an older Frenchman – a thin, pale little man, who was a ballet-master at one of the large theatres on the other side of the water. The old Frenchman took a fancy to little Polly, and seeing that she was pretty, well limbed, and graceful, asked her if she would join his class.

. . . Polly told him that her father could not afford to pay for her tuition, and the pale little Frenchman said that he did not require payment, but that he would teach her for nothing, because she was like a little lady he had known long years ago, and a long way off . . .

. . . The only scion of the house of Daubray was wrong to fall in love with a young woman who earned eighteen shillings per week, and whose father was known as Sodden Sammy, for a mile round Astley's amphitheatre . . . (pp. 167–70)

Mr Eccles was a dirty-looking old villain, with the flavour of last night's tap-room strong upon him. His address was unpleasing, fawning, and sham-propitiatory. Daubray saw the blackguard under his too-civil, over-deferential manner, and wondered why for the sake of his own comfort he – Eccles – did not wash himself oftener. The girls considered their father a good average sort of parent; a little tipsified, but that they were used to; and certainly somewhat eccentric, which was proved by his frequent personal castigation of his daughters – Polly, as the oldest and most habituated, being his favourite for punishment; but a very clever man for all that, and who could have done wonders – had he liked. (p. 175)

Ensign Daubray's regiment was ordered to the Crimea. Lady Clardonax kissed her son's forehead, and pressed his hand as she told him that she was sure he would do his duty . . .

. . . Fairfax Daubray was a brave, stupid, good-natured young man, and adored by the men under his command. A finer-hearted gentleman, or a more incapable officer never buckled on a sword-belt . . . (pp. 177–8)

. . . The mother had hardly recovered [from the birth of her baby] when the fatal letter reached England; but Jenny, when she saw that the address was not in the usual handwriting, guessed instantly at its contents. She opened it and read it, and kept it from her sister for some days . . .

[Eccles spends the money intended for Polly and the child.] A stormy scene ensued between father and daughter. Mrs Daubray asked him if he wished to see his grandson starve? To which Eccles replied that after all he had done for her, the position he had raised her to, she was ungrateful, and hoped that she might live to feel how sharper than a serpent's tooth was a thankless child.

. . . Major Swynton returned to England with one of his coat sleeves empty. Almost his first call was on his comrade's widow . . . (pp. 180–1)

A carriage stood before the door of the little house in Stangate. Lady Clardonax ntroduced herself, and desired that her son's son might go back with her. Mrs Daubray fired up and refused. The old grandmother was haughty and imperious; he young mother passionate and proud; a violent altercation ensued, and Mrs Daubray, in a flood of tears, desired Lady Clardonax to leave the house.

'Part with *him*, *my boy*!' she panted, 'I'd sooner die!'

'You can see him when you wish to do so,' said the lady.

'Better do what the good lady asks you, my dear,' suggested the amiable Mr Eccles, who was present, and desired to make himself agreeable to the owner of a arriage and pair; 'for sure she's advising you for your good, and for the child's likewise.'

'My good creature,' urged Lady Clardonax, 'you surely cannot intend to bring p my son's son in a place like this?'

'It *is* a poor place,' sighed Mr Eccles, 'and we are poor people, that's sure enough. Ve ought not to fly in the face of our pastors and masters, our pastresses and nastresses.'

'*Do* hold your tongue!' said Jenny, who felt a strong inclination to assault both ady Clardonax and her father at the same time.

'Master Fairfax Daubray,' said Mrs Daubray, hugging the infant who was erenely unconscious of the storm around him, 'Master Fairfax Daubray will remain rith his mother!'

'But you've no money. Fairfax's father and Fairfax himself so dipped the estate hat it will be ten years before it is got round. How do you intend to live?' asked the ld lady.

'Turn Columbine,' replied the mother; 'go on the stage again and dance!'

This last speech was too much for Lady Clardonax, who beat a precipitate treat; at the bottom of the stairs Mr Eccles overtook her, and requested the loan f the sum of a sovereign until that day week.

'Go away,' said the old lady, as she stepped into her carriage and drove off. p. 181–2)

APPENDIX II Mr Eccles's musical and literary allusions

It will be readily appreciated that Eccles's speeches in act III of *Caste* are heavily seasoned with quotations from and parodies of a wide variety of popular songs and verses of the period, many no doubt acquired while frequenting ''Armonic Meetin's at taverns'. George Honey who played the part in the original production was a talented operatic singer, and no doubt had some say in creating Eccles's repertoire. It has therefore been illuminating to track down as many allusions as can be easily identified, as reflecting (if only on a fictional level) something of the popular taste of the period.

p. 164 *'A carpenter said', etc.*: not directly traced, but Roger L'Estrange's version of *Aesop's Fables* (1692) gives the anecdote: 'There was a council of mechanics called upon to advise about the fortifying of a city . . . Up starts a currier; Gentlemen, says he, when y'ave said all that can be said, there's nothing in the world like leather . . . '

p. 164 *'For a' that', etc.*: Eccles switches to a garbled version of lines 5–8 of Robert Burns's well-known poem which run:

For a' that, and a' that;
Our toil's obscure, and a' that;
The rank is but the guinea stamp;
The man's the gowd for a' that.

The third line of Eccles's version is a memory of line 22 of the original:

His riband, star, and a' that.

p. 165 *'Who ran to catch me', etc.*: cf. lines 21–4 of 'My Mother' by Ann Taylor (1782–1866), from *Original Poems for Infant Minds* by Jane and Ann Taylor (1804):

Who ran to help me when I fell,
And would some pretty story tell,
Or kiss the place to make it well?
My Mother.

p. 170 *'I'll stand by my friend', etc.*: untraced, but the sentiment is typical of countless Victorian ballads; cf. Felix McGlennon's 'Comrades'.

p. 170 *'Strike on this grey head'*: just possibly a reminiscence of line 35 of 'Barbara Frietchie' by James Greenleaf Whittier (1807–92), published in *In War Time* (1864): 'Shoot, if you must, this old grey head'.

p. 170 *'Britons, strike home'*: a song by Henry Purcell (1659–95) from *Bonduca, or the British Heroine*, an adaptation of a play probably by John Fletcher.

p. 170 *'A long pull', etc.*: title of a song by F. Alexander.

p. 170 *'They have given thee to a plumber', etc.*: a parody of the song by George Linley (1798–1865), which begins:

They have giv'n Thee to another,
They have broken ev'ry vow,
They have giv'n Thee to another,
And my heart is lonely now . . .

Oh! was it well to leave me?
Thou could'st not so deceive me!
Long and sorely I shall grieve Thee
Lost, lost Rosabel!

p. 170 *'For I know that the angels', etc.*: untraced but the line might occur in almost any sentimental parlour-ballad of the period.

p. 171 *'Be kind to thy father', etc.*: possibly a parody of 'Be kind to each other', a ballad by Charlotte M. Hewke, published in 1866, but the original is more likely to have read 'Be kind to thy mother'.

p. 171 *'When I heard she was married', etc.*: cf. 'When I heard he was married', words by Thomas Haynes Bayly, music by George Alexander Lee, published *c.* 1835.

THE PRINCIPAL PLAYS OF TOM ROBERTSON

(For much of the detail contained in this list I am indebted to Maynard Savin's *Thomas William Robertson: His Plays and Stagecraft*, Providence, Rhode Island: Brown University, 1950, pp. 121–37.)

The Battle of Life, adapted from the short story by Charles Dickens. Produced Boston, Lincs, 1843–7; Theatre Royal, Norwich, 23 January 1847.

The Haunted Man, adapted from the short story by Charles Dickens. Produced Boston, Lincs, 1843–8; Queen's Theatre, London, 1 January 1849.

The Chevalier de St George, adapted from a play by 'M. Mélesville' (Anne H.J. Duveyrier) and Roger de Beauvoir. Produced Princess's Theatre, London, 20 May 1845.

Noémie, adapted from a play by Dennery and Clément. Produced as *Ernestine*, Princess's Theatre, London, 14 April 1846.

A Night's Adventure; or, Highways and Byways, based on Bulwer-Lytton's novel *Paul Clifford*. Produced Lyceum Theatre, London, 25 August 1851.

The Ladies' Battle, adapted from the play *La Bataille des Dames* by Scribe and Legouvé (see note * below).

Faust and Marguerite, adapted from a play by Michel Carré. Produced Princess's Theatre, London, 19 April 1854.

Castles in the Air. Produced City of London Theatre, Bishopsgate, London, 29 April 1854.

My Wife's Diary, adapted from a play by Dennery and Clairville. Produced Lyceum Theatre, London, 18 December 1854.

The Star of the North, adapted from a play by Eugène Scribe. Produced Sadler's Wells Theatre, London, 5 March 1855.

The Clockmaker's Hat, adapted from a play by Emilie de Giradin. Produced Adelphi Theatre, London, 7 March 1855.

Peace at Any Price. Produced Strand Theatre, London, 13 February 1856.

The Muleteer of Toledo. Produced Grecian Saloon, London, 6 May 1856.

The Half-Caste; or, The Poisoned Pearl. Produced Surrey Theatre, London, 8 September 1856.

The Cantab. Produced Strand Theatre, London, 14 February 1861.

Jocrisse the Juggler, adapted from a play by Dennery and Brésil. Produced as *Magloire the Prestigiator*, Adelphi Theatre, London, 1 April 1861.

David Garrick, adapted from the play *Sullivan* by 'M. Mélesville' (Anne H.J. Duveyrier). Produced Prince of Wales's Theatre, Birmingham; then Theatre Royal, Haymarket, London, 30 April 1864.

Constance, with music by Frederick Clay. Produced Covent Garden Theatre, London, 23 January 1865.

Society. Produced Prince of Wales's Theatre, Liverpool, 8 May 1865; then Prince of Wales's Theatre, London, 11 November 1865.

Ours. Produced Prince of Wales's Theatre, Liverpool, 23 August 1866; then Prince of Wales's Theatre, London, 15 September 1866.

Shadow-Tree Shaft. Produced Princess's Theatre, London, 6 February 1867.

A Rapid Thaw, adapted from the play *Le Dégel* by Victorien Sardou. Produced St James's Theatre, London, 2 March 1867.

A Dream in Venice. Produced Royal Gallery of Illustration, 18 March 1867.

Caste, based on Robertson's short story, 'The Poor-Rate Unfolds a Tale'. Produced Prince of Wales's Theatre, London, 6 April 1867.

For Love. Produced Holborn Theatre, London, 5 October 1867.

The Sea of Ice; or, The Prayer of the Wrecked. Produced Colosseum Theatre (?), Glasgow.

Play. Produced Prince of Wales's Theatre, London, 15 February 1868.

Passion Flowers, adapted from the play *On Ne Badine Pas Avec L'Amour* by Alfred de Musset. Produced Theatre Royal, Hull, 28 October 1868.

Home, based on the play *L'Aventurière* by Emile Augier. Produced Theatre Royal, Haymarket, London, 14 January 1869.

School, based on the theme of the play *Aschenbrödel* by Roderick Benedix. Produced Prince of Wales's Theatre, London, 16 January 1869.

My Lady Clara. Produced Alexandra Theatre, Liverpool, 22 February 1869; as *Dreams*, Gaiety Theatre, London, 27 March 1869.

A Breach of Promise. Produced Globe Theatre, London, 10 April 1869.

Dublin Bay. Produced Theatre Royal, Manchester, 18 May 1869.

Progress, adapted from the play *Les Ganaches* by Sardou. Produced Globe Theatre, London, 18 September 1869.

The Nightingale. Produced Adelphi Theatre, London, 15 January 1870.

MP. Produced Prince of Wales's Theatre, London, 23 April 1870.

Birth. Produced Theatre Royal, Bristol, 5 October 1870.

War. Produced St James's Theatre, London, 16 January 1871.

Policy. Produced Theatre Royal, Glasgow, 13 February 1871.

Not At All Jealous. Produced Court Theatre, London, 29 May 1871.

Other Days. Produced Theatre Royal, Hull, 12 April 1883.

A Row in the House. Produced Toole's Theatre, London, 30 August 1883.

Cinderella. Produced Theatre Royal, Newcastle-upon-Tyne, 15 August 1892.

Over the Way. Produced Court Theatre, London, 20 January 1893.

**Note:* Savin is probably in error when he states that Robertson's translation of *La Bataille des Dames* was that performed at the Theatre Royal, Haymarket, on 18 November 1851. In PDW it is acknowledged that the version presented at the Olympic Theatre on 7 May 1851 was made by Charles Reade; according to Malcolm Elwin's *Charles Reade A Biography* (London, 1931, pp. 72–6), Reade attended the Paris première of the piece during the spring of 1851, and shortly afterwards submitted his adaptation to Mrs Fanny Stirling whom he envisaged in the part of the Comtesse d'Autreval. The play was revived (with Reade directing rehearsals) at the Theatre Royal, Haymarket, on 18 November, and ran for three weeks, but it is not likely (though not impossible) that Robertson had any hand in it. Unless he collaborated with Reade on the first translation or some revised version, it would seem unwise to attribute any of the 1851 text to him. His rendering, which differs materially from Reade's, was not published by Lacy until 1867.

SELECT BIBLIOGRAPHY

Editions

The Principal Dramatic Works of Thomas William Robertson, with a memoir by his son, 2 vols, London: Sampson Low, Marston, & Co., and Samuel French, 1889

Society and *Caste*, ed. T. Edgar Pemberton, Boston and London: D.C. Heath & Co., 1905 (Belles Lettres Series III)

Books on Robertson

Pemberton, T. Edgar. *The Life and Writings of T.W. Robertson*. London: Richard Bentley & Son, 1893

Savin, Maynard. *Thomas William Robertson: His Plays and Stagecraft*. Providence, Rhode Island: Brown University, 1950 (Brown University Studies XIII)

Articles etc. on Robertson

Anonymous. 'Thomas William Robertson and the Modern Theatre', *Temple Bar* XLIV (1875), 199–209

Archer, William. *English Dramatists of To-Day*. London: Sampson Low, 1882, pp. 21–6

The Old Drama and the New. An Essay in Re-Valuation. London: William Heinemann, 1923, pp. 257–69

Armstrong, Cecil Ferard. *Shakespeare to Shaw: studies in the life's work of six dramatists of the English stage*. London: Mills & Boon, 1913, pp. 168–205

Beerbohm, Max. 'More in Sorrow – ', *The Saturday Review* 85 (14 January 1899), 44–5; repr. in *Around Theatres*, London: Hart-Davis, 1953, pp. 15–19 (review of a revival of *School*, Globe Theatre, London, 7 January 1899)

Booth, Michael. Introduction to *English Plays of the Nineteenth Century*, vol. III *Comedies*. Oxford: Clarendon Press, 1973, pp. 33–43

Durbach, Errol. 'Remembering Tom Robertson (1829–1871)', *Educational Theatre Journal* XXIV (1973), 284–8

Friswell, J. Hain. *Modern Men of Letters Honestly Criticised*. London: Hodder & Stoughton, 1870, pp. 345–56

Harrison, Dale. 'Tom Robertson: a Centenary Criticism', *Contemporary Review* 135 (March 1929), 356–61

Jones, W. Wilding. 'Robertson as a Dramatist', *The Theatre* New Series II (1879), 355–60

Meier, Erika. *Realism and Reality*. Bern: Francke Verlag, 1967, pp. 7–40.

Rahill, Frank. 'A Mid-Victorian Regisseur', *Theatre Arts Monthly* XIII (1929), 838–44

Shaw, G.B. 'Robertson Redivivus', *The Saturday Review* 83 (19 June 1897), 685–7; repr. in *Our Theatres in the Nineties*, London: Constable & Co., 3 vols,